KAPLAN

Other Kaplan Books Relating to Law School Admissions

John Douglas's Guide to Careers in the FBI

Law School Admissions Adviser

LSAT

Scholarships

Yale Daily News Guide to Fellowships and Grants

2 Real LSATs*

EXPLAINED

By the Staff of Kaplan, Inc.

Simon & Schuster

NEW YORK · LONDON · SINGAPORE · SYDNEY · TORONTO

Kaplan Books
Published by Simon & Schuster
1230 Avenue of the Americas
New York, NY 10020

The material in this book is up-to-date at the time of publication. Law School Admission Council may have instituted changes after this book was published. Please read all material you receive regarding the LSAT carefully.

Contributing Editors: Charlene Garrett, Trent Anderson
Editor: Ruth Baygell
Desktop Publishing Manager: Michael Shevlin
Production Editor: Maude Spekes
Managing Editor: Dave Chipps
Executive Editor: Del Franz

Special thanks to Charlene Garrett, Eric Goodman, Ben Paris, David Rodman, Bob Verini, David Wilkerson

Manufactured in the United States of America
Published simultaneously in Canada

October 2000

10 9 8 7 6 5 4 3 2

ISBN 0-7432-0271-6

Contents

About the Authors

Trent Anderson is the vice president of e-Ventures Group and publisher for Kaplan, Inc. He has worked extensively with LSAT and admissions consulting (for business school, law school, and graduate school). He has been teaching LSAT, developing innovative and effective pedagogy, and creating LSAT material since 1989. He has scored in the ninety-ninth percentile every time he has taken the LSAT and has helped tens of thousands of people get into law school. He received his B.A. from the University of California, Los Angeles and his J.D. and M.B.A. from the University of Southern California. He is a member of the California Bar, the Federal Districts Courts for the Central District of California, and the Ninth Circuit Court of Appeals.

Eric Goodman has been teaching the Kaplan LSAT course for nine years and works for Kaplan, Inc. as a product consultant. When not teaching or writing for Kaplan, Eric works as a composer and musician in New York City.

Benjamin Paris was recently a curriculum director responsible for the LSAT at Kaplan, Inc. He received his B.A. from Bowdoin College, completed the general course at the London School of Economics, and received his J.D. from New York University. He has taught thousands of students how to succeed on standardized tests, and develops content and pedagogy for Kaplan's LSAT course.

Bob Verini is currently director of academic development for the western U.S. and a national training associate for Kaplan, Inc. Since 1980, Bob has taught thousands of students how to ace the LSAT. He also trains new Kaplan instructors nationally, works in course development, and serves as an academic counselor in Kaplan's one-on-one Admissions Consulting program. He holds a B.A. from SUNY/Albany and an M.F.A. from Indiana University. When he takes a break from the LSAT, Bob is a writer, actor, and director, with several films and extensive stage experience to his credit. Bob is also one of the biggest money winners in the history of the game show Jeopardy!™ and was the winner of the 1987 Tournament of Champions.

Why This Book Is Different

Only *2 Real LSATs Explained* includes *actual* exam questions *plus* Kaplan's exclusive explanations. No other book contains both. This gives you an edge that no other resource can.

The LSAT (Law School Admission Test) is a standardized test. That means that law schools must be able to compare any two people's scores, even if the two people took the test at very different times (even years apart!). For LSAT scores to be comparable, the LSAT must test the same basic content. It wouldn't be possible (or fair) to compare two scores that were based on two very different tests. If you were tested on your knowledge of economics and another applicant were tested on her knowledge of legal history, law schools couldn't compare your test scores. So each exam must test the same set of skills, and the content of the test must remain the same from exam to exam.

Since the content of the exam is consistent, each previous exam gives you the chance to get a sneak preview of future tests. Granted, the exact questions in *2 Real LSATs Explained* will not appear on *your* LSAT. However, the concepts tested on these LSATs will be the same concepts tested on your LSAT. For this reason, your preparation for the LSAT should include working with released questions. But are released questions enough?

No way. Released questions are great, but they won't do any good if you don't know how to *use* them. To improve your score on the LSAT you need to identify the concepts and technique that underlie the exam, and you need focused practice with those concepts and techniques. This is where Kaplan comes in. Kaplan invented LSAT prep in 1969, and our proven methods have helped over 600,000 people prepare for law school. Anyone can acquire released tests, but only Kaplan can help you use those released tests to acquire the skills you'll need for the test.

Anyone can claim to be a "test-prep expert," and anyone can claim to have strategies that will help you get a higher score on the test. But if you're not using actual exam questions, how do you know that those strategies will work on *your* test? With *2 Real LSATs Explained*, you know you're working with real test questions, and you have the proven methods of Kaplan, the world's leader in test prep.

How to Use This Book

Step One: Get an Overview

Read the LSAT Basics and Strategy Overview chapters. We'll discuss why you have to take the LSAT, review the structure of the LSAT, and introduce you to the general strategies and proper state of mind you'll need to master the LSAT. We'll show you how to handle the test mechanics so that you have a framework in which to apply the question strategies that you will learn in Step Two.

Step Two: Work Through the Topical Chapters

In each chapter we give you the nuts and bolts of LSAT preparation—the strategies and techniques for every question type on the test. We'll also give you a look at the best way to approach the unscored section of the LSAT—the Writing Sample. For each of the multiple-choice sections—Logical Reasoning, Logic Games, and Reading Comprehension—we'll teach you:

- **Basic Principles**
  We explain each question type, it's purpose on the test, and general test-taking strategies.
- **The Kaplan Method**
  We'll teach you a step-by-step method for attacking every question. We'll also teach you a method for attacking every section. By the day of the test, you'll have powerful flexible strategies and a strategic modus operandi for attacking the test.
- **Crucial Question Types**
  Certain question types appear again and again. We'll make sure you know which questions to expect and how to handle them quickly, confidently, and accurately.

After you finish each chapter, we've given you a practice set so that you can immediately practice applying what you've learned.

Step Three: Put It All Together

In the Putting It All Together chapter, we'll review what you've learned and pull it all together, marshaling your strategies and expertise with the right mindset, so that you're in control of the entire test. With the proper test mentality, you can have everything at your fingertips—from the contrapositive to gridding techniques, from sequencing game strategies to pacing methods. We'll also outline all of the subtle attitudinal factors, often overlooked, that are nonetheless integral so that you can perform your absolute best on the test.

Step Four: Take, Then Review, Each Real LSAT

The two real LSATs in this book will make the difference between your being ready to take the test and being ready to ace it. There's no better way to prepare for the LSAT than by taking, then reviewing, past exams. And only Kaplan has strategic explanations to every question. You'll take the tests one at a time. Then you'll spend several hours carefully reviewing each. After working through Kaplan's exclusive explanations, you'll review the appropriate chapters in this book to relearn or refine your test-taking skills. By the day of the test, you'll be ready to maximize your score.

A Special Note for International Students

In recent years, U.S. law schools have experienced an increase in inquiries from non-U.S. citizens, some of whom are already practicing lawyers in their own countries. This surge of interest in the U.S. legal system has been attributed to the spread of the global economy. When business people from outside the United States do business with Americans, they often find themselves doing business under the American legal system. Gaining insight into how the American legal system works is of great interest around the world.

This new international interest in the U.S. legal system is having an effect on law schools. Many schools have developed special programs to accommodate the needs of this special population of lawyers and students from around the globe. If you are an international student or lawyer interested in learning more about the American legal system, or if you are considering attending law school in the United States, Kaplan can help you explore your options. For more help with applying to law school and other vital information on the 178 law schools accredited by the American Bar Association (ABA), see Kaplan's guide to United States law schools, *Law School Admissions Adviser.*

Getting into a U.S. law school can be especially challenging for students from other countries. If you are not from the United States, but are considering attending law school in the United States, here is what you'll need to get started.

- If English is not your first language, you'll probably need to take the TOEFL (Test of English as a Foreign Language), or provide some other evidence that you are proficient in English. Most law schools require a minimum computer TOEFL score of 250 (600 on the paper-based TOEFL) or better.
- Depending on the program to which you are applying, you may also need to take the LSAT (Law School Admissions Test). All law schools in the United States require the LSAT for their J.D. programs. LL.M. programs usually do not require the LSAT. Kaplan will help you determine if you need to take the LSAT. If you must take the LSAT, Kaplan can help you prepare for it.
- Since admission to law school is quite competitive, you may want to select three or four programs and complete applications for each school.
- You should begin the process of applying to law schools or special legal studies programs at least eighteen months before the fall of the year you plan to start your studies. Most programs will have only September start dates.
- In addition, you will need to obtain an I-20 Certificate of Eligibility from the school you plan to attend if you intend to apply for an F-1 Student Visa to study in the United States.

Kaplan International Programs

If you need more help with the complex process of law school admissions, assistance preparing for the LSAT or TOEFL, or building your English language skills in general, you may be interested in Kaplan's programs for international students.

General Intensive English

These classes are designed to help you improve your skills in all areas of English and to increase your fluency in spoken and written English. Classes are available for beginning to advanced students, and the average class size is 12 students.

English for TOEFL and University Preparation

This course provides you with the skills you need to improve your TOEFL score and succeed in an American university or graduate program. It includes advanced reading, writing, listening, grammar and conversational English, plus university admissions counseling. You will also receive training for the TOEFL using Kaplan's exclusive computer-based practice materials.

LSAT Test Preparation Course

The LSAT is a crucial admission criteria for law schools in the United States. This course includes the skills you need to succeed on each section of the LSAT, as well as access to Kaplan's exclusive practice materials.

Legal English Communication Review Course

This program is for international legal professionals and law students. Lessons include: mastering pronunciation, building your legal vocabulary, and developing presentation and legal writing skills.

Other Kaplan Programs

In addition to the above programs, Kaplan offers courses to prepare for the SAT, GMAT, GRE, MCAT, DAT, USMLE, NCLEX, and other standardized exams at locations throughout the United States.

Applying to Kaplan International Programs

For more information, or to apply to any of Kaplan's programs, contact us at:
Kaplan International Programs
888 Seventh Avenue, New York, NY 10106 USA
Telephone: (212) 492-5990
Fax: (212) 957-1654
E-mail: world@kaplan.com
Web: www.studyusa.kaplan.com

Kaplan is authorized under federal law to enroll nonimmigrant alien students, and is authorized to issue Form IAP-66 needed for a J-1 (Exchange Visitor) visa. Kaplan is accredited by ACCET (Accrediting Council for Continuing Education and Training). Test names are registered trademarks of their respective owners.

SECTION ONE

Preparation for the LSAT

CHAPTER 1

LSAT Basics

The Law School Admission Test (LSAT) is required for admission by all Law School Admission Council law schools (over 190 of them)—including every American Bar Association approved law school. It is probably unlike any other test you have ever taken. Most of the tests you've encountered in high school and college have been knowledge-based tests—that is, tests requiring you to recall and be conversant with a certain body of facts, formulas, theorems, or other acquired knowledge. However, there is no math or vocabulary on the LSAT. It doesn't ask you to spit back memorized facts. It doesn't ask you to apply learned formulas to specific problems. In fact, all you'll be asked to do on the LSAT is think—thoroughly, quickly, and strategically.

Sign up for the LSAT

You'll need a copy of the *LSAT/LSDAS Registration and Information Book.* It's free and available at designated distribution points, such as undergraduate advising offices, law schools, and Kaplan centers (call 800-KAP-TEST for locations). You can also call Law Services at (215) 968-1001 or visit its Web site at http://www.LSAC.org.

The LSAT is designed to measure skills that are considered essential for success in law school: the reading and comprehension of complex texts with insight and accuracy; the organization and management of information and the ability to draw reasonable inferences from it; the ability to reason critically; and the analysis and evaluation of the reasoning and arguments of others. These are skills that you already possess to some extent; you've acquired them gradually over the many years of your education. However, most people haven't fully developed the skills necessary for success on the LSAT.

And that's where test preparation—and this book—comes in. We'll not only help you to develop the reading and reasoning skills you'll need, we'll also show you how to apply the skills you already have to the very specific and idiosyncratic tasks required by the LSAT. For example, you already know how to read. But we'll show you how to read critically in the way the test demands—we'll show you how to most effectively unlock the dense but highly structured arguments and passages that appear on the LSAT. Similarly, while you've probably developed plenty of sound, logical ways of analyzing problems in everyday life, we'll teach you how to apply your natural deductive and analytical skills to the unusual demands of the Logic Games and Logical Reasoning sections of the LSAT.

Quarterly
The LSAT is offered four times each year: February, June, late September or early October, and December.

Before we begin developing your skills, though, it's important that you be familiar with the purpose and format of the LSAT. Why? First, because understanding the exam is the first step in mastering it. Second, because there are a lot of rumors floating around about the LSAT—most of which are pernicious myths. Listening to, and worse, believing these rumors can be debilitating and destructive. Do any of these sound familiar?

> "The LSAT has nothing to do with law school."
> "They just want to make it impossible for us."
> "Logic Games? Oh, they're all about drawing the right picture."
> "It's smart to skip one Logic Game or Reading Comprehension passage."
> "Reading Comprehension? Nobody can teach you how to improve that."
> "You're supposed to choose the best answer, but there's always more than one."
> "No law school reads the writing sample."
> "You can't prepare for the LSAT."

In this chapter, we'll make sure you are comfortable with the format of the LSAT. We'll also tackle some of these common LSAT myths, and show you how wrong (and damaging to your score!) they are. Throughout this book, we will continue to empower you by debunking the most common LSAT myths.

For now, let's start with the biggest myth of all: *"The LSAT has nothing to do with Law School."* The test makers have designed the LSAT to mimic or reflect the reading and reasoning skills necessary for success in the first year of law school. These skills can be measured with precision and fairness because the first-year curricula of all law schools are virtually identical, as is the thinking that first-year law students ("1-Ls") must demonstrate. Therefore, the test makers know what skills are required by law students and can design a test to evaluate this well-defined set of skills.

Studies show that LSAT scores help to predict which students will do well in law school! This is why law schools place such extraordinary emphasis on the LSAT. In fact, your LSAT score may determine as much as 50 percent or more of a school's decision whether to admit you.

Many "self-proclaimed" test preparation experts like to claim that the LSAT is nothing more than an arbitrary obstacle. Why? It's an appealing message. Most people like to believe that if they don't do well on the test, it's not their fault. They can blame the test—after all, it's arbitrary, right? We know, from almost 30 years of experience helping over 600,000 people prepare for law school, that people who scoff or show contempt for the LSAT don't do well. Mockery is the retreat of the insecure; it allows the mocker to retain his status.

On the other hand, you shouldn't venerate or be intimidated by the exam, either. Instead, understand the exam and take control of it. Our strategies—and this book—will help you understand and take command of the LSAT.

Now let's tackle another myth: *"You can't prepare for the LSAT."* Once again, this simply isn't true. The LSAT is a standardized test. A 158 on the June 1992 exam must mean the same thing as a 158 on the December 1996 exam. Therefore, the content of the test must remain the same from exam to exam. It wouldn't be possible (or fair) to compare two scores that were based on two very different tests. Every exam must test the same set of skills.

This is great news for you. It means you *can* prepare for test. Even the people who administer the LSAT (Law Services) believe it is important to prepare. In its *Registration and Information Book,* Law Services states that "although it is impossible to say when you are sufficiently prepared for the LSAT, very few people achieve their full potential without preparing."

We know what will appear on your test and as you work through this book, we'll teach you what you need to know to score your best. If you begin your studies assuming you can't improve, you won't. If you believe that you can improve, you will. It's that simple. At Kaplan, we've helped over 600,000 people improve their LSAT scores and we'll help you.

Now that you know *why* you need to take the test and that you *can* prepare for it, let's talk about the test itself.

What Is the Structure of the LSAT?

The LSAT consists of five sections of multiple-choice questions (175 minutes total), plus a 30-minute writing sample. The writing sample is always administered last. However, the five 35-minute multiple-choice sections can appear in any order. Add in the administrative details at both ends of the testing experience, plus a break of 10–15 minutes between sections three and four, and you can count on being in the test room for at least four and a half to five hours. It's a long day, to say the least. And if you can't approach it with confidence and rigor, you'll quickly lose your composure. That's why it's so important that you take control of the test.

Section	Number of Questions	Time in Minutes
Logical Reasoning	24–26	35
Logical Reasoning	24–26	35
Reading Comp	26–28	35
Logic Games	23–24	35
"Experimental"	24–28	35
Writing Sample	—	30

Each of the two scored Logical Reasoning sections contains 24 to 26 short passages ("stimuli"). The Reading Comprehension section consists of four passages, each about 450 words long, with five to eight questions per passage. The Logic Games section contains four games with five to seven questions per game.

The experimental section is unscored and allows Law Services to test questions that they may use on future tests. It will look exactly like a scored section of the same question type, so on the day of the test *don't spend time trying to figure out which section is experimental.*

We'll talk more about each of these question types in later chapters. For now, realize that you'll be answering about 125 questions during three intense hours. That's only a little over one minute per question! And that doesn't include time to read passages or set up games. Clearly, you're going to need to move quickly. But don't let yourself get careless. To take control of the LSAT you must increase speed without sacrificing accuracy.

How Is the LSAT Scored?

The scoring scale for the LSAT runs from 120 to 180; 120 is the lowest possible score and 180 the highest. Your scaled score is based on your raw score, the number of total questions that you get right. (Remember, the Writing Sample doesn't receive a numerical score and the Experimental section, no matter what question type it contains, doesn't count.) All questions are weighted equally. (So, as we'll talk about later, you should never leave a question blank.) Your scaled score also corresponds to a percentile ranking, which allows law schools to see where your score places you in the applicant pool.

Get the Score

Your LSAT score will be mailed to you about four weeks after you take the test. But you can call in earlier to get your score. Call LSAT TelScore at (215) 968-1200 for details.

Your raw score is the number of questions that you answer correctly. Your raw score is multiplied by a complicated scoring formula (which is different for each test to accommodate differences between tests) to yield the scaled score—the one that will fall somewhere in that 120–180 range. This scaled score is reported to the schools as your LSAT score.

Since the test is graded on a preset curve, the scaled score will always correspond to a certain percentile, which will also be given on your score report. A score of 160, for instance, corresponds roughly to the eightieth percentile, meaning that 80 percent of test takers scored at or below your level. The percentile figure is important because it allows law schools to get a sense quickly of where you fall in the pool of applicants.

SOME SAMPLE PERCENTILES

Percentile	Approx. Scaled Score (Range 120–180)	Approx. Raw Score
99th percentile	172	~91 correct out of 101
95th percentile	167	~84 correct out of 101
90th percentile	164	~80 correct out of 101
80th percentile	160	~73 correct out of 101
75th percentile	158	~69 correct out of 101
50th percentile	152	~59 correct out of 101

Note: Exact percentile-to-scaled-score relationships vary from test to test.

As there's no penalty for wrong answers on the LSAT, *always select an answer choice for every question.* This means that you should always fill in an answer for every question, whether you get to that question or not! Never let time run out on any section without filling in an answer for every question!

What's a Good LSAT Score?

Of course, what you consider to be a "good" LSAT score depends on your own expectations and goals, but here are a few interesting statistics. If you get about half of the questions right (about 50), you'll score in approximately the thirtieth percentile, approximately a 147—not a great score. But on the LSAT a little improvement counts for a lot. If you get only one more question right every ten minutes during the exam, you'll jump to the sixtieth percentile (about 64 questions right)—a huge improvement. Just a few additional correct answers can make a big difference in your score.

However, you don't have to be perfect, or nearly so, to do well. In fact, on most LSATs you can get as many as 28 questions wrong and score above the eightieth percentile, and as many as 21 wrong and score above the ninetieth percentile! Even students who score in the 99.9th percentile usually get a handful of questions wrong.

Although many factors influence whether a law school will accept you, your LSAT score is probably the most important. So, typically, an "average" score isn't good enough. While the median LSAT score is about a 151, you'll need a score of 160 or above to be considered competitive at many law schools. And if you're competing for the top schools, you'll probably have to do even better.

What Kinds of Questions Are on the LSAT?

Now let's take a quick look at each question type you'll encounter on the test. We'll provide you with strategies and techniques in coming chapters. For now, just familiarize yourself with the kinds of questions asked on each section.

Logical Reasoning

What It Is

Each of the two scored Logical Reasoning sections consists of 24 to 26 questions based on short passages ("stimuli"). Each stimulus takes the form of an argument—that is, a conclusion based on evidence. You need to understand the stimulus argument to answer the one or two questions based on it. Although you don't need to know the technical terms of formal logic, you do need critical reasoning skills to analyze an argument and make judgments accordingly.

Why It's on the Test

The law schools want to see whether you can understand, analyze, evaluate, and manipulate arguments, and draw reliable conclusions—as every law student and attorney must. It's important to note that this question type makes up half of your LSAT score, so you know that the law schools value these skills.

What It's Like

Here are the directions to the section, along with a sample question:

Don't Read the Directions

These are the actual directions that appear on the LSAT. Read them now. But, don't waste your time reading them on the day of the test.

> Directions: The questions in this section are based on the reasoning contained in brief statements or passages. For some questions, more than one of the choices could conceivably answer the question. However, you are to choose the best answer; that is, the response that most accurately and completely answers the question. You should not make assumptions that are by commonsense standards implausible, superfluous, or incompatible with the passage. After you have chosen the best answer, blacken the corresponding space on your answer sheet.

A study of 20 overweight men revealed that each man experienced significant weight loss after adding SlimDown, an artificial food supplement, to his daily diet. For three months, each man consumed one SlimDown portion every morning after exercising, and then followed his normal diet for the rest of the day. Clearly, anyone who consumes one portion of SlimDown every day for at least three months will lose weight and will look and feel his or her best.
Which one of the following is an assumption on which the argument depends?

(A) The men in the study will gain back the weight they lost if they discontinue the SlimDown program.
(B) No other dietary supplement will have the same effect on overweight men.
(C) The daily exercise regimen was not responsible for the effects noted in the study.
(D) Women will not experience similar weight reductions if they adhere to the SlimDown program for three months.
(E) Overweight men will achieve only partial weight loss if they do not remain on the SlimDown program for a full three months.

Choice (C) is correct. We'll show you how to approach Logical Reasoning questions like this in a later chapter.

Logic Games

What It Is

There are 23 to 24 questions in the Logic Games (a.k.a. Analytical Reasoning) section, and these are based on four games, with five to seven questions each. They require an ability to reason clearly and deductively from a given set of rules or restrictions, all under strictly timed conditions.

Why It's on the Test

The section tests your command of detail, your formal deductive abilities, your understanding of how rules limit and order behavior (which is the very definition of law itself), and your ability to cope with many pieces of data simultaneously in the course of solving problems.

What It's Like

What follows are directions to the Logic Games section as well as a shortened sample game and questions:

> Directions: Each group of questions in this section is based on a set of conditions. In answering some of the questions, it may be useful to draw a rough diagram. Choose the response that most accurately and completely answers each question and blacken the corresponding space on your answer sheet.

Don't Read the Directions

These are the actual directions that appear on the LSAT. Read them now. But, don't waste your time reading them on the day of the test.

Five workers—Mona, Patrick, Renatta, Saffie, and Will—are scheduled to clean apartments on five days of a single week, Monday to Friday. There are three cleaning shifts available each day—a morning shift, an afternoon shift, and an evening shift. No more than one worker cleans in any given shift. Each worker cleans exactly two shifts during the week, but no one works more than one cleaning shift in a single day.

Exactly two workers clean on each day of the week.
Mona and Will clean on the same days of the week.
Patrick doesn't clean on any afternoon or evening shifts during the week.
Will doesn't clean on any morning or afternoon shifts during the week.
Mona cleans on two consecutive days of the week.
Saffie's second cleaning shift of the week occurs on an earlier day of the week than Mona's first cleaning shift.

1. Which one of the following must be true?

(A) Saffie cleans on Tuesday afternoon.
(B) Patrick cleans on Monday morning.
(C) Will cleans on Thursday evening.
(D) Renatta cleans on Friday afternoon.
(E) Mona cleans on Tuesday morning.

2. If Will does not clean on Friday, which one of the following could be false?

(A) Renatta cleans on Friday.
(B) Saffie cleans on Tuesday.
(C) Mona cleans on Wednesday.
(D) Saffie cleans on Monday.
(E) Patrick cleans on Tuesday.

(Note that there are only two questions accompanying this game; a typical logic game will have five to seven questions.)

For Question 1, the answer is (C); for Question 2 it's (E). Games are highly amenable to systematic technique and the proper use of scratch work, which we'll discuss in detail later.

Reading Comprehension

What It Is

The Reading Comprehension section consists of four passages, each about 450 words long, with five to eight questions. These long excerpts of scholarly passages are reminiscent of the kind of prose found in law texts. The topics are chosen from the areas of social sciences, humanities, natural sciences, and law.

Why It's on the Test

The purpose of the section is to see whether you can quickly get the gist of long, difficult prose—just as you'll have to do in law school.

What It's Like

Here are the directions and a sample passage. Note that the passage below is just an excerpt from a full-length passage; standard passages are generally longer.

> Directions: Each passage in this section is followed by a group of questions to be answered on the basis of what is stated or implied in the passage. For some of the questions, more than one of the choices could conceivably answer the question. However, you are to choose the best answer; that is; the response that most accurately and completely answers the question, and blacken the corresponding space on your answer sheet.

Don't Read the Directions

These are the actual directions that appear on the LSAT. Read them now. But, don't waste your time reading them on the day of the test.

> It has been suggested that post–World War II concepts of environmental liability, as they pertain to hazardous waste, grew out of issues regarding municipal refuse collection and disposal and industrial waste disposal in the period 1880–1940. To a great degree, the remedies available to Americans for dealing with the burgeoning hazardous waste problem were characteristic of the judicial, legislative, and regulatory tools used to confront a whole range of problems in the industrial age. At the same time, these remedies were operating in an era in which the problem of hazardous waste had yet to be recognized. It is understandable that an assessment of liability was narrowly drawn and most often restricted to a clearly identified violator in a specific act of infringement of the property rights of someone else. Legislation, for the most part, focused narrowly on clear threats to the public health and dealt with problems of industrial pollution meekly if at all. . . .

> According to the passage, judicial assessments of liability in waste disposal disputes prior to World War II were usually based on
>
> (A) excessively broad definitions of legal responsibility
> (B) the presence of a clear threat to the public health
> (C) precedents derived from well-known cases of large-scale industrial polluters
> (D) restricted interpretations of property rights infringements
> (E) trivial issues such as littering, eyesores, and other public nuisances

(Note that the above passage is an abbreviated example; on the test, a passage has approximately 450 words.)

The answer is choice (D). We'll show you how to approach the Reading Comp questions later.

The Experimental Section

The experimental (unscored) section allows Law Services to test questions for use on future tests. This section will look just like one of the others—either Logical Reasoning, Logic Games, or Reading Comprehension—so don't try to figure out which section is experimental and then just cruise through that section. That's an extremely risky proposition. Just do as well as you can on every section, and you're covered.

The Writing Sample

What It Is

The Writing Sample comes at the end of your LSAT day. You'll be given a scenario followed by two possible courses of action, and you'll have 30 minutes to make a written case that one course of action is superior.

Why It's on the Test

The writing sample shows the law schools whether you can argue for a position while breaking down the argument of an opponent. This essay is not graded, but is sent to law schools along with your LSAT score.

What It's Like

Here's a sample topic for a Writing Sample:

> The *Daily Tribune,* a metropolitan newspaper, is considering two candidates for promotion to business editor. Write an argument for one candidate over the other with the following considerations in mind:
>
> - The editor must train new writers and assign stories.
> - The editor must be able to edit and rewrite stories under daily deadline pressure.
>
> Laura received a B.A. in English from a large university. She was managing editor of her college newspaper and served as a summer intern at her hometown daily paper. Laura starting working at the *Tribune* right out of college and spent three years at the city desk covering the city economy. Eight years ago the paper formed its business section and Laura became part of the new department. After several years covering state business, Laura began writing on the national economy. Three years ago, Laura was named senior business and finance editor on the national business staff; she is also responsible for supervising seven writers.
>
> Palmer attended an elite private college where he earned both a B.S. in business administration and an M.A. in journalism. After receiving his journalism degree, Palmer worked for three years on a monthly business magazine. He won a prestigious national award for a series of articles on the impact of monetary policy on multinational corporations. Palmer came to the *Tribune* three years ago to fill the newly created position of international business writer. He was the only member of the international staff for two years and wrote on almost a daily basis. He now supervises a staff of four writers. Last year, Palmer developed a bimonthly business supplement for the *Tribune* that has proved highly popular and has helped increase the paper's circulation.

Obviously, there can be no right or wrong "answer" to the Writing Sample topic, but there are good and bad responses. We'll show you one possible response to this topic later, in the Writing Sample chapter.

What's Next?

Now that you are familiar with the format, scoring, and question types of the LSAT, let's turn our attention to strategies for mastering each section.

CHAPTER 2

Strategy Overview

Now that you have an idea of why you need to take the LSAT and how it's set up, let's talk about strategies to help you maximize your score on the test. First, we'll look at adopting the proper state of mind for LSAT success and general strategies for tackling the test. Then, in the topical chapters (Logical Reasoning, Logic Games, Reading Comprehension, and Writing Sample), we'll teach you the specific strategies you'll need for each type of question. In the chapter on Putting It All Together, we'll pull all of the section and question strategies you've learned into a cohesive plan of attack. Finally, we'll have you work through the two real LSATs applying what you've learned. By the day of the test, you'll be confident and totally prepared.

The LSAT Mindset
Knowing strategies for each question is only the beginning. You also have to approach the test with the proper attitude—a proactive, take-control kind of thinking we call the "LSAT mindset."

Let's get started. The first thing you need is the proper mental attitude. Knowing what questions will appear and how to answer them isn't enough. To do your best on the LSAT, you have to approach the entire test with the right mindset.

The LSAT Mindset

The LSAT mindset is something you want to bring to every question, passage, game, section, and full-length test (including the actual exam). Being in the LSAT mindset means reshaping your test-taking experience so that you are in control. It means:

- answering questions *if* you want to (by guessing on the most difficult questions rather than wasting time on them)
- answering questions *when* you want to (by saving tough but doable games, passages, and questions for later, coming back to them after racking up points on the easy ones)
- answering questions *how* you want to (by using our shortcuts and strategies to get points quickly and confidently, even if those methods aren't exactly what the test makers had in mind)

In order to do your best on the LSAT, you need to control the test, rather than allow the test and the test makers to control you. Don't worry; we'll teach you everything you need to know to attack the test in this proactive, take-control manner. Here are the overriding principles of the LSAT mindset that will be covered *in depth* in the chapters to come:

- Read actively and critically.
- Translate prose into your own words.
- Prephrase answer choices so you know what to look for.
- Save the toughest questions, passages, and games for last.
- Know the test and each of its components inside and out.
- Allow your confidence to build on itself.
- Take full-length practice tests the week before the test to break down the mystique of the real experience.
- Learn from your mistakes; it's not how much you practice, it's how much you get out of the practice.
- Look at the LSAT as a challenge, the first step in your legal career, rather than as an arbitrary obstacle to it.

And that's what the LSAT boils down to: taking control. Being proactive. Being on top of the test experience so that you can get as many points as you can as quickly and as easily as possible.

How to Take Control of Each Section

For most tests you've taken, you at least *tried* every question. If a question seemed particularly difficult, you spent significantly more time on it, since you probably got more points for answering it correctly. Not so on the LSAT. Remember, every LSAT question, no matter how difficult (or basic), is worth a single point. And since there are so many questions to do in so little time, you'd be a fool to spend three minutes getting a point for a hard question and then not have time to get a couple of quick points from two easy questions later in the section.

Guess

If you can't answer a question or you are running out of time, guess! There's no penalty if you're wrong, and you will get a point if you guess correctly.

Given this combination—limited time and all questions equal in weight—you've got to develop a way of handling the test sections to make sure you get as many points as you can as quickly and easily as you can. You need to take control. Here are the principles that will help you do that:

- Attack the questions in any order that strikes you as logical.
- Learn to recognize and seek out questions you're good at.
- Know that test questions are written to different levels of difficulty.
- Control time instead of letting time control you.

Attack the Questions in Any Order That Strikes You as Logical

One of the most valuable strategies for finishing the sections in time is recognizing and dealing first with the questions, games, and passages that are easier and more familiar to you. That means temporarily skipping those that promise to be difficult and time consuming. You can always come back to these at the end, and if you run out of time, you're much better off not getting to questions you may have had difficulty with, rather than missing relatively easy material. Of course, since there's no wrong-answer penalty, always fill in an answer to every question on the test, whether you get to it or not. And remember, unlike some other standardized tests, the questions on the LSAT *don't* appear in increasing order of difficulty. In fact, the last question could be the easiest.

Learn to Recognize and Seek out Questions You're Good At

LSAT questions, games, and passages, unlike items on the SAT and other standardized tests, are not presented in order of difficulty. There's no rule that says that you have to work through the questions in any particular order. In fact, the test makers scatter the basic and difficult questions throughout the section, in effect rewarding those who actually get to the end. Don't lose sight of what you're being tested for along with your reading and thinking skills: efficiency and cleverness. If you find sequencing games particularly easy, for example, seek out the sequencing game on the Logic Games section and do it first. Similarly, if you just love formal logic questions, head straight for such questions when you first turn to the Logical Reasoning sections.

Pop Quiz

Every question is worth the same amount. But question difficulty varies dramatically. Given that the LSAT is a timed test, which questions should you answer: basic or hard?

Know That the Test Questions Are Written to Different Levels of Difficulty

It's imperative that you remain calm and composed while working through a section. You can't allow yourself to be rattled by one hard game or reading passage so that it throws off your performance on the rest of the section. Expect to find at least one difficult passage or game on every section, but remember, you won't be the only one to have trouble with it. The test is curved to take the tough material into account. Having trouble with a difficult game isn't going to ruin your score—but getting upset about it and letting it throw you offtrack will. When you understand that part of the test maker's goal is to reward those who keep their composure, you'll recognize the importance of not panicking when you run into challenging material.

Don't Be Macho

It's difficult to concede defeat—to give up on a tough, time-consuming question. But, to score your best, you must. Every question is worth the same amount, so rack up easy, quick points first.

Control Time Instead of Letting Time Control You

Of course, the last thing you want to happen is to have time called on a particular section before you've answered half the questions. It's essential, therefore, that you pace yourself, keeping in mind the general guidelines for how long to spend on any individual question, passage, or game (we'll give you those guidelines). No one is saying that you should spend, for instance, exactly one and a quarter minutes on every Logical Reasoning question. But you should have a sense of how long you have to answer each question, so you'll know when you're exceeding the limit.

Keeping track of time is also important for guessing. Remember, there's no penalty for a wrong answer on the LSAT! So it pays to leave a little time at the end to guess on the questions you couldn't answer. For instance, let's say you don't get a chance to do the last game on a Logic Game section. If you were to leave the answer grids for those questions blank, you would get no points for that entire game. If, on the other hand, you were to give yourself a little time at the end to fill in a guess for each of those questions, you would have a very good chance of getting lucky on at least one or two questions. That would up your raw score by one or two points—which translates into a higher scaled score.

So, when working on a section, always remember to keep track of time. Don't spend a wildly disproportionate amount of time on any one question or group of questions. Also, give yourself 30 seconds or so at the end of each section to fill in answers for any questions you didn't get to. After all, a correct guess is worth just as much as any other correct answer.

Logical Reasoning

Section Expertise: Logical Reasoning

The important LR section strategies that will allow you to take control are:

- Spend an average of one and a quarter minutes per question.
- Save for last the questions that are the toughest for you.
- Try starting with the stimuli that have two questions (a double question) first.

Time Per Question

There are 24 to 26 questions to answer in 35 minutes, which works out to roughly a minute and a quarter per question. Keep in mind, though, that this is only an average; there are bound to be some questions that take less time and some that take more. It's okay if the occasional question takes you two minutes, if you're able to balance it out with a question that takes 45 seconds. Remember, too, that every question is worth the same, so don't get hung up on any one question. No single point on this section is worth three minutes of your valuable time, that's for sure. And think about it—if a question is so hard that it takes you that long to answer it, chances are you may get it wrong anyway. In that case, you'd have nothing to show for your extra time but a lower score.

Managing the Section

What kind of Logical Reasoning questions should you skip? Certainly questions containing stimuli that are indecipherable to you after a quick reading. It might be a good idea to skip questions that contain extra-long stimulus arguments, especially if you're running behind on time. But don't automatically be intimidated by the sheer length of a stimulus; often, the long ones are uncomplicated and easy to understand. Often, a good stimulus to start with is one that comes with two questions attached. There are usually two to four double-question stimuli on each Logical Reasoning section. Working through these, as opposed to single-question arguments, saves a little time, as you can potentially rack up two points for reading only one stimulus.

Logic Games

Time Per Game

There are four games to get through in 35 minutes, which works out to roughly eight and a half minutes per game. Remember, just as in Logical Reasoning, this is an average—some games may take a little more time, while some may take a little less.

Section Expertise: Logic Games

The best way to manage your time on the LG section:

- Preview the section before you start.
- Start with the easiest game.
- Allocate eight and a half minutes per game.
- Skip complex, difficult, or time-consuming questions.

Managing the Section

First, and most important, is the necessity of previewing the section. By this we mean that you should flip through the pages and glance at each game in order to decide which games look the easiest and most familiar to you. Previewing, of course, is not foolproof; a game that looks fairly straightforward at first glance could turn out to be more difficult. However, you should be able to get a general sense of a game's difficulty in just a few seconds. The ideal goal is to tackle the games in order of difficulty, from basic to hardest. But if you achieve nothing more than saving the hardest game for last, then you've come out way ahead.

So how can you tell which games might be difficult? The best way is to know the game types (which we will discuss in the Logic Games section), and to know which types you're good at and which types you should avoid like the plague (until the end, of course). A game that doesn't look familiar could simply be an oddball game—a good one to postpone. And don't necessarily be scared off by games with a lot of rules; sometimes, this works to your advantage. The more rules they give you, the more definite and concrete the game situation is, and the easier it will be to answer the questions. It's the games with few rules that often turn out to be tough, because they're inherently ambiguous.

Finally, remember what we said about the way the test makers test efficiency. They're crafty—they'll sometimes put an intentionally time-consuming question at the end of a game, possibly one involving a rule change that requires you to backtrack and set up the game all over again. Bear in mind that when this happens, they may not be testing your ability to get the right answer. Instead, you may be rewarded for your clever decision to skip the killer question in order to devote precious time to the next game, with a possible payoff of six or seven points.

Reading Comprehension

Time Per Passage

The Reading Comp format is similar to that of Logic Games: four passages in 35 minutes, which means about eight and a half minutes per passage. The Reading Comp strategies and techniques in the RC chapter should help you to get through each passage as quickly as possible, but here are a few additional suggestions for

Section Expertise: Reading Comprehension

Here are the strategies needed to maximize your RC score:

- Preview the section, as in LG, to assess relative difficulty.
- Do tough or time-consuming passages last.
- Spend about eight and a half minutes per passage (including questions).
- Don't get mired in the details of a passage. Read for structure and main idea and relocate details as required.

tackling a full section.

Managing the Section

It's a little more difficult to preview the Reading Comp section than it is to preview a Logic Games section. But it is possible to know that it's time to move on if the first third of a passage is extraordinarily confusing—or simply boring to the point of distraction. Concentration is a major key in Reading Comp, and if you simply can't "lock onto" the ideas in a passage, then it's time to put that one aside and look for friendlier territory. As in Logic Games, the goal is to save the most difficult stuff for last.

Quite often, you'll encounter Reading Comprehension passages that contain a preponderance of technical details or difficult concepts, only to find that few if any questions deal with the part of the passage that's so dense. Again, the test makers aren't necessarily trying to find out who's smart enough to understand that section of the passage. They may be trying to find out who's clever enough to skim past those details and focus on the more important aspects of the passage instead. If you keep this in mind, you'll be less likely to get mired in extraneous details.

What's Next

We've covered the proper LSAT mindset and section strategies for taking control of the LSAT. Let's now move to question strategies. We'll begin with the most important question type on the LSAT: Logical Reasoning. On the day of the test, you'll get two scored sections of LR that will make up about half of your LSAT score. The principles and strategies you'll learn in the LR chapter will also form the foundation for much of your work on the other question types. After LR, we'll work on Reading Comprehension, then move to Logic Games. We'll also spend a chapter teaching you the best way to handle the unscored Writing Sample. Finally, we'll tie together everything you've learned and prepare you to apply it to the two real LSATs.

CHAPTER 3

Logical Reasoning

You will get two *scored* Logical Reasoning sections on the day of the test (remember, though, you could see three sections, two scored and one unscored, if your experimental section is LR). Each section will contain 24 to 26 questions.

Don't Read the Directions

Part of what will allow you to move quickly and efficiently through LR is familiarity with the format of the section and the directions. We discussed both in the section on LSAT basics; if you need to review it quickly, do so now, before you continue.

LR constitutes half of your LSAT score! That's why we're starting this book with it and why this chapter is the longest. The fact that Logical Reasoning comprises half of your LSAT score is actually good news, because you already have most of the Logical Reasoning skills you need for the test. In fact, we all do. But as we pointed out in the section on LSAT basics, the LSAT tests your ability to use those skills thoroughly, quickly, and strategically in the context of a strictly timed, multiple-choice test.

On the LSAT, as in law school and in your legal career, you'll need the ability to see and understand complex reasoning. It's not enough to sense whether an argument is logically strong or weak; you'll need to analyze precisely why it is so. This involves an even more fundamental skill, one that's called on by nearly every Logical Reasoning question—the ability to isolate and identify the various components of any given argument.

First of all, let's clarify what's meant by the word "argument." We don't mean a conversation in which two or more people are shouting at one another. No, the word "argument" in Logical Reasoning means any piece of text where an author puts forth a set of ideas and/or a point of view, and attempts to support it.

You Have What It Takes

There's nothing unique about the skills you need for Logical Reasoning. You already can think in the way the test maker rewards. You just need to learn to apply the skills you already have to the peculiar requirements of a timed, standardized test.

Nearly, every LSAT Logical Reasoning stimulus—that is, every argument—is made up of two basic parts:

- the conclusion (the point that the author is trying to make)
- the evidence (the support that the author offers for the conclusion)

Everything's an Argument
Almost all LR stimuli are arguments, consisting of evidence and conclusion.

Success in LR hinges on your ability to identify these parts of the argument. There is no general rule about where conclusion and evidence appear in the argument—the conclusion could be the first sentence, followed by the evidence, or it could be the last sentence, with the evidence preceding it, or any sentence in between. Consider the following short stimulus.

> The Brookdale Public Library will require extensive physical rehabilitation to meet the new building codes passed by the town council. For one thing, the electrical system is inadequate, causing the lights to flicker sporadically. Furthermore, there are too few emergency exits, and even those are poorly marked and sometimes locked.

Let's suppose that the author of the argument above was only allowed one sentence to convey her meaning. Do you think that she would waste her lone opportunity on the statement: "The electrical system at the Brookdale Public Library is inadequate, causing the lights to flicker sporadically"? Would she walk away satisfied that she got her main point across? Probably not. Given a single opportunity, she would have to state the first sentence: "The Brookdale Public Library will require extensive physical rehabilitation. . . ." This is her conclusion. If you pressed her for her *reasons* for making this statement, she would then cite the electrical and structural problems with the building. This is the evidence for her conclusion.

But does that mean that an evidence-statement such as, "The electrical system at the Brookdale Public Library is inadequate" can't be a conclusion? No; we're saying that it's not the conclusion for this particular argument. Every idea, every new statement, must be evaluated in the context of the stimulus in which it appears. For the sake of argument (no pun intended), let's see what a stimulus would look like in which the statement above serves as the conclusion:

> The electrical wiring at the Brookdale Public Library was installed over forty years ago, and appears to be corroded in some places *(evidence)*. An electrician, upon inspection of the system, found a few frayed wires as well as some blown fuses *(evidence)*. Clearly, the electrical system at the Brookdale Public Library is inadequate *(conclusion)*.

Structural Signals
Certain words and phrase can tell you what the evidence and conclusion are; learn to recognize them. Clues that signal evidence: "because," "since," "for," "as a result of," "due to," etcetera. Clues that signal the conclusion: "consequently," "hence," "therefore," "thus," "clearly," "so," "accordingly," etcetera.

To succeed in Logical Reasoning, you have to be able to determine the precise function of every sentence in the stimulus. Use structural signals, or keywords, when attempting to isolate evidence and conclusion. Words in the stimulus such as "because," "for," and "since" usually indicate evidence is about to follow, while words such as "therefore," "hence," "thus," and "consequently" usually signal a conclusion.

Be aware however, that not every sentence or idea in a stimulus may contribute something to the argument (evidence and conclusion). The test makers often repeat information, include extraneous material, or try to distract you. Cut through the surplus words to the heart of the argument. Your goal is to discover the two basic parts to every argument: the evidence and the conclusion. Consider the following stimulus:

> The Brookdale Public Library is a beautiful building, but very old *(extraneous)*. Unfortunately, it has fallen into disrepair in recent years *(distracting)*. The electrical wiring at the Brookdale Public Library was installed over forty years ago, and appears to be corroded in some places *(evidence)*. Recently, city inspectors evaluated the plumbing and electrical systems in the building *(extraneous)*. An electrician, upon inspection of the system, found a few frayed wires as well as some blown fuses *(evidence)*. Clearly, the electrical system at the Brookdale Public Library is inadequate *(conclusion)*.

The evidence and conclusion are the same as in the previous example. But, this sample stimulus clearly includes sentences that don't contribute to the author's argument. For instance, the first sentence states that the building is beautiful. This is extraneous to the author's conclusion (that the electrical system is inadequate). The fact that the building is old, also from the first sentence, is also extraneous. Finally, knowing that the electrician who inspected the wiring was a city inspector doesn't really contribute anything to the conclusion that the electrical system is inadequate. Maybe his opinion carries more weight, but heck, his opinion could be worth less—he does work for the city after all.

It's *critical* to break down every LR argument into evidence and conclusion because knowing what is important and what is extraneous or irrelevant will allow you to answer questions quickly and accurately. You will be able to prephrase an answer to the question and pick the correct choice with confidence. Also, wrong answer choices often deal with extraneous and distracting words or ideas. If you don't understand the argument before looking at the answer choices, it is much more likely that you will be tempted by one of the wrong choices. The explanations throughout this book, especially for the two real LSATs at the end, will help you to focus on the essential evidence and conclusion in each argument. Pay close attention. The best way to learn to read critically is to review explanations to actual LSAT questions.

The Importance of Careful Review

As you practice for the test, it is *extremely* important that you carefully review the explanation to every question—both for the questions you got wrong *and* the questions you got right. You don't learn anything by answering a question; you merely test your ability to answer that question. It's only through review that you can *improve* your score. Did you get a question right for the right reasons or was it a lucky guess? You want to be able to *repeat* your performance on the day of the test. If you got a question right for the wrong reason, how will you know if you can get it right on the day of the test? And if you got a question right for the right reasons, was there a quicker way to get the same result?

You Don't Learn Anything by Answering a Question!
It's only through careful review that you can improve your score.

After we introduce you to the Kaplan Four-Step Method for Logical Reasoning, we'll spend a little time explaining why explanations are so valuable and how to use them to improve your score. For now, let's learn the method of attack that you will use for every question that appears on the test.

The Kaplan Four-Step Method for Logical Reasoning

The Kaplan Four-Step Method for Logical Reasoning is the same method we teach in our live classes. Hundreds of thousands of Kaplan students have successfully applied this method to real LSAT questions. Now we will teach it to you. Here are the four steps:

The Kaplan Four-Step Method for Logical Reasoning
1. Preview the question stem.
2. Read the stimulus.
3. Prephrase an answer.
4. Choose an answer.

1. Preview the question stem.
2. Read the stimulus.
3. Try to prephrase an answer.
4. Choose an answer.

Step One: Preview the Question Stem

Previewing the stem (but not the answers) is a great way to focus your reading on the stimulus, so that you know exactly what you're looking for. In effect, it gives you a jump on the question. You'll know what is important in the argument and what is extraneous, so that you can focus your efforts, save time, and improve accuracy. For example, let's say the question attached to the original library argument above asked the following:

> The author supports her point about the need for rehabilitation at the Brookdale Library by citing which of the following?

Know What You're Looking For
By previewing the question stem before you read the stimulus, you'll know what you need to do in advance. This will save time and improve your accuracy. Don't, however, preview the answers.

If you were to preview this question stem before reading the stimulus, you would know what to look for in advance—namely, evidence, the "support" provided for the conclusion. Similarly, if the question asked you to find an assumption that the author is relying on, this would tell you in advance that there was a crucial piece of the argument missing, and you could begin to think about it right off the bat.

Previewing the stem allows you to set the tone of your attack on each particular question, and thus will help you save time in the long run. As you'll soon see, this technique will come in especially handy when we discuss approaches to the various question types.

Don't, however, preview the answer choices. Whereas reading the question stem, by itself, is very helpful, previewing the answer choices is not. Since wrong answers are written to look tempting, it's dangerous to read them before you have a solid understanding of the argument.

Step Two: Read the Stimulus

With the question stem in mind, read the stimulus, paraphrasing as you go. Remember to read actively and critically, pinpointing evidence and conclusion. Also get a sense for how strong or weak the argument is.

Remember, you must read actively, not passively, on the LSAT. Active readers are always thinking critically, forming reactions as they go along. They constantly question whether the author's argument seems valid or dubious. On a section where many of the questions deal with finding flaws in the author's reasoning, it's imperative to read with a very critical eye.

For instance, how persuasive is the argument in the library stimulus? Well, it's pretty strong, since the evidence certainly seems to indicate that certain aspects of the library's structure need repair. But without more evidence about what the new building codes are like, we can't say for sure that the conclusion of this argument is valid. So this is a strong argument, but not an airtight one.

Part of what you're called on to do in this section is to evaluate arguments, so don't allow yourself to fall into the bad habits of the passive reader—reading solely for the purpose of getting through the stimulus. Those who read this way are clueless when it comes to answering the questions, and invariably find themselves having to read the stimuli twice or even three times. Then they wonder why they run out of time on the section. Read the stimuli right the first time—with a critical eye and an active mind.

After you read the stimulus, you'll want to paraphrase the author's main argument—that is, restate the author's ideas in your own words. Frequently, the authors in Logical Reasoning (and in Reading Comprehension, as we'll see) say pretty simple things in complex ways. But if you mentally translate the verbiage into a simpler form, you'll find the whole thing more manageable.

In Your Own Words
It's often much easier to understand and remember an argument if you restate it, simply, in your own words.

In the library argument, for instance, you probably don't want to deal with the full complexity of the author's stated conclusion:

> The Brookdale Public Library will require extensive physical rehabilitation to meet the new building codes just passed by the town council.

Instead, you probably want to carry a much simpler form of the point in your mind, something like:

> The library will need fixing up to meet new codes.

Often, by the time you begin reading through answer choices, you run the risk of losing sight of the gist of the stimulus. After all, you can only concentrate on a certain amount of information at one time. Restating the argument in your own words will not only help you get the author's point in the first place, but it will also help you hold on to it until you've found the correct answer.

Step Three: Try to Prephrase an Answer

The Art of the Prephrase
You don't need to be elaborate or even very specific. Your goal is just to get an idea of what you're looking for, so that it's easier to find the correct answer.

This step is crucial. You must try to approach the answer choices with at least a faint idea of what the answer should look like. This is not to say that you should ponder the question for minutes until you're able to write out your own answer; it's still a multiple-choice test, so the right answer is there on the page. Just try to get in the habit of instinctively framing an answer to each question. This step will enable you to scan the choices for the right answer quickly and confidently. In the alternative, it will make it *much* easier to identify and eliminate incorrect answers (process of elimination).

If you can come up with a prephrase of a possible answer, scan the choices. The correct answer will undoubtedly be worded differently and will be fleshed out more than your little seed of an idea. But if it matches your thought, you'll know it in a second. And you'll find that there's no more satisfying feeling in Logical Reasoning than prephrasing correctly, allowing you to choose the correct answer quickly and confidently. For instance, let's say a question for the library argument went like this:

> The author's argument depends on which one of the following assumptions about the new building codes?

Having thought about the stimulus argument, an answer to this question may have sprung immediately to mind—namely, the assumption that the new codes apply to existing buildings as well as to new buildings under construction. After all, according to the author, the library will have to be rehabilitated to meet the new codes. Clearly, the assumption is that the codes apply to existing buildings. And that's the kind of statement you would look for among the choices.

By the way, don't be discouraged if not all questions are good candidates for prephrasing answers. Some questions just won't have an answer that jumps out at you. But if used correctly, prephrasing can work on many, many questions. It will really boost your confidence and increase your speed on the section when you can come up with a glimmer of what the right answer should look like, and then have it jump right off the page at you.

Step Four: Choose an Answer

Process of Elimination
If you can't prephrase an answer, use the process of elimination.

If you were able to prephrase an answer, skim the choices looking for something that sounds like what you have in mind. If you couldn't think of anything, use process of elimination: read and evaluate each choice, throwing out the ones that are outside the scope of the argument. After settling on an answer, you may wish to double-check the question stem briefly to make sure that you're indeed answering the question that was asked.

Answer the Question Asked!

It's disheartening when you fully understand the author's argument, and then blow the point by supplying an answer to a question that wasn't asked. For example, when you're asked for an inference supported by the argument, it does you no good to pick the choice that strengthens the author's conclusion. Likewise, if you're asked for an assumption, don't be fooled into selecting a choice that looks vaguely like a piece of the author's evidence.

When asked why they made a particular wrong choice, students sometimes respond by saying such things as, "Well, it's true, isn't it?" and "Look, it says so right there," pointing to the stimulus. Well, that's simply not good enough. The question stem doesn't ask, "Which one of the following looks familiar?" It always asks for something very specific. It's your job to follow the test makers' line of reasoning to the credited response.

Also, be on the lookout for "reversers"—words such as "not" and "except." These little words are easy to miss, but they entirely change what kind of statement you're looking for among the choices.

Use the Scope of the Argument to Eliminate Wrong Choices

One of the most important Logical Reasoning skills, particularly when you're at the point of actually selecting one of the five choices, is the ability to focus on the scope of the argument. The majority of wrong choices on this section are wrong because they are "outside the scope." In everyday language, that simply means that these choices contain elements that don't match the author's ideas, or that simply go beyond the context of the stimulus.

Some common examples of scope problems are choices that are too narrow, or too broad, or literally have nothing to do with the author's point. Also, watch for and eliminate choices that are too extreme to match the argument's scope; they're usually signaled by words such as "all," "always," "never," "none," and so on. Choices that are more qualified are often correct for arguments that are moderate in tone, and contain words such as "usually," "sometimes," "probably," etcetera.

Scope It Out
A significant number of wrong answers in LR can be eliminated because they are outside the scope. Eliminate answers that are too extreme, that don't match the stimulus' tone or subject, or that have nothing to do with the author's point.

To illustrate the scope principle, let's look again at the question mentioned above:

> The author's argument depends on which one of the following assumptions about the new building codes?

Let's say one of the choices reads as follows:

> (A) The new building codes are far too stringent.

Knowing the scope of the argument would help you to eliminate this choice very quickly. You know that this argument is just a claim about what the new codes will require—that the library be rehabilitated. It's not an argument about whether the requirements in the new codes are good, or justifiable, or ridiculously strict. That kind of value judgment is outside the scope of this argument.

Recognizing scope problems is a great way of eliminating dozens of wrong answers quickly. Make sure you pay special attention to the scope issues discussed in the explanations throughout this book.

The Importance of Proper Review

As we told you earlier, it is *extremely* important that you carefully review the explanation to every question—both for the questions you got wrong *and* the questions you got right. Remember, you don't learn anything by answering a question; you merely test your ability to answer that question.

Study the Explanations

Answering a practice question won't improve your score. Studying the explanation to that same question will.

By taking a practice test and scoring it, you'll know you missed a certain question, but will you know *why* you missed it? More importantly, will you know how to avoid missing the same type of question on the day of the test? You know you got the question right, but do you know *how* you answered it correctly? And most importantly, do you know how to *repeat* this success on the same type of question on the day of the test?

Kaplan's explanations break each stimulus down into evidence and conclusion and show you how to identify and choose the right answer. We'll also show you why the wrong answers are wrong so that you won't be tempted to choose similar traps on the test. With Kaplan's exclusive explanations, you'll soon learn to recognize and avoid these common wrong choices that the test makers create to ensnare the unwary. We've included explanations that detail the Kaplan Four-Step Method to every question in this book. Use them, and you'll see your score increase!

Now you're ready to try applying the Kaplan Method to a question. Afterwards, learn from the experience by reviewing the strategic explanation that follows.

Applying the Kaplan Four-Step Method for Logical Reasoning

Try applying the Kaplan Method to this genuine Logical Reasoning question:

> A study of 20 overweight men revealed that each man experienced significant weight loss after adding SlimDown, an artificial food supplement, to his daily diet. For three months, each man consumed one SlimDown portion every morning after exercising, and then followed his normal diet for the rest of the day. Clearly, anyone who consumes one portion of SlimDown every day for at least three months will lose weight and will look and feel his or her best.
>
> Which one of the following is an assumption on which the argument depends?
>
> (A) The men in the study will gain back the weight they lost if they discontinue the SlimDown program.
>
> (B) No other dietary supplement will have the same effect on overweight men.
>
> (C) The daily exercise regimen was not at least partially responsible for the effects noted in the study.

(D) Women will not experience similar weight reductions if they adhere to the SlimDown program for three months.
(E) Overweight men will achieve only partial weight loss if they do not remain on the SlimDown program for a full three months.

Step One: Preview the Question Stem

We see, quite clearly, that we're dealing with an assumption question. Good. Immediately, we can adopt an "assumption mindset," which basically means that, before even reading the first word of the stimulus, we know that there is a gap between the supporting evidence and the conclusion. We can now turn to the stimulus, already on the lookout for this missing link.

Step Two: Read the Stimulus

The first sentence introduces a study of 20 men using a food supplement product, resulting in weight loss for all of them. The second sentence describes how they used it: once a day, for three months, after morning exercise. So far so good; it feels as if we're building up to something. The word "clearly" (a structural signal) usually indicates that some sort of conclusion follows, and in fact it does: the author concludes in the third sentence that anyone who has one portion of the product daily for three months will lose weight, too.

You must read critically! Notice that the conclusion doesn't say that anyone who follows the *same routine* as the twenty men will have the same results; it says that anyone who simply *consumes the product* in the same way will have the same results. You should have begun to sense the inevitable lack of crucial information at this point. The evidence in the second sentence describes a routine that includes taking the supplement after daily exercise, whereas the conclusion focuses on the supplement and entirely ignores the part about the exercise. The conclusion, therefore, doesn't stem logically from the evidence in the first two sentences. This blends seamlessly into Step Three.

Step Three: Prephrase an Answer

As expected, the argument is beginning to look as if it has a serious shortcoming. Of course, we expected this because we previewed the question stem before reading the stimulus.

In overly simplistic terms, the argument proceeds like so: "A bunch of guys did A and B for three months, and had X result. If anyone does A for three months, that person will experience X result, too." Sound a little fishy? You bet. The author must be assuming that A (the product), not B (exercise), must be the crucial thing that leads to the result. If not, the conclusion makes no sense.

So, you might prephrase the answer like this: "Something about the exercise thing needs to be cleared up." That's it. Did you think your prephrasing had to be something fancy and glamorous? Well, it doesn't. All you need is an inkling of what the question is looking for, and in this case, it just seems that if we don't shore up the exercise issue, the argument will remain invalid and incomplete. So, with our vague idea of a possible assumption, we can turn to Step Four, which is . . .

Step Four: Choose an Answer

Since we were able to prephrase something, it's best to skim the choices looking for it. And, lo and behold, there's our idea, stated very LSAT-like, in choice (C). Choice (C) clears up the exercise issue. Yes, this author must assume (C) to make the conclusion that eating SlimDown alone will cause anyone to lose weight.

At this point, if you're stuck for time, you simply choose (C) and move on. If you have more time, you may as well quickly check the remaining choices, to find (we hope) that none of them fits the bill. Of course, once you grasp the structure of the argument and have located the author's central assumption, you should be able to answer any question they throw at you. This one takes the form of an assumption question. But it could just as easily have been phrased as a weaken-the-argument question:

> Which one of the following, if true, casts the most doubt on the argument above?

Answer: Daily exercise contributed significantly to the weight loss experienced by the men in the study. And here's a flaw question that could have been based on the same stimulus:

> The author's reasoning is flawed because it

Answer: Overlooks the possibility that the results noted in the study were caused, at least in part, by daily exercise rather than by the consumption of SlimDown alone.

The Nine Crucial LR Question Types

Now that you're familiar with the Kaplan Four-Step Method to Logical Reasoning, let's look at the most common types of questions you'll see. Certain question types crop up over and over again on the LSAT, and it pays to be familiar with them. Of the types discussed below, the first three (Assumption, Strengthen the Argument/Weaken the Argument, and Inference) appear the most frequently.

Assumption Questions

The Missing Link

If an argument is missing a link between evidence and conclusion, the author is making an assumption—a necessary but unstated premise.

An assumption bridges the gap between an argument's evidence and conclusion. It's a piece of support that isn't explicitly stated, but that is required for the conclusion to remain valid. When a question asks you to find an author's assumption, it's asking you to find the statement without which the argument falls apart.

In order to test whether a statement is assumed by an author, we can employ the Kaplan Denial Test. Here's how it works: simply deny or negate the statement and see if the argument falls apart. If it does, that choice is the correct assumption. If, on the other hand, the argument could still be true, the choice is wrong. Consider, as an example, this simple stimulus:

> Allyson plays volleyball for Central High School. Therefore, Allyson must be more than 6 feet tall.

You should recognize the second sentence as the conclusion, and the first sentence as the evidence for it. But is the argument complete? Obviously not. The piece that's missing—the unstated link between the evidence and conclusion—is the assumption, and you could probably prephrase this one pretty easily:

> All volleyball players for Central High School are more than 6 feet tall.

To test whether this really is an assumption necessary to the argument, let's apply the Kaplan Denial Test, by negating it. What if it's not true that all volleyball players for Central High School are more than 6 feet tall? Can we still logically conclude that Allyson must be taller than 6 feet? No, we can't. Sure, it's possible that she is, but just as possible that she's not. By denying the statement, then, the argument falls to pieces; it's simply no longer valid. And that's our conclusive proof that the statement above is a necessary assumption of this argument.

As we've just seen, you can often prephrase the answer to an Assumption question. By previewing the question stem, you'll know what to look for. And stimuli for Assumption questions just "feel" like they're missing something. Often, the answer will jump right out at you, as in this case. In more difficult Assumption questions, the answers may not be as obvious. But in either case, you can use the Kaplan Denial Test to check quickly whichever choice seems correct.

Assumption Questions at a Glance

- There are four or five Assumption questions per section.
- They break down the argument into evidence and conclusion.
- They find the necessary but unstated premise that links the evidence to the conclusion.
- The assumption must be true in order for the conclusion to be true.
- They can be identified by using the Kaplan Denial Test.

Sample Stems

Here are some of the ways in which Assumption questions are worded:

> Which one of the following is assumed by the author?
>
> Upon which one of the following assumptions does the author rely?
>
> The argument depends on the assumption that
>
> Which one of the following, if added to the passage, will make the conclusion logical?
>
> The validity of the argument depends on which one of the following?
>
> The argument presupposes which one of the following?

Practice Assumption Question

Apply the Kaplan Four-Step Method to the following Assumption question:

> Video arcades, legally defined as video parlors having at least five video games, require a special city license and, in primarily residential areas such as Eastview, a zoning variance. The owners of the Video Zone, popular with Eastview teenagers, have maintained that their establishment requires neither an arcade license nor a zoning variance, because it is really a retail outlet.
>
> Which one of the following is an assumption on which the argument of the Video Zone's owners is based?
>
> (A) The existing Eastview zoning regulations are unconstitutionally strict.
> (B) At no time are more than four video games in operation at the Video Zone.
> (C) Stores like the Video Zone perform an important social function.
> (D) Many of the Video Zone's games were developed after the city's zoning laws were written.
> (E) Retail establishments require no special licenses or zoning variances in Eastview.

Step One: Preview the Question Stem
You're looking for an assumption. Read for evidence and conclusion and look for the necessary but unstated premise.

Step Two: Read the Stimulus
Video Zone's owners are concluding that their operation is exempt from the requirement to have an arcade license and a zoning variance in Eastview. Their evidence is the fact that they are a retail outlet.

Step Three: Try to Prephrase an Answer
To connect this evidence to this conclusion, they must assume that no "retail outlet" is required to obtain either the license or the variance, which is choice (E). If retail outlet *are* subject to the requirement, then Video Zone's owners are still on the hook.

Step Four: Choose an Answer
Choice (E) matches our prephrase. If you had used the process of elimination, you could have ruled out the other answer choices as follows.

Choice (A): The owners have implicitly accepted the community's zoning and other regulations; although they interpret the ordinances in a manner that might be open to question, they are not criticizing the regulations themselves.

Choice (B): We can surmise that the contrary is the case; that is at least five video games are in operation at some time. Otherwise, the Video Zone would simply not fall under the community's definition of "video parlor," and the issue of the possible need for an arcade license would not have arisen.

Choice (C): There is no suggestion in the owners' argument that they believe, or expect others to believe, that the business can be viewed as performing a social function. Their argument concerns classification, not social value.

Choice (D): Attractive as this line of reasoning might be in certain legal situations, we have no evidence here that Video Zone's owners have considered the issue of *when* the zoning laws were written.

Strengthen the Argument and Weaken the Argument Questions

Determining an argument's necessary assumption, as we've just seen, is required to answer assumption questions. But it also is required for other common question types: Strengthen the Argument and Weaken the Argument questions.

Strengthen/Weaken Questions at a Glance

- There are four or five Weaken the Argument and one or two Strengthen the Argument questions per section.
- Both question types often involve an assumption: Weaken questions may ask you to point out an assumption, while Strengthen questions may ask you to shore up a missing assumption.
- Correct answers don't prove or disprove the argument; they simply strengthen or weaken the argument.

One way to weaken an argument is to break down a central piece of evidence. Another way is to attack the validity of any assumptions the author may be making. The answer to many Weaken the Argument questions is the one that reveals an author's assumption to be unreasonable. Conversely, the answer to many Strengthen the Argument questions provides additional support by affirming the truth of an assumption or by presenting more persuasive evidence.

Let's take the same stimulus we used before, but look at it in the context of these other question types.

> Allyson plays volleyball for Central High School. Therefore, Allyson must be more than 6 feet tall.

Remember the assumption holding this argument together? It was that all volleyball players for Central High School are more than 6 feet tall. That's the assumption that makes or breaks the argument. So, if the question asked you to weaken the argument, you would want to attack that assumption.

> Which one of the following, if true, would most weaken the argument?

Answer: Not all volleyball players at Central High School are more than 6 feet tall. We've called into doubt the author's basic assumption, thus damaging the argument. But what about strengthening the argument? Again, the key is the necessary assumption.

> Which one of the following, if true, would most strengthen the argument?

Answer: All volleyball players at Central High School are more than 6 feet tall. Here, by making explicit the author's central assumption, we've in effect bolstered the argument.

Bait and Switch

A common trap in LR is to have an answer choice that obviously weakens the argument in a Strengthen the Argument question (and the reverse, an answer that obviously strengthens the argument in a Weaken the Argument question). Don't fall for the trap! Answer the question asked.

Extra Tips

Weaken the Argument questions tend to be more common on the LSAT than Strengthen the Argument questions. But here are a few concepts that apply to both question types:

- Weakening an argument is not the same thing as disproving it, while strengthening is not the same as proving the conclusion to be definitely true. A strengthener tips the scale toward believing in the validity of the conclusion, while a weakener tips the scale in the other direction, toward doubting the conclusion.
- The wording of these question types usually takes the form: "Which one of the following, if true, would most [weaken or strengthen] the argument?" The "if true" part means that you have to accept the truth of the choice right off the bat, no matter how unlikely it may sound to you.
- Don't be careless. Wrong answer choices in these questions often have exactly the opposite of the desired effect. That is, if you're asked to strengthen a stimulus argument, it's quite likely that one or more of the wrong choices will contain information that actually weakens the argument. By the same token, weaken questions may contain a choice that strengthens the argument. So once again, pay close attention to what the question stem asks.

Sample Stems

The stems associated with these two question types are usually self-explanatory. Here's a list of what you can expect to see on the test.

Weaken the Argument Stems

- Which one of the following, if true, would most weaken the argument above?
- Which one of the following, if true, would most seriously damage the argument above?
- Which one of the following, if true, casts the most doubt on the argument above?
- Which one of the following, if true, would most undermine the argument above?

Strengthen the Argument Stems

- Which one of the following, if true, would most strengthen the argument?
- Which one of the following, if true, would provide the most support for the conclusion in the argument above?
- The argument above would be more persuasive if which one of the following were found to be true?

Practice Weaken the Argument Question

Apply the Kaplan Four-Step Method to the following Weaken the Argument question:

> Whitley Hospital's much publicized increase in emergency room efficiency due to its new procedures for handling trauma patients does not withstand careful analysis. The average time before treatment for all patients is nearly forty minutes—the highest in the city. And for trauma victims, who are the specific target of the guidelines, the situation is even worse: the average time before treatment is nearly half an hour—more than twice the city average.
>
> Which of the following, if true, would most seriously weaken the conclusion about the value of the new procedures?
>
> (A) The city hospitals with the most efficient emergency rooms utilize the same procedures for handling trauma patients as does Whitley Hospital.
> (B) After the new procedures went into effect, Whitley's average time before treatment for trauma patients and patients in general dropped by nearly 35 percent.
> (C) Because trauma patients account for a large percentage of emergency room patients, procedures that hasten their treatment will likely increase overall emergency room efficiency.
> (D) Due to differences in location and size of staff, not all emergency rooms can be expected to reach similar levels of efficiency.
> (E) The recently hired administrators who instituted the new procedures also increased Whitley's emergency room staff by nearly fifteen percent.

Step One: Preview the Question Stem
We know from reading the question stem that we want to weaken the argument. So, we'll read with an eye toward weakening the link between the author's evidence and conclusion.

Step Two: Read the Stimulus
The author contests Whitley's claims about increased emergency room (ER) efficiency due to new procedures. The author's conclusion is that the new procedures haven't made Whitley's ER more efficient. All of the evidence is intended to show that Whitley's ER moves at a snail's pace, and thus that efficiency isn't up. Does it really show this, however? No. Just because Whitley has the slowest ER in the city doesn't mean that Whitley's efficiency hasn't grown by leaps and bounds. Evidence comparing Whitley to other hospitals (which is all the author presents) is irrelevant. What's important is how Whitley's *present* efficiency compares to its *previous* efficiency.

Step Three: Try to Prephrase an Answer
The problem here is a mismatch between evidence and conclusion. In light of our analysis above, we should look for an answer that compares Whitley's *present* efficiency to its *previous* efficiency.

Step Four: Choose an Answer
Skim the answer choices and look for one that matches our prephrase. If (B) is true, then Whitley's efficiency is up, and this seems likely to be the result of

the new procedures. Even though it's still the slowest ER around, it has improved markedly.

Choice (A)'s claim that these procedures are used in the best ERs does *not* show that the procedures are good, and therefore, are responsible for the improvements at Whitley. One, the other ERs could be fast for reasons other than the procedures. Two, even if the procedures generally increase efficiency, Whitley's staff could be so incompetent that the procedures are ineffective. The key is information about *Whitley's past ER efficiency*, not information about other hospitals.

In (C), even if the procedures are intended to speed the treatment of trauma victims (that's not actually said, you notice), there's no reason to assume that they worked at Whitley.

As for (D), while it might excuse Whitley for offering below-average care, it gives us no reason to think that Whitley's care has improved, which is what we need.

Finally, (E) tells us that the new procedures have been accompanied by new administrators and more staff. So if there has been an increase in efficiency, this complicates things a bit; we wouldn't know exactly what accounted for the increase. The problem, though, is that (E) provides no reason to believe that there *has* been an increase in efficiency.

Practice Strengthen the Argument Question

Apply the Kaplan Four-Step method to the following Strengthen the Argument question:

> The state lawmakers' critics warned that if the lawmakers carried out their plan to overturn the existing legislation requiring all mental health personnel to report patients' murder threats to the potential victims, there would be an increase in the number of homicides in the state. Since the legislation has just been overturned, the state should prepare itself for an increase in the murder rate.
>
> Which one of the following, if true, would most strengthen the argument above?
>
> (A) The vast majority of people who make murder threats do not intend to carry them out.
> (B) During the first year the legislation was enacted, violent crime fell by nearly 5 percent.
> (C) Most violent patients of mental health personnel are confined to high security psychiatric institutions.
> (D) Many patients of mental health professionals make numerous threats against others, often against individuals personally unknown to them.
> (E) A positive correlation between warning a potential murder victim, and the later prevention of the threatened murder, has been shown to exist.

Step One: Preview the Question Stem
We want to bolster the link between evidence and conclusion.

Step Two: Read the Stimulus
The author believes that the state will very likely see an increase in the murder rate. Why? A law requiring mental health personnel to warn potential victims of the murder threats made by their patients has just been overturned. Critics of the lawmakers warned that the repeal would lead to an increase of murders, and the author agrees.

Step Three: Try to Prephrase an Answer
To strengthen this argument, we need to look for a choice that would explain why overturning the established laws will result in a higher incidence of murders. We want a choice that screams, "Bring back the laws!"

Step Four: Choose an Answer
Choice (E) fits the bill. If there's a positive correlation between warning a potential murder victim and saving that potential victim's life, then the laws were doing good work, and with their repeal we can expect a higher murder rate.

Choice (A) seems to be saying that a murder threat is nothing to get too alarmed about. If that's the case, then it's less likely that laws requiring the report of murder threats were necessary or even useful. So (A) hardly argues for the importance of the old laws.

Choice (B), which deals with *violent crime* in general, is out of the scope. We're talking about murders, not all violent crime. So even if the law had some effect on violent crime (which is still uncertain), (B) is off-point with respect to the incidence of murders.

Choice (C) implies that dangerous patients are safely isolated in high-security institutions. This would tend to weaken the argument, showing that these people are unlikely to kill anyone, warning or no.

Finally, choice (D) just points to the number of threats made by mental health patients, while leaving open the question of whether these threats are later carried out. If the threats are not carried out, then there is little to worry about, even though the laws have been repealed.

Inference Questions

Another common question type on the LR section is the Inference question. The process of inferring is a matter of considering one or more statements as evidence, and then drawing a conclusion from them.

Sometimes the inference is very close to the author's overall main point. Other times, it deals with a less central point. A valid inference is something that must

Inference Questions at a Glance

- Expect about 4 or 5 per section on the test
- The right answer must be true based on the stimulus.
- The right answer is often a paraphrase of the author's main point.
- The question stems for inference questions vary considerably.
- A valid inference can be checked with the Kaplan Denial Test.

be true if the statements in the passage are true—an extension of the argument rather than a necessary part of it. For instance, let's take a somewhat expanded version of the volleyball team argument:

> Allyson plays volleyball for Central High School, despite the team's rule against participation by nonstudents. Therefore, Allyson must be over 6 feet tall.

Inference: Allyson is not a student at Central High School. Clearly, if Allyson plays volleyball despite the team's rule against participation by nonstudents, she must not be a student. Otherwise, she wouldn't be playing despite the rule; she would be playing in accordance with the rule. But note that this inference is not an essential assumption of the argument, since the conclusion about Allyson's height doesn't depend on it.

So be careful; unlike an assumption, an inference need not have anything to do with the author's conclusion—it may simply be a piece of information derived from one or more pieces of evidence. However, the Kaplan Denial Test works for inferences as well as for assumptions: a valid inference always makes more sense than its opposite. If you deny or negate an answer choice, and it has little or no effect on the argument, chances are that choice is not inferable from the passage.

Sample Stems

Inference questions probably have the most varied wording of all the Logical Reasoning question stems. Some question stems denote inference fairly obviously. Others are more subtle, and still others may even look like other question types entirely. Here's a quick rundown of the various forms that Inference questions are likely to take on your test:

- Which one of the following is inferable from the argument above?
- Which one of the following is implied by the argument above?
- The author suggests that
- If all the statements above are true, which one of the following must also be true on the basis of them?
- The author of the passage would most likely agree with which one of the following?
- The passage provides the most support for which one of the following?
- If the statements above are true, which one of the following conclusions can be properly drawn on the basis of them?

Stay in Line!

A valid inference:

- stays in line with the gist of the passage
- stays in line with the author's tone
- stays in line with the author's point of view
- stays within the scope of the argument or the main idea
- is neither denied by, nor irrelevant to, the argument or discussion
- always makes more sense than its opposite (the Kaplan Denial Test)

Practice Inference Question

Apply the Kaplan Four-Step Method to the following Inference question:

> Hypnotic drugs, which are meant to restore normal sleep patterns, sometimes accumulate in the blood and lead to insomnia. Opioid drugs, which are used to blunt sensory awareness, occasionally result in heightened tactile sensations. Stimulants designed to decrease appetite and combat fatigue can cause both fatigue and ravenous hunger.
>
> Which one of the following conclusions can be most reasonably drawn from the passage above?
>
> (A) The three major categories of drugs are hypnotics, opioids, and stimulants.
> (B) Regardless of their stated purpose, very few drugs have a single, easily defined effect.
> (C) Hypnotic and opioid drugs tend to have effects that are the opposite of those of stimulants.
> (D) Some drugs can actually have effects roughly the opposite of their usual, expected effects.
> (E) Drugs that can produce both their intended effect, and its opposite, should be taken in combination with other drugs.

Step One: Preview the Question Stem

A conclusion that "can be most reasonably drawn" is just another way of saying "inference." So we'll attack the question stem looking for what *must be true.*

Step Two: Read the Stimulus

Do you see a pattern? Some drugs intended to restore normal sleep patterns lead to insomnia. Some drugs meant to decrease sensory awareness actually increase it, and, irony of ironies, stimulants designed to decrease appetite can cause both fatigue and hunger.

Step Three: Try to Prephrase an Answer

Prephrasing an answer to an Inference question is always difficult, and this question is no exception. You might have noticed the pattern above and concluded that at least some drugs can have an effect that is the opposite of their intended effect.

Step Four: Choose an Answer

Choice (D) can be reasonably inferred. Hypnotics, opioids, and stimulants are all drugs, and they all can have effects roughly the opposite of their intended effects, and so it is safe to say that *some* drugs can have roughly the opposite of their intended effect. Choice (D) may not be as sweeping or broad as the other (wrong) choices, but it has the quality you need for an Inference question. It must be true.

(A): The passage only *mentions* these types of drugs, but for all we know, there are other "major" categories of drugs.

(B): This is too extreme. The author only mentions three kinds of drugs, so a conclusion about virtually all drugs is unwarranted.

(C): Stimulants combat fatigue, which isn't quite the opposite of restoring normal sleep patterns. In any case, opioids blunt sensory awareness, which has no clear opposite among the listed effects of stimulants.

(E): This is a strange recommendation that might even be a little dangerous. Taking drugs in combination *might* produce the intended effect, there's nothing in the stimulus to suggest that this is a safe bet.

Flaw Questions

This question type—known also as a Critique the Logic question—asks you to recognize what's wrong with an argument. There are two basic types: general and specific.

In the general type of Flaw question, the correct choice will critique the reasoning by pointing out that it contains a classic fallacy (for example, "The argument attacks the source of an opinion, rather than the opinion itself."). In this case, the flaw falls into a general, well-defined category. In the specific type of Flaw question, the correct choice won't refer to a classic fallacy, but rather will attack a specific piece of the argument's reasoning. An example of this would be: "It cannot be concluded that the number of male turtles has increased simply because the percentage of turtles that are male has increased."

Flaw Questions at a Glance

- You'll see about four Flaw questions per section on the test.
- Think: "What's wrong with the argument?"
- The right answer could be either a common flaw or specific to the particular argument.
- Understanding the structure of the argument is key.

Notice that the subject of the above statement isn't turtles; it's the author's faulty reasoning about turtles. Similar to many other question types, the required skill is the ability to identify the structure of the author's argument—specifically, where the argument goes wrong.

Practice Flaw Question

Apply the Kaplan Four-Step Method to the following Flaw question:

> It doesn't surprise me that the critic on our local radio station went off on another tirade today about the city men's choir. This is not the first time that he has criticized the choir. But this time his criticisms were simply inaccurate and unjustified. For ten minutes, he spoke of nothing but the choir's lack of expressiveness. As a professional vocal instructor, I have met with these singers individually; I can state with complete confidence that each of the members of the choir has quite an expressive voice.
>
> Which one of the following is the most serious flaw in the author's reasoning?
>
> (A) He directs his argument against the critic's character rather than against his claims.
> (B) He ignores evidence that the critic's remarks might, in fact, be justified.
> (C) He cites his own professional expertise as the sole explanation for his defense of the choir.
> (D) He assumes that a group will have a given attribute if each of its parts has that attribute.
> (E) He attempts to conclude the truth of a general situation from evidence about one specific situation.

Step One: Preview the Question Stem
We're told to look for the most serious flaw, so we don't have to ask *whether* the author's argument is faulty. Instead, we can focus on determining *how* it is faulty.

Step Two: Read the Stimulus
Each of the singers has an expressive voice, therefore all the choir, as a group, must be expressive and the critic must be wrong. But just because each voice is expressive alone doesn't necessarily mean that all the voices will be expressive *together.*

Step Three: Try to Prephrase an Answer
The flaw in the author's reasoning lies in his reasoning from part to whole.

Step Four: Choose an Answer
Choice (D), therefore, is correct. Something that's true about every individual element need not be true about the whole, and that's just the faulty claim that was made.

(A): Although the author is rather vehement in disputing the critic's claims, he doesn't address the critic's character, so (A) is out.

(B): There isn't any evidence provided in support of the critic's remarks; the flaw is not that the author ignores evidence that might hurt his argument, but that he uses evidence that doesn't really prove anything.

(C): This is a little tough because the author *does* provide his own professional opinion as his only explanation. Yet, he is a professional vocal instructor, and we have no reason to doubt his qualifications.

(E): This sounds a little like (C), but there's no mention of specific situations here—the evidence is about *all* the individual singers within the choir.

Method of Argument Questions

Method of Argument questions bear a similarity to Flaw questions. Once again, you'll be asked to demonstrate an understanding of how an author's argument is put together. However, unlike flaw questions, Method of Argument questions don't always involve faulty logic. You're simply asked to pick the choice that describes how the author goes about presenting his or her case. The key skill—once again—involves being able to analyze the structure of an argument. If you can't identify the evidence and conclusion, you'll have difficulty describing how an argument works.

Method of Argument Questions at a Glance

- There are two or three per section.
- The key to answering them is understanding the structure of the argument.
- Questions will ask either about the author's intentions or the way in which the author makes his or her argument.

Also like Flaw questions, there are two distinct types of Method of Argument questions—one general, one specific. The first deals with classic arguments. These are the classic argumentative structures, such as, "arguing from a small sample to a larger group," or "inferring a causal relationship from a correlation." The other type of Method of Argument question gives you a description of the argument in much more specific terms. An example of this might read, "The author presents the case of his mother in order to show that not all astronauts are men."

Focus on the following: "What is the evidence? What is the conclusion? How does the author link the evidence and conclusion together?" These are the questions you have to ask yourself in order to determine the author's method of argument.

Practice Method of Argument Question

Apply the Kaplan Four-Step method to the following Method of Argument question:

> There is no way to predict the ups and downs of the stock market. Although many of us cannot help but listen to and be intrigued by analysts' optimistic claims, we should bear in mind the source of these claims. After all, analysts make their living by deceiving naive investors; in fact, many have gone to jail for their dishonest practices.
>
> The above argument relies on which one of the following argumentative strategies?
>
> (A) directing the argument against its opponents rather than against its opponents' claim
> (B) offering evidence suggesting that the information analysts impart is often inaccurate
> (C) demonstrating that its opponents' claims are dishonest by providing evidence that such claims are never accurate
> (D) creating a causal connection between the opponents' dishonest claims and their legal troubles
> (E) pointing out a weakness in the opponents' claims by advancing an analogous position

Step One: Preview the Question Stem
We're asked to identify the argumentative strategy, or method of argument, used by the author. So we'll keep our focus on *how* the author presents the argument.

Step Two: Read the Stimulus
The conclusion is announced in the first sentence: playing the stock market is a game of pure chance. Granted there are some who claim that there is a method to the madness, but those people are professional analysts who have a financial incentive in convincing investors that they know what they are doing. Besides, some of those analysts have gone to jail for their unethical behavior.

Step Three: Try to Prephrase an Answer
The author doesn't present any positive proof to support the claim that the path of the stock market cannot be predicted. Rather, the entire argument revolves around an attack on the motives and character of analysts. So look for a choice that mentions an attack on the analysts.

Step Four: Choose an Answer
(A): This choice identifies that the author attacks the analysts themselves, and not their claim that the market can be predicted. So (A) is correct.

(B) and (C): There's no evidence being presented against the analysts' claims *at all*, so choices (B) and (C) are both incorrect.

(D): The author probably assumes that dishonest claims will eventually lead to legal troubles, but there's no stated causal connection here.

(E): What analogous position?

Parallel Reasoning Questions

Parallel Reasoning questions require you to identify the answer choice that contains the argument most similar, or parallel, to that in the stimulus in terms of the reasoning employed. To do this kind of question, you need to grasp the distinction between an argument's form and its content. "A causal relationship concluded from a correlation" is a form—a type—of reasoning. Any argument with this form can contain virtually any content. Your task is to abstract the stimulus argument's form, with as little content as possible, and then locate the answer choice that has the form most similar to that of the stimulus. Don't let yourself be drawn to a choice based on its subject matter. A stimulus about music may have an answer choice that also involves music, but that doesn't mean that the reasoning in the two arguments is similar.

Parallel Reasoning Questions at a Glance

- There are two per section.
- They must mimic structure or form, not content, of stimulus.
- They are sometimes amenable to algebraic symbolization.
- The key is to summarize the argument's overall form and match it to that of the correct choice.

A good approach to these questions is to see first if the argument can be symbolized algebraically, using Xs and Ys. Take the following example:

> All cows eat grass. This animal eats grass. Therefore, it must be a cow.

This (flawed) argument can be symbolized like so:

> All X do Y. This does Y. Therefore, this must be an X.

If the stimulus can be symbolized this way, your job will be to search for the choice that can be symbolized in the same way. Your answer might look something like this:

> Every politician (all X) tells lies (does Y). Stegner is lying (this does Y). So he must be a politician (therefore, this must be an X).

Notice how the exact wording doesn't have to match ("all X" means "every X"), and notice that the subject matter doesn't have to match in the least. What's important is the parallel structure.

Sometimes, though, an argument's reasoning isn't amenable to symbolization. In such a case, see if you can put a label on the type of argument being used, such as "arguing from a part to a whole," or "circular reasoning (evidence and conclusion are identical)." Naming the argument will often help eliminate two or three choices that don't even come close to this general form.

But whatever way you choose, as long as you can summarize the argument's form without including content, you're well on your way to finding the parallel argument among the choices.

Extra Tips

Here are a few more tips on parallel reasoning:

- All elements of the original argument must be present in its parallel. For example, if the original argument made a generalization to a specific case, a second argument, no matter how similar in structure otherwise, cannot be parallel unless it makes a comparable generalization.
- Stay away from answer choices written about the same subject matter as the original. This is an old trick of the test makers, intended to catch those who mistakenly try to mimic the content rather than the structure of the stimulus.
- Statements that are logically parallel don't have to have all logical elements in the same sequence. Provided all elements of the first argument exist in the second, even in a different order, the two arguments are parallel.

Same-Topic Trap

On some Parallel Reasoning questions, one of the wrong choice may be on the same topic although the logic is very different. Don't fall for the trap. Find the structure, not the content, that is parallel.

Practice Parallel Reasoning Question

Apply the Kaplan Four-Step Method to the following Parallel Reasoning question:

The Valley Theatre Company has selected Brenda Huber for the female lead of its new play. Since the cast of the play in which Brenda Huber previously appeared is known for excellent acting, the Valley Theatre Company can be fully assured that the woman chosen for the female lead of the new play is an accomplished actress.

Which one of the following contains flawed reasoning most parallel to that contained in the passage?

(A) One trait common to all Spanish terriers is a slight hip displacement that can cause long-term mobility impairment. Since Trent's dog has a hip displacement that could result in a long-term mobility impairment, Trent's dog must therefore be a Spanish terrier.

(B) Since the Pacific division of Failsafe Insurance has exceeded this year's revenue expectations, it is therefore certain that Ben London's office, which is part of Failsafe's Pacific division, must have exceeded revenue expectations as well.

(C) All members of the Scholars' Program have achieved a mark of 95 or better on each of their first-year examinations. Since Alicia is a member of the Scholars' Program, she therefore must have scored at least a 95 on her first-year chemistry examination.

(D) Gordon spent the entire day visiting the City Museum, which is currently showing a nationally known collection of Northern European Renaissance paintings. Gordon is an avid admirer of Northern European Renaissance painting, and so he must have seen the collection.

(E) Clark Abrams works as a door-to-door salesperson selling a variety of household goods. Since only a licensed vendor can sell goods door-to-door, it is certain that Mr. Abrams has a license.

Step One: Preview the Question Stem
Previewing the question stem is always important, but this strategy is absolutely critical for Parallel Reasoning questions. By reading the question stem first, we know that we need to look for the choice that duplicates the *shape* of the argument. We also get a bonus: since we are looking for a parallel flaw, we also know that the stimulus and the right answer contained flawed arguments.

Step Two: Read the Stimulus
Brenda Huber was part of a cast that as a whole was known for excellent acting. Therefore, Brenda must have that quality as well.

Step Three: Try to Prephrase an Answer
We're looking for something like this: "Since an individual entity was part of a group that as a whole was known for some quality, we can therefore conclude that the individual entity has that quality as well."

Step Four: Choose an Answer
Choice (B) fits the bill. Since Ben London's office was part of the Pacific division, a group that as a whole was known for exceeding revenue goals, we can therefore conclude that Ben London's office has that quality as well. This reasoning is flawed, and in the same way as that of the stimulus.

(A): In this choice, the author concludes that since X (Spanish terrier) implies Y (hip displacement), then Y (hip displacement) implies X (Spanish terrier). This is flawed reasoning, but not the kind in the stimulus.

(C): This is not flawed. If all members of the Scholar's Program did X (score a 95 or higher) on each of their first-year exams, then it is logical to conclude that a given member of the Scholar's Program did X on any given first-year exam.

(D): This makes a prediction of Gordon's behavior based on information concerning his preferences, which has no parallel in the original.

(E): This is not flawed. If only licensed vendors can sell door-to-door, then selling goods door-to-door guarantees that one has a license.

Paradox Questions

A paradox exists when an argument contains two or more seemingly inconsistent statements. You'll know you're dealing with a paradoxical situation if the argument ends with what seems to be a bizarre contradiction. Another sure sign of a paradox is when the argument builds to a certain point, and then the exact opposite of what you would expect to happen happens.

In a typical Paradox question, you'll be asked either to find the choice that "explains the paradoxical result" or "resolves the apparent discrepancy." Basically, this will be the choice that reconciles the seemingly inconsistent statements that

Paradox Questions at a Glance

- You'll usually get one per section.
- The correct answer will explain the apparent contradiction.
- The correct answer often requires you to realize that two groups, which are presented as identical, actually aren't.

make up the argument while still allowing them to be true. Take the following question:

> Fifty-seven percent of the registered voters in this district claimed to support the Democratic candidate, and yet the Republican candidate won the election with 55 percent of the vote.
>
> Which of the following would resolve the apparent discrepancy above?

The stimulus seems paradoxical since the Republican won the election, even though more registered voters preferred the Democrat. But do all registered voters vote? No. So a correct answer for this question might read something like this:

> Because of an intensive get-out-the-vote effort in traditionally Republican neighborhoods, a disproportionate number of registered Republicans actually voted in the election.

This statement reconciles the seemingly contradictory elements of the argument by showing that the group of registered voters is not identical to the group of people who actually voted in the election.

Extra Tips

Here are a few tips for handling Paradox questions:

- Before attempting to resolve a paradox, make sure you have a good grasp of what the paradox is. If it doesn't hit you right off the bat, look hard for an unexpected result, or what seems to be a blatant contradiction between the author's evidence and conclusion.
- Resolving paradoxes is often a matter of recognizing that two things that are being compared aren't really similar. Read critically to note these subtle distinctions.
- In Paradox questions, avoid choices that merely amplify points already raised in the argument.

Practice Paradox Question

Apply the Kaplan Four-Step method to the following Paradox question:

> Human beings are the ultimate predators. We have virtually devastated the conch population of the West Indian barrier reef region, brought the North American caribou to the verge of extinction, and nearly wiped out the mountain lion native to the hills of Appalachia. Legislation could be enacted to prohibit killing the lions, but even if the law could be enforced effectively, the lions would become extinct anyway, and the blame would still be ours.
>
> Which one of the following, if true, would provide the most logical explanation of the apparent paradox?
>
> (A) Hunters throughout the Appalachian region are notoriously resentful of what they consider government intrusion and will try to circumvent the law.

(B) The mountain lion is really not native to the Appalachian region and plays no essential role in the total environment of the area.
(C) The problems with the conch population and the North American caribou are quite distinct and cannot usefully be compared with the problem of the mountain lion.
(D) Because of urban development and industrial pollution, the mountain lion no longer has the large hunting territories and abundance of small game the species needs to survive.
(E) The natural evolution of the region, rather than the intrusions of human beings, has been responsible for the decline of the mountain lion population.

Step One: Preview the Question Stem
Knowing that we have to resolve an apparent paradox tells us that the evidence will seem to conflict with the conclusion, but we'll have to show how they could be consistent.

Step Two: Read the Stimulus
The paradox in the paragraph is that the author asks us to stop killing mountain lions while predicting that the animals will die off anyway, thanks to us.

Step Three: Try to Prephrase an Answer
If not by direct acts of killing, therefore, humans must in some *other* fashion be contributing to the extinction of the species.

Step Four: Choose an Answer
Choice (D) gives a plausible explanation of this apparent paradox by noting that humans, by *indirectly* destroying game with pollution, and reducing the lions' hunting areas through urban development, would indeed be responsible for the threat of extinction, even if they stopped killing them directly. So (D) is correct.

(A): This does not explain the paradox; it simply suggests that the proposal to ban direct killing will not be honored by everyone. But the passage says that humans would be responsible even if the law *could* be effectively enforced across the board.

(B): This is irrelevant to the argument, which has focused on human responsibility for the death of a species, not on the importance of the species to the local ecology.

(C): This addresses a secondary aspect of the passage. Indeed, the conch and the caribou are mentioned as examples of species threatened by humans, but the essential paradox of the passage applies, so far as we are told, only to the case of the mountain lion.

(E): This contradicts the stimulus by asserting that nature, not humans, is responsible for the threat to the lion. If that were true, why would humans still be responsible for the fate of the lions?

Principle Questions

Principle questions involve fitting a specific situation into a global generality (or, occasionally, vice versa). Usually, you'll be given an argument, and then asked to find the principle that seems to justify the author's reasoning. For example, suppose that an author's evidence leads to this conclusion in the final sentence of the stimulus:

Principle Questions at a Glance

- There are usually one or two per section.
- The logic required is similar to that which judges use to decide cases.
- The correct answer almost always reflects the author's key idea.

> Therefore, Marvin should provide a home for his ailing grandmother until she gets back on her feet.

The question stem might read:

> The author's position most closely conforms to which one of the following principles?

In other words, what principle best accounts for or justifies the author's position? The answer could sound like this:

> If a close relative is in need, one should always do his or her best to help that person, regardless of personal inconvenience.

On the other hand, the question stem might read:

> Which one of the following principles would justify Marvin's refusal to follow the author's recommendation?

In this case, the answer may sound something like this:

> No person should be obligated to provide support for another person, even if that other person is a close relative.

Notice the general nature of both principles. While they don't specifically mention Marvin or his grandmother, or the exact conditions of the stimulus per se, the general situation (helping a relative in need) is addressed in both.

The correct answer to Principle questions is usually the one that expresses the key concepts and contains the key terms that the other choices leave out. Be extremely wary of choices that are outside the scope of the argument. Most of the wrong choices contain principles that sound very formal and look good on the page by themselves, but that don't address the author's main concern.

Practice Principle Question

Apply the Kaplan Four-Step Method to the following Principle question:

Dunwich: The Dunwich Rare Book Collection was painstakingly built by my family over generations. Now, however, the family estate has fallen into such financial difficulties that we will be forced to sell some of the books in order to keep the bulk of the collection in the family's possession.

Saunderson: But you have no right to do that. That library is a national artistic treasure and a precious resource for scholars. If your family cannot afford to keep the whole collection, you ought to sell the whole thing as a unit rather than break it up and scatter it around the world.

Which one of the following principles, if established, does the most to justify Saunderson's reply?

(A) An historic collection of art or antiquities should always be preserved as the original collector intended.
(B) The obligation to preserve the unity of an historic collection of art or antiquities transcends the right of possession of its traditional owners.
(C) The most important consideration when disposing of an historic collection of art or antiquities is to maximize the number of people who have access to it.
(D) If the safety of an historic collection of art or antiquities is threatened by the owners of that collection, then the national government has the right to take possession of the collection.
(E) People should not purchase an historic collection of art or antiquities unless they intend to preserve it as a whole.

Step One: Preview the Question Stem
We're looking for a rule that would support *Saunderson's* claim.

Step Two: Read the Stimulus
So what is Saunderson's claim? Saunderson believes that Dunwich has no right to sell part of the collection, which is a national treasure and scholarly resource. Saunderson feels that, rather than break the collection up in order to keep most of it, the family is obligated to sell the collection as a whole.

Step Three: Try to Prephrase an Answer
If Saunderson is to prevail, the historical and/or academic importance of the library must outweigh the rights of the owner.

Step Four: Choose an Answer
Choice (B) matches our prephrase. If the preservation of the Rare Book Collection is more important than Dunwich's rights of ownership, then Saunderson's position would be more justified.

(A): This doesn't apply; the Dunwich Rare Book Collection was built up over generations, so we can't pinpoint an "original collector." Moreover, we don't know how any of the many collectors *intended* the collection to be preserved.

(C): If Saunderson formulated a recommendation based on this principle, he probably would be in favor of splitting up the collection. After all, that would probably maximize access to it better than keeping the entire collection in one place, as Saunderson actually argues for. This principle therefore seems to run counter to Saunderson's reasoning. (Also, "disposing of" is a little strong for this scenario; it would apply better if Dunwich was simply looking to throw the whole thing out rather than hesitantly siphon off part of the collection for financial reasons.)

(D): Ouch. There's no hint that the "safety" of the collection is being threatened, and Saunderson says nothing about the rights and duties of "the national government."

(E): This doesn't help Saunderson. The Dunwich family never purchased the *collection* as a whole, they built it up over generations. Now Dunwich is interested in selling some of the collection, and (E) says nothing about why those who already happen to own an historic collection should not feel free to sell part of it.

Formal Logic Questions

The manner in which formal logic is tested on the LSAT has evolved over the last few years. Gone (at least for now) are the days when the test makers would line up formal if/then and all/some/none statements and ask you what can, must, or cannot be true on the basis of them. Now, the test makers bury formal statements in the context of a casual argument, asking for an inference that can be drawn from the passage. You may not easily recognize formal logic when you see it, and questions of this nature are fewer in number than in the past. But formal logic skills are tested in Logic Games as well, so it's best to get a solid handle on it now.

Formal Logic Questions at a Glance

- There are usually zero to two Formal Logic questions per section.
- Although the logic is "formal," the stimulus is almost always casual.
- The correct answer in a Formal Logic question often involves the contrapositive of a statement in the stimulus.

Let's look at an example:

> Ian will go to the movies only when his wife is out of town. He'll go to a matinee alone, but will see a movie at night only if accompanied by Ezra and Mabel.

This simple stimulus looks like any other casual argument in Logical Reasoning, but in fact, it's made up of a couple of formal-logic statements, each fraught with its own implications. Statements in Formal Logic questions resemble rules in Logic Games. Be on the lookout for Logical Reasoning stimuli that contain sentences that can be boiled down to such hard-and-fast rules. When you come across examples of these, you can apply the following principles of formal logic to help you arrive at the correct answer.

The Contrapositive

For any if/then statement—or a statement that can be translated into if/then form—the contrapositive of the statement will result in an equally valid second statement. This is a nice shortcut to employ when faced with Formal Logic questions on the test.

The contrapositive can be formed by reversing and negating the terms of any if/then statement. The general model goes like this: "If X, then Y." The contrapositive of this statement is: "If *not* Y, then *not* X."

The contrapositive of a valid if/then statement will always be valid itself. Let's illustrate this with a simple example. Consider the following strict formal statement:

> If the building has vacancies, then the sales office will be open.

To form the contrapositive, reverse and negate the terms, like so:

> If the sales office is NOT open, then the building does NOT have vacancies.

This would be a valid inference based on the original statement. The contrapositive, while quite a fancy term, is nothing more than everyday common sense.

Now let's apply the contrapositive to the first sentence of the earlier example. Here's the original:

> Ian will go to the movies only when his wife is out of town.

This is a little trickier, because it's not stated in the form of a true if/then statement. But we can translate this statement into an if/then statement without changing its original meaning:

> If Ian goes to the movies, then his wife must be out of town.

If the statement above is true, which statement must be true on the basis of it? Why, the contrapositive of it, of course:

> If Ian's wife is not out of town, then Ian does not go to the movies.

Simple enough, right? One caveat: wrong answers often result from either forgetting to switch around the terms before negating them, or negating only one of the terms. For example, in the above example, if Ian doesn't go to the movies, we can't infer anything about whether his wife is in or out of town. Similarly, if Ian's wife *is* out of town, we can't tell for sure whether Ian goes to the movies.

If one part of the Formal Logic statement contains a compound phrase, then both parts of the phrase must be taken into account. For example, let's take the other part of the stimulus above:

> Ian will see a movie at night only if accompanied by Ezra and Mabel.

Translation: If Ian sees a movie at night, then he's accompanied by Ezra and Mabel.

Contrapositive: If Ian is not with Ezra and Mabel, then he does not see a movie at night.

Correct Interpretation: If either Ezra or Mabel is missing, then Ian's out of luck. If he's with only one of them, or neither of them, then he can't go to a night movie.

Finally, if one part of a Formal Logic statement is already in the negative, the same rules that apply to math apply to forming the contrapositive: negating a negative yields a positive.

> If the sun is shining, then Samantha does not wear green.

Contrapositive: If Samantha is wearing green (if she's *not* not wearing green), then the sun is not shining.

Necessary Versus Sufficient Conditions

For success in formal logic, it's crucial that you distinguish clearly between necessary and sufficient conditions. Here are examples of each:

> Sufficient: If I yell loudly at my cat Adrian, he will run away.
> Necessary: The TV will work only if it is plugged in.

My yelling loudly is a sufficient condition for Adrian to run away. It's all I need to do to get the cat to run; it's sufficient. But it's not necessary. My cat will run if I throw water at him, even if I don't yell loudly.

The TV's being plugged in, on the other hand, is a necessary condition of its working. My TV won't work without it, so it's necessary. But it's not sufficient. Other conditions must apply for the TV to work (for example, the electricity to the house must be on).

You must be clear on what kinds of deductions you can and can't make from statements of necessary and sufficient conditions. For instance, sufficient conditions are usually signaled by an if/then statement, which means that the contrapositive can be used.

> If I yell loudly at my cat Adrian, he will run away.

Given that the above statement is true, which one of the following statements must also be true?

Not Valid: If I don't yell loudly at my cat Adrian, he will not run away.
Not Valid: If my cat Adrian has run away, then I yelled loudly at him.
Valid: If my cat Adrian has not run away, then I did not yell loudly at him.

The third statement is the contrapositive, and is the only one of the three statements that's inferable from the original. My yelling loudly is sufficient to make Adrian run away, but it's not necessary; that is, it'll do the trick, but it's not the only thing that will make him head for the hills. If I squirt him with a water gun, he'll also run away. This is why the first two statements are not inferable from the original statement.

Necessary conditions, on the other hand, are usually signaled by the word "only":

> The TV will work only if it is plugged in.

Given that the above statement is true, which one of the following statements must also be true?

Not Valid: If my TV is plugged in, it will work.
Not Valid: If my TV is not working, then it must not be plugged in.
Valid: If my TV is working, then it must be plugged in.
Valid: If my TV is not plugged in, then it won't work.

Plugging the TV in is necessary for the TV to work. To work, the TV needs to be plugged in. However, plugging in the TV is not sufficient to make the TV work. True, the TV won't work without plugging it in, but plugging it in is not a guarantee that the TV will work. What if other conditions interfere? Maybe the picture tube is broken. Maybe my electricity is out due to a hurricane. So the first two statements above are not inferable from the original statement, while the last two are.

Practice Formal Logic Question

Apply the Kaplan Four-Step Method to the following Formal Logic question:

> The moment a broker is found guilty of stock manipulation, he will be fined and his license will be revoked.
>
> If the statement above is true, which one of the following statements must also be true?
>
> (A) If a broker is not fined, then his license is not revoked.
> (B) If a broker is not fined, then he has not been found guilty of stock manipulation.
> (C) If a broker's license is revoked, then he has been found guilty of stock manipulation.
> (D) If a broker is fined, then he has been found guilty of stock manipulation.
> (E) If a broker's license is not revoked, then he is not fined.

Step One: Preview the Question Stem
We're looking for a statement that must be true based on the stimulus.

Step Two: Read the Stimulus
This is a straightforward if/then statement. Remember, though, that the consequent has two parts: if the broker is guilty, then both things occur (he is fined *and* his license is revoked).

Step Three: Try to Prephrase an Answer
Whenever you see an if/then statement, think about the contrapositive. Often, the correct answer to a Formal Logic question is merely the contrapositive of one of the statements in the stimulus. Since being found guilty of stock manipulation inevitably leads to the two penalties, if it is *not* the case that *both* things occur, then it cannot be true that the broker was found guilty of stock manipulation.

Step Four: Choose an Answer
Choice (B) describes the contrapositive of the original statement—if the broker is not fined, then it is *not* the case that *both* things occur, and therefore it cannot be true that the broker was found guilty of stock manipulation.

(A) and (E): Either of the two penalties (a fine or a license revocation) could possibly be administered without the other, provided the crime in question is not stock manipulation.

(C) and (D): The administration of either penalty alone (or both together, for that matter) is not enough to tell us whether the broker has been found guilty of stock manipulation. For all we know, many other miscues could lead to fines and/or license revocation.

What's Next

So there you have it—a quick demonstration of how to use the strategies and techniques outlined in this chapter to work through the complete Logical Reasoning process. Try to apply these techniques as best you can on the following practice set. Pay careful attention to all of the written explanations, even those for the ones you got right.

After the practice set, we'll move on to another major section of the test, Logic Games.

Logical Reasoning Practice Set

Directions: This test consists of questions that ask you to analyze the logic of statements or short paragraphs. For each question, choose the answer you consider best on the basis of your common-sense evaluation of the statement and its underlying assumptions. Although a question may seem to have more than one acceptable answer, there is only one best answer, and that is the one that does not entail making any illogical, extraneous, or conflicting assumptions about the question.

1. The mural in the executive dining room was painted more than forty years ago, and its subsequent exposure to extremes of heat and humidity has caused some of the once-vivid colors to fade. Fortunately, the muralist's preliminary studies included precise instructions for mixing pigments. Using these instructions and his leftover paints, skilled preservationists will be able to restore the mural to its original hues.

   Which one of the following is an assumption on which the conclusion logically depends?

   (A) The preservationists will be able to duplicate the muralist's technique.
   (B) The wide fluctuations in temperature and humidity typical of food-service areas make the executive dining room a poor location for a mural.
   (C) The artist foresaw that the colors would fade with time.
   (D) The paints left over from the mural's creation have not themselves changed color.
   (E) Humidity-control technology was insufficient at the time of the mural's painting to prevent its subsequent fading.

   Ⓐ Ⓑ Ⓒ Ⓓ Ⓔ

2. Many undeveloped areas of the world suffer from air pollution, even though there are no factories or combustion engines in use. Evidently, the connection between industrialization and air pollution has yet to be proved to the dispassionate observer.

   Which one of the following most closely parallels the reasoning in the argument above?

   (A) A few of his analyses of our capitalization program were overly optimistic. I think we can agree that he does not have the steadiness necessary to manage our banking division.
   (B) When the new diet drink was tested at the shopping mall, some people detested the taste. It is safe to assume that most people will like it very much.
   (C) Many people who rarely eat red meat have developed cardiac problems. We may conclude, therefore, that a diet including much red meat is not demonstrably harmful to the heart.
   (D) Even if more students sign up for gymnastics, the school will still be buying the same amount of equipment for the sport. We must urge our gymnasts to scout out alternative sites for practice.
   (E) At first, we hired a famous violinist to teach the music class, but few students improved dramatically. We should have just hired someone who knew only fundamentals.

   Ⓐ Ⓑ Ⓒ Ⓓ Ⓔ

3. When we returned home after our six-month vacation abroad, we found several drinking glasses shattered in place on the kitchen shelf—something that can only happen during a sonic boom or when there is an earth tremor. This must have been the loud noise that we heard not long after we drove off to the airport our last night in this country. Since there was no report on the car radio that night about tremors in the area, which always receive great attention, the glasses must have been shattered by a sonic boom, an occurrence so common that it is never reported.

The speaker's conclusion about the "loud noise" assumes which one of the following?

(A) It is easy to tell the difference between glass shattered by an earth tremor and that shattered by a sonic boom.
(B) A sonic boom always causes more damage in the house than does an earth tremor.
(C) No earth tremor has occurred since the night the family left on their vacation.
(D) The drinking glasses on the shelf were shattered because they were not securely protected.
(E) Every time there is an earth tremor in the area, some of the kitchen glassware will be shattered.

Ⓐ Ⓑ Ⓒ Ⓓ Ⓔ

4. Educators have too eagerly embraced the rise, after a decade of decline, in median SAT scores. Unfortunately, this encouraging statistic is actually yet another indictment of our educational system. The scores have risen because fewer students take the tests. In particular, students with disadvantaged backgrounds have become discouraged and have given up their hopes for attending colleges that require the tests. In other words, the low scorers have dropped out of competition, and today's higher median scores reflect an increasingly homogeneous test-taking population of privileged students.

The author argues primarily by

(A) denying the accuracy of his opponents' figures
(B) finding an alternative explanation for his opponents' evidence
(C) refining an existing argument
(D) defending an argument against the claims of his opponents
(E) suggesting that his opponents may be unduly influenced by self-interest

Ⓐ Ⓑ Ⓒ Ⓓ Ⓔ

5. Recent studies have indicated that a certain type of freshwater cod has more tumors than other species of fish in the Hudson River. Long before this phenomenon was recognized, significant strides had been made in clearing the river of chemical and other kinds of industrial pollution thought to promote tumorous growth.

   Which one of the following conclusions can most reliably be drawn from the statements above?

   (A) There is no causal link between chemical pollution and the tumors on the freshwater cod.
   (B) A sudden change in the river environment has had a drastic effect on the freshwater cod.
   (C) Efforts to clear the Hudson of chemical and other kinds of industrial pollution have not been vigorous enough.
   (D) No other fish but the freshwater cod is susceptible to the effects of chemical and other kinds of industrial pollution.
   (E) The mentioned studies provide no evidence that the number of tumors in the freshwater cod is related to the level of industrial pollution in the river.

   Ⓐ Ⓑ Ⓒ Ⓓ Ⓔ

<u>Questions 6–7</u>

The people behind this movement to impeach me charge that I drastically exacerbated our state's unemployment problems. By raising corporate taxes, they claim, I singlehandedly forced many labor-intensive industries to move out of the state. What they fail to realize, however, is that my purpose in increasing the corporate income tax was to raise revenues to fund a statewide jobs program. The remarks I made two years ago before the legislature would bear me out, if my detractors would read the Legislative Record. But no, they prefer to persecute me for wanting to create jobs and ease our state's economic woes.

6. Which one of the following is most similar in logical features to the response the author makes above?

   (A) Emperor Hirohito's claim that, though he was opposed to Japan's invasion of Manchuria, he was powerless to restrain the military from launching it
   (B) Benedict Arnold's declaration that, while he did not originally intend to betray the revolutionary army, the injustices he suffered had forced him to do so
   (C) Galileo's assertion that he had renounced his true beliefs before the Inquisition because failure to do so would have resulted in his conviction as a heretic
   (D) Alfred Nobel's contention that he had invented dynamite to be used as a tool of peacetime technology rather than as the destructive weapon it later became
   (E) Charles I's pronouncement on the scaffold that his duty had been to care for his subjects as a loving father, and that he had done so to the best of his ability

   Ⓐ Ⓑ Ⓒ Ⓓ Ⓔ

7. Which one of the following points out the principal flaw in the reasoning of the argument?

   (A) There is no guarantee that a statewide jobs program would be effective in eliminating unemployment.
   (B) The number of jobs created by a statewide jobs program would not necessarily offset the number of jobs lost as a result of the tax increase.
   (C) The author's constituents want to impeach him because of the effects of his tax increase, and not because of the intent of his tax increase.
   (D) The author's claim concerning the intent of his tax increase is impossible to verify.
   (E) Raising taxes is not an effective method of creating jobs in industry.

Ⓐ Ⓑ Ⓒ Ⓓ Ⓔ

Questions 8–9

Government support for the arts cannot help but interfere with the free flow of the creative process. Monies, inevitably channeled at the dictates of the politically powerful, will accumulate around the established institutions, when a certain philosophy prevails, or just as swiftly revert to the more experimental groups, when the political pendulum swings. Individual creators will swerve willy-nilly, pursuing the funds at the expense of their own sure and inner-directed development.

8. The author's logic in the argument would be most weakened if it were argued that

   (A) approximately the same number of individual creative artists are associated with so-called established institutions as with the more experimental groups
   (B) in assigning monies to the arts, politicians in power heed the advice of committees composed of artists who are well known in their fields
   (C) while it can be argued that political ideas swing in and out of fashion, it is equally arguable that trends in the arts are often short-lived
   (D) Artists do not typically tailor their efforts to attract monies, either private or public
   (E) many people who would not otherwise experience the arts have had the opportunity to do so because of increased government funding over the past few years

Ⓐ Ⓑ Ⓒ Ⓓ Ⓔ

9. Which one of the following conclusions to a final sentence beginning, "As a result, the creative process in this country . . ." would be most appropriate, given the logic of the rest of the paragraph?

(A) would be continually diverted, distracted, and otherwise degraded by the intrusion of governmental decisions into the world of art
(B) would become the plaything of the politically powerful, inevitably and irretrievably captured by the established institutions
(C) would dry up entirely in those regions where political representation is weakest and thrive wholesomely in areas dominated by aggressive, successful political leaders
(D) would be seen at its most exuberant when the political pendulum swings toward support of the experimental groups, and at its most moribund when the reverse is true
(E) might become, at last, the expression of the individual's own inner-directed development rather than a pale reflection of the prevailing political philosophy

Ⓐ Ⓑ Ⓒ Ⓓ Ⓔ

10. Those who oppose psychological testing of schoolchildren, alleging that teachers will unconsciously "write off" pupils labeled as slow, overlook the fact that a self-fulfilling prophecy is necessarily also a true one. Information about a student's probable development can only help his or her teacher to arrange an appropriate remedial program.

Which one of the following arguments is most similar in logical structure to that above?

(A) Opponents of long-term testing of newly developed drugs maintain that intensive short-term testing is sufficient to identify possibly dangerous side effects. This ignores the possibility that some side effects may become evident only after decades of use.
(B) There are risks involved in the arms limitation talks, but they are risks worth taking. We should always err on the side of survival, rather than on the side of patriotically inspired self destruction.
(C) Claims that hospital diets are often unbalanced and even harmful, because of their high sodium and starch content, are beside the point, since hospitals hire trained nutritionists to design their menus.
(D) The majority of contact lens wearers agree that the benefits of improved vision and physical appearance outweigh the admitted inconveniences of the lenses in comparison to traditional eyeglasses.
(E) Whether the possibility of contagion through door handles and water faucets touched by many people is real or imagined, installation of swinging doors and pedal-controlled wash basins in public restrooms is an easy way to allay such fears.

Ⓐ Ⓑ Ⓒ Ⓓ Ⓔ

11. It is barbarous in the extreme to equate murder with simple acquiescence in the choice of a pain-wracked, dying friend to find self-deliverance from an onerous life. To assist a friend in suicide is to give solace, to respect the individual's free choice; to murder, of course, is to perform the ultimate act of disrespect for individual civil rights. Both our legislators and our justices must be urged to use reason rather than to respond as they have with traditional prejudice.

    It can be inferred from the passage that

    (A) the concept of murder in any given society is related to that society's interpretation of the idea of individual rights
    (B) terminally ill patients frequently contemplate suicide
    (C) our legislators and our justices do not agree with the author of the passage that assisting a suicide is not an act of murder
    (D) suicide should always be considered an act of self-deliverance, just as murder should be considered an act of disrespect for individual civil rights
    (E) whether or not suicide can be considered a legal act depends upon whether or not the suicide victim is suffering great pain

    Ⓐ Ⓑ Ⓒ Ⓓ Ⓔ

12. Without the profound structural changes in the Irish agricultural economy that began with the first grudging acceptance of the potato into the human diet, the great Potato Famine of the 1840s would never have been the disaster it was. Although other staples continued to be cultivated, primarily for export to England, the total dependence of much of the Irish population on potatoes turned the blight-induced failure of several potato crops in the latter part of the decade into a sweeping sentence of death or emigration.

    Which one of the following conclusions can most reliably be drawn from the statements in the passage?

    (A) The adoption of the potato as the staple of the Irish diet represented a nationalistic rejection of English social patterns.
    (B) Other staples are less susceptible to crop failure than is the potato.
    (C) Reliance on a single crop made Ireland a fertile ground for revolutionary activity when that crop failed.
    (D) Much of the Irish population was left without adequate alternative food sources when the potato crops failed.
    (E) Those who resisted the potato when it was introduced into Ireland did so to forestall the potential dangers of a restructured agricultural system.

    Ⓐ Ⓑ Ⓒ Ⓓ Ⓔ

13. Samuel Taylor Coleridge must have found the inspiration for "The Rime of the Ancient Mariner" in Hakluyt's 1600 edition of the real-life sea narrative, *The Southern Voyage of John Davis.* Although the poet did not mention the 200-year-old work in his notes, both "Mariner" and *Southern Voyage* prominently feature a tale of misfortune resulting from the murder of a bird, a rotting ship drifting out of control in the tropics, and a scene of a dying man cursing his fate. Furthermore, Wordsworth, Coleridge's good friend and occasional collaborator, had an interest in books about actual historical sea voyages and may have owned a copy of Davis's story.

    The author of the passage makes his point primarily by

    (A) drawing an analogy between literature and seafaring
    (B) reinterpreting a classic literary work
    (C) paralleling an author's work with the events of the author's life
    (D) supporting a claim with circumstantial evidence
    (E) documenting a controversial claim of literary influence

    Ⓐ Ⓑ Ⓒ Ⓓ Ⓔ

14. Deviations from social norms, particularly in such emotionally charged areas as eating, are usually accompanied by defensiveness, self-justification, and attempts at proselytizing others. That meat eating is still fundamental to mainstream American culture can be seen from the fact that most vegetarians, regardless of the specific motivation underlying their diet, express strong feelings about the rightness of their eating pattern and its potential benefits for others.

    A logical critique of the argument above would most likely emphasize which one of the following?

    (A) the difference between proselytizing and educating others
    (B) the failure to consider that not all proselytizers are deviants
    (C) the failure to define "mainstream American culture"
    (D) the author's evident prejudice against vegetarians
    (E) the actual number of vegetarians in America today

    Ⓐ Ⓑ Ⓒ Ⓓ Ⓔ

Answers

1. D	6. D	11. C
2. C	7. C	12. D
3. C	8. D	13. D
4. B	9. A	14. B
5. E	10. B	

Explanations

1 (D) is correct. In this passage we read that a forty-year-old mural has faded because of exposure. It is thought that the vividness of the original colors can be restored by using the muralist's leftover paints and mixing them according to his surviving instructions. Can this ploy work? Only if the leftover paints have not themselves deteriorated or otherwise altered over the years; otherwise, the mixing instructions, however precise, would result in colors unlike the original. Therefore, choice (D) is an assumption that is critical to the preservationists' plans.

Choice (A), on the other hand, is an unnecessarily sweeping assumption. The point is to restore color, not to try to emulate the muralist's personal technique of painting; while commendable, the latter goal is not the focus of the argument of the passage. Choice (B) takes the unwarranted line that the executive dining room must have suffered "extremes of heat and humidity" because of side effects from the serving of food. In fact, the extremes could have occurred throughout the entire building or, for that matter, at any building in the area. The cause of the exposure is not an essential part of the argument, so (B) is not assumed. In (C), we are invited to assume that the muralist left his original paints and instructions for the use of later generations, but the "precise instructions" may actually have been for his own use, and we have no indication that the paints were set aside for future restoration. They may simply have been found. Finally, (E) may be so, but is not necessarily so, on the basis of the passage. Perhaps technology was sufficient to prevent fading, but the company did not invest in any form of humidity control.

2 (C) is correct. In this question you are being asked to select an argument that resembles in *logic* the argument about air pollution. Note the logical shape of this argument. According to the writer, we cannot (if dispassionate) make a connection between industrialization and air pollution if the latter occurs without the presence of the former. In other words, we cannot say that a specific cause (X) has a specific effect (Y) unless that specific cause (X) is *always* associated with that specific effect (Y). Without evaluating the logic of this kind of argument, you will note that it resembles the argument of correct choice (C). In this case, the contention is that we cannot say that eating red meat (the specific cause X) leads to cardiac problems (the specific effect Y) because some people who have cardiac problems (Y) do not eat red meat (X).

In choice (A) the logical structure is quite different. Someone is described as giving occasional evidence of a certain characteristic (unwarranted optimism); this evidence is interpreted or redefined as another quality (lack of requisite steadiness). The argument of choice (B) can be broken down this way: if a small portion of a sampling responds one way (for example, detests the diet drink), the larger portion will have a completely opposite reaction (like it very much). Remember, it is not the *quality* of logic that concerns us here, but the *shape* of the argument being advanced in each case; in that regard, (B) does not resemble the original argument. Choice (D) argues that if more gym students have the same amount of practice equipment available, some will have to go elsewhere to practice. In other words, if there is more demand for a constant supply of a resource, the demand will require other sources of the resource. Equally dissimilar in structure to the stimulus is choice (E), in which the cause (a famous violinist) has little effect, so it is argued that a lesser cause (the teacher schooled only in fundamentals) would have a greater effect.

3 (C) is correct. This passage makes clear that the phenomenon of the shattered glasses could only have been caused by either a sonic boom or an earth tremor. The speaker heard a loud noise just as he was leaving for a vacation abroad, but did not

turn back to investigate. The car radio carried no mention of earth tremors, which are always reported in the area; the speaker assumes that the noise was therefore a sonic boom, which would not have gained broadcast attention. In other words, it is assumed that the noise heard was connected with the shattering of the glassware. This assumption ignores the possibility that the glasses were broken some time *later*, either by another sonic boom or by an earth tremor, while the speaker was in another country and unlikely to hear a report about such a local phenomenon. Choice (C) states this assumption.

Choice (A) proposes a distinction that is not necessary for the argument to work. In fact, if it were possible to tell the difference as suggested in this answer choice, there would be no need for the speculation of the speaker's concluding sentence. Choice (B) also suggests a distinction that is not an assumption of the speaker's; on the contrary, the *extent* of the damage is not seen as a clue to its cause, which (on that basis alone) could be either an earth tremor or a sonic boom. It is of course possible that more secure protection might have prevented the shattering of the glasses, as suggested in (D), but we have no indication that the speaker assumes so. The assumption in (E) is not essential to the speaker's conclusion, which designates a sonic boom rather than an earth tremor as the cause of the shattering. In any event, the speaker states that the breaking of glassware is "something that can only happen during a sonic boom or when there is an earth tremor"—not something that inevitably *must* happen.

4 (B) is correct. For this passage you are asked to describe the type of argument used by the author. First, it is important to understand the intent of the passage, which concerns the nationwide rise in median SAT scores. The trend has gratified educators, we read, but the author contends that an accurate interpretation reveals a disturbing truth: scores have not risen because all students have improved as test takers, but because an increasing number of potentially low scorers no longer take the tests, leaving the field to the more privileged students. In other words, the author accepts the basic evidence of optimistic educators—the rise in test scores—but offers a contrasting explanation. The correct answer is therefore choice (B).

Choice (A) is incorrect because it is essential to the author's argument that he accept "the accuracy of his opponents' figures." Choice (C) would suggest that the author has clarified an explanation of the statistic; in fact, he offers an original explanation that flies in the face of the educators' optimistic reading of the test results. Because his argument is original, (D) cannot apply in this case, for he is articulating a new idea rather than defending one previously stated. As for (E), don't be misled by the author's somewhat facetious reference to the educators' all too eager embrace. Although he has adopted a dry tone toward his opponents and hints that they may have been hasty in their judgment, he in no way suggests that self-interest has clouded their ability to interpret the rise in median SAT scores (remember that the question asks for the author's primary method of argument).

5 (E) is correct. There are only two sentences in this brief paragraph. Assuming that one logically follows from the other, what conclusion can reasonably be drawn? First, we are told that one Hudson River fish, a cod, suffers more from tumors than do other fish in the river. Second, we learn that pollution thought to cause such growths was being cleaned out of the river long before the cod tumors were discovered. What relationship does the second fact have to the first? The correct choice is (E): there is no evident relationship at all between the two facts, at least as far as we can tell from the study. There is certainly no proof of a connection between cod tumors and Hudson River pollution; the former were discovered *after* the latter began to abate. This is not to say that there *isn't* a relationship, merely that we have no evidence of a relationship.

The other answer choices offer unwarranted conclusions. In (A), for example, the lack of evidence is taken to an illogical extreme; that is, since there is no *evidence* that pollution causes the tumors, there must be no connection. But a lack of evidence for one possibility does not prove that its opposite is true. Choice (B) is not only an unjustified conclusion but also plays fast and loose with the facts. There was no "sudden change" in the river, so far as we know. Rather, the passage suggests, if anything, an impressive but gradual change in the amount of pollution. More to the point, sudden or not, the change cannot be linked to the appearance of the tumors, simply on the basis of the information in the passage. The tumors may have existed long before they were discovered, or may have been undetectable in their early stages. There is no indication that choice (C) is a reasonable conclusion; on the contrary, the author cites the "significant strides" made. It is always possible that the efforts could be more vigorously pursued, but we have no reason to suspect that to be the case. Choice (D) rides roughshod over logic in two ways—by making the assumption that the Hudson River pollution causes the cod tumors, and by assuming that the alleged causal relationship would *only* affect the freshwater cod. The latter error, presumably, would result from a misreading of the statement that one type of cod has *more* tumors than other fish swimming the same waters.

6 (D) is correct. The author (who is obviously a politician) is defending herself against a call for her impeachment. The call for her impeachment is a response to the author's having raised corporate taxes, and thereby forced many industries out of the state. The resulting loss of jobs has exacerbated the state's unemployment problems. The author's defense consists not of disputing the alleged *effects* of her corporate tax increase, but of pointing out her *intentions* in raising the tax. She responds to the impeachment call with the reason behind her tax increase. So the form of the reasoning is something like this: "Regardless of the effects of my actions, I had good intentions behind them." Choice (D) mirrors this reasoning: Alfred Nobel created dynamite, which has led to much death and suffering, but he originally intended it to be used in peaceful pursuits.

Choice (A) describes an example where someone (Hirohito) claims not to be responsible for some wrong-headed undertaking. This is different from the stimulus plea because in the stimulus the politician never denies responsibility for the tax increase. Choice (B) has Benedict Arnold *changing* his intentions. This is not the same as having good intentions, yet seeing them go unfulfilled in practice. Choice (C) just provides a sensible reason for Galileo's renunciation. There's no idea here of a distinction between effects and original intentions, so (C) cannot be correct. And (E) is incorrect because Charles I was not making a plea to escape responsibility. His intention had presumably been to carry out his duty, and he claimed to have done so as well as he could. There is no hint here of a plea to ignore the effects of his policies in favor of his original intent.

7 (C) is correct. The principal flaw in the author's reasoning is her unreasonable assumption that her constituents want to impeach her because of her original intentions. This is very unlikely. What has angered her constituents is the *effect* of the author's policy. Thus (C) is correct; the issue here is the effects of the tax increase, and not the purpose behind it.

Choices (A) and (B) are attacks upon the strategy of increasing the corporate tax rate. Yet the author did not imply that this was guaranteed, choice (A), to eliminate unemployment. She merely thought it *likely* to *reduce* unemployment. And (B) points out that the plan could fail, and the state wind up with higher unemployment. Well, this doesn't weaken the author's argument because she is not arguing that the plan was foolproof, merely that it was well intentioned. Choice (D) is both false and irrelevant. The author tells us that the Legislative Record can verify her claim, and even if it couldn't, the real problem is the *nature* of her claim—that her intentions are what is important—and not its verifiability. And choice (E) is incorrect because the author does not believe that raising taxes itself will create jobs. The author's idea was that raising taxes will provide revenues, and that these revenues could fund a statewide jobs program. Choice (E) is too simplified. Furthermore, it ignores the author's principle mistake—the mistake of thinking that her *intentions* are important to the issue of her *competence.*

8 (D) is correct. With some force, the author of the passage criticizes government funding of the arts on two counts. First, it will be distributed according to the views of those temporarily in power; second, as a necessary consequence, artists will produce according to the changing political realities. In other words, government agencies will support, not the *best* artists, but those whose ideas are most *acceptable* at any given moment; artists will produce, not truly individual works, but what is currently acceptable. The logic of this argument would be seriously weakened if artists tend to ignore the lure of government funds, or, as in choice (D), the influence of either private or public monies. Thus, (D) weakens the contention that, overall, "the free flow of the creative process" will be interfered with.

The information in (A) would put equal numbers of working artists at each extreme of the political spectrum, but does not address their motives. Did they join an institution or group as a means of getting funding? Do most remain with a group, even when it loses funding? Without more information, then, choice (A) cannot qualify as a refutation of the argument in the passage. As for (B), the artists who are "well known in their fields" might well share the political philosophies of the "politicians in power." The participation of the advisory committees would, in that case, exacerbate the problem outlined by the author; politicians and artists of a certain stripe might tend to channel monies to artists or groups of the same stripe. Nor does choice (C) weaken the argument of the passage; it is simply not directly relevant. Interesting as it may be that both politics and the arts may be characterized by rapid shifts in fashion, that fact would not change the relationship described in the passage between government money and interference with individual creativity. On the contrary, if there were a provable *connection* between political and artistic trends in their brevity, the author's argument might be *strengthened.* Choice (E) changes the focus by referring to another aspect of government arts funding, the effect upon audience, rather than the effect upon artists. The author has not addressed this issue. While audiences may have increased, they could have been experiencing only those performances or exhibits which had found political favor or had been created, as the author fears, to appeal to the tastes of those disbursing government funds.

9 (A) is correct. For this question, you are being asked to choose a comprehensive summation of the passage about government funding's possibly harmful effect on the arts. The topic sentence that opens the paragraph lays down the basic charge, that such support interferes with creativity. The author, as we have seen, expands upon the point by describing how it can or will do so. As stated in choice (A), a logical conclusion of the argument is that the type of interference with the creative process will be diverting, distracting, and otherwise degrading. These rather overheated terms are in keeping with the polemical tone of the writing; they follow logically from the author's picture of "willy-nilly" pursuit of government funds.

The first half of (B) seems to follow logically, both in tone and in substance; the author suggests that politicians would adopt a condescendingly proprietary attitude toward the arts. The second half of (B), however, misses an important point; rather than be "inevitably and irretrievably captured" by one type of institution, the arts would, in the author's view, become the plaything of whichever group held power at a particular moment in a continually shifting process. Choice (C), at first glance, seems logical enough. The author does believe that "the politically powerful" can control arts funding; it would seem likely that the most powerful leaders would divert funds to their own legislative districts. But we must remember that the author does not believe that increased arts funding always correlates with wholesomely thriving art. Far from it. The passage makes clear that, to the author, arts funding is likely to produce debased or insincere art. In choice (D), there is a misreading of the second sentence of the passage. Experimental groups and established institutions are apparently equal, from the author's point of view; neither is more likely than the other to encourage the individual artist to pursue his or her own path. Choice (E) directly contradicts the intent of the passage. This answer choice describes the state of affairs that the author would *like* to see occur, but is the *reverse* of the supposed effect of government funding of the arts as denounced in the passage. There, the paramount suggestion is that such government action will indeed encourage artists to render a pale reflection of the prevailing political philosophy.

10 (B) is correct. As in two earlier questions, the point here is to grasp the essential structure of the argument in the passage, then compare it with the logical structure of each of the answer choices. Here, you are asked to select the answer choice with a structure *most* similar to that of the passage given, in which the author argues that the possible danger of psychological testing of schoolchildren is outweighed by the likelihood that the results of such testing will benefit students. In other words, an activity should be pursued if the good effects will probably be greater than the possible bad effects. Similarly, (B) states that arms limitation talks should be pursued because increased chances of survival outweigh the possible risks involved. The subjects of the two arguments are different, but the logical structures are similar.

By contrast, (A) does not argue in favor of pursuing a certain activity (intensive short-term testing of drugs) but attacks it, bringing up an objection which, to the author, affirms the need for the alternative program of long-term testing. In choice (C), the claim being discussed—that hospitals serve high-sodium, high-starch diets—is merely dismissed with the counterclaim that hospital menus are designed by trained nutritionists (the assumption being that trained nutritionists would not design harmful meals). The structure of (D) at first seems roughly similar to that of the passage. The good results (improved vision, improved appearance) are contrasted with the bad effects, the inconveniences as compared with eyeglasses. But "inconveniences" do not weaken the possible good of wearing lenses; this is a side effect, not something detrimental to the essential aim of improved vision. In addition, the argument, unlike that of the paragraph, includes a comparison between two alternatives, rather than merely discussing the merits and possible drawbacks of only one. Choice (E) is an argument for adding devices (swinging doors, pedal-controlled wash basins) to make another device (the public restroom) *appear* less dangerous, or contagious, than people think it is. Rather than weigh a greater good against a possible lesser evil, this argument contends that the public should be distracted from concern over a perceived, but possibly nonexistent, evil.

11 (C) is correct. This author argues that an individual ought to be allowed to help a "pain-wracked, dying friend" to commit suicide. To do so would not be an act of murder, according to the author, but a giving of solace and a mark of respect for an individual's free choice. The correct inference can be drawn from the final sentence of the passage, where the author concludes that lawmakers and judges must treat such cases reasonably, instead of responding "as they have with traditional prejudice." We can infer, then, that lawmakers and judges disagree with the author (otherwise, the author would not be trying to win them over to his side). Choice (C) is thus the correct answer: lawmakers and judges, according to the author, feel that assistance of suicide *is* murder, and the author wishes to change their minds.

Choice (A) is sensible but cannot be *inferred* from the passage. A logical inference must be provable *solely* on the basis of the given information. The author never discusses his idea in the context of other societies, so we cannot infer a universal application for it. Choice (B) is far off the mark. The passage tells us nothing about the thoughts and feelings of the terminally ill; perhaps very few contemplate suicide. Choice (D) goes too far. The author very carefully describes exactly the type of assistance of suicide he thinks is justified, and never implies that the act of suicide is *always* an act of self-deliverance. Choice (E) also tries to cover too much ground. The author's case for the legality of suicide assistance rests on the free *choice* of the victim, not on the amount of pain the victim is suffering.

12 (D) is correct. The author argues that, since much of the Irish population had become totally dependent on the potato for the bulk of its diet, successive failures of the yearly potato crop resulted in a national famine. The question asks for the most logical conclusion of this argument. Choice (D) is the best conclusion, because if much of the population was totally dependent on the potato for its diet, then it follows that much of the population was left without alternative sources of food when the potato crops continued to fail.

There's no reason to conclude that the adoption of the potato as a staple of the Irish diet represented a rejection of English social patterns, choice (A), because the author never discusses either nationalism or social patterns. Similarly, the passage tells us nothing about the relative susceptibility of various staples to crop failure, choice (B). All the author tells us about other crops is that they continued to be cultivated, but "primarily for export to England." Choice (C) is also unwarranted; the author never implies that the great Potato Famine caused any revolutionary activity. Instead, the disastrous consequence of the Potato Famine, according to the author, was "a sweeping sentence of death or emigration." Finally, (E) cannot be concluded because although the author asserts that the potato was grudgingly accepted as a staple of the Irish diet, the passage tells us nothing of those who resisted the potato, or their motivation in doing so.

13 (D) is correct. To prove that a particular sea narrative was partial inspiration for a Coleridge poem, the author of the passage first lists several concrete characteristics that the two works have in common. In addition, he notes that the poet's good friend Wordsworth might have owned a copy of the narrative; the implication is that he shared it with Coleridge. Similar qualities have appeared in works written two centuries apart, and the earlier work could have been available to the author of the more recent work; however, no connection between events has actually been documented in the passage. In other words, the argument relies entirely upon the citation of evidence that is circumstantial, as stated in correct answer choice (D).

Choice (A) is incorrect because the author doesn't create an analogy between seafaring and literature; the author is comparing two literary works about seafaring. The statement in choice (B) introduces an element that is not found at all in the paragraph. The author has not attempted to reinterpret the poem, but merely to explain its genesis; no attention is paid to the meaning of the work. Choice (C) is incorrect because the parallels adduced in the passage are between two works rather than between one work, "The Rime of the Ancient Mariner," and the life of its creator, Coleridge. The reference to his real-life friendship with Wordsworth is not presented as a parallel to any aspect of the poem, although the author implies that the relationship could have had an effect upon the work. As we have seen, precisely what the argument in the passage lacks is concrete documentation for this new claim about literary influence; answer choice (E) is therefore incorrect.

14 (B) is correct. In effect, this question asks you to determine what is illogical about the passage. The author begins by claiming that the attempt to proselytize or convert others is, among other characteristics, a likely trait of people whose behavior may not be strictly normal. As an example, she cites the case of vegetarians, who are, in her view, mostly proselytizers. This very tendency, she says, proves that vegetarianism is a deviation from the American social norm of meat eating. What logical objection can be raised to this argument? As expressed in answer choice (B), the author has neglected the possibility that, while social deviation may indeed create proselytizers, it is not therefore true that all proselytizers have been created by a deviation from the social norm. Social deviation may be one cause, but not the only cause, of the urge to proselytize.

The objection cited in choice (A) is less damaging, since it merely offers a less pejorative expression than "proselytizing" without addressing the question of whether or not the activity of expressing strong feelings, however termed, is always associated with social deviation. Softening the term "proselytizing" does not change the form of the author's reasoning. In (C), there is the suggestion that an important term in the author's argument is too vague. In context, however, what she means by "mainstream American culture" is perfectly clear, since it is, by definition, that part of society that follows the social norms. Choice (D) brings an unwarranted charge. Although the author might seem to feel that social deviants in general have some unattractive qualities, as set forth in the first sentence, she does not reveal a prejudice against vegetarians *per se*. There is no evidence that her characterization of the behavior of vegetarians is unfair. Choice (E) seems an attractive choice because, if statistics showed that more than half of all Americans no longer eat meat, the author's conclusion would indeed be mistaken; vegetarianism would be a mainstream activity. This objection cannot be raised, however, if the figures are otherwise. Since we do not know which is the case, we cannot be certain that "the actual number" would weaken the author's main argument.

CHAPTER 4

Logic Games

Nothing inspires more fear in the hearts of LSAT test takers than Analytical Reasoning—affectionately known as Logic Games. Why? Partly, it's because the skills tested on this section seem so unfamiliar: you need to turn a game's information to your advantage by organizing your thinking and spotting key deductions, and that's not easy to do. Predominantly, however, it's because most test takers don't have a clearly defined method of attack so that they can move through the section quickly and confidently.

That's where Kaplan's Five-Step Method for Logic Games comes in. We're going to teach you the principles, strategies, and techniques you need to rack up points quickly and confidently.

Every Logic Games section consists of four games and usually 24 total questions. The format and directions never change; so, make sure you are familiar with both. We discussed format and directions in the section on LSAT basics; if you need to review them, do so now before you continue.

The following are the major analytical skills that the Logic Games section is intended to measure:

- Organization—the ability to efficiently assimilate, both in your head and on the page, the formidable amount of data associated with each game
- Mental agility—the ability to keep track of multiple pieces of information simultaneously, and still maintain enough flexibility to shuffle the pieces around in different ways for each question
- Memory—the ability to retain the work done in the setup stage while focusing on the new information in each question stem
- Concentration—the ability to keep focused on the task at hand and not let your mind wander

You've probably heard many people complain: "If only I had more time, I could do these!" Well, this is no consolation on the day of the test, when you simply won't have any extra time. You can spend as much time on a game as you like when you're sitting in your own living room, but when your proctor says, "You have thirty-five minutes . . . begin," he or she is not kidding around. Remember, the test makers aren't testing just to see who can answer the LG questions correctly, but also who can do so in 35 minutes.

Logic Games is perhaps the most speed-sensitive section of the test. The test makers know that if you could spend hours methodically trying out every choice in every question, you'd probably get everything right. But what does that prove? Nothing. Who's going to get the sought-after legal position or win the important client—the person who can write the legal brief and prepare the court case in four days, or the person who can do the same job in four hours? It's all about efficiency, both on the test and in your future career. Our step-by-step approach is designed to help you tackle the games section quickly and efficiently.

You will probably improve the most in Logic Games because it is the least familiar initially and the most coachable of all of the question types. We begin our discussion of games by teaching you the Kaplan Five-Step Method. We'll then help you to apply the method to actual games.

The Kaplan Five-Step Method for Logic Games

As we said, the key to improvement in games is having a systematic approach to attacking them. Based on more than 25 years of experience with over 600,000 students in our classes, we've developed the following Kaplan Five-Step Method for Logic Games:

1. Get an overview.
2. Visualize and map out the game.
3. Consider the rules individually.
4. Combine the rules.
5. Work on the questions systematically.

The Kaplan Five-Step Method for Logic Games

1. Get an overview.
2. Visualize and map out the game.
3. Consider the rules individually.
4. Combine the rules.
5. Work on the questions systematically.

Another key to success on the Logic Games section (and on all the sections!) is to carefully review the past LSATs using Kaplan's exclusive explanations. No one else (not even the creators of the LSAT) provides you with this question-by-question insight into released LSATs. Following the review of Kaplan's Five-Step Method for Logic Games, we'll go into just why these explanations are so valuable and how you can best use them.

Step One: Get an Overview

Put your pencil down. Most people assume that the key to Logic Games is doodling. Actually, nothing could be farther from the truth. Think about it: if Logic Games was about how well you can draw, the test makers would give you an empty box to draw in and then would grade (or give you partial credit) for your diagram. The truth is that the test makers don't even give you scratch paper!

Scratch work is only needed if it helps you answer a question. It's a means to an end, not an end in itself. And you won't know whether it will be helpful until you first understand the game and what you are being asked to do. So, begin by carefully reading the game's introduction *and* rules to establish the "cast of characters," the "action," and the number limits governing the game. Keep the following somewhat paradoxical-sounding, Logic Games principle in mind: *to go faster, slow down.*

To gain time in Logic Games, you must spend a lot of time thinking through and analyzing the setup and the rules. This is not only the most important principle for logic games success, it's also the one that's most often ignored, probably because it just doesn't seem right intuitively: people having timing difficulties tend to speed up, not slow down. But by spending a little extra time up front thinking through the stimulus, the "action" of the game, and the rules, you'll be able to recognize the game's key issues and make important deductions that will actually save you time in the long run.

Take Your Time

We know it sounds paradoxical, but you really do save time in the games section by slowing down!

Step Two: Visualize and Map out the Game

Make a mental picture of the situation and let it guide you as you create a sketch or other kind of scratchwork. Now (after your overview) you are ready to put pencil to page, if necessary, to keep track of the rules and to handle new information.

The proper use of scratchwork can help you do your best on Logic Games. The directions state: "You may wish to draw a rough sketch to help answer some of the questions." Notice that they use the wording "rough sketch," not "masterpiece," "work of art," or "classic picture for the ages." The LSAT is not a drawing contest; remember, you get no points for creating beautiful diagrams on the page.

It's Not About How Well You Can Draw

You don't have to make elaborate diagrams in Logic Games and there is not just one correct sketch. However, good scratchwork can help you get points quickly and accurately.

However, although some games aren't amenable to scratchwork, for most games you'll find that it is helpful to create a master sketch, one that encapsulates all of the game's information in one easy-to-reference picture. Typically, you should create your master sketch at the top of the page near the rules. Doing so will not only give your eye a place to gravitate toward when you need information, but it will also help to solidify in your mind the action of the game, the rules, and whatever deductions you come up with up front.

Keep your scratchwork simple—the less time you spend drawing, the more time you'll have for thinking and answering questions. Pay careful attention to the scratchwork suggestions in the explanations we've provided in this book. You'll notice that most games only require minimal scratchwork.

Part of your scratchwork should involve jotting down on your page a quick and shortened form of most rules. Shorthand is a visual representation of a mental thought process and is useful only if it reminds you at a glance of the rule's meaning. Whether you write a rule in shorthand or commit it to memory, you should never have to look back at the game itself once you get to the questions.

The goal of the entire scratchwork process is to condense a lot of information into manageable, user-friendly visual cues. It's much easier to remember rules written in shorthand like so:

B → E
No G in 2

than rules written like so:

If Bob is chosen for the team, then Eric is also chosen.
Box 2 does not contain any gumdrops.

This is helpful as long as you know, for instance, what the arrow from B to E means, and you're consistent in using it. If you can develop a personal shorthand that's instantly understandable to you, you'll have a decided advantage on the day of the test. We'll discuss the best ways to write rules in shorthand following this introduction to the Kaplan Five-Step Method to Logic Games.

Step Three: Consider the Rules Individually

As you think through the meaning and implications of each rule, you have three choices. You can:

- build it directly into your sketch of the game situation
- jot down the rule in shorthand form to help you remember it, or
- underline or circle rules that don't lend themselves to the first two techniques

Don't Be a Parrot
To fully grasp a rule, you must know more than just what it says. You must know what the rule means in the context of the game and in combination with other rules.

But, you won't be able to manipulate and apply the rules unless you understand what a rule means, not just what it says. Don't simply rewrite a printed rule, understand what it means. This is essential. Legal practitioners and scholars (as well as effective LSAT test takers) don't merely read a statement and then spit it back verbatim. You'll never see this on the LSAT:

Rule: Arlene is not fifth in line.
Question: Which one of the following people is not fifth in line?
Answer: Arlene

True, some LG questions are easy—but not that easy. The LSAT, after all, measures the critical thinking skills deemed necessary for success in law school. Virtually every sentence in Logic Games has to be filtered through some sort of analytical process before it will be of any use, just as you'll be asked to filter dense, complicated prose in law school. You may have to use the information about Arlene to help you eliminate a choice or lead you to the right answer, but even in the simplest of cases, this will involve the application, as opposed to the mere parroting, of the rule.

So, it's not enough just to copy a rule off the page (or write it in shorthand); it's imperative that you think through its exact meaning, including any implications it might have. And don't limit your interpretation to the indented rules; statements in the games' introductions are very often rules in and of themselves, and warrant the same meticulous consideration.

For instance, let's say a game's introduction sets up a scenario in which you have three boxes, each containing at least two of the following three types of candy: chocolates, gumdrops, and mints. Then you get the following rule:

> Box 2 does not contain any gumdrops.

What does that rule say? That there aren't any gumdrops in Box 2. But what does that rule mean, when you think about it in the context of the game? That Box 2 *does* contain chocolates and mints. Each box contains at least two of three things, remember. Once you eliminate one of the three things from any particular box, therefore, you know that the other two things must be in that box.

Part of understanding what a rule means, moreover, is grasping what the rule doesn't mean. For example, take the rule we mentioned earlier:

> If Bob is chosen for the team, then Eric is also chosen.

This means: "Whenever Bob is chosen, Eric is, too." This *doesn't* mean: "Whenever Eric is chosen, Bob is, too."

Remember the discussion of formal logic in the Logical Reasoning chapter? If I yell loudly at my cat Adrian, he will run away. That does mean that whenever I yell at him loudly, he runs away. But it *doesn't* mean that whenever he runs away, I've yelled at him loudly.

Understanding what each rule means and not just what it says is key. You'll get plenty of practice interpreting rules throughout this book. Read the explanations to the questions carefully, and compare your interpretation to ours. Don't get discouraged if you find it difficult at first. We'll give you plenty of practice interpreting rules when we apply the Five-Step Method to some sample games, and when you take the two real LSATs toward the end of the book.

Know the Rules Cold

You must know what each rule means, how it impacts other rules, and it's implications before you move to the questions.

Focus on the Important Rules

Not all rules are equal; some are inherently more important than others. Try to focus first on the concrete ones and the ones that have the greatest impact on the situation, specifically the ones that involve the greatest number of the entities. These are also the rules to turn to first whenever you're stuck on a question and don't know how to set off the chain of deduction.

Step Four: Combine the Rules

Look for common elements among the rules; that's what will lead you to make deductions. Treat these deductions as additional rules, good for the whole game.

Rules that contain common elements are often the ones that lead to deductions. Consider the following three rules:

> If Sybil goes to the party, then Edna will go to the party.
> If Jacqui goes to the party, then Sherry will not go to the party.
> If Edna goes to the party, then Dale will go to the party.

Rules 1 and 2 have no entities in common, which is a sure sign that we can't deduce anything from combining them. The same goes for Rules 2 and 3. But since Rules 1 and 3 have Edna in common, a deduction is possible (although not guaranteed). In this case, combining Rules 1 and 3 would allow us to deduce another rule: if Sybil goes to the party, then Dale will go also.

Look for Common Elements

Look for rules that deal with the same entity. Often you can combine the rules to make an important deduction.

Games are structured so that, in order to answer the questions quickly and correctly, you need to search out relevant pieces of information that combine to form valid new statements, called deductions. Now, you can either do this once, up front, and then utilize the same deductions throughout the game, or you can choose to piece together the same basic deductions—essentially repeating the same work—for every single question. For instance, let's say that two of the rules for a Logic Game go as follows:

> If Bob is chosen for the team, then Eric is also chosen.
> If Eric is chosen for the team, then Pat will not be chosen.

You can, as you read through the rules of the game, just treat those rules as two separate pieces of independent information. But there's a deduction to be made from them. Do you see it? If Bob is chosen, Eric is, too. If Eric is chosen, Pat is not. That means that, if Bob is chosen, Pat is not chosen. That's an important deduction—one that will undoubtedly be required from question to question. If you don't take the time to make it up front, when you're first considering the game, you'll have to make it over and over again, every time it's necessary to answer a question. But if you do take the time to make this deduction up front, and build it into your entire conception of the game, you'll save that time later. You won't be doing the same work several times.

The choice is yours; but, most test takers find that the rush-to-the-questions method is inefficient, time consuming, and stress inducing.

So, always try to take the game scenario and the rules as far as you can before moving on to the questions. Look for common elements among the rules (like Eric in the rules above)—this will help you combine them and pull out major deductions. The stimulus creates a situation, and the rules place restrictions on what can and cannot happen within that situation. If you investigate the possible scenarios, and look for and find major deductions up front, you'll then be able to rack up points quickly and confidently.

Step Five: Work on the Questions Systematically

Read the question stems carefully! Take special notice of words such as "must," "could," "cannot," "not," "impossible," and "except." As always, use the hypothetical information offered in if-clauses to set off a chain of deduction.

When hypothetical information is offered in a question stem, try to use it to set off a chain of deductions. Consider the following question. (Since this question is excerpted without the accompanying introduction and rules, ignore the specific logic of the discussion; it's just presented to make a point.)

> If the speedboat is yellow, which one of the following must be true?
>
> (A) The car is green.
> (B) The airplane is red.
> (C) The train is black.
> (D) The car is yellow.
> (E) The train is red.

The question stem contains a hypothetical, which is an if-clause offering information pertaining only to that particular question. The wrong approach is to acknowledge that the speedboat is yellow, and then proceed to test out all of the choices. The muddled mental thought process accompanying this tragic approach might go something like this:

> "All right, the speedboat's yellow, does the car have to be green? Well, let's see, if the speedboat's yellow, and the car is green, then the train would have to be yellow, but I can't tell what color the airplane is, and I guess this is okay, I don't know, I better try the next choice. Let's see what happens if the speedboat's yellow and the airplane is red. . . ."

Don't do this kind of dithering! Notice that the question doesn't ask, "What happens if, in addition to this, the car is green?" or "What happens if this is true and the airplane is red?" So why is the confused test taker above intent on answering all of these irrelevant questions? Never begin a question by trying out answer choices; that's going about it backwards. Only if you're entirely stuck, or are faced with a question stem that leaves you no choice, should you resort to trial-and-error.

Most Logic Games questions are amenable to a more efficient and systematic methodology. The correct approach is to incorporate the new piece of information into your view of the game, creating one quick sketch if you wish. How do you do this? Simple—apply the rules and any previous deductions to the new information in order to set off a new chain of deductions. Then follow through until you've taken the new information as far as it can go. Just as you must take the game and rules as far as you can before moving on to the questions, you must carry the information in a question stem out as far as you can before moving on to the choices.

Don't Use Trial-and-Error Unless You Have To

It's normally much quicker to follow the deduction chain until you reach the credited response. In some questions, trial-and-error is the only way to find the answer. But, don't turn to it unless you must.

So make sure to stay out of answer-choice land until you have sufficiently mined the hypothetical. If the question stem contains a hypothetical, then your job is to get as much out of that piece of information as you can before even looking at the choices. This way, you dictate to the test, and not the other way around. You'll then be able to determine the answer and simply pick it off the page.

Know the Forms of Question Stems

You must have a solid command of the various forms of Logic Games question stems. When you take a few seconds to think through what kind of statements would be the right and wrong answers to a particular question, your work becomes more time efficient. You're also less likely to slip up at the last minute and pick the wrong thing. The following should clear up any misconceptions you may have regarding what the choices should look like for each of the major types of questions:

- If the question reads: "Which one of the following statements could be true?" the right answer will be a statement that could be true, and the four wrong choices will be statements that definitely cannot be true (that is, statements that must be false).
- If the question reads: "Which one of the following statements cannot be true?" the right answer will be a statement that cannot be true, and the four wrong choices will be statements that either must be true or merely could be true.
- If the question reads: "Which one of the following statements must be true?" the right answer will be a statement that must be true, and the four wrong choices will be statements that either cannot be true or merely could be true.
- If the question reads: "All of the following statements could be true EXCEPT?" the right answer will be a statement that cannot be true, and the four wrong choices will be statements that either could be true or even must be true.
- If the question reads: "All of the following statements must be true EXCEPT?" the right answer will be a statement that either cannot be true, or merely could be true, and the four wrong choices will be statements that must be true.
- If the question reads: "Which one of the following statements could be false?" the right answer will be a statement that cannot be true or could be either true or false, and the four wrong choices will be statements that must be true.
- If the question reads: "Which one of the following statements must be false?" the right answer will be a statement that cannot be true, and the

four wrong choices will be statements that either must be true or merely could be true.

Tackle Easier Questions First

The questions don't appear in order of difficulty, so tackle them in whatever order makes sense to you. We advise Kaplan students to answer Logic Game questions in the following order:

1. Questions that ask which of the answer choices is an acceptable order of the characters, such as:

   Which one of the following is an acceptable list of the seven names in order from first to last?

   (A) Suzi, Ryan, Matt, Ned, Paula, Laura, Tom

2. Questions that ask what must be true based solely on the rules (but whose answer choices *aren't* phrased in "if . . . then" form) such as:

   Which one of the following statements must be true?

   What is the total number of athletes whose exact finish position in the race can be deduced?

3. Questions that provide hypothetical information, such as:

   If garage Y contains six cars, which one of the following must be true?

   If the ranks of A, B, and C are consecutive, then which of the following statements must be false?

4. Other question types, such as:

   Which of the following is a complete and accurate list of the days on which Olive's interview could be scheduled?

   Which of the following must be true?

   (A) If Toyais interviewed on Saturday, then Pat is interviewed on Thursday.

   . . .

   If P finished the race before J, then what is the maximum possible number of athletes whose finish positions could be determined?

   Assume that the condition requiring that Sam finishes the race before Mary is suspended. If all other conditions remain the same and if Peter finishes the race fourth, which one of the following CANNOT be true?

No "Best" Choice

Unlike the answer choices in Logical Reasoning and Reading Comprehension, in which the correct answer is the "best" choice, the answers in Logic Games are objectively correct or incorrect. Therefore, when you find an answer that's definitely right, have the confidence to circle it and move on, without wasting time to check the other choices. This is one way to improve your timing on the section.

Kaplan's Exclusive Explanations for Released LSATs

Only Kaplan offers extensive diagnoses of every question on released LSATs (or PrepTests). After taking a PrepTest, you know that you missed a certain question, but do you know *why* you missed it? More importantly, do you know how to avoid missing that same type of question on the day of the test? You know that you got a question right, but do you know *how* you answered it correctly? And most importantly of all, do you know how to *repeat* this success on the same type of question on the day of the test? Kaplan's explanations break each question down and shows you what's wrong with each incorrect choice and why the credited response is right. Using the explanations, you can identified what tricked you into picking a wrong choice, and you can ensure that you got a question right for *repeatable* reasons. If you got lucky and guessed right on a question, how will that aid you on the day of the test? It won't. Every time our students work on a PrepTest, they are able to review the test using the explanations. With Kaplan's help, soon they are able to recognize the common wrong choices and avoid these common traps that the test makers create to snare the unwary. They are able to solidify their technique for pinpointing the credited response. However, to get to this point, you must be diligent in your use of Kaplan's explanations. It's not enough to review the questions you got wrong. It's vital that you also know why you got a question right. Practice tests are just that, practice. They don't count. What matters (and what should be your overriding focus) is the LSAT itself.

Crucial LG Skills

Although the number of different types of games that can appear on the LSAT may seem limitless, the test makers focus on three primary skills: sequencing, grouping, and matching, either individually or in combination (a hybrid game). We'll provide you with the logic behind each skill and a sample game so that you can practice applying the Kaplan Five-Step Method to a game that involves each skill.

Sequencing

Logic Games that require sequencing skills have long been a favorite of the test makers. No matter what the scenario in games of this type, the common denominator is that in some way, shape, or form, they all involve putting entities in order. In a typical sequencing game, you may be asked to arrange the cast of characters numerically from left to right, from top to bottom, in days of the week, in a circle, and so on. The sequence may be a sequence of degree—say, ranking the eight highest-scoring test takers from one to eight. On the other hand, the sequence may be based on time, such as one that involves the order of shows broadcast on a radio station. In some cases, there are two or even three orderings to keep track of in a single game.

Fixed and Unfixed Sequences

There are generally two types of sequence games: the fixed, or standard, sequence, and the unfixed, or free-floating, sequence. In a fixed-sequence game, the placement of entities is very strictly defined. We may be told, for example, that "A is third," or that "X and Y are in adjacent lanes," and so on. These are definite, concrete pieces of information, and the game centers around placing as many entities into definite spots as possible. In contrast to this, in an unfixed or free-floating sequence game, our job is to rank the entities only in relation to one another. We're usually never asked to fully determine the ordering of the cast of characters. Instead, the relationships between the entities constitute the crux of the game.

Sequencing at a Glance

- Sequencing games appear on almost every exam.
- Sequencing requires that you put entities in order.
- Sequencing can be fixed or free floating.
- Sequencing can be in time (for example, the sequence of shows), space (for example, people in line), or degree (for example, shortest to tallest, worst to best, etcetera).

Typical Issues

The following is a list of the key issues that underlie sequencing games. Each key issue is followed by a corresponding rule—in some cases, with several alternative ways of expressing the same rule. At the end, we'll use these rules to build a miniature Logic Game, so that you can see how rules work together to define and limit a game's "action." These rules all refer to a scenario in which eight events are to be sequenced from first to eighth:

- Which entities are concretely placed in the ordering?

  X is third.

- Which entities are forbidden from a specific position in the ordering?

  Y is not fourth.

- Which entities are next to, adjacent to, or are immediately preceding or following one another?

  X and Y are consecutive.
  X is next to Y.
  No event comes between X and Y.
  X and Y are consecutive in the ordering.

- Which entities cannot be next to, adjacent to, or immediately preceding or following one another?

  X does not immediately precede or follow Z.
  X is not immediately before or after Z.
  At least one event comes between X and Z.
  X and Z are not consecutive in the sequence.

- How far apart in the ordering are two particular entities?

  Exactly two events come between X and Q.

- What is the relative position of two entities in the ordering?

> Q comes before T in the sequence.
> T comes after Q in the sequence.

How a Sequence Game Works

Let's see how rules like those above might combine to create a simple Logic Game.

> Eight events—Q, R, S, T, W, X, Y, and Z—are being ordered from first to eighth.
>
> X is third.
> Y is not fourth
> X and Y are consecutive.
> Exactly two events come between X and Q.
> Q occurs before T in the sequence.

How would you approach this simplified game? Well, what are you asked to do? With eight events to sequence from first to eighth, you would probably want to draw eight dashes in the margin of your test booklet, maybe in two groups of four (so you can easily determine which dash is which). Then take the rules in order of concreteness, starting with the most concrete of all—Rule 1—which tells you that X is third. Fill that into your sketch:

_ _ X _   _ _ _ _

Jump to the next most concrete rule, Rule 4, which tells you that exactly two events come between X and Q. Well, since Q can't obey this rule coming before X, it must come after X—in the sixth space.

_ _ X _   _ Q _ _

Rule 5 says that Q comes before T. Since Q is sixth, T must be either seventh or eighth. To indicate this, under the sketch, write T with two arrows pointing to the seventh and eighth dashes. Meanwhile, Rule 3 says that X and Y are consecutive. X is third, so Y will be either second or fourth. Rule 2 clears up that matter. Y can't be fourth, says Rule 2, so it will have to be second:

_ Y X _   _ Q _ _
\ T /

And this is how the rules work together to build a sequence game. The questions might then present hypothetical information that would set off the "chain of deduction" we mentioned in the basic principles section.

Now try applying the Kaplan Five-Step Method to the following sequence game.

Eight children—Mallory, Ned, Oona, Paula, Quentin, Robert, Sam, and Terrance—slide down a waterslide, one at a time, at a local amusement park. Each child slides down the waterslide exactly once according to the following conditions:

Mallory slides down before Robert.
Sam slides down before Quentin.
Oona slides down after both Robert and Terrance.
Quentin slides down before Ned and Paula.

1. How many children could have been the first child to slide down the waterslide?

(A) 1
(B) 2
(C) 3
(D) 4
(E) 5

2. If Terrance is the seventh child to slide down the waterslide, then which one of the following must be false?

(A) Mallory slides down the waterslide before Sam.
(B) Ned slides down the waterslide before Terrance.
(C) Oona slides down the waterslide before Paula.
(D) Quentin slides down the waterslide before Robert.
(E) Robert slides down the waterslide before Sam.

3. If Oona slides down the waterslide before Quentin, then what is the maximum number of children that can slide down the waterslide before Robert?

(A) 1
(B) 2
(C) 3
(D) 4
(E) 5

4. If Oona slides down the waterslide fourth, then which one of the following must be true?

(A) Ned slides down the waterslide last.
(B) Paula slides down the waterslide last.
(C) Robert slides down the waterslide second.
(D) Sam slides down the waterslide fifth.
(E) Terrance slides down the waterslide second.

5. Which one of the following must be true?

   (A) If Mallory slides down the waterslide before Sam, then Robert slides down the waterslide before Ned.
   (B) If Oona slides down the waterslide before Paula, then Mallory slides down the waterslide before Ned.
   (C) If Quentin slides down the waterslide before Robert, then Sam slides down the waterslide before Oona.
   (D) If Quentin slides down the waterslide before Terrance, then Oona slides down the waterslide before Sam.
   (E) If Terrance slides down the waterslide before Ned, then Quentin slides down the waterslide before Robert.

Step One: Get an Overview

We need to determine the order in which eight children, abbreviated M, N, O, P, Q, R, S, and T slide down a waterslide. This is an unfixed or free-floating sequence game. It is concerned with the relationships between the entities—who slides down the waterslide before and after whom—rather than focusing on who is first, second, third, etcetera. A fixed-sequence game would have rules that place entities into definite slots—for example, "Marty works on Tuesday."

Step Two: Visualize and Map Out the Game

One of the challenges in a free-floating sequence game, is how to organize the information. A common Kaplan approach to this type of game involves making use of a vertical sketch, in this case by placing the earlier children above the later children and connecting them with solid lines. We suggest working vertically, because most people can easily remember that the children who slide down first are above the children who slide down later. If you are more comfortable working horizontally with the earlier children to the left of the later ones, feel free to organize your sketch in that way.

You Are in Charge

As long as the sketch you choose is neat and accurate, and the information is readily accessible, the final form is totally up to you.

Step Three: Consider the Rules Individually

With a free-floating sequence game, the first thing you need to do is find the entity that could be on top of your sketch. Look for the child who is not prohibited by any of the rules from sliding down after any other child. This is the child who you'll put at the top of your sketch. Mallory, Sam, and Terrance all fit the bill. Since Mallory is in Rule 1 and Sam is in Rule 2, we'll start by putting an "M" and an "S" at the top of our sketch. As we're told by a rule that a child slides down after Mallory or Sam, we'll just draw a line down to the letter representing that child's name.

Rules 1 and 2 should be pretty straightforward. Mallory slides down before Robert, and Sam slides down before Quentin. Starting with the "M" and "S" in our sketch, build this information into the sketch.

Rule 3 is really two rules in one. When you're give a rule that has multiple parts, break it down and consider each piece individually. Oona must slide down after

Robert and Oona must slide down after Terrance. Robert is already a part of the sketch, so it's a simple matter to add the first part of this rule into the sketch. And once the first part is added, you can add the second part.

According to Rule 4, Q must come before both N and P, but we don't know anything about the relationship between N and P. Since Q is already a part of the sketch under S, all we have to do is add the new information.

Step Four: Combine the Rules

We've already done the combing as we considered each rule. The game breaks down into two separate rankings—Mallory, Oona, Robert, and Terrance in one, and Ned, Paula, Quentin, and Sam in the other. Rules 1 and 3 combine nicely to give us this:

Rules 2 and 4 result in this ordering:

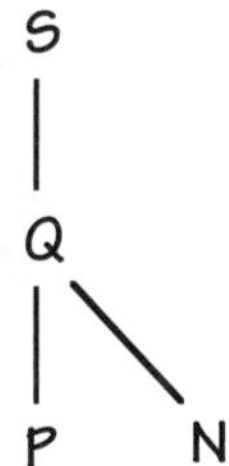

This game is a fairly easy example of an unfixed sequence game, but be careful to be flexible in your placement of children relative to the children from the other ranking. For example, even though Oona is at the bottom of the first ranking above, she can still slide down before everyone in the second ranking.

Step Five: Work on the Questions Systematically

A Kaplan-trained student would handle the questions in roughly the following order: 1, 4, 2, 3, 5. Question 1 appears to be the easiest; it asks for what must be true based solely on the rules. Question 5 definitely looks to be the most time consuming. Although the question stem sounds simple, each of the answer choices is an if/then statement. Question 4 is a straight if/then question, asking for what must be true. Figuring out what must be true is simpler for most students than trying to deduce what must be false, as is required by Question 5. But Questions 4 and 5 promise to be more straightforward than Question 3, which gives only relative information in the stem (Oona slides down before Quentin) and asks an abstract question (What's the maximum number of kids that could slide down before Robert?).

Note, however, that the differences between Questions 2, 3, and 4 are slight. As long as you recognized that Question 1 promised to be the easiest and Question 5 the most time consuming, you could have tackled the middle three questions in order.

Question 1
Any child who has no child definitely sliding before him or her is free to be the first child down the waterslide, and the only children who fit this description are Mallory, Sam, and Terrance. Robert and Quentin can at best be second, Paula and Ned can at best be third, and the earliest Oona can go is fourth. The answer is 3, choice (C).

Question 4
In the ranking that results from Rules 1 and 3, Oona slides down later than exactly three children—Mallory, Robert, and Terrance. So in order for Oona to be fourth, she must follow those three, and the children from the other part of the sketch must all come after her, like so:

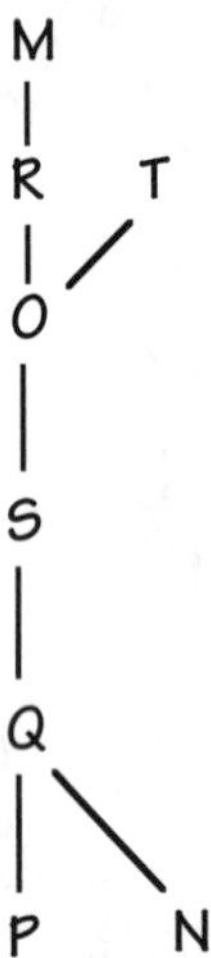

The true statement that conforms to this arrangement is choice (D): Sam *must* immediately follow Oona down the waterslide, making him fifth. As for the others, either Terrance or Robert (or Mallory, for that matter) could be second, which kills choices (C) and (E), and either Ned or Paula could be last, which eliminates (A) and (B).

Question 2
If Terrance is seventh, and Oona, according to rule 3, is after Terrance, then Oona must be eighth, which makes choice (C) the impossibility—Oona, who is last, cannot go before Paula. Choice (C) must be false, while each of the other choices are possible.

Question 3
If Oona slides down before Quentin, then Robert and Mallory must slide down before Quentin as well. That means that Paula and Ned must come after Robert, so the only children who could slide down before Robert are Mallory, Sam, and the wild card Terrance. The correct answer is therefore 3, which is choice (C).

Question 5

We get no new information in the stem of Question 5, so we might as well test out the choices, looking for one that must be true. In (A), Mallory slides down before Sam, but Robert could still slide down after Ned. In (B), Oona's sliding down before Paula does not affect Mallory's position relative to Ned's—nothing prohibits Ned from going before her. However, in (C), if Quentin goes before Robert, then Sam must in fact slide down before Oona, because Sam is before Quentin and Oona comes after Robert. So (C) is the true statement. If this were the day of the test, you shouldn't waste time checking out the others. For practice here, though, you may want to verify that the remaining choices need not be true, and you'll confirm that (C) indeed is correct.

Grouping

All games begin with a set of entities. What sets grouping apart is the "action" of the game, or specifically, what you're asked to do with the entities. In a pure grouping game, unlike sequencing, there's no call for putting the entities in order. Instead, you'll usually be required to "select" a smaller group from the initial group, or "distribute" the entities in some fashion into more than one subgroup. As a distinct skill, grouping differs from sequencing in that you're not really concerned with what order the entities are in, but rather how they're grouped—who's in, who's out, and who can and cannot be with whom in various subgroups.

Grouping at a Glance

- Grouping appears in almost every test.
- Grouping can be selection (which entities) or distribution (where the entities go).
- Number rules are crucial (how many chosen, how many in each group, etcetera).
- Don't forget the contrapositive if you see an if/then rule.

Grouping Games of Selection and Distribution

In selection games, you'll be given the cast of characters and told to select from them a smaller group, based, of course, on a set of rules. For example, a game may include eight musical cassettes, from which you must choose four. Sometimes the test makers specify an exact number for the smaller group, and other times they don't. A small variation of this type occurs when the initial group of entities is itself broken up in groups to begin the game. An example would be a farmer choosing three animals from a group of three cows and five horses.

In distribution games, we're more concerned with who goes where than we are with who's chosen and who isn't—who's in and who's out, in other words. Sometimes, every entity will end up in a group—an example is placing or distributing eight marbles into two jars, four to a jar. On the other hand, it's perfectly viable for a game to mandate the placement of three marbles in each jar, leaving two marbles out in the cold.

It's important for you to be aware of the numbers that govern each particular grouping game, because although all grouping games rely on the same general skills, you have to adapt these skills to the specific situations of each. Still, all grouping games revolve around the same basic questions. Is this entity in? Is it out? If it's not in this group, is it in that one?

Like sequencing games, grouping games have a language all their own, and it's up to you to speak that language fluently when you come across games that require this particular skill on your test.

Grouping Games of Selection: Typical Issues

The following is a list of the key issues that underlie grouping games of selection. Each key issue is followed by a corresponding rule—in some cases, with several alternative ways of expressing the same rule. These rules all refer to a scenario in which you are to select a subgroup of four from a group of eight entities—Q, R, S, T, W, X, Y, and Z. (At the end, again, we'll use these rules to build a miniature Logic Game.)

- Which entities are definitely chosen?

  Q is selected.

- Which entities rely on a different entity's selection in order to be chosen?

  If X is selected, then Y is selected.
  X will be selected only if Y is selected.
  X will not be selected unless Y is selected.

Note: A common misconception surrounds the rule, "If X is selected, then Y is selected." This works only in one direction; if X is chosen, Y must be, but if Y is chosen, X may or may not be. Remember, understand what a rule means, but also what it doesn't mean!

- Which entities must be chosen together, or not at all?

  If Y is selected, then Z is selected, and if Z is selected, then Y is selected.
  Y will not be selected unless Z is selected, and vice versa.

- Which entities cannot both be chosen?

  If R is selected, then Z is not selected.
  If Z is selected, then R is not selected.
  R and Z won't both be selected.

How Grouping Games of Selection Work

We can combine these rules to create a rudimentary grouping game of selection:

> A professor must choose a group of four books for her next seminar. She must choose from a pool of eight books—Q, R, S, T, W, X, Y, and Z.
> Q is selected.
> If X is selected then Y is selected.
> If Y is selected, Z is selected, and if Z is selected, then Y is selected.
> If R is selected, Z is not selected.

One good way of dealing with this kind of game is to write out the eight letters—four on top, four on the bottom—and then circle the ones that are definitely selected while crossing out the ones that are definitely not selected. Thus, Rule 1 would allow you to circle the Q:

(Q) R S T

W X Y Z

The other rules can't be built into the sketch just yet, since they describe eventualities (what happens if something else happens). Here's where you would want to use shorthand:

- Rule 2 translates as, "**If X, then Y**" or "**X ——> Y**"
- Rule 3 might be rendered as, "**YZ together**" (as a reminder to choose them together, if at all).
- Rule 4 could be noted as, "**Never RZ**" (since R and Z are mutually exclusive).

The rules would then be poised to take effect whenever a question would add new hypothetical information, setting off a chain of deduction. For instance, let's say a question read like so:

If R is selected, which of the following must be true?

This new information would put the rules into motion. R's inclusion would set off Rule 4—"**Never RZ**"—so we would have to circle R and cross out Z:

Q (R) S T

W X Y ~~Z~~

This would in turn set off Rule 3—"**YZ together**." Since Z is out, Y is out, because they must be chosen together or not at all:

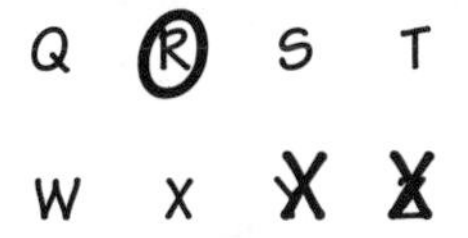

Q (R) S T

W X ~~Y~~ ~~Z~~

Now Rule 2 comes into play. "**X ——> Y**" means that if Y is not chosen, X can't be either (since X's inclusion would require Y's). So we can take the chain of deduction one step further:

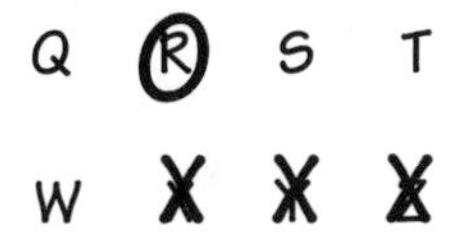

Q (R) S T

W ~~X~~ ~~Y~~ ~~Z~~

A correct answer to this question, then, might be "X is not selected." And that, in a nutshell, is how a (simplified) grouping game of selection works.

Grouping Games of Distribution: Typical Issues

Here are the issues involved in the other kind of grouping game—grouping games of distribution—along with the rules that govern them. These rules, by the way, refer to a scenario in which the members of our old favorite group of eight entities—Q, R, S, T, W, X, Y, Z—have to be distributed into three different classes:

- Which entities are concretely placed in a particular subgroup?

  X is placed in Class 3.

- Which entities are barred from a particular subgroup?

  Y is not placed in Class 2.

- Which entities must be placed in the same subgroup?

  X is placed in the same class as Z.
  Z is placed in the same class as X.
  X and Z are placed in the same class.

- Which entities cannot be placed in the same subgroup?

  X is not placed in the same class as Y.
  Y is not placed in the same class as X.
  X and Y are not placed in the same class.

- Which entity's placement depends on the placement of a different entity?

  If Y is placed in Class 1, then Q is placed in Class 2.

How Grouping Games of Distribution Work

The above rules, neatly enough, also can combine to form a miniature grouping game of distribution.

> Eight students—Q, R, S, T, W, X, Y, and Z—must be subdivided into three different classes—Classes 1, 2, and 3.
> X is placed in Class 3.
> Y is not placed in Class 2.
> X is placed in the same class as Z.
> X is not placed in the same class as Y.
> If Y is placed in Class 1, then Q is placed in Class 2.

A good scratchwork scheme for games of this type would be to draw three circles in your booklet, one for each of the three classes. Then put the eight entities in the appropriate circles as that information becomes known.

Here again, start with the most concrete rule first, which is Rule 1, which definitively places X in Class 3. Rule 2 just as definitively precludes Y from Class 2, so build that into the scratchwork, too:

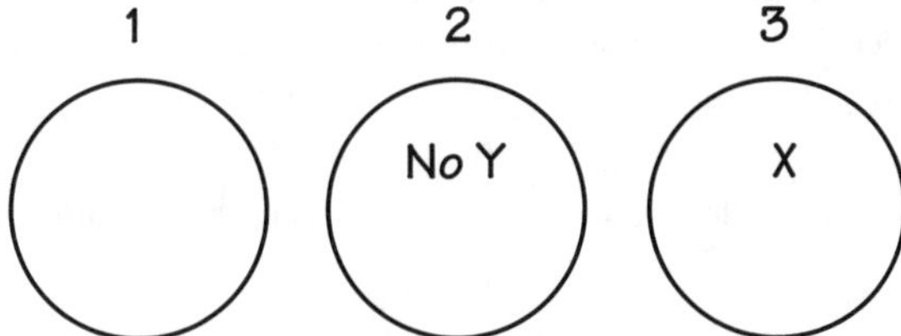

Rule 3 requires Z to join X in Class 3:

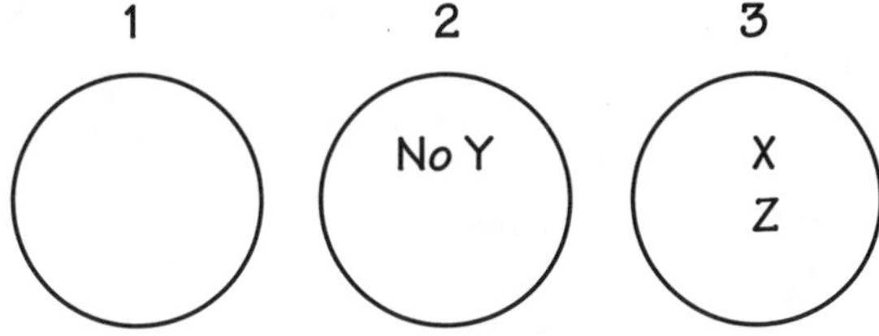

Rule 4, prohibiting Y from being in the same class as X, means that Y can't be in Class 3. But we already know that Y can't be in Class 2. We can deduce, therefore, that Y must go in Class 1. That in turn puts Rule 5 into play: if Y is in Class 1 (as it is here), Q is in Class 2:

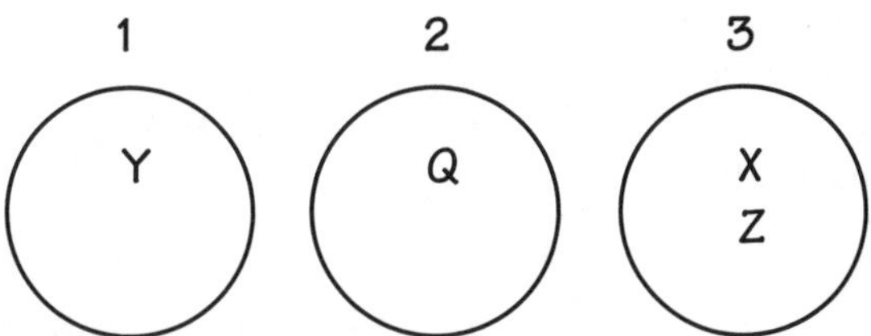

And that is the dynamic of most grouping games of distribution (though, again, in much simplified form).

Now try applying the Kaplan Five-Step Method to the following grouping game.

The creative director of the Midtown Ad Agency must select two two-person teams to work on a new campaign. Each team is to contain one writer and one artist. The available writers are Alan, Beatrice, Cindy, and Dalen. The available artists are Enid, Felicity, and Godfrey.

Alan and Beatrice will not both work on the campaign.

Enid and Beatrice will not work on the same team, though they are willing to work on the campaign together.

Cindy and Godfrey will not work on the same team, though they are willing to work on the campaign together.

If either Dalen or Felicity is selected to work on the campaign, the other must also be selected.

1. Which one of the following is an acceptable assignment of campaign workers?

	First Team	Second Team
(A)	Cindy	Alan
	Godfrey	Enid
(B)	Dalen	Alan
	Felicity	Beatrice
(C)	Beatrice	Dalen
	Enid	Felicity
(D)	Cindy	Beatrice
	Enid	Godfrey
(E)	Alan	Enid
	Cindy	Godfrey

2. If Beatrice works on the first team of the campaign and Felicity on the second, the other two workers must be

(A) Dalen and Godfrey
(B) Cindy and Godfrey
(C) Dalen and Enid
(D) Cindy and Enid
(E) Alan and Godfrey

3. If Alan works on the campaign, which of the following pairs of workers CANNOT work on the campaign?

(A) Felicity and Dalen
(B) Cindy and Enid
(C) Felicity and Cindy
(D) Dalen and Enid
(E) Cindy and Godfrey

4. If Cindy works on the second team, which of the following CANNOT be the members of the first team?

(A) Dalen and Godfrey
(B) Dalen and Felicity
(C) Beatrice and Godfrey
(D) Alan and Godfrey
(E) Alan and Enid

5. If Felicity works on the first team and Enid works on the second, which of the following could be true?

   (A) Dalen works on the first team and Beatrice works on the second.
   (B) Alan works on the first team and Cindy works on the second.
   (C) Godfrey works on the first team and Dalen works on the second.
   (D) Beatrice works on the first team and Dalen works on the second.
   (E) Beatrice works on the first team and Cindy works on the second.

Step One: Get an Overview

We must pick two two-person teams, four people total, from the seven people available. So, three of the people won't be assigned to a team. Each team must have exactly one writer and one artist. Thus, this is a grouping game of selection. The line in the opening paragraph that tells us that each team must be composed of one writer and one artist is an example of a very important rule that is hidden in the opening paragraph. You can never turn off your critical reading. Though most rules are in the normal indented form, often important rules are written into the introduction. If you gloss over them, you could cause yourself problems. You really have to be on your toes with this game, since there are some pairs of workers who won't work together at all, and some who will cooperate on the campaign, though not on the same team.

Step Two: Visualize and Map Out the Game

If you were the creative director of the Midtown Ad Agency, how would you keep track of the two two-person teams? You would probably want to keep it simple for easy reference. Simple is good in real life and it's good on the LSAT. Just draw a couple of lines for the two members of each time and list the entities off to the side. We recommend using capital letters for the writers and lowercase for the artists to help you keep them separate:

First Team	Second Team	
______ (artist)	______ (artist)	e f g
______ (writer)	______ (writer)	A B C D

Step Three: Consider the Rules Individually

From the overview, you should have picked up the fact that some workers won't work together at all, and that some will work together but not on the same team. As always, make sure you *think over* each rule. Using shorthand is not enough. Remember that there is not only one right way to sketch a game. We've provided two alternatives below. Use whichever you feel most comfortable with.

Rule 1: NOT A and B
Rule 2: NOT e and B on same team, but OK

Rule 3: NOT C and g on same team, but OK

Rule: 4: (Df)

You could also note the first and fourth rules as follows:

CAMPAIGN

A ≠ B (Df) or ~~Df~~

The second and third rules—the ones about people who will work together on a campaign though not on the same team—could look like this:

TEAM
Can't have: eB Cg

Step Four: Combine the Rules

Although we have several rules that involve the same character, for instance Rules 1 and 2, we can't make any further deductions before moving to the questions. It's possible that on the test, you'll get a game like this in which you can't combine rules. After spending a few moments searching for deductions in vain, have the confidence in your abilities to give up on your search and hit the questions. Just make sure you have a solid understanding of the rules individually and can manipulate them quickly and effectively.

Step Five: Work on the Questions Systematically

As is so happens, the order in which these questions appear is the best order in which to attack them. The acceptability question, Question 1, is a great place to start your work, and in Question 5, the stem and the choices are all two-parters. This level of complexity makes Question 5 a great place to *end* your work. Questions 2, 3, and 4 are all roughly equivalent on the surface, harder than Question 1 but easier than Question 5.

Question 1

Use the rules in order to narrow down the answer choices. In violation of Rule 1, Alan and Beatrice work on the same campaign in (B). In violation of Rule 2, Enid and Beatrice work on the same team in (C). Rule 3 prohibits Cindy and Godfrey on the same team, which is what we get in (A). And while the four workers in (E) are O.K., they're paired up improperly: we can't have two writers on one team and two artists on the other. That leaves (D), which violates no rules.

Question 2

Felicity is working on the second team. Rule 4 says that Dalen will have to work on the campaign if Felicity does, so Dalen will have to be brought on (and she'll work with Felicity, since we already have one writer, Beatrice, on the other team). Right off the bat you can eliminate (B), (D), and (E) because they neglect to mention the necessary Dalen. So: D and f are one team. Who can team up with Beatrice on the first team? Not Enid—remember, e ≠ B thanks to Rule 2. All that's left is (A), D and g, Dalen with Felicity and Godfrey with Beatrice, and that's the correct answer.

Question 3

Begin with A, a writer, and exclude B because of Rule 1. Since the chain of deductions seems to stop there, you can simply add in the pairs from each answer choice and check the resulting group against the rules. Obviously, we expect four out of five of them to work; only one pair, the correct answer, will not. The pairs in choices (A), (B), (D), and (E) are all possible to complete an acceptable group starting with A. Choice (C), however, is impossible, because if f and C work on the campaign, then D would also have to, because of the last rule. This would give us A, C, D, and f, a group consisting of three writers and one artist, when we always need exactly two writers and two artists. So (C) contains the violation, and we take it as our answer and move on.

Question 4

This question is similar to its predecessor: who could *not* be members of the first team. We're told by the stem that Cindy is on the second team. Rule 3 comes into play and tells us that either Godfrey won't work at all or he will work on the first team. Again the chain of deductions seems to stop, so try out each choice. (A) is all right: D-g as the first team would necessitate C-f as the second (since f = D). (B) is fine, too: D-f as team one would leave C-e for the second team (since C ≠ g). In (C), B g as the first team would allow C to pair up with e; (D)'s suggestion that A-g be the first team would be complemented by C-e as the second. By a somewhat lengthy process of elimination, we're left with (E) as the correct choice. A-e as the first team would leave C to be paired up with f (no good because f = D) or g (but c ≠ g). So (E) contains the forbidden pair.

Question 5

If f works on the first team and e works on the second team, we know a few things immediately that will help us to eliminate choices that cannot be true. First of all, f needs D, so choices (B) and (E), which both leave out D when filling in the remaining two workers, can't be true. Furthermore, e and B can't work on the same team, so choice (A) is out also. Choice (C) cannot be true; a group consisting of e, f, g, and D contains three artists and one writer, no good. The answer, therefore, is (D): B-f/D-e is a perfectly acceptable group, violating none of the given rules.

Matching

The third skill tested is matching. Matching games have haunted LSAT test takers since they came into favor some years ago. As the name implies, matching games ask you to match up various characteristics about a group of entities. They often require you to distribute many characteristics at once. For example, a game may involve three animals, each assigned a name, a color, and a particular size. It's no wonder test takers get bogged down in these types—there's often a lot to keep track of.

Matching at a Glance

- These are often complicated. If so, leave them until the end of the section.
- Don't forget the contrapositive if you see an if/then rule.
- A table or grid is often the best way to keep track of the information.

Some people dislike matching games because they feel as if they're being bombarded with information, and they don't know where to start. Organization is important in any game, but it is crucial for matching games. A table or grid can be helpful, but for some games you need to rely on your instincts to organize the information efficiently based on the particulars of the game. If you do use a sketch, and this goes for any game, remember that thinking must always precede writing. A visual representation of a mental thought process can be invaluable, whereas scribbling thoughtlessly for the sake of getting something down on the page is useless, and even detrimental.

One matching hint is to try to center the game around the most important characteristic—the one with the most information attached to it. Going back to the example above, don't necessarily assume that you should organize your thinking, or a sketch, around the animals—there may be a better attribute, one that you know more about, that should take center stage. An efficient test taker spends less time panicking and being intimidated by all of the information in a matching game, and more time visualizing the action and creating a mental picture or a sketch on the page that places the elements into a logical order. If you think through the scenarios and don't get scared off by their seeming complexity, you should find matching games accessible and even fun.

Matching Games: Typical Issues

The following is a list of the key issues that underlie matching games. Each key issue is followed by a corresponding rule or set of rules. All of these rules refer to a situation in which we have three animals—a dog, a cat, and a goat. Each animal has a name (Bimpy, Hank, and Sujin), a color (brown, black, or white), and a size (large or small):

- Which entities are matched up?

  The dog is brown.
  The black animal is small.

- Which entities are not matched up?

  Bimpy is not white.
  The goat is not large.

- Which entity's matchups depend on the matchups of other entities?

  If the cat is large, then Hank is brown.
  If the white animal is small, then Sujin is not the dog.

Notice that these last rules take the form of if/then statements, which, based on our discussion of Logical Reasoning in the previous chapter, means that the contrapositive can be employed. Whenever rules take this form, you should always work out the contrapositive and then add the result, as a valid deduction, to your view of the game. Remember, the contrapositive can be formed by reversing and negating the terms of an if/then statement. For the first, we get:

If Hank is NOT brown, then the cat is NOT large.

Taking the contrapositive of the second rule results in this statement:

If Sujin IS the dog, then the white animal is NOT small.

The Contrapositive
Make the contrapositive of all if/then rules. It will almost always yield an important deduction.

Both of these new pieces of information are just as powerful as any of the indented rules given in the game's introduction.

How Matching Games Work

You know the drill by now. Let's take some of the rules above and form them into a mini-logic game:

> A rancher owns three animals—a dog, a cat, and a goat. The animals are named Bimpy, Hank, and Sujin, though not necessarily in that order. One of the animals is brown, one is black, and one is white. Two of the animals are large and one is small.
> The dog is brown.
> The black animal is small.
> Bimpy is not white.
> The goat is not large.
> If the cat is large, then Hank is brown.

A good way to approach this game would be to set up a grid or chart to keep track of all of the attributes to be matched up:

(animal)	Dog	Cat	Goat
(name) B H S			
(size) L L S			
(color) br bl wh			

Notice that Rules 1 and 4—the most concrete rules—can be built into the sketch immediately.

(animal)	Dog	Cat	Goat
(name) BHS	B		
(size) LLS			S
(color) br bl wh			

But remember, think about what Rule 4 means, not just what it says. There are only two sizes here—small and large. If the goat is not large, it must be small, and since there are two large and only one small animal, we can deduce the size of the other two as well:

(animal)	Dog	Cat	Goat
(name) BHS	B		
(size) LLS	L	L	S
(color) br bl wh			

Once we know that the cat is large, moreover, Rule 5 kicks in, telling us that Hank is brown. And since we've already deduced that the brown animal is the large dog, we know that Hank is the large brown dog.

And that's how a simple matching game works. The third game of the Logic Games section in each of the real LSATs in this book is a typical matching game for you to work on. Pay careful attention to the way in which it's set up, as outlined in the written explanations.

Now apply the Kaplan Five-Step Method to the following matching game.

Fawn, Ginger, Hamish, and Isaac are students at Eastern University. Each of them has one faculty adviser, either Professor Steele or Professor Tatum. One of the students lives in Keeble Hall, another lives in Ling Hall, and the other two live in Jasper Hall. The following restrictions must be observed:

Exactly three of the students have 4.0 averages.

Two of the students are English majors, two are math majors, and no one majors in both subjects.

Only the two students who live in Jasper Hall are advised by Professor Steele.

Both math majors, one of whom is Fawn, have 4.0 averages.

Hamish lives in Ling Hall.

1. The student who does not have a 4.0 average must be which one of the following?

(A) Ginger
(B) one of the students advised by Professor Tatum
(C) one of the English majors
(D) one of the students living in Jasper Hall
(E) the student living in Ling Hall

2. Hamish must be which one of the following?

(A) one of the math majors
(B) one of the English majors
(C) one of the students advised by Professor Steele
(D) one of the students advised by Professor Tatum
(E) one of the students with a 4.0 average

3. If Ginger lives in Keeble Hall, then which one of the following must be true?

(A) Isaac is advised by Professor Steele.
(B) Ginger is advised by Professor Steele.
(C) Both math majors live in Jasper Hall.
(D) Ginger has a 4.0 average.
(E) The student who does not have a 4.0 average lives in Jasper Hall.

Ⓐ Ⓑ Ⓒ Ⓓ Ⓔ

4. If the student who lives in Keeble Hall does not have a 4.0 average, all of the following must be true EXCEPT:

(A) Fawn lives in Jasper Hall.
(B) The student who does not have a 4.0 average is advised by Professor Tatum.
(C) Fawn is advised by Professor Steele.
(D) Hamish has a 4.0 average.
(E) Ginger is a math major.

5. If neither math major lives in Jasper Hall, then all of the following must be true EXCEPT:

   (A) Ginger lives in Jasper Hall.
   (B) Isaac has a 4.0 average.
   (C) Both English majors are advised by Professor Steele.
   (D) Two of the students who have 4.0 averages are advised by Professor Tatum.
   (E) The student who does not have a 4.0 average lives in Jasper Hall.

   Ⓐ Ⓑ Ⓒ Ⓓ Ⓔ

Step One: Get an Overview

There are five, count them five, attributes to link up in this matching game—students, advisers, residence halls, majors, and grade point averages. Yikes! Don't panic. You know an effective way to deal with matching games (discussed above). Use it. Continue your overview by reading each rule so that you get the big picture, then return to the introduction to visualize and map out the game.

Step Two: Visualize and Map Out the Game

Where to begin? Probably the attribute with the most concrete information connected to it is the students, so your sketch probably should be centered around them. Also, it makes sense that students would have majors, GPAs, and advisors, and live in residence halls. It seems silly to think of a hall having a major or a GPA or an advisor.

	Fawn	Ginger	Hamish	Isaac	
halls					K L J J
advisors					S or T
majors					math math eng. eng.
GPAs					4.0 4.0 4.0 ~~4.0~~

Step Three: Consider the Rules Individually

Here's a game in which seeking out concrete information and acting on it is much more effective than working doggedly through the rules in their given order. Drop in what you know for sure: the number of students per hall, and the one resident confirmed by a rule (Rule 5); also recognize that since only the Jasper Hall students get Steele as an adviser (Rule 3), the others must get Tatum. The story so far:

	Fawn	Ginger	Hamish	Isaac
halls			Ling	
advisors			Tatum	
majors				
GPAs				

K/T J/S J/S

math math eng. eng.

4.0 4.0 4.0 ~~4.0~~

The rest of the information, *once analyzed in detail*, can be jotted down off to the side for future use.

Step Four: Combine the Rules

If three students have 4.0s (Rule 1), then exactly one does *not*. And that one will be an English major—the "big deduction" in this mess. Both math majors, one of whom is Fawn, have 4.0s (Rule 4), which accounts for two of the three 4.0s in the game; it will have to be true that one English major has a 4.0 and the other doesn't. This means:

MATH	ENGLISH
F 4.0	_ 4.0
_ 4.0	_ NOT 4.0

If you organized your information by student, your sketch might look something like this:

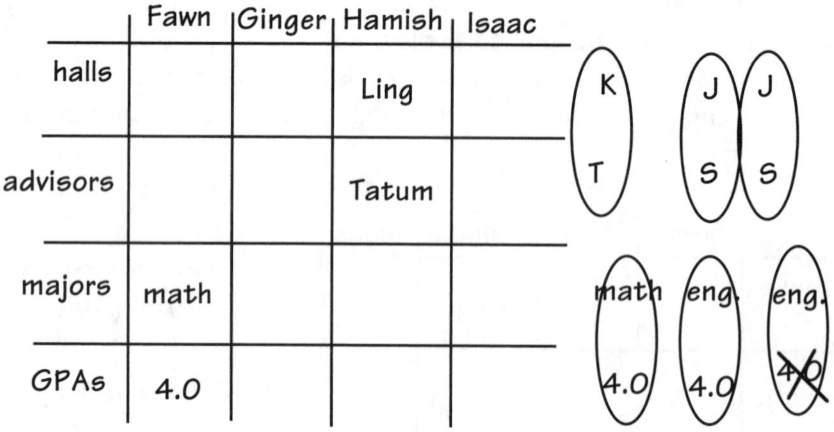

	Fawn	Ginger	Hamish	Isaac
halls			Ling	
advisors			Tatum	
majors	math			
GPAs	4.0			

Step Five: Work on the Questions Systematically

A Kaplan-trained student would, as was the case for the grouping game, answer these questions in the order in which they appear. Question 1, which tests for a big deduction, and Question 2, which can be answered solely from your work with the setup, are good candidates to be answered first. The remaining questions are all roughly equivalent hypothetical questions.

Question 1

Question 1 was answered above in the introductory analysis of the game. There are exactly two math majors, and both of them have 4.0 averages. But there are exactly three students with 4.0 averages, so the third must be one of the other students. Those "others" are two English majors, so one of them must have a 4.0, and the other must be the student who does not have a 4.0. Choice (C) has it right. The student without a 4.0 must be an English major.

Question 2

Hamish definitely lives in Ling Hall, according to Rule 5, and we deduced from Rule 3 that the students in Keeble Hall and Ling Hall must be advised by Professor Tatum, since Jasper is the only residence hall to get Professor Steele. The logical outgrowth of this is that Hamish, who lives in Ling, is advised by Tatum, choice (D). Hamish could be an English major or a math major, so (A) and (B) need not be true. Choice (C), as we've just seen, is patently false, and (E) is only possible—Hamish *could* be the English major who doesn't have the 4.0. But again, the best way to tackle this question was to actively pursue the answer found in choice (D).

Question 3

If Ginger lives in Keeble Hall, and Hamish as always lives in Ling, then the other two students, Fawn and Isaac, live in Jasper. (*Never forget the rules that are built into the opening paragraph:* we're told that Jasper Hall gets two students and the others get one each.) Since we know who advises the students in which halls, we know enough to confirm (A) as a true statement—not to mention (B) as a false one: Ginger, as a Keeble resident, gets Tatum, and Isaac gets Steele. *One* math major, Fawn, lives in Jasper, but contrary to (C), the other could be Ginger in Keeble, or Hamish in Ling. Choices (D) and (E) are likewise only possibly true. If, for instance, Ginger is the English major without a 4.0, then both (D) and (E) are false.

Question 4

If the student in Keeble is the single person without the 4.0, then that student must be an English major. This means that Fawn, whom we know to be a math major, must live in Jasper Hall. (Ling Hall is filled, as always, by Hamish.) Isaac and Ginger are left to occupy the slot in Keeble and the remaining slot in Jasper, but we don't know who is who. What we *do* know looks like this:

	Fawn	Ginger	Hamish	Isaac		
halls	J		Ling		K	J
advisors	S		Tatum		T	S
majors	math		eng. or math		eng.	eng. or math
GPAs	4.0		4.0		~~4.0~~	4.0

All of the choices are definitely true except for (E): Ginger *could* be a math major, but it's just as likely that she's the English major in Keeble Hall.

Question Five

Fawn, a math major, must live in Keeble Hall if, as we're told, neither math major lives in Jasper (Ling Hall is filled, as always, by Hamish.). The two students in Jasper Hall must be English majors. There are now two students left to place, and two spots in need of students in Jasper Hall, so Ginger and Isaac must take those spots and live in Jasper. Choice (A) is true, and we can cross it off because this is a "must be true EXCEPT" question. Ginger and Isaac are the English majors in this one, and living in Jasper Hall they do have Professor Steele as adviser, so (C) is true as well. Choice (D) must be true, as Fawn and Hamish, who are the 4.0 math majors this time, do have Professor Tatum as adviser. Ginger and Isaac, who are in Jasper, are the English majors, so one of them has a 4.0 and the other one doesn't. Either way, the student without the 4.0 lives in Jasper Hall, so (E) is true, which makes (B) the correct answer. Isaac could be the English major with the 4.0 average, but he could also be the English major without the 4.0 average, so (B) only could be true, and therefore is correct.

Hybrid Games

Many games are what you might call "hybrid games," requiring you to combine sequencing, grouping, and/or matching skills (we'll have a look at one later on when we talk about the five-step method). Keep in mind that while we try to recognize games as a particular type, it's not necessary to attach a strict name to every game you encounter. For example, it really doesn't matter if you categorize a game as a sequencing game with a grouping element or as a grouping game with a sequencing element, as long as you're comfortable with both sets of skills. The first of the following games is an example of a hybrid game.

Try Applying the Kaplan Five-Step Method to this hybrid game.

Five workers—Mona, Patrick, Renatta, Saffie, and Will—are scheduled to clean apartments on five days of a single week, Monday to Friday. There are three cleaning shifts available each day—a morning shift, an afternoon shift, and an evening shift. No more than one worker cleans in any given shift. Each worker cleans exactly two shifts during the week, but no one works more than one cleaning shift in a single day.

Exactly two workers clean on each day of the week.
Mona and Will clean on the same days of the week.
Patrick doesn't clean on any afternoon or evening shifts during the week.
Will doesn't clean on any morning or afternoon shifts during the week.
Mona cleans on two consecutive days of the week.
Saffie's second cleaning shift of the week occurs on an earlier day of the week than Mona's first cleaning shift.

1. Which one of the following must be true?

(A) Saffie cleans on Tuesday afternoon.
(B) Patrick cleans on Monday morning.
(C) Will cleans on Thursday evening.
(D) Renatta cleans on Friday afternoon.
(E) Mona cleans on Tuesday morning.

2. If Will does not clean on Friday, which one of the following could be false?

(A) Renatta cleans on Friday.
(B) Saffie cleans on Tuesday.
(C) Mona cleans on Wednesday.
(D) Saffie cleans on Monday.
(E) Patrick cleans on Tuesday.

(A) (B) (C) (D) (E)

(Note that there are only two questions accompanying this game; a typical logic game will, of course, have five to seven questions. As we have already discussed both sequencing and grouping, the two skills this game tests, we kept this game short.)

Step One: Get an Overview

We need to schedule five workers, abbreviated M, P, R, S, and W, in a particular order during a five-day calendar week, Monday to Friday. The ordering element tells us we're dealing with a sequencing task, though there is a slight grouping element involved in that a couple of the rules deal with grouping issues—namely, which people can or cannot clean on the same day of the week as each other. That makes this a "hybrid" game—but remember, it doesn't matter what you call it, as long as you can do it.

What's in a Name?

You don't get points for correctly categorizing a game. So, don't worry about what to call a game; simply decide which skills are required.

Be very careful about the numbers governing this game; they go a long way in defining how the game works. There are to be exactly two workers per day (never cleaning on the same shift). Each worker must clean exactly two shifts, and since workers are forbidden to take two shifts in the same day, this means that each worker will clean on exactly two days. So, in effect, ten out of the 15 available shifts will be taken, and five will be left untouched.

Step Two: Visualize and Map out the Game

Go with whatever you feel is the most efficient way to keep track of the situation. Most people would settle on a sketch of the five days, each broken up into three shifts, like so:

	M	Tu	W	Th	F
Morn.					
Aft.					
Eve.					

Into this sketch—one letter per box—each entity will have to go twice (each worker does two shifts, remember). So your pool of entities to place would be: MMPPRRSSWW. You might want to include five Xs (or Øs) for the five shifts that won't be taken by anyone.

Step Three: Consider the Rules Individually

We've already dealt with some of the number-related rules hidden in the game's introduction. Now let's consider this statement from the intro:

> No more than one worker cleans in any given shift.

Make sure you interpret rules like this correctly. You may have to paraphrase, in your own words, its exact meaning. In this case: two workers per shift is no good, three is out of the question, etcetera. But it doesn't mean that any given shift must have a worker. If the test makers meant to imply that, they would have written, "Exactly one worker cleans on every given shift." Notice the difference in wording. It's subtle, but it has a huge impact on the game.

Let's consider the other rules:

Rule 1: We've already handled Rule 1. You may wish to jot down "2 a day," or something like that, to remind you of this important information.

Rule 2: Mona and Will clean on the same days, and that holds for both of the days they clean. Note this any way that seems fitting (one suggestion is to draw MW with a circle around it on your page).

Rules 3 and 4: We can handle these two rules together because they're so similar. You can note these rules as they are, but you would be doing yourself a great disservice. Instead, first work out their implications, which is actually a pretty simple matter. If Patrick doesn't clean afternoons or evenings, he must clean mornings. If Will doesn't clean mornings or afternoons, he must clean evenings. Always take the rules as far as you can, and then jot down their implications on your page for reference.

Rule 5: This one is pretty self-explanatory; Mona's shifts must be on consecutive days, such as Thursday and Friday. MM might be a good way to note this.

Rule 6: Here's another sequencing rule; you must place both Ss for Saffie on earlier days of the week than the two Ms, for Mona. That means that Saffie and Mona can't clean on the same day (although we already knew that from Rule 2), and that Mona's shifts can't come before Saffie's. Try noting this as (S...S...MM).

Step Four: Combine the Rules

This is the crucial stage for most games. Here, notice that Mona appears in three of the six indented rules; that's a good indication that combining these rules should lead somewhere useful. Combining Rule 2 and Rule 5 gives us two Mona/Will days in a row. Will must be scheduled for evening shifts (remember, we turned Rule 4 into this positive statement). That means that Mona would take the morning or afternoon shift on these consecutive days.

Rule 6 concerns Mona as well: two Saffies before the two Monas. How is this possible? We need two Ss on different days to come before the two consecutive Ms. If Saffie's cleaning shifts are as early in the week as possible, she'll clean on Monday and Tuesday. That means that the earliest day that Mona can clean (and Will as well, thanks to Rule 2) is Wednesday. There's our first really key deduction: Mona and Will cannot clean on Monday and Tuesday; they must clean Wednesday, Thursday, or Friday.

Do we stop there? No, of course not. The difference between the Logic Games expert and the Logic Games novice is that the expert knows how to press on when further deductive possibilities exist. If you relate this deduction back to Rule 5, it becomes clear that Mona and Will must clean on Wednesday and Thursday, or on Thursday and Friday. This brings us to another big deduction: either way, Mona and Will must clean on Thursday. Thanks to Rule 4, we can slot Will in for Thursday evening. Mona will then take Thursday morning or afternoon. The other Mona/Will day must be either Wednesday or Friday, to remain consecutive.

The following sketch shows what your completed sketch may look like, with as many of the rules built into it as possible.

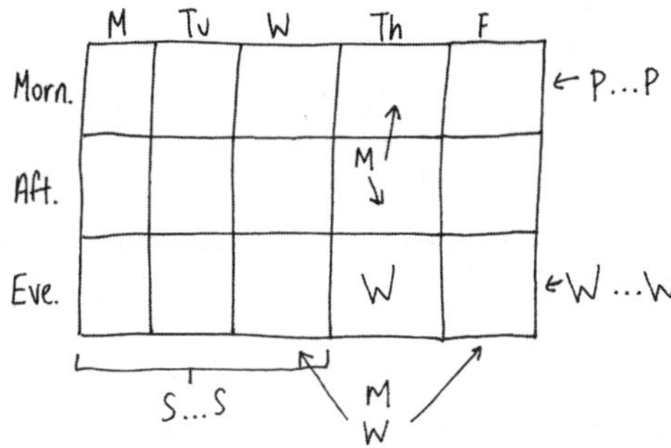

Now that we've combined the rules and have even uncovered a few big deductions, it's time to move on to the questions.

Step Five: Work on the Questions Systematically

Now you'll see how all the work we did up front pays off. Question 1 offers no hypothetical information; it simply asks what must be true. And since we've already deduced a few things that must be true, we can scan the choices for one that matches any one of our newly discovered pieces of information. It doesn't take long to spot choice (C)—it's our big deduction staring us right in the face. You shouldn't even waste time checking the other choices. Instead, have the confidence that you've done the right work the right way, and circle (C) and move on. [Just for the record, for those of you who are curious, (A), (B), and (D) could be true, but need not be, while (E), as we discovered earlier, is an impossibility.]

Question 2 contains a hypothetical: no Will on Friday. One glance at our sketch tells us that the second Mona/Will cluster must therefore be placed on Wednesday, next to the Thursday Mona/Will group. Saffie must then clean on Monday and Tuesday, in order to satisfy Rule 6 (although we don't yet know the exact shifts she takes during those days).

That brings us to the two questions that test takers ask all too infrequently: "Who's left?" and more importantly, "Where can they go?" Two Ps and two Rs are left to place, with one spot on Monday, one spot on Tuesday, and two spots on Friday open to place them. How can this be done? Friday can't get both Ps or both Rs (from the last sentence in the introduction), so it will have to get one of each, with P in the morning and R in either the afternoon or evening. The other P and the other R will join S on Monday or Tuesday, in either order. Of course, whichever day P is on, he must be in the morning, whereas the exact shifts for R and S are ambiguous.

Look at how far the chain of deductions takes us, beginning with the simple statement in the question stem:

If Will doesn't clean on Friday, then . . .

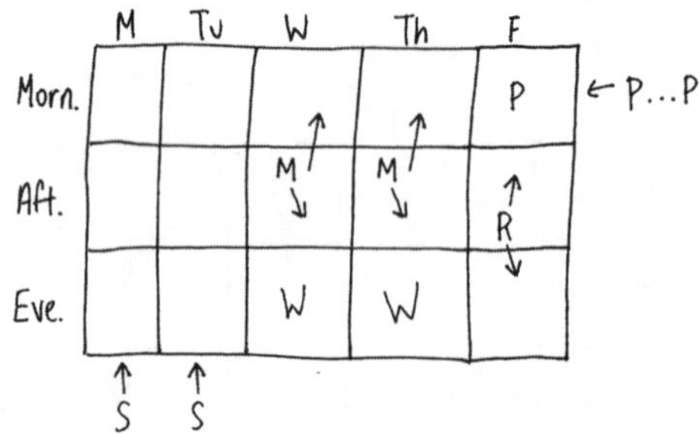

With all of this information at our disposal, there's not a question in the world we can't answer correctly. This one asks for a statement that could be false—which means that the four wrong choices will all be things that must be true. And in fact, choices (A) through (D) match the situation in this question perfectly, while (E) merely could be true: Patrick's first cleaning shift of the week could be on Tuesday, but it just as easily could be on Monday as well. (His second shift must be on Friday, of course.) Choice (E) is therefore the only choice that could be false.

Other Game Types

Occasionally, you will run across a game that doesn't seem to fit into one of the categories above. For instance, occasionally you'll see a game that asks you to place people around a circular table, a game with a diagram (a spatial arrangement), or a game that doesn't seem to require any type of diagram at all because it describes a process. Don't panic. The powerful thing about Kaplan's Five-Step Method is that it can get you through any game, no matter what the type.

Try Applying the Kaplan Five-Step Method to the following game.

> A botanist is testing the effects of sunlight on four plants. At the beginning of the first month of the experiment, the plants—F, G, H, and I—are in front of the north window, the east window, the south window, and the west window, respectively. The botanist will rotate the plants exactly once a month, at the end of each month, in one of the following two ways:
>
> Rotation 1: The plant in front of the north window will be moved to the east window. The plant in front of the east window will be moved to the south window. The plant in front of the south window will be moved to the west window. The plant in front of the west window will be moved to the north window.
>
> Rotation 2: Plant F will be moved to the window that H was in front of during the previous month. Plant H will be moved to the window that Plant I was in front of during the previous month. Plant I will be moved to the window that G was in front of during the previous month. Plant G will be moved to the window that F was in front of during the previous month.

1. Which one of the following could be the window locations for the four plants at the beginning of the second month?

	north	east	south	west
(A)	F	G	H	I
(B)	F	I	H	G
(C)	G	F	I	H
(D)	I	F	G	H
(E)	I	G	F	H

2. If G is in front of the north window at the beginning of the second month, which one of the following must be true?

   (A) F is in front of the east window.
   (B) F is in front of the west window.
   (C) H is in front of the east window.
   (D) I is in front of the east window.
   (E) I is in front of the west window.

(Note that there are only two questions accompanying this game; a typical logic game will, of course, have five to seven questions. Since games other than sequencing, grouping, and matching games are much less common, we kept this game short.)

Step One: Get an Overview

This is a process game, a type of game that first appeared in 1994. You are given an initial placement of the plants, and you're told that the plants will move from window to window over the months of the experiment. The plants will be rotated exactly once per month, at the end of the month. This change over time is one of the big clues that you have a process game on your hands. Some questions are asking you to look forward in the process and follow the steps through to a result, while others—generally the tougher ones—tell you what the result of the process was, and ask you to work backwards to reconstruct the situation that made this result possible. Since only two questions are included with this game, you will be asked only to look forward in the process.

Step Two: Visualize and Map out the Game

As with most process games, you can't rely solely on sketching. Get down the initial placement of plants, and keep your thinking sharp:

N
F

W I G E

H
S

Step Three: Consider the Rules Individually

Rule 1: Here you're given the first rotation method. Take your time when you sort out the information. In essence, each plant will simply move one space clockwise along the compass. The north plant will go to the east. The east plant will go to the south. The south plant will go to the west. The west plant will go to the north.

Rule 2: And here's the second rotation: Plant F will move to plant H's previous location. Plant H will move to plant I's previous location. Plant I will move to plant G's previous location, and plant G will move to plant F's previous location.

Step Four: Combine the Rules

There're usually not many deductions in process games, and that's the case here. If you find the game's workings confusing, you can go through what would happen based on the two rotation methods. For instance, here's what would happen if Rotation 2 was used after the first month:

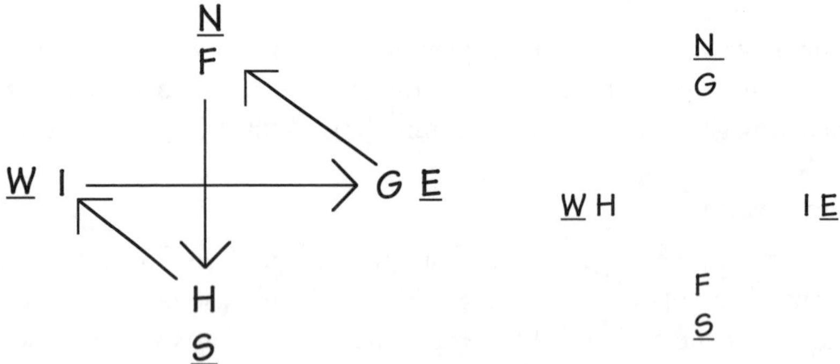

Finally, don't assume anything that you're not explicitly told. There's no rule saying that the botanist can't use the same rotation for consecutive months. In fact, since there's not a rule forbidding it, the same rotation could be used throughout the entire experiment.

Step Five: Work on the Questions Systematically

What does "at the beginning of the second month" in Question 1 mean? If the plants are rotated exactly once a month, at the end of each month, this means that at the beginning of the second month the plants have gone through one rotation from their initial placements. So grab an entity and see where it could have gone under each rotation. F starts at the north window, so under Rotation 1 it would go to the east, and under Rotation 2 it would go to the south. Cross off any choice that has F someplace other than east or south. Good-bye (A) and (B). G starts at the east window, so under Rotation 1 it would go to the south, and under Rotation 2 it would go to the north. Cross off (E), which tries to put G at the east window. Plant I starts off at the west window, so under Rotation 1 it would go to the north, and under Rotation 2 it would go to the east. Eliminate (C) which tries to put I at the south window. Choice (D) remains and is the answer.

In Question 1, the plants have undergone one rotation, and G is at the north window. G starts at the east. If Rotation 1 was used, G would go south, so Rotation 2 must have been used. Under Rotation 2, G goes to the north (F's previous location), F goes to the south (H's old home), H goes to the west (I's last spot), and I goes to the east (G's old location). I at the east window is choice (D), the answer.

What's Next

This concludes our general discussion of the Logic Games section. Apply the Five-Step Method, and all of the techniques mentioned in this chapter, when you work through the following practice set. Pay careful attention to all of the written explanations, even those for the ones you got right.

After the practice set, we'll move on to the final major section of the test, Reading Comprehension.

Logic Games Practice Set

Directions: Each group of questions in this section is based on a set of conditions. In answering some of the questions, it may be useful to draw a rough diagram. Choose the response that most accurately and completely answers each question.

Questions 1–7

A class of eight students—girls Q, R, S, and T, and boys U, V, W, and X—is divided into two teams, Team Blue and Team Gold.

Each team consists of exactly four students.
T and X are on different teams.
V and W are on the same team.
R is on Team Gold.
Each team consists of at least one boy and at least one girl, and consists of an unequal number of boys and girls.

1. Which one of the following represents the possible membership of Team Gold?

(A) Q, R, T, and X
(B) Q, R, T, and U
(C) R, T, V, and W
(D) R, S, T, and V
(E) Q, V, W, and X

Ⓐ Ⓑ Ⓒ Ⓓ Ⓔ

2. If Q, T, and U are on Team Blue, which one of the following is the fourth member of Team Blue?

(A) R
(B) S
(C) V
(D) W
(E) X

Ⓐ Ⓑ Ⓒ Ⓓ Ⓔ

3. If T and V are on Team Blue, which one of the following is the membership of Team Gold?

(A) Q, R, S, and X
(B) Q, R, S, and U
(C) R, S, U, and W
(D) R, S, U, and X
(E) R, U, W, and X

Ⓐ Ⓑ Ⓒ Ⓓ Ⓔ

4. If R and W are on the same team, all of the following must be true EXCEPT:

(A) T is on Team Blue.
(B) Q and U are on the same team.
(C) W is on Team Gold.
(D) R and V are on the same team.
(E) S is on Team Gold.

Ⓐ Ⓑ Ⓒ Ⓓ Ⓔ

5. If X is on Team Blue, which one of the following pairs of students CANNOT be together on a team?

(A) X and V
(B) X and Q
(C) S and V
(D) Q and S
(E) U and T

Ⓐ Ⓑ Ⓒ Ⓓ Ⓔ

6. Assume that Team Blue consists of Q, V, W, and X and that Team Gold consists of R, S, T, and U. Which one of the following pairs of students may switch teams without violating any conditions?

(A) Q and T
(B) S and Q
(C) U and W
(D) T and X
(E) R and Q

Ⓐ Ⓑ Ⓒ Ⓓ Ⓔ

7. Which one of the following must be true?
   (A) If Q is on Team Gold, then S is on Team Gold.
   (B) If T is on Team Blue, then X is on Team Blue.
   (C) If U is on Team Blue, then V is on Team Blue.
   (D) If V is on Team Gold, then X is on Team Gold.
   (E) If W is on Team Blue, then X is on Team Blue.

Ⓐ Ⓑ Ⓒ Ⓓ Ⓔ

Questions 8–13

A travel agency has put together travel packages for four customers—Mr. Abbott, Ms. Bellow, Mr. Chandra, and Ms. Dean. Each package includes at least one of the following: airfare, hotel, rental car, and shopping discount coupons. The following facts are known about the four packages:

Exactly three of the packages include a hotel.
Exactly two of the packages include a rental car.
Bellow's and Dean's packages include airfare.
Chandra's package includes a hotel, a rental car, and shopping discount coupons.
The package that does not include a hotel does include shopping discount coupons.

8. Which one of the following could possibly be the complete package made up for Bellow?
   (A) hotel only
   (B) airfare only
   (C) airfare and rental car only
   (D) airfare and hotel only
   (E) rental car, hotel, and shopping discount coupons only

Ⓐ Ⓑ Ⓒ Ⓓ Ⓔ

9. If Dean's package does not include hotel, which one of the following must be true?
   (A) Abbott's package includes a rental car.
   (B) Abbott's package includes a hotel.
   (C) Bellow's package does not include a rental car.
   (D) Bellow's package includes shopping discount coupons.
   (E) Chandra's package does not include a hotel.

Ⓐ Ⓑ Ⓒ Ⓓ Ⓔ

10. If none of the packages includes both airfare and a rental car, all of the following must be true EXCEPT:
   (A) Abbott's package includes a rental car.
   (B) Dean's package does not include a rental car.
   (C) Abbott's package does not include airfare.
   (D) Exactly three of the packages include airfare.
   (E) Bellow's package does not include a rental car.

Ⓐ Ⓑ Ⓒ Ⓓ Ⓔ

11. If every package that includes airfare also includes a hotel, which one of the following must be true?
   (A) Abbott's package includes shopping discount coupons.
   (B) Abbott's package includes airfare.
   (C) Bellow's package includes shopping discount coupons.
   (D) Bellow's package includes a rental car.
   (E) Chandra's package includes airfare.

Ⓐ Ⓑ Ⓒ Ⓓ Ⓔ

12. If Bellow's and Chandra's packages are the only two that include shopping discount coupons, and if no package includes both airfare and a rental car, all of the following must be true EXCEPT:

    (A) Abbott's package includes hotel.
    (B) Abbott's package includes a rental car.
    (C) Chandra's package does not include airfare.
    (D) Dean's package does not include a rental car.
    (E) Dean's package does not include a hotel.

13. If Dean's is the only package that does not include shopping discount coupons, which one of the following must be false?

    (A) Abbott's and Chandra's packages are identical.
    (B) Dean's package includes a hotel.
    (C) Bellow's and Chandra's packages are identical.
    (D) Bellow's package includes a rental car.
    (E) Abbott's and Bellow's packages are identical.

Answers

1. B	6. B	11. A
2. B	7. D	12. E
3. A	8. D	13. E
4. E	9. B	
5. D	10. D	

Explanations

Student Teams (Questions 1–7)

This game begins straightforwardly enough: you've got eight kids who are to be distributed into two groups of four. The most significant rule—the one that has the most impact on the course of the game—is the last one, and there's an important deduction to be derived from it. Did you see it?

If you must have four people on a team, and can't have equal numbers of boys and girls on any one team, then the teams must be divided in a 3:1 ratio like so:

One Team: three boys, one girl
Other Team: three girls, one boy

(Notice that one other possibility—that of a team of four boys and a team of four girls—is excluded by the final rule.) From here, it's just a matter of thinking through the other, more detail-oriented rules, perhaps using capital letters for one gender and lowercase letters for the other.

About those detail-oriented rules: it's critical that, every step of the way, you remember that T and x join different teams; that v and w will join the same team; and that R is always on Team Gold.

1 (B) is correct. The possible membership of Team Gold depends on its roster not violating any rules, so the most efficient approach is to take each rule and throw out the choices that violate it. Since T and x must be on different teams (Rule 2), and choice (A) puts them together, (A) is incorrect. And v and w are supposed to be on the same team (Rule 3), but choice (D) violates that. Since R must be on Team Gold (Rule 4), and choice (E) omits R, choice (E) can be rejected. We need unequal numbers of boys and girls (Rule 5), but choice (C)'s ratio is 2:2, so (C) is out. So choice (B), the only one remaining, must be acceptable. And it is.

2 (B) is correct. Assuming that Q, T, and u are on Team Blue, the fourth and final person has to be a girl (because another boy would give us the forbidden 2:2 ratio), and since R is already on Team Gold, the only girl left is S, choice (B).

3 (A) is correct. If T is on Team Blue, then R will have to be joined on Team Gold by X (Rule 2). And putting v on Team Blue, which the question stem also does, means that w will be on Team Blue as well (Rule 3). So far Team Blue consists of two boys (v and w) and a girl (T); it will need a third boy, and the only one available is u. So Team Blue consists of T, u, v, and w, and Team Gold gets everyone else—Q, R, S, x, which is choice (A).

4 (E) is correct. The team that R and w are both on will be Team Gold because of Rule 4. Wherever we find w we find v (Rule 3), so Team Gold so far has two boys and a girl. Another boy will be needed to avoid a 2:2 ratio; and since we need to separate T and x, Team Gold will have to consist of R, v, w, and x, leaving Q, S, T, and u on Team Blue. Of the five choices, (E) is the only one that contradicts what we've deduced, so it's what we want as our answer.

5 (D) is correct. Putting X on Team Blue means that T goes onto Team Gold (Rule 2) along with R (Rule 4). Team Gold will have to be rounded out by one boy and one girl to preserve the 3:1 ratio; that boy will be u (since v and w will be together, on Team Blue), while the girl can be either S or Q. Hence, choices (A) and (E) must be true, choices (B) and (C) could be true, but choice (D) is impossible. The S-Q pair will be on different teams, so (D) is correct.

6 (B) is correct. The challenge is to see which "switch"—which pair of people exchanging teams—would not violate any rules. Using the process of elimination, we find that executing choice (A) would put T and x together on a team, violating Rule 2; choice (C) would put v and w on different teams, violating Rule 3; choice (D) would give each team two boys and two girls, a violation of Rule 5; and choice (E) would put R onto Team Blue, a violation of Rule 4. Only choice (B)'s exchange would cause no damage—and it's no accident that neither S nor Q is mentioned in the rules. That's mainly what makes it possible for them to switch without a problem.

7 (D) is correct. Questions like this need to be evaluated choice by choice. In choice (A), we need to know if placing Q on Team Gold requires us to place S on Team Gold. Back in Question 1, we had the following acceptable arrangement: Blue: Svwx; Gold: QRTu. If it could be true then, it could be true now, so we know that we can have Q on Team Gold without having S on Team Gold. Choice (B) cannot be true, since T and x cannot be on the same team, according to Rule 2. Choice (C) asks whether placing u on Team Blue forces us to place v on Team Blue. The grouping in Question 2 had u on Team Blue and v on Team Gold, so we know that choice (C) need not be true. Choice (D) asks us if placing v on Team Gold forces us to place x on Team Gold. If v is on the Team Gold, then w is on Gold as well (Rule 3). With two males on Gold, we need a third, and the two remaining candidates are u and x. If we picked u, then the Gold Team would be v, w, u, and R (R is always on Gold). That would force both T and x onto the Blue Team, which is not allowed according to Rule 2. Therefore, the third male on Gold cannot be u; it must be x and choice (D) must be true.

On the day of the test, you wouldn't even check choice (E). In case you're wondering why placing w on Team Blue doesn't force us to place x on Team Blue, go back to your work for Question 3, where our possible arrangement had w on Team Blue and x on Team Gold.

Travel Packages (Questions 8–13)

You begin this game by learning that four travelers (A, B, C, and D) have individual travel packages, each composed of a maximum of four features (a, h, r, and c); your job is to figure out the contents of each person's package. The difficulty, of course, is that you're not told everything you'd like to know. How many features does Dean's package contain, for instance? How many sets of coupons are available? And so on. To overcome this ambiguity, you should always take refuge in what you know for sure. In other words, instead of dwelling on what you're not told, you should always try to determine as much definite information as you can, before going on to the questions.

When we mine Rules 3 and 4 for concrete information, we learn that Bellow's and Dean's lists must each contain airfare (or a), and we learn that Chandra's list contains the symbols h, r, and c (for "coupons"). (Incidentally, when reading Rule 4, did you assume that it means that Chandra's package cannot include airfare? Rule 4 doesn't say it necessarily presents a complete picture of Chandra's package, so we can't use Rule 4 to rule out airfare there.)

Meanwhile, Rules 1 and 2 tell us that a hotel is part of three people's packages and a rental car is part of two packages. Well, Chandra's package already contains both features, so Rule 1 really means "Chandra and two others are given a hotel," and Rule 2 means "Chandra and one other will rent a car."

Finally, take note of Rule 5: whichever one of the packages doesn't include a hotel—Abbott's, Bellow's, or Dean's—will get coupons. If you sketch it all out, maybe it looks something like this (note, on the right, the roster of symbols to be inserted and the reminder of Rule 5):

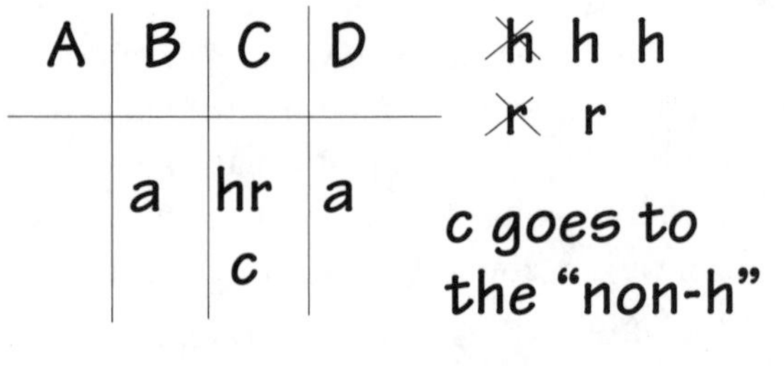

A	B	C	D
	a	hr c	a

~~h~~ h h
~~r~~ r

c goes to the "non-h"

8 (D) is correct. About Bellow's package, we know for certain only that it contains airfare (so choices (A) and (E) can be discarded as the possible complete contents—each fails to mention airfare). Could it contain airfare only, choice (B)? Certainly not: three of the packages contain a hotel (Rule 1), and the package that doesn't contain a hotel contains coupons (Rule 5). Thus choice (B) is unacceptable. For that matter, equally unacceptable is airfare and rental car only, choice (C); that combination would force a violation of one rule or another. We're left with choice (D), and if Bellow has a and h (as one possibility), Abbott has c only, Dean has a, h, and r, and Chandra has only what Rule 4 gives him, then no rules are violated. Choice (D) is therefore correct.

9 (B) is correct. The news that Dean's package doesn't include a hotel has dual impact: it means that the other three people's packages contain a hotel, and that Dean is the one mentioned in Rule 5, the one with coupons. Having done that much deduction, you should stop and see if the correct answer has yet emerged; in this case it has. Choice (B) must be true.

Choices (A) and (C) are possibly true, but we have no way of knowing which of the three people besides Chandra is renting a car. Choice (D) is also possible, but Bellow need not get coupons. Choice (E), of course, is downright wrong, an explicit violation of Rule 4.

10 (D) is correct. The premise that no one gets both airfare and rental car links up with Rule 2 and Rule 3. Rule 2 tells us we need one more rental car besides Chandra's, but that car cannot go to Bellow or Dean, each of whom is given airfare by Rule 3. Choices (B) and (E) must be true, therefore, and can be crossed out. Abbott, the only one remaining, must therefore receive a rental car in his package in order to ensure two rental cars, so choice (A) must also be true. Abbott, now the proud renter of a car, is therefore prohibited by the question stem to receive airfare, so choice (C) is true and choice (D) must be false, as this leaves only two of the customers, Bellow and Dean,

eligible to receive airfare. Since we're looking for the choice that need not be true, (D) gets the nod.

11 (A) is correct. Airfare and hotel are to go hand in hand. That means that Bellow and Dean, granted airfare by Rule 3, will receive a hotel as well. Meanwhile, Chandra was given a hotel by Rule 4, so in this question it is Abbott who is the traveler without a hotel, the traveler who will therefore receive coupons (Rule 5). That's precisely what choice (A) states, so (A) is correct. Of the other choices, (B) is false—giving Abbott airfare would require four hotels, not three—while the remaining statements could be true, but need not be.

12 (E) is correct. This question's very length guarantees you a lot of useful information. If (as the stem says) only Bellow and Chandra receive coupons, then Bellow is the person Rule 5 is talking about—the one with coupons but without a hotel. This leaves Abbott and Dean to receive hotels in their packages (Rule 1). Next, the question tells us that no one receives both airfare and a rental car. This, too, is helpful, because we know Bellow and Dean each have the former, while Chandra has the latter. Therefore it must be Abbott who receives the second and final rental car (Rule 2). We have now confirmed all the choices except for (E). Choice (E) is false—Dean's package does in fact include a hotel—so that's the credited answer.

13 (E) is correct. If only Dean doesn't receive coupons, then we know that the other three people do. But more importantly, we can be sure that Dean's is one of those packages with a hotel. [Remember Rule 5: packages without hotels get coupons, so getting no coupons means that one must get a hotel (that's the contrapositive).] Choice (B), therefore, cannot be false. Yet to be determined are:

- Who gets the second and last rental car?
- Which package, Abbott's or Bellow's, does not include hotel?
- Does anyone other than Bellow and Dean get airfare?

Scanning the choices, we see that Abbott and Bellow, choice (E), cannot be given identical packages, since only one of them can include a hotel. This is therefore the statement that must be false, and the correct answer.

As for the others: if Abbott gets a hotel and the rental car, then he and Chandra—choice (A)—would have identical packages. On the other hand, if it's Bellow who gets both a car and a hotel, not only is choice (D) possible, but then her package and Chandra's—choice (C)—could match (as long as Chandra gets airfare in addition to the hotel, car, and discount coupons already assigned to him in the rules).

CHAPTER 5

Reading Comprehension

Every Reading Comprehension (RC) section consists of four passages; each approximately 450 to 500 words in length. You'll be asked five to eight questions about each passage; a total of 26 to 28 questions for the section. Remember, the format and directions for RC never change, so make sure you are familiar with both. You'll save time and be more confident when you open your test booklet on the day of the LSAT and see *exactly* what you expect. We discussed both format and directions in the section on LSAT Basics; if you need to review them quickly, do so before you continue.

Don't Read the Directions

The directions for the Reading Comprehension section were discussed in the LSAT Basics chapter. If you need to review them quickly, do so before you continue.

Reading Comprehension requires you to make sense of dense, unfamiliar prose. These passages tend to be long, wordy, and difficult—not unlike at least some of the material you'll face in law school. The topics for RC passages are taken from four areas:

- social sciences
- natural sciences
- humanities
- law

While it might be possible to break down the Reading Comprehension section into the types of passages that appear, this isn't the best way to master the section. Don't try to learn a different approach for each passage type; you'll be wasting your time (and worse, hurting your score). In Logic Games, categorizing the games is helpful because each of the game types has a distinct logical pattern. Therefore, we teach you distinct strategies for handling each game type. Such differences don't exist in Reading Comprehension. The structure of a humanities passage is the same as that for a natural science passage, and the same as that for a social science or law passage. The topics may be different, but the critical reading techniques needed for success are the same for each. Therefore, we'll teach you one powerful method for handling any passage. We'll then teach you effective strategies for handling every type of question that appears.

Improvement in Reading Comprehension requires practice and patience. You might not see dramatic improvement after only one practice section. Don't get discouraged. With ongoing practice, the principles we show you will help you increase your skill, confidence, and score. Many people simply give up on Reading Comprehension by adopting a defeatist attitude: "*I can't change the way I read.*" This may protect their egos; by setting low expectations, they aren't as disappointed with poor results. But it doesn't improve their score.

Have an Attitude

If you believe you can improve, you will. Reading Comprehension is a great opportunity to improve your score.

The Reading Comp section is a great opportunity for you to differentiate yourself from (read "score higher than") other test takers. Since many people don't prepare for Reading Comprehension, or assume they can't prepare, it's easy for you to improve your overall LSAT score (compared to those people) by preparing for Reading Comp.

Before we teach you the Kaplan Three -Step Method though, let's talk first about the type of reading that you will be required to do on the LSAT. It is probably very different from the type of reading you currently do.

What Type of Reading Does the LSAT Reward?

"Reading Comprehension" is actually a little misleading because you aren't being asked to read and understand every word in every passage. Instead, the test makers are really testing your ability to read critically. In fact, the single most important skill needed to master RC is critical reading. But what is critical reading?

Ask different people what "reading critically" means, and you're likely to get a wide variety of responses. So, let's sum it up in a way that will be the most useful for you on the LSAT.

Read Critically

The LSAT is a timed test. You don't have the luxury of being able to read and digest the passages leisurely. In fact, the test makers design the exam so that you can't possibly finish the section if you read as you normally would. Therefore, you need to develop the ability to read critically in the way that the test makers reward.

Critical Reading = Perspective

At Kaplan, we use the word "perspective" to sum up the concept of critical reading. Gaining perspective means stepping back from the text, carefully evaluating why the author wrote the piece and how she put it together, instead of concentrating on the content. "Perspective" is a useful word because it conjures up a variety of LSAT-relevant tasks:

- Reading for structure: How is the prose put together?
- Reading for purpose and idea: Why is the author writing? What is his or her main point?
- Reading for detail only when questions demand it (since details are present only to support broader points).
- Reading between the lines: What's implied by the text?

Why is all of this such a big deal and why is it such a major part of the LSAT? First, if the test makers simply wanted to test whether you could repeat what's on the page, the exam would be very simple. All but the most careless readers would get every question right.

The LSAT is designed to test something much subtler, however. Law schools need to know whether applicants can think about what they read, as opposed to simply reading, absorbing, and memorizing. Law students are asked to interpret facts, not just to regurgitate them. So when you think about prose—when you paraphrase it, analyze it, evaluate it, and compare it to what you already know about the world—you're reading critically, and reading in a way that law school will require. It's as simple (and complex) as that.

The other reason that reading critically is fundamental to LSAT success is almost as simple: most of us don't do it very often. Think about it—when was the last time you read an article and asked yourself such questions as:

- What's the main idea?
- What's the purpose of the third paragraph?
- How does the subsection on pages 40–41 relate to the author's primary purpose?
- Why does the author quote Antoine de Saint-Exupéry in paragraph two?

If you ask yourself these kinds of questions all the time, then congratulations. You are already a full-time critical reader. But you're surely in a minority! What goes through most people's minds during their everyday reading is very different—not nearly as disciplined and not nearly as stressful. Put simply, most everyday reading is done for one of two purposes:

- to learn something
- for entertainment

Neither of those purposes has anything to do with the LSAT. So when you turn your attention from everyday prose to LSAT prose, you have to change the reason you read. And don't get us wrong: you are, or have been, a critical reader, or you never would have made it through high school and college. You do know how to take apart difficult prose, look at it with a sense of perspective, and evaluate it. The point, once again, is just that you need to read critically throughout the LSAT—under timed conditions and without losing focus—in order to rack up points on the test.

Reading Critically

Use What You Already Know

You don't need to know anything about the topics covered in the passages; everything you'll need to answer every question is included in the passages themselves. However, the passages are always logical, and always reflect ideas that you have heard about and can understand. Don't read in a vacuum; relate what you read to the world, and recognize the common sense of the text. One warning, though: the questions test your understanding of the author's points, not your previous understanding or personal point of view on the topic. Answer choices never conflict with what is true in the real world, but realize that various opinions do exist for most issues.

So use your own knowledge and experience to help you to comprehend the passages, but be careful not to let it interfere with answering questions correctly.

Critical Reading = Perspective

Critical reading involves perspective—the ability to step back from a piece of prose and carefully evaluate it. On the RC section, critical reading includes:

- **Reading for purpose and idea:** Why is the author writing? What's his or her point of view or main idea?
- **Reading for structure:** How is the passage put together?
- **Reading between the lines:** What is implied by the text?

The following are ways in which you can improve the specific critical reading skills necessary for success on Reading Comprehension:

- **Get a handle on the "spirit" of the passage.** Is it passionate? Neutral? Is it academic, conversational, or poetic in tone? What does the author favor? Disapprove of?
- **Keep paraphrasing key ideas.** Make sure you can put the author's most important concepts into your own words.
- **Keep anticipating where the author is going.** Each step of the way, ask yourself, "What could or must follow?"
- **Don't let complex-sounding words and sentences scare you.** Most passages consist of pretty simple ideas, written to sound impressive.
- **Read carefully for the gist or main point.** Read loosely for everything else—details, etcetera.
- **Remember that authors are repetitious.** Not every sentence they write adds a new idea.
- **Use keywords.** Like LR arguments, RC passages are full of structural signals—words or phrases whose main function is to help the author string ideas together logically. They allow you to infer a great deal about con-

tent, even if that content is obscure or difficult. Conclusion signals ("therefore," "consequently," "thus") and evidence signals ("because," "since") are extremely helpful, as are contrast signals ("but," "however," "although," "by contrast"), which indicate an opposition or shift in ideas.

Attack—Don't Just Read—the Passages

Always remember that you get no points for just "getting through" the passage. Don't be the kind of test taker who views reaching the end of a passage as a moral victory—this type of victory is short-lived when you find you can't answer any questions.

Attack the Passage
The test makers design the passages to reward people who read actively—who attack the passage.

No, you must attack—not simply read—the passages. The former embodies the winning mindset: you're entering the passage for the sole purpose of picking up the author's key ideas that will enable you to rack up points. By thinking in terms of attack, you're less likely to be diverted from this mission or to let the densely worded prose distract you.

Attacking a passage involves the application of all of the strategies mentioned in the previously stated principles. It also means reading actively. Active readers keep their minds working at all times, while trying to anticipate where the author's points are leading. Typically when we read—say, a newspaper—we start with the first sentence and read the article straight through. The words wash over us and are the only things we hear in our minds. This is typical of the passive approach to reading.

Active reading, on the other hand, involves doing more than just reading the words on the page—it means thinking about what you're reading as you read it. It means paraphrasing the complicated-sounding ideas and jargon. It means asking yourself questions as you read:

- What's the author's main point here?
- What's the purpose of this paragraph? Of this sentence?

When you read actively, there's a running commentary going on in your mind as you read. You may want to jot down notes or underline. When you read actively, you don't absorb the passage, you attack it!

Improving Critical Reading Skills

In addition to the practice you do to prepare for the test, you can, and should, work on your critical reading skills whenever you read. No matter what you are reading, or for what purpose, apply the skills discussed above.

At least three times a week, read critically for one hour. A good test of your critical reading skills is often the editorial page of your local newspaper. Or, if the writing isn't very vigorous, study editorials from the *New York Times*, the *Washington Post*, the *Chicago Tribune*, or the *Los Angeles Times*; these papers are usually available nationally at bookstores, newspaper stands, and local libraries). Ignore the headline, which often gives away the reason the author is writing, and attack the editorial or opinion essay by asking yourself the questions we discussed above. If you get in the habit of reading opinionated prose with these things in mind, you'll be doing the type of reading that the LSAT requires and rewards.

Read Critically

Get in the habit of reading editorials and opinion essays, asking as you go along, "What's the author's main point here? What is the purpose of this paragraph?"

At least once a week, read *way* over your head. You can do so by locating one of the many sources that the test makers use for actual reading passages. They're usually legal or technical journals, such as the following:

University of Kansas Law Review
University of Pennsylvania Law Review
California Law Review
The Journal of the AMA
Tulane Law Review
The Georgetown Law Review
UCLA Journal of Environmental Law and Policy
The Economist

Sit down with an article from one of these publications, or with a policy journal such as *Foreign Affairs*, for an hour or so. As you read, try to get through it quickly, answering the critical reasoning questions above.

Of course LSAT passages, which are about 450 words in length, are simply excerpted from these sources, so don't fret; you won't have to tackle an entire 25-page article. But spending time looking over highly specialized, technical prose, and thinking critically about it will make your adjustment to the demands of LSAT reading that much more painless.

You could also watch a debate on television once or twice per week. Excellent for that purpose is CNN's *Crossfire* or PBS's *Firing Line*, but it can be any show in which clear antagonists engage in the art of putting over their point of view while rebutting that of their opponents. Avoid empathizing with whichever side reflects your own views, and try to analyze the rhetoric critically. What is each side's main thesis? What evidence is used? What assumptions are being made by each side? The more practice you get in exercising these skills, the easier and more effective your LSAT prep will be.

The Kaplan Three-Step Method for Reading Comprehension

Now that you know the type of reading that the LSAT requires, we'll teach you a step-by-step method for attacking every passage and every question: Kaplan's Three-Step Method for Reading Comprehension.

1. **Attack the first third of the passage.**
2. **Read the rest of the passage.**
3. **Answer the questions efficiently.**

It's that simple and easy to remember. Yet, it is very powerful. Let's go through each step in detail. We'll then have you apply Kaplan's Three-Step Method to an actual Reading Comprehension passage. Finally, we'll give you a few practice passages so that you can refine the technique before you tackle the two real LSATs in this book.

Step One: Attack the First Third of the Passage

Read the first part of the passage with care, in order to determine the main idea and purpose. The first third of any passage usually introduces the topic and scope, the author's main idea/primary purpose, the author's tone, and almost always hints at the structure that the passage will follow. Let's take a closer look at these crucial elements of a Reading Comprehension passage.

Zooming In

Reading the first third of the passage is a zooming-in process. First, you get a sense of the general topic. Then you pin down the more specific scope of the passage. Finally, you glean the author's purpose in writing the passage—and the main idea that he or she is trying to get across about that particular subject.

Topic, Scope, and Purpose

Topic and scope are both objective terms, meaning they include no specific reference to the author's point of view. The difference between them is that the topic is broader; the scope narrows the topic. Scope is particularly important because answer choices that depart from it will always be wrong. The broad topic of "The Battle of Gettysburg" would be a lot to cover in 450 words. We should ask, "What aspect of the battle does the author take up?"—and, because of length limitations, it's likely to be a pretty small chunk. Whatever that "chunk" is—the prebattle scouting, or how the battle was fought, or the effects of the battle on the U.S. political scene—is the passage's scope. Answer choices that deal with anything outside of this narrowly defined chunk are wrong.

The topic/scope distinction ties into the all-important author's purpose. The author deliberately chooses to narrow the scope by including certain aspects of the broader topic and excluding others. Why the author makes those choices has to do with why the passage is being written in the first place. We can say that the topic is broadly stated and objective (for instance, a passage's topic might be "solving world hunger"). Scope is also objective, but narrower (a new technology for solving world hunger) and leads rather quickly to the author's subjective purpose (the author is writing in order to describe a new technology and its promising uses). And this is what turns into the author's main idea, which will be discussed at greater length in the next principle.

All this leads to a clear point of attack. Don't just "read" the passage; instead, try to do the following three things: *identify the topic; narrow it down to the precise scope that the author includes; and make a hypothesis about why the author is writing and where she is going with it.* A clear conception of these three things translates directly into points.

Structure and Tone

In a quest to master the content side of the passages—namely, *what* the author says—test takers are notorious for ignoring the less glamorous but just as important structural side—namely, *how* the author says it. One of the keys to success on this section is to understand not only the purpose, but also the structure of each passage. Why? Simply because the questions ask both what the author says, and how he or she says it. The following is a list of the classic LSAT passage structures:

Don't Be Tone Deaf

Some passages have a strong tone—i.e., the author has a definite viewpoint on the topic and is expressing it with emotion. Other passages have a more even tone—they report information without much emotion or a discernible angle. Distinguishing one from the other is an important skill in Reading Comprehension.

- passages based on a strong opinion
- passages based on a serious problem or situation
- passages based on differing opinions
- passages based on significant new findings (often a science passage)

Many LSAT passages have been based on one of these classic structures, or a variation thereof. You've most likely seen these structures at work in passages before, even if unconsciously. Your task is to seek them out actively as you begin to read a passage; usually, the structure is announced within the first third of the passage. Let these classic structures act as a "jump start" in your search for the passage's "big picture" and purpose.

As for how the author makes his or her point, try to note the author's position within these structures, usually indicated by the author's tone. For example, in the third structure (passages based on differing opinions), the author may simply relate the two sides of the story, or may at some point jump in and take a side, or even reject the conflicting opinions in favor of his or her own. In the first structure (passages based on a strong opinion), the opinion could be the author's, in which case the author's tone may be opinionated, argumentative, heated, passionate. On the other hand, the author could simply be describing the strongly held opinions of someone else. This author's writing style would be more descriptive, factual, and even-handed. His or her method may involve mere storytelling—the simple relaying of information—which is altogether different from the former case.

Notice the difference in tone between the two types of authors. Correct answer choices for a Primary Purpose question in the former case would use terms such as "argue for," "propose," and "demonstrate," whereas correct choices for the same type of question in the latter case would use terms such as "describe" and "discuss." Correct answers are always consistent with the author's tone, so noting the author's tone is a good way to score points.

Focus on the Main Idea

Almost every passage boils down to one big idea. We discussed above how topic leads to scope, and then in turn to the author's purpose in writing the passage. An author's primary purpose and main idea are forever intertwined. Take, for example, the hypothetical passage stated above, in which the author had the following purpose:

> The author is writing in order to describe a new technology and its promising uses.

The main idea is simply a restatement of this without the active verb structure:

> Biochemical engineering (or whatever new technology is discussed) can help solve world hunger.

Your job is to get past the fancy wording and focus on this big idea.

What's the Big Idea?
You should always keep the main idea in mind, even when answering questions that don't explicitly ask for it. Correct answers on even the detail questions tend to echo the main idea in one way or another.

Most often, the main idea will be presented in the first third of the passage. But occasionally the author will build up to it gradually, in which case you may not have a solidified conception of the author's purpose or big idea until the very end. And, occasionally a passage won't include a main idea, which itself is a strong hint that the passage is more of a descriptive, story-telling type of passage, with an even-handed tone and no strong opinions. Bottom line: don't panic if you can't immediately pin down the author's main idea and purpose. Read on.

Unless it's solely descriptive, the main idea must appear somewhere in the passage, and when it does, you must take conscious note of it. For one thing, the purpose of everything else in the passage will be to support this idea. Furthermore, many of the questions—not only Main Idea questions or Primary Purpose questions, but all kinds of questions—are easier to handle when you have the main idea in the forefront of your mind. Always look for choices that sound consistent with the main idea. Wrong choices often sound inconsistent with it.

Step Two: Read the Rest of the Passage

Don't obsess over details. There are differences between the reading skills required in an academic environment and those useful on standardized tests. In school, you probably read to memorize information for an exam. This kind of reading most likely includes taking note of and memorizing details.

It's an Open-Book Test
Don't feel that you have to memorize or understand every little thing as you read the passage. Remember, you can always refer to the passage later to clarify the meaning of any detail.

But this is not the type of reading that's good for getting points on Reading Comprehension. On the test, you'll need to read for short-term, as opposed to long-term, retention. When you finish the questions on a certain passage, that passage is over, gone, done with. You're free to promptly forget everything about it.

What's more, there's certainly no need to memorize details—it's an open-book test, after all. You always have the option to relocate details if a particular question requires you to do so. If you have a good sense of a passage's structure and paragraph topics, and your mental map is clear in your mind, then you should have no problem navigating back through the text when the need arises.

Get the Gist of Each Paragraph

The paragraph is the main structural unit of any passage. After you've read the first third of the passage carefully, you need only find the gist, or general purpose, of each succeeding paragraph, and then attempt to relate each paragraph to the passage as a whole. To find the gist of each paragraph, ask yourself:

Make a Map

Try labeling each paragraph, so that you know what's covered in each and how it fits into the overall structure of the passage. This will help you to get a fix on the passage as a whole, and it will help you locate the specific details later.

- Why did the author include this paragraph?
- What shift did the author have in mind when moving on to this paragraph?
- What bearing does this paragraph have on the author's main idea?

This process allows you create a "mental map" of the passage, which ties in strongly with the structure and main idea. When questions arise that require you to look back into the passage, having a mental map will help you locate the place in the text that contains the answer. For example, it's helpful to know that, say, the author's critique of a recommendation is in the third paragraph. Doing so will allow you to zero in on the relevant information quickly. The art of not trying to understand every little thing in the passage brings us to our next principle.

Step Three: Answer the Questions Efficiently

Quickly scan the question stems for Global questions, specifically Main Idea or Primary Purpose questions. Doing these questions first will often help you solidify your conception of the author's main idea and purpose, and you're more likely to answer them correctly now, while the passage is still fresh in your mind.

If there are any other global types, such as questions regarding the author's overall tone or the organization of the passage, you may benefit from seeking out and handling those next. Explicit Text questions, especially those with line references, are good candidates to tackle after that. Many test takers benefit from leaving the more difficult inference questions for last. So, answer questions in the following order:

All Questions Are Not Created Equal

Those who always answer the questions in the order in which they appear are not taking control of the test. It does matter which questions you choose to do first.

1. Global questions
2. Explicit Text questions
3. Inference questions

This, of course, is only a rough order based on question type. You may want to revise this order to account for the difficulty level of each individual question. For example, on any given passage, some inference questions may be easier than some Explicit Text questions. So, for each question, quickly ask yourself: "Can I answer this question quickly?" Shop around—tackle the questions that you think will get you quick points first, and leave the others for later. This reinforces the all-important LSAT mindset—your conscious decision to take control of the test.

Three main question types accompany each passage: Global, Explicit Text, and Inference. Let's look at each of these more closely.

Global Questions

A Global question asks us to sum up the author's overall intentions, ideas, or passage structure. It's basically a question whose scope is the entire passage. Global questions account for 25 to 30 percent of all RC questions.

In general, any answer choice to a Global question choice that grabs onto a small detail—or zeros in on the content of only one paragraph—will be wrong. Often, scanning the verbs in the Global question choices is a good way to take a first cut at the question. The verbs must agree with the author's tone and way in which he or she structures the passage, so scanning the verbs can narrow down the options quickly. The correct answer must be consistent with the overall tone and structure of the passage, whereas the wrong choices will go beyond the scope or focus on a detail or be inconsistent with the author's tone. You'll often find Global questions at the beginning of question sets, and often one of the wrong choices will play on some side issue discussed at the tail end of the passage. We suggest doing Global questions first because you can often use their answers to help you on the Explicit Text and Inference questions.

Global Questions at a Glance

- GQs represent 25–30 percent of Reading Comp questions.
- GQs sum up the author's overall intentions or passage structure.
- Nouns and verbs must be consistent with the author's tone and the passage's scope.
- Types of GQs: Main Idea, Primary Purpose, Title, Structure, Logic, and Tone.

The different types of Global questions are Main Idea, Primary Purpose, Title, Structure, Logic, and Tone questions. Let's briefly review each.

Main Idea and Primary Purpose Questions

The two main types of Global questions are Main Idea and Primary Purpose questions. We discussed these ideas earlier, noting that main idea and purpose are inextricably linked, because the author's purpose is to convey his or her main idea. The formats for these question types are pretty self-evident:

- Which one of following best expresses the main idea of the passage?
- The author's primary purpose is to . . .

Title Questions

A very similar form of Global question is one that's looking for a title that best fits the passage. (This question type disappeared for a while from the LSAT, but has started to make a comeback.) A title, in effect, is the main idea summed up in a brief, catchy way. This question may look like this: "Which of the following titles best describes the content of the passage as a whole?"

Be sure not to go with a choice that aptly describes only the latter half of the passage; a valid title, like a main idea and primary purpose, must cover the entire passage.

Structure Questions

Another type of Global question is one that asks you to recognize a passage's overall structure. Here's what this type of question might sound like, "Which of the following best describes the organization of the passage?"

Answer choices to this kind of Global question are usually worded very generally; they force you to recognize the broad layout of the passage as opposed to the specific content. For example, here are a few possible ways that a passage could be organized:

- A hypothesis is stated and then analyzed.
- A proposal is evaluated and alternatives are explored.
- A viewpoint is set forth and then subsequently defended.

When choosing among these choices, literally ask yourself: "Was there a hypothesis here? Was there an evaluation of a proposal, or a defense of a viewpoint?" These terms may all sound similar, but in fact, they're very different things. Learn to recognize the difference between a proposal, a viewpoint, and so on. Try to keep an eye on what the author is doing as well as what the author is saying, and you'll have an easier time with this type of question.

Logic Questions

Logic questions are those that ask about *why* the author does something—cite a source, bring up a detail, put one paragraph before another, etcetera. Choices that discuss the content or a detail will be wrong for these questions.

Tone Questions

The last type of Global question is the Tone question, which asks you to evaluate the style of the writing or how the author sounds. Is the author passionate, fiery, neutral, angry, hostile, opinionated, low key? Here's an example: "The author's tone in the passage can best be characterized as . . ."

Make sure you don't confuse the nature of the content with the tone in which the author presents the ideas—a social science passage based on trends in this century's grisliest murders may be presented in a cool, detached, strictly informative way. Once again, it's up to you to separate what the author says from how he or she says it.

Explicit Text Questions

The second major category of Reading Comprehension questions is the Explicit Text question. As the name implies, an Explicit Text question is one whose answer can be directly pinpointed and found in the text. This type makes up roughly 10 to 20 percent of the questions on the section. It's fairly simple to identify an Explicit Text question from its stem:

- According to the passage/author . . .
- The author states that . . .
- The author mentions which one of the following as . . .

Often, these questions provide very direct clues as to where an answer may be found, such as a line reference or some text that links up with the passage structure. (Just be careful with line references—they'll bring you to the right area, but usually the actual answer will be found in the lines immediately before or after the referenced line.) Detail questions are usually related to the main idea, and correct choices tend to be related to major points.

Explicit Test Questions at a Glance

- ETQs represent 10–20 percent of Reading Comp questions.
- ETQ answers can always be found in the text.
- ETQs sometimes include line references to help you locate the relevant material.
- ETQs are concrete, and therefore the easiest RC question type for most.

Now, you may recall that we advised you to skim over details in Reading Comprehension passages in favor of focusing on the big idea, topic, and scope. But, here's a question type that's specifically concerned with details, so what's the deal? The fact is, most of the details that appear in a typical passage aren't tested in the questions. Of the few that are, you'll usually either remember them from your reading or be given a line reference to bring you right to them. Even in those instances when you have to search for the important details, your mental map and understanding of the purpose of each paragraph will help you quickly locate the relevant detail and then choose an answer. And even if that fails, you have the option, as a last resort, of putting that question aside and returning to it later, if and when you have the time to search through the passage more rigorously. The point is, even with the existence of this question type, the winning strategy is still to note the purpose of details in each paragraph's argument, but not to attempt to memorize the details themselves.

Most people find Explicit Text questions to be the easiest type of RC question, since they're the most concrete. Unlike inferences, which hide somewhere between the lines, explicit details reside in the lines themselves. For this reason, we suggest placing Explicit Text questions high on your list of priorities, above Inference questions but below Global questions, when choosing the order in which you tackle the questions.

Inference Questions

Inference questions make up 55 to 60 percent of the Reading Comprehension section, and are very similar to those found in Logical Reasoning. An inference is something that is almost certainly true, based on the passage, but that is contained "between the lines." The answer is something that the author strongly implies or hints at, but does not state directly. Often the right answer is a paraphrase of what the author says. Furthermore, the Kaplan Denial Test, which was introduced earlier for Logical Reasoning Assumption and Inference questions, works for Inference questions in Reading Comprehension as well. The right answer, if denied, will contradict or significantly weaken the passage. So in those two respects, Logical Reasoning and RC inferences are similar. The differences?

- RC Inference questions can focus on either major or minor points, whereas LR Inference questions tend to focus on only major elements of the stimulus.
- RC text is tougher to get through than LR prose, which is much briefer. So RC Inference questions are tougher, since it can be difficult to know where in the passage to look for the answer.

Inference Questions at a Glance

- IQs represent 55–60 percent of Reading Comp questions.
- IQs are similar to Logical Reasoning inferences.
- IQs test ability to read between the lines.
- The Denial Test works to test choices.
- IQs often boil down to translating the author's points.
- The IQ question stem usually provides a clue as to where in the passage the answer will be found
- IQs will ask for either something that can be inferred from a specific part of the passage, or else for something with which the author would agree.

The same rules that apply to inferences in Logical Reasoning also apply to inferences in Reading Comprehension. A good inference:

- stays in line with the gist of the passage
- stays in line with the author's tone
- stays in line with the author's point of view
- stays within the scope of the passage and its main idea
- is neither denied by, nor irrelevant to, the ideas stated in the passage
- always makes more sense than its opposite

Extracting valid inferences from RC passages requires the ability to recognize that information in the passage can be expressed in different ways. The ability to bridge the gap between the way information is presented in the passage and the way it's presented in the correct answer choice is vital. In fact, Inference questions often boil down to an exercise in translation. Remember, the best answers to Inference questions are often paraphrases of what the author said.

Standard Inference Questions

The most common type of Inference question simply asks what can be inferred from the passage, but does so in a variety of ways:

- It can be inferred from the passage that . . .
- The passage/author suggests that . . .
- The passage/author implies that . . .
- The passage supports which one of the following statements . . .

Usually, some specific information will complete these question stems, so you'll almost always have a clue as to which idea or set of ideas from the passage is the key to the answer. When evaluating the answer choices, keep the relevant ideas firmly in mind. The farther you stray from them to endorse a choice, the more likely it is that this choice will be wrong. Occasionally, the stem won't contain specific information, in which case you simply have to work your way through the choices until you find the one that's most consistent with the passage.

Agreement Questions

Another common form of Inference question is one that asks you to find a statement that the author (or some character or group mentioned in the passage) would agree with. Once again, the question stem will usually provide a hint as to which part of the passage contains the answer.

Choose an Answer

Prephrase an answer to the question, and skim the answer choices looking for something similar. After settling on an answer, briefly reread the question stem to ensure that you are answering the question that was asked.

Process of Elimination

Ideally, you want to prephrase an answer before looking at the choices. However, in practice, this doesn't always happen, especially under the pressures of taking the test. So, it's important to recognize the most common types of wrong answer choices that appear for all three question types. This will allow you to eliminate answer choices quickly and efficiently until you are left with one choice, the credited response. If you aren't able to prephrase an answer to a question, remember to eliminate the following:

- choices that go beyond the author's scope
- choices that are "half-right, half-wrong"
- choices that use the wrong verb
- choices that distort the passage's ideas
- choices that say the exact opposite of what you are looking for

Throughout the explanations to the questions in this book, we've indicated which questions are good candidates for process of elimination. Pay attention to the way in which wrong answer choices are crafted so that you can eliminate them quickly and confidently on the day of the test.

Even if you can only narrow down the choices to two or three by using the process of elimination, you've improved your odds of guessing correctly. So, never abandon a question if you can't prephrase an answer. Quickly eliminate as many choices as possiblem, guess randomly from the remaining choices, and move to the next question.

Applying the Kaplan Three-Step Method

Apply the Kaplan Three-Step Method to the following LSAT-type RC passage. We've only included the question stems of the questions attached to this passage because we want you to decide the order in which you will answer the questions. We'll then work through a couple of the actual questions so that you can practice applying your question strategies.

It has been suggested that post–World War II concepts of environmental liability, as they pertain to hazardous waste, grew out of issues regarding municipal refuse collection and disposal and industrial waste disposal in the period 1880–1940. To a great degree, the remedies available to Americans for dealing with the burgeoning hazardous waste problem were characteristic of the judicial, legislative, and regulatory tools used to confront a whole range of problems in the industrial age. At the same time, these remedies were operating in an era in which the problem of hazardous waste had yet to be recognized. It is understandable that an assessment of liability was narrowly drawn and most often restricted to a clearly identified violator in a specific act of infringement of the property rights of someone else. Legislation, for the most part, focused narrowly on clear threats to the public health and dealt with problems of industrial pollution meekly if at all.

Nevertheless, it would be grossly inaccurate to assume that the actions of American politicians, technologists, health officials, judges, and legislators in the period 1880–1940 have had little impact on the attempts to define environmental liability and to confront the consequences of hazardous waste. Taken as a whole, the precedents of the late nineteenth through the mid-twentieth century have established a framework in which the problem of hazardous waste is understood and confronted today. Efforts at refuse reform gradually identified the immutable connection between waste and disease, turning eyesores into nuisances and nuisances into health hazards. Confronting the refuse problem and other forms of municipal pollution forced cities to define public responsibility and accountability with respect to the environment. A commitment to municipal services in the development of sewers and collection and disposal systems shifted the burden of responsibility for eliminating wastes from the individual to the community. In some way, the courts' efforts to clarify and broaden the definition of public nuisance were dependent on the cities' efforts to define community responsibility itself. The courts retained their role as arbiter of what constituted private and public nuisances. Indeed, fear that the courts would transform individual decisions into national precedents often contributed to the search for other remedies. Nonetheless, the courts remained an active agent in cases on the local, state, and national level, making it quite clear that they were not going to be left out of the process of defining environmental liability in the United States. In the case of hazardous waste, precedents for behavior and remedial action were well developed by 1940. Even though the concept of hazardous waste is essentially a post–World War II notion, the problem was not foreign to earlier generations. The observation that the administrative, technical, and legal problems of water pollution in the 1920s were intertwined is equally applicable to today's hazardous waste problem.

1. According to the author, the efforts by cities to define public responsibility for the environment resulted in which of the following?
2. Which of the following, if substituted for the word "immutable" (line 21), would LEAST alter the author's meaning?
3. With which one of the following statements would the author be most likely to agree?
4. The author's primary purpose is to discuss
5. The tone of the author's discussion of early attempts to deal with waste and pollution problems could best be described as
6. According to the passage, judicial assessments of liability in waste disposal disputes prior to World War II were usually based on
7. The passage suggests that responses to environmental problems between 1880 and 1940 were relatively limited in part because of

Step One: Attack the First Third of the Passage

The first few sentences introduce the topic: hazardous waste. The scope, as you recall, is the specific angle the author takes on the topic, and this seems to be the post–World War II concept of environmental liability associated with hazardous waste. The author points out that it's been suggested that this concept of liability has some connection to issues from the time period 1880–1940; latter-day remedies for hazardous waste are "characteristic of the judicial, legislative, and regulatory tools used to confront a whole range of problems in the industrial age." Since hazardous waste liability concepts of the postwar era had their roots in an era that predated the recognition of hazardous waste problems, the author finds it understandable that liability assessment and the ensuing legislation regarding hazardous waste were both "narrowly drawn."

All of this comes out of the first paragraph. In some cases, this would be enough to cover the "first third of the passage" reading. However, the keyword "nevertheless" at the beginning of the next paragraph indicates that it may be helpful to include this sentence in your initial reading as well. This sentence harks back to and solidifies the connection between the actions and policies from the period 1880–1940 and the concept of environmental liability associated with hazardous waste. This connection is the author's main idea.

Step Two: Read the Rest of the Passage

The sentence from lines 18 to 20—"Taken as a whole. . . ."—is simply another restatement of the main idea. It's followed by a description of the gradual recognition of the hazardous waste problem, and some of the repercussions of the cities' and courts' efforts to define the problem and to assign responsibility for it. Note that there's some talk in the paragraph about individual versus community responsibility, and the role of cities, but don't fuss over the specifics. If there's a question on these issues, you'll know where to look.

The first part of the last paragraph deals mainly with the courts' role in defining environmental liability. The last three sentences of the passage reinforce the main idea; namely that there's a historical context for the ways in which hazardous waste problems are viewed today.

Step Three: Answer the Questions Efficiently

Let's look at the seven question stems attached to this passage:

1. According to the author, the efforts by cities to define public responsibility for the environment resulted in which of the following?
2. Which of the following, if substituted for the word "immutable" (line 21), would LEAST alter the author's meaning?
3. With which one of the following statements would the author be most likely to agree?
4. The author's primary purpose is to discuss
5. The tone of the author's discussion of early attempts to deal with waste and pollution problems could best be described as
6. According to the passage, judicial assessments of liability in waste disposal disputes prior to World War II were usually based on
7. The passage suggests that responses to environmental problems between 1880 and 1940 were relatively limited in part because of

Global Questions

Quickly scan the question stems for Global questions, specifically Main Idea or Primary Purpose questions. You should attempt Question 4 first, while the author's big idea is fresh in your mind:

4. The author's primary purpose is to discuss

 (A) contrasts in the legislative approaches to environmental liability before and after World War II
 (B) legislative trends that have been instrumental in the reduction of environmental hazardous wastes
 (C) the historical and legislative context in which to view post–World War II hazardous waste problems
 (D) early patterns of industrial abuse and pollution of the American environment
 (E) the growth of an activist tradition in American jurisprudence

Choice (C) has the elements of a right answer: the connection (denoted by "the historical and legislative context . . . to view . . . waste problems") that represents the author's main idea, and the correct topic and scope—hazardous waste, post-World War II. Choice (B) is tempting; legislative trends were discussed, but not in enough depth to constitute the author's primary purpose. More damaging to (B) is the fact that the discussion hinges on defining liability for hazardous wastes, and doesn't specifically discuss any factor instrumental in the reduction of environmental wastes. Meanwhile, (A) misinterprets the passage structure—there is no such contrast presented, while (D) and (E) both violate the topic and scope of the passage (notice that neither one even mentions the topic of hazardous wastes).

Question 5, focusing on tone, is another Global question that you might want to answer early on. Continuing to scan the question stems, the one with the line reference, Question 2, may have caught your eye. This type simply tests your understanding of a certain word in a particular context, and since it tells us exactly where in the passage the word is, you would be justified in trying this one next. Questions 1 and 6 are clearly Explicit Text questions, so you should do those next, beginning with the one that seems the most familiar. Questions 3 and 7, the Inference questions, are good candidates to be saved for last.

We've already discussed one of the Global questions, so let's now conclude this discussion of Reading Comprehension with a brief look at one Explicit Text question and one Inference question.

Explicit Text Question

Here's the complete form (with answer choices) of Question 6:

6. According to the passage, judicial assessments of liability in waste disposal disputes prior to World War II were usually based on

    (A) excessively broad definitions of legal responsibility
    (B) the presence of a clear threat to the public health
    (C) precedents derived from well-known cases of large-scale industrial polluters
    (D) restricted interpretations of property rights infringements
    (E) trivial issues such as littering, eyesores, and other public nuisances

Pre–World War II judicial assessments of liability should ring a bell; they were discussed in the first paragraph. The correct answer, choice (D), is a direct paraphrase of the passage: ". . . an assessment of liability was narrowly drawn and most often restricted to a clearly identified violator in a specific act of infringement of the property rights of someone else."

Watch for Traps

Same-wording and *au contraire* wrong choices are common. Recognize them and avoid them.

Choice (E) is a common type of wrong answer; it consists of wording taken straight from the passage, but unfortunately, the wrong part of the passage. Don't choose an answer simply because you recognize some of the words or phrases in it; this is a common trap that snags many careless test takers.

Choice (B) is another classic wrong answer —the *au contraire* choice. This choice actually represents the opposite of what's stated or implied in the passage. According to the author, pre–World War II was "an era in which the problem of hazardous waste had yet to be recognized."

Inference Question

Finally, let's take a quick look at Question 3, an Inference question, and its answer choices:

3. With which one of the following statements would the author be most likely to agree?

    (A) The growth of community responsibility for waste control exemplifies the tendency of government power to expand at the expense of individual rights.
    (B) Although important legal precedents for waste control were established between 1880 and 1940, today's problems will require radically new approaches.
    (C) While early court decisions established important precedents involving environmental abuses by industry, such equally pressing matters as disposal of municipal garbage were neglected.
    (D) Because environmental legislation between 1880 and 1940 was in advance of its time, it failed to affect society's awareness of environmental problems.
    (E) The historical role of U.S. courts in defining problems of hazardous waste and environmental liability provides valuable traditions for courts today.

Remember the basic rule for inferences: an inference must stay in line with the author's tone as well as the passage's topic and scope. The author's tone in this passage—factual, even-handed—doesn't seem to fit with choices (A) and (B). Choice (A) offers a judgment taken from the community/individual responsibility issue, something the author never does; he or she simply says that the burden shifted from one to the other.

There's no reason to believe that the author would agree with (B), either. While he or she would certainly agree with the first part, there's nothing that indicates that the author would advocate radical new approaches for today's problems. Both of these choices fail to match the author's tone, and are slightly outside the scope of the passage as well.

Notice how correct choice (E) sounds like an offshoot of the author's main idea. The first sentence of the second paragraph says that it would be wrong to assume that the actions of judges and legislators, among others, had little impact on defining liability and confronting the issue of hazardous waste. This implies that the courts had a positive impact, which is bolstered by lines 33 to 35. Combine that with the statement in lines 18 to 20: "Taken as a whole, the precedents of the late nineteenth through the mid-twentieth century have established a framework in which the problem of hazardous waste is understood and confronted today." All of this points towards (E) as a statement that the author would agree with, and therefore the answer to this Inference question.

What's Next?

We've introduced you to the type of reading that the test makers require, given you a powerful method for dealing with RC passages and questions, and walked you though application of the method to a Reading Comprehension passage. Now, it's time for you to practice applying Kaplan's Three-Step Method. The following practice passages and full explanations will help you refine your technique.

When you are done, turn to the Putting It All Together chapter, where we'll discuss timing, guessing, gridding, section management, and the proper LSAT mindset. This will help you to tie together everything you've learned about the three question types so that you can tackle the two real LSATs.

Reading Comprehension Practice Set

<u>Directions</u>: Each selection in this test is followed by several questions. After reading the selection, choose the best response to each question and mark it on your answer sheet. Your replies are to be based on what is <u>stated</u> or <u>implied</u> in the selection.

The basic theory of plate tectonics recognizes two ways continental margins can grow seaward. Where two plates such as the African plate and the South American plate are moving away from a mid-ocean rift that separates them, the continental margins on those plates are said to be passive, or rifted. Such continental margins grow slowly from the accumulation of riverborne sediments and of the carbonate skeletons of marine organisms, which are deposited as limestone. Suites—unbroken sequences—of such accretions, consisting of nearly flat strata, are called miogeoclinal deposits. Since most miogeoclinal deposits are undeformed and exhibit an unbroken history, it is evident that passive margins are generally not associated with mountain building.

Along active, or convergent, margins, such as those that ring most of the Pacific basin, continents tend to grow much faster. At an active margin an oceanic plate plunges under a continental plate, with the continental plate scraping off deep-ocean sediments and fragments of basaltic crust that then adhere to the continental margin. Simultaneously the plate plunging under the continental margin heats up and partially melts, triggering extensive volcanism and mountain-building. A classic example is the Andes of the west coast of South America.

In the original plate-tectonic model western North America was described as being a passive margin through the late Paleozoic and early Mesozoic eras (roughly 350 to 210 million years ago) after which it became an active margin. It was assumed that the continent grew to a limited extent along this margin as sedimentary and igneous rocks of oceanic origin were accreted in a few places, as in the Coast Ranges of California. The model was successful in explaining such disparate features as the Franciscan rocks of the California Coast Ranges, formed by local subduction processes, and the granite rocks of the Sierra Nevada, farther to the east, which clearly originated as the roots of volcanoes similar to those of the Andes.

The basic plate-tectonic reconstruction of the geologic history of western North America remains unchanged in the light of microplate tectonics (the process by which the edge of a continent is modified by the transport, accretion and rotation of large crystal blocks called terranes), but the details are radically changed. It is now clear that much more crust was added to North America in the Mesozoic era (248 to 65 million years ago) than can be accounted for by volcanism along island arcs and by the simple accretion of sediments from the ocean floor. It has also become evident that some terranes lying side by side today are not genetically related, as would be expected from simple plate tectonics, but almost certainly have traveled great distances from entirely different parts of the world.

1. Which of the following best expresses the main idea of the passage?

   (A) The margin of the west coast of North America developed through a combination of active and passive mechanisms.
   (B) The growth of continental margins is only partially explained by the basic theory of plate tectonics.
   (C) Continental margins can grow seaward in two ways, through sedimentation or volcanism.
   (D) The introduction of microplate tectonics poses a fundamental challenge to the existing theory of how continental margins are formed.
   (E) Continental margins grow more rapidly along active margins than along passive margins.

   Ⓐ Ⓑ Ⓒ Ⓓ Ⓔ

2. The passage supplies information for answering all of the following questions regarding continental margins EXCEPT:

(A) How have marine organisms contributed to the formation of passive continental margins?
(B) What were some of the processes by which the continental margin of the west coast of North America was formed?
(C) Are miogeoclinal deposits associated with mountain building along continental margins?
(D) Were the continental margins of the east and west coasts of South America formed by similar processes?
(E) Did the west coast of North America grow faster than the east coast prior to the late Paleozoic era?

Ⓐ Ⓑ Ⓒ Ⓓ Ⓔ

3. According to the passage, which of the following is true about the formation of the Sierra Nevada Mountains?

(A) They developed through the deposition of terranes.
(B) They were formed during the Paleozoic era.
(C) Their geologic origin is analogous to that of the Andes.
(D) Their history can be traced back to the accretion of miogeoclinal deposits.
(E) They are similar in structure to the Coast Ranges.

Ⓐ Ⓑ Ⓒ Ⓓ Ⓔ

4. The author mentions the Franciscan rocks of the California Coast Ranges (lines 42-43) in order to make which of the following points?

(A) The basic theory of plate tectonics accounts for a wide variety of geologic features.
(B) The original plate tectonic model falls short of explaining such features.
(C) Subduction processes are responsible for the majority of the geologic features found along the west coast of North America.
(D) Passive margins can take on many geologic forms.
(E) The concept of microplate tectonics was first introduced to account for such phenomena.

Ⓐ Ⓑ Ⓒ Ⓓ Ⓔ

5. Which of the following does the author mention as evidence for the inadequacy of the original plate tectonic model to describe the formation of continental margins?

(A) Nearly flat, undeformed crystal blocks have been found along some continental margins where there are mountains further inland.
(B) Sediments and fragments from the depths of the ocean accumulate along continental margins.
(C) Large pieces of the Earth's crust that appear to be completely unrelated are found in the same area today.
(D) Undeformed miogeoclinal deposits are usually not linked to mountain building.
(E) Oceanic plates drop beneath continental plates along active margins.

Ⓐ Ⓑ Ⓒ Ⓓ Ⓔ

6. According to the passage, a passive margin is more likely than an active margin to be characterized by which of the following?

   (A) rapid growth
   (B) mountain building
   (C) the aggregation of oceanic rocks
   (D) carbonate deposits
   (E) the accretion of terranes

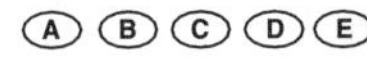

7. The author seems to regard the basic theory of plate tectonics as

   (A) outdated
   (B) unassailable
   (C) insufficient
   (D) revolutionary
   (E) unlikely

Opponents of the pocket veto allege that it grants the president too much power. They describe it as an absolute veto, a prerogative of the English kings that the Framers vehemently despised. In its most favorable light, the argument also embraces a vast body of commentary on the "imperial presidency," that is, the growing accumulation of power in the executive relative to the legislative branch. The presidential dominance arguments misrepresent the pocket veto. Unlike the royal prerogative, the pocket veto is exercised by a democratically elected leader pursuant to a clearly defined constitutional procedure. Congress may arrange presentation of a bill to thwart the president's opportunity to use the pocket veto. Moreover, an absolute veto forecloses further action on a proposal; the Congress, however, may overcome a pocket veto by reintroducing and passing the rejected bill.

The "imperial presidency" developed from the extension of executive action into areas where it has been assumed that the legislative branch retains supremacy. The legislative process, however, spells out shared responsibility between the president and Congress. Presidential power to block legislation is not of the same quality as presidential power to substitute executive judgment for congressional authorization. The latter threatens the constitutional system of checks and balances; the former situation, typified by the pocket veto, is a part of that system of checks and balances.

The pocket veto's flaw, if any, is that it permits the president to block legislation when Congress would almost certainly override a return veto. The arguments raised in *Kennedy* and *Barnes* implicitly claim that a return veto would be overridden, or not exercised at all. Consequently, the pocket veto grants the president a special political tool against "popular will." Herein lies the fundamental disagreement over the pocket veto. Opponents press for the president to defer to the seemingly inevitable congressional victory. The president, in contrast, stands behind the historical use of the pocket veto to delay legislation he thinks unwise.

Not every bill pocket vetoed would be subjected to a return veto. And not every return veto of a bill that was overwhelmingly popular in the Congress would be overridden. But in those cases in which the president would use the return veto, and Congress would vote to override that return, the pocket veto acts to stop or delay popular legislation. If legislative supremacy is the most important value to protect, then the pocket veto is wrong. On the other hand, if circumspection and deliberation are the more valued aspects of the law-making process, even the most blatantly political use of the pocket veto passes muster. Historical practice favors the president's role as an interloper.

8. The primary purpose of this passage is to

   (A) examine and reject arguments against the pocket veto
   (B) show that the pocket veto must be reconsidered in the light of the development of the "imperial presidency"
   (C) contrast English and American usages of the pocket veto
   (D) demonstrate the importance of the pocket veto
   (E) respond to arguments raised against the pocket veto in *Kennedy* and *Barnes*

   Ⓐ Ⓑ Ⓒ Ⓓ Ⓔ

9. The author would consider a "blatantly political use of the pocket veto" (lines 61–62) to be

   (A) unjustified, since the will of the congressional majority should be respected
   (B) unwise, since the president should be perceived to stand above partisan politics
   (C) appropriate if the president has pledged in advance to block the legislation in question
   (D) justifiable only when Congress is not supported by public opinion
   (E) legitimate because it can force further consideration of a bill the president opposes

   Ⓐ Ⓑ Ⓒ Ⓓ Ⓔ

10. Which of the following can be inferred about the pocket veto from the passage?

   (A) The president may use it for political purposes different from those of the return veto.
   (B) It was frequently used by the British monarchs.
   (C) The Congress is powerless to prevent the president from using it.
   (D) It is only advantageous to the president in cases where a return veto could be overridden by the Congress.
   (E) It is used by the president more frequently than the return veto.

   Ⓐ Ⓑ Ⓒ Ⓓ Ⓔ

11. It can be inferred that the author considers which of the following to be the strongest argument AGAINST the positions opposing the pocket veto taken in *Barnes* and *Kennedy?*

(A) A return veto of the legislation in question would not have been overridden.
(B) A return veto of the legislation in question would probably have been overridden.
(C) The president would have been unlikely to use a return veto, because of fear of public opinion.
(D) In certain cases, the Constitution allows the president to delay legislation that has majority support.
(E) The pocket veto is an extension of presidential power into an area of congressional authority.

Ⓐ Ⓑ Ⓒ Ⓓ Ⓔ

12. The author would be most likely to agree with which of the following statements about the "imperial presidency"?

(A) It represents an unprecedented threat to the continuity of American institutions.
(B) It is more in keeping with the present English system of government than with the American.
(C) The pocket veto is not really an example of tendencies toward an "imperial presidency."
(D) It has been the cause of increasingly frequent use of the pocket veto.
(E) It is the most compelling argument in defense of the pocket veto.

Ⓐ Ⓑ Ⓒ Ⓓ Ⓔ

13. The author's attitude toward the opponents of the pocket veto could best be described as one of

(A) dissent
(B) condescension
(C) concurrence
(D) deep respect
(E) mild alarm

Ⓐ Ⓑ Ⓒ Ⓓ Ⓔ

Answers

1. B	6. D	11. D
2. E	7. C	12. C
3. C	8. A	13. A
4. A	9. E	
5. C	10. A	

Explanations

Plate Tectonics

This passage may have posed some problems for you initially, since it's cluttered with technical terms and somewhat hard to get through. But don't get caught up in the jargon—read for the main idea, and try to get a handle on the topic of each paragraph. The passage describes the basic theory of plate tectonics, and ultimately suggests that the theory falls short of explaining all the phenomena of growing continental margins. The first paragraph states that according to the basic theory of plate tectonics, there are two ways in which continental margins can grow seaward, one of which is by passive margins. The second paragraph describes the other way, by active margins. The third paragraph uses a concrete example (western North America) to illustrate how the two ways together can describe the growth of a continental margin. Then, the final paragraph introduces the concept of microplate tectonics, and explains to the reader how it helps to explain certain phenomena that "simple" or "basic" plate tectonics cannot account for.

1 (B) is correct. While the basic theory of plate tectonics explains much about the growth of continental margins, the fourth paragraph suggests that it cannot fully explain certain geologic details. Choice (B) captures this, and is the correct answer.

Although (A) is stated in the third paragraph, the focus on the west coast of North America is merely a detail mentioned in support of the main idea. Choice (C) distorts the two ways that continental margins can grow: through passive or active margins. Though the first paragraph mentions sedimentation as an example of passive margins, and the second paragraph states that volcanism often results from active margin growth, the author never goes so far as to say that sedimentation and volcanism are the two ways that continental margins grow. Choice (D) is incorrect because the first sentence of the fourth paragraph states that the basic plate tectonic theory remains unchanged in light of microplate tectonics; it's the *details* that are radically changed, not the basic theory. And while choice (E) represents a true statement, it's a detail, not the passage's main idea.

2 (E) is correct. (A) is covered in the first paragraph, which describes the growth of passive margins. There, the author says that passive margins grow, in part, through the accumulation of the carbonate skeletons of marine organisms. Choice (B) is the subject of the third paragraph—the continental margin of the west coast of North America grew at first as a passive margin, and then as an active margin. Choice (C) is answered in the last sentence of the first paragraph: miogeoclinal deposits are associated with passive margins and are "generally not associated with mountain building." You have to search a bit for the answer to choice (D): the first paragraph suggests that the eastern edge of the South American plate is a passive margin, while the last sentence of the second paragraph says that the west coast of South America is an active margin.

Only the last answer choice, (E), cannot be answered with information contained in the passage. The passage says nothing about the east coast of North America, so we don't know if that coast grew more slowly than did the west coast.

3 (C) is correct. To answer this detail question, focus on the third paragraph, since that's where the author mentions the Sierra Nevada Mountains. The end of that paragraph states that the Sierra Nevada Mountains "clearly originated as the roots of volcanoes similar to those of the Andes." This is correctly stated in answer choice (C).

Choice (A) is incorrect because there is no mention of terranes in reference to the Sierra Nevada Mountains. Choice (B) contradicts the author's statement that the Sierra Nevada Mountains originated as the roots of volcanoes, formed by the processes of active continental margins *after* the Paleozoic era. Choice (D) is incorrect because miogeoclinal deposits are associated with passive continental margins, whereas the Sierra Nevada Mountains were formed while the west coast was an active margin. Choice (E) is wrong because the author states in the third paragraph that the Coast Ranges and the Sierra Nevada Mountains are "disparate features," formed by two different processes.

4 (A) is correct. The Coast Ranges of California are introduced in the third paragraph to give an example of the variety of geologic features that the original plate-tectonic model could successfully explain: the Franciscan Rocks, formed by local subduction, and the granite rocks of the Sierra Nevada, formed by volcanic action. Thus, (A) is the correct answer choice.

Choice (B) is wrong because the problems with the basic plate tectonic model are discussed in the fourth paragraph, where the California Coast Ranges are never mentioned. Choice (C) is incorrect because it distorts a detail through exaggeration. We don't know if subduction processes are responsible for the *majority* of the west coast's geologic features; we're only told that they are responsible for some, such as the Coast Ranges. Choice (D) is wrong because the Coast Ranges were formed by local subduction processes, according to the third paragraph, not by the actions of passive margins. As for choice (E), the concept of microplate tectonics was introduced to account for phenomena that the basic, or original, plate tectonic model could not adequately explain. But the Coast Ranges are features that the basic model *can* account for, so (E) is incorrect.

5 (C) is correct. The inadequacy of the plate tectonic model is introduced in the final paragraph of the passage. Genetically distinct pieces of the earth's crust are found in the same area, a fact

that the original plate tectonic model cannot explain, making (C) the right answer.

The original plate tectonic model can account for (A)—see the third and fourth paragraphs. Choices (B), (D), and (E) are true statements—see the first and second paragraphs—but none of these statements has a direct bearing on the issue of the inadequacy of the original plate tectonic model.

6 (D) is correct. In the first sentence of the second paragraph, the author states that *active* margins tend to grow much faster than passive ones; choice (A) contradicts this fact, so it's incorrect. The second-to-last sentence characterizes *active* margins as associated with mountain building, and the last sentence of the first paragraph states that passive margins are "generally not associated with mountain building," so (B) is also not correct. The aggregation of oceanic rocks is something that microplate tectonics is involved with, as mentioned in the first sentence of the last paragraph, so you can eliminate choice (C).

But choice (D) correctly states a likely characteristic of passive margins, but not of active margins—carbonate deposits—as stated in the third sentence of the first paragraph. Choice (E) is incorrect because it states a phenomenon associated with microplate tectonics, not with passive or active margins.

7 (C) is correct. This question asks you to identify the author's attitude toward the basic theory of plate tectonics. Since the passage as a whole suggests that the basic theory of plate tectonics is useful, but not complete, choice (C), "insufficient," best captures the author's attitude and tone.

Choice (A) is incorrect because the author never suggests that the basic theory of plate tectonics is outdated, just that it's incomplete. "Unassailable" means something that is incapable of being disputed or disproven, but the author clearly does think that there is a slight problem with the basic theory of plate tectonics, so (B) is incorrect. Choice (D) is incorrect because the author never suggests that the basic theory of plate tectonics is revolutionary; if anything's revolutionary, it's the theory of microplate tectonics. Finally, choice (E) is wrong because although the author thinks that the basic theory does not sufficiently explain certain phenomena, it is presented as a sound theory capable of explaining many features, not an unlikely theory, as (E) suggests.

Pocket Veto

As always, read the opening lines carefully. The first several lines give you the topic: arguments against the pocket veto. They also give you the author's point of view, because the word "allege" means the author disagrees and will answer the arguments later. The second and third paragraphs cover two of the major arguments against the pocket veto: that it is an absolute veto, and that it is an example of trends toward an "imperial presidency." The fourth and fifth paragraphs cover what the author thinks is a more substantive question: the president's ability to use the pocket veto to thwart the will of Congress.

8 (A) is correct. As just noted, the author defends the pocket veto against certain arguments made against it. These arguments are variations on the basic idea that, as the first sentence says, the pocket veto "grants the president too much power." The first three paragraphs rebut the specific arguments raised in the first paragraph. The fourth paragraph partly acknowledges "the pocket veto's flaw"—the fact that "it permits the president to block legislation when Congress would override a return veto"—but then the author goes on in this paragraph and the next one to argue that this flaw is not a conclusive argument against the pocket veto. So choice (A) best expresses the author's intention.

Choice (B) misrepresents the author's discussion of the "imperial presidency": the author rejects this idea as an argument against the pocket veto. The passage does not compare the use of the pocket veto in England and in America, as (C) claims; the passage merely says that critics of the pocket veto have compared it to the absolute veto of the English kings. The author is not concerned to demonstrate the importance of the pocket veto, as (D) would have it; the author takes the importance of the pocket veto for granted, and attempts to demonstrate its *legitimacy*. The author's response to the arguments raised in *Kennedy* and *Barnes* (E) is a supporting detail; it is not the main purpose of the passage.

9 (E) is correct. The phrase cited in this question appears near the end of the passage, where the author says that such use of the pocket veto "passes muster" if one considers it important to promote "circumspection and deliberation." Choice (E) expresses this idea.

Choice (A) is wrong because, in the same sentence, the author implicitly rejects the idea that "legislative supremacy is the most important value to protect." Choice (B) is wrong because the author clearly says that this political use of the pocket veto "passes muster" (that is, is acceptable), and nowhere does the author say that the president should be perceived as standing above partisan politics. Choice (C) suggests an idea that is not mentioned in the passage. Choice (D) is wrong for two reasons. Firstly, since the president vetoes acts of Congress, we must assume that "popular will" (line 42) means the will of the people *as manifested in Congress*, and therefore that the idea of Congress not being supported by "public opinion" is not relevant here. Secondly, and more importantly, even if the "public opinion" of the question were the same as the "popular will" of the passage here, the author rejects the idea that the president must always bow to "popular will."

10 (A) is correct. The basis for choice (A) is in the first sentence of the last paragraph, where the author says that "not every bill pocket vetoed would be subjected to a return veto." In the next two sentences the author indicates that the pocket veto, unlike the return veto, allows the president to block legislation that is overwhelmingly favored by Congress. This justifies the statement made in (A).

The author does not say that the English kings frequently used the pocket veto, as (B) states. The author only says that some critics have claimed that the pocket veto is *like* the English kings' absolute veto. Choice (C) is contradicted by the author's statement that "Congress may arrange presentation of a bill to thwart the president's opportunity to use the pocket veto." The passage does not support choice (D); the passage says that this is a possible application of the pocket veto, but not that it is the only application. As for choice (E), there is no evidence in the passage of how often pocket and return vetoes are used.

11 (D) is correct. The arguments against the pocket veto raised in *Kennedy* and *Barnes* are alluded to in the second and third sentences of the fourth paragraph. By inference, they come down to the idea that the president should not be able to block legislation that has enough support in Congress for Congress to override a veto. Choice (D) gets to the heart of this argument: it says that the president has a right to delay legislation, even when that legislation has majority support. This view is stated first in the last sentence of the fourth paragraph, and more extensively in the last two sentences of the fifth paragraph. The author doesn't say specifically that this is his or her opinion, but we infer that this is the case because of how the final paragraph is structured: the author's "last word" is that the pocket veto promotes "circumspection and deliberation" and is supported by historical precedent.

Choice (A) refutes what we are told is a major point in *Barnes* and *Kennedy*—the implicit claim that a return veto would have been overridden. But it fails to get to the heart of the matter: the implication of the last three sentences of the last paragraph is that even if it were true that "a return veto would be overridden, or not exercised at all," the president would still have the right to use the power of the pocket veto to block legislation that the president considers unwise. Choice (B), which says the exact opposite of (A), is clearly wrong because it confirms the claim that a return veto would be overridden, instead of refuting it; hence, it *strengthens* the arguments in *Barnes* and *Kennedy*. Choice (C) would also have the effect of strengthening the argument against the pocket veto instead of weakening it, because it implies that the pocket veto gives the president added power to thwart the will of the Congress and of the people. Choice (E) restates one of the arguments against the pocket veto, whereas this question is asking for a rebuttal of such arguments.

12 (C) is correct. The author speaks of the "imperial presidency" in the first and third paragraphs, and defines it as "the growing accumulation of power in the executive relative to the legislative branch."

Choice (A) is wrong because it overstates the case without specific support: the author never says that this increase in the power of the president would be as terrible a threat as (A) claims. Choice (B) is wrong because the passage doesn't provide any basis for deciding how appropriate the "imperial presidency" might be for the present English system of government. Choice (C), however, is correct. The point of the third paragraph is that the pocket veto is a part of the "constitutional system of checks and balances," whereas the "imperial presidency" involves an "extension" of executive power at the expense of the legislative branch which "threatens" the checks and balances system; therefore, as (C) says, the pocket veto is not an example of the "imperial presidency." There is no evidence in the passage that there has been an increasingly frequent use of the pocket veto, so choice (D) is wrong. The author does not cite the "imperial presidency" as a defense of the pocket veto, so (E) is wrong.

13 (A) is correct. The author disagrees with the opponents of the pocket veto; the passage as a whole is devoted to answering their arguments, in a respectful but firm fashion. This is best expressed by "dissent," choice (A).

"Condescension," choice (B), implies a disrespectful tone that is not present in the passage. "Concurrence," choice (C), means "agreement"—the opposite of the truth. Choice (D) is too positive; the author is respectful but within the context of disagreement. And choice (E) overstates the author's disagreement with the opponents of the pocket veto: he or she expresses no fear (even a mild one) about their ideas or influence.

CHAPTER 6

The Writing Sample

The Writing Sample is the last section you will handle on the day of the test. The proctors will collect the multiple-choice portion of the test and distribute a separate essay booklet. The topic of the Writing Sample always consists of a scenario followed by two possible courses of action. You'll have 30 minutes to make a written case for one of the choices. This section tests your ability to write a clear, concise, persuasive argument. No outside knowledge is required.

You'll receive a pen to write the essay, as well as scrap paper to plan out your response before you actually write it. Your essay must be confined to the space provided, which is roughly the equivalent of one sheet of standard lined paper. Your essay must fit within the lined space; you won't be given additional paper, so must keep your argument concise. Usually, two or three paragraphs will be enough. Note that there's really no time or space to change your mind or radically alter your essay once you've begun writing, so plan your argument carefully before beginning to write. Write as legibly as you can.

Does It Really Matter?
The Writing Sample may not matter in some admissions decisions, but in others it can be influential. Don't take a chance; take it seriously.

The Writing Sample is ungraded, but a photocopy is sent to the law schools to which you apply along with your LSAT score. Many law schools use the Writing Sample to help make decisions on borderline cases, or to decide between applicants with otherwise comparable credentials. Granted, it may not carry the same weight as the scored sections of the test, but since it can impact on your admission chances, your best bet is to take it seriously.

You'll be allowed to take a copy of your essay home with you. Our advice: don't reread it. Put it in a file drawer and forget about it. Your essay is ungraded and you can't do anything to change what you wrote after the fact.

Sample Topic

The structure of every Writing Sample topic is the same. First, a brief introduction outlines the choice to be made. That's followed by two criteria that should guide your decision. Finally, the two alternatives that you're to choose between are described in a paragraph each.

The following is an example of a Writing Sample topic:

> The *Daily Tribune,* a metropolitan newspaper, is considering two candidates for promotion to business editor. Write an argument for one candidate over the other with the following considerations in mind:
>
> - The editor must train new writers and assign stories.
> - The editor must be able to edit and rewrite stories under daily deadline pressure.
>
> Laura received a B.A. in English from a large university. She was the managing editor of her college newspaper and served as a summer intern at her hometown daily paper. Laura starting working at the *Tribune* right out of college and spent three years at the city desk covering the city economy. Eight years ago the paper formed its business section and Laura became part of the new department. After several years covering state business, Laura began writing on the national economy. Three years ago, Laura was named senior business and finance editor on the national business staff; she is also responsible for supervising seven writers.
>
> Palmer attended an elite private college where he earned both a B.S. in business administration and an M.A. in journalism. After receiving his journalism degree, Palmer worked for three years on a monthly business magazine. He won a prestigious national award for a series of articles on the impact of monetary policy on multinational corporations. Palmer came to the *Tribune* three years ago to fill the newly created position of international business writer. He was the only member of the international staff for two years and wrote on almost a daily basis. He now supervises a staff of four writers. Last year, Palmer developed a bimonthly business supplement for the *Tribune* that has proved highly popular and has helped increase the paper's circulation.

The Eight Basic Principles of Writing Sample Success

What follows are the most important rules-of-thumb to remember when attacking the Writing Sample.

1. Use Scrap Paper to Plan Your Essay

The proctors give you scrap paper for a reason. Use it! Make yourself a rudimentary outline, listing the points you want to make in each paragraph. Ideally, you should know what you want to say and how you want to say it before putting pen to paper.

2. Don't Obsess over Making Your Choice

Nobody really cares which choice you make (for example, whether you choose to support Laura or Palmer in the sample above). What's important is how well you support the choice you make. Generally, the alternatives are written to be pretty evenly matched, so there's no right or wrong answer—just a well-supported or ill-supported position.

Nobody Cares

The admissions officers don't care which alternative you choose; they care *how* you support your choice. Make your choice quickly.

3. Get Right to the Point

The first sentence should immediately offer a solid endorsement of one choice over the other. Assume that the reader is already familiar with the situation; there's no need to waste time describing the scenario and the alternatives.

4. Use a Clear, Simple Essay Format

Since all the essay topics have the same structure, you can decide in advance how you will structure your response. One possibility is the "winner/loser" format, in which the first paragraph begins with a statement of choice and then discusses the reason why your choice (the winner) is superior. The next paragraph focuses on why the other alternative (the loser) is not as good, and should end with a concluding sentence reaffirming your decision. Another possibility is the "according to the criteria" format, in which the first paragraph would discuss both the winner and the loser in light of the first criterion, and the second paragraph would discuss them both in light of the second criterion.

Whether you adopt one of these formats or use one of your own, the most important thing is that your essay be coherent, and not all over the map in its reasoning. The more organized your essay is, the more persuasive it will be.

No Points for Spontaneity

The writing sample structure is always the same. So, decide in advance exactly how you will structure your response. This will save you time and allow you to write your best possible essay.

5. Mention, but Downplay, the Loser's Strengths and the Winner's Weaknesses

Use sentence structures that allow you to do this, such as, "Even though Palmer won a prestigious national award . . ." and then attempt to demonstrate why this is really no big deal. This is an example of mentioning yet downplaying one of the loser's strengths. Try to do the same thing for at least one of the winner's obvious weaknesses. Doing so demonstrates that you see the full picture. Recognizing and dealing with possible objections makes your argument that much stronger.

6. Don't Simply Repeat Facts About the Candidates

Try instead to offer an interpretation of the facts in light of the stated criteria. If you're arguing for Laura in the topic above, you can't state simply that "Laura was named senior business and finance editor on the national business staff" and expect the reader to infer that that's a good thing. For all we know, being in that position may be a detriment when it comes to the criteria—training new writers and working under daily deadline pressure. It's up to you to indicate why certain facts about the winner are positive factors in light of the criteria, and vice versa for facts about the loser. Merely parroting what's written in the topic won't win you any points with the law schools.

7. Write Well

It sounds obvious, of course, but you should try to make your prose as clean and flawless as you can. Some people get so entangled in content that they neglect the mechanics of essay writing. But spelling, grammar, and writing mechanics are important. Use structural signals to keep your writing fluid and clear, and use transitions between paragraphs to keep the entire essay unified. Above all, write legibly. Nothing annoys essay readers more than an illegible essay.

Appearance Does Count

If you think your poor handwriting doesn't matter, think again. Readers are often prejudiced against writing that is difficult to decipher.

8. Budget Your Time Wisely

We suggest spending roughly five to seven minutes reading the topic, making a decision, and planning out your essay. As we suggested, use the scrap paper provided to jot down a quick outline of the points you intend to make. Then spend about 20 minutes writing the essay. This should be plenty of time; remember, we're only looking at two or three paragraphs at the most. This schedule will leave about three to five minutes at the end to proofread your essay for spelling and grammar.

A Note on Finishing

Before leaving the topic of the Writing Sample, we want to make one more important point: make sure you finish your essay. Some students find that time is called while they're still writing. Bad move. Not only does that leave you with an incomplete essay, it also hints to the admissions officers that your organization and time-management skills aren't stellar. So don't make this classic error. Give yourself plenty of time to finish the essay.

So, Clearly the Job Must Go To—

Don't get cut off. It's a mistake to leave your essay unfinished. Allocate several minutes at the end to review your essay.

Writing Sample DON'Ts and DOs

These important DON'Ts for your LSAT Writing Sample are based on comments from Kaplan teachers nationwide (who have read hundreds of these samples) as well from law school admissions personnel (who have read *thousands*). Don't make these mistakes:

DON'T start writing right away. Think and plan. By fairly universal agreement, the most impressive LSAT Writing Samples are the ones that show some forethought, notwithstanding the time constraints.

DON'T ask yourself, "Which one is the correct choice?" Each of the two alternatives is adequate. Your essay won't be better received if you choose one over another.

DON'T treat the criteria as hard-and-fast rules. They're guidelines. Be guided by them.

DON'T try to write a first draft; there just isn't enough time. You might want to swing a first draft of your opening sentence, however.

DON'T restate the situation, alternatives, and criteria in your introduction. Get right into your choice and the reasons behind it.

DON'T make unsupported assertions. Provide evidence for your claims.

DON'T quote text from the topic directly. Paraphrase it, so that you indicate that you have thought about the text and are trying to interpret it.

DON'T fail to discuss why the alternative you *didn't* choose isn't as good as the one you did choose.

DON'T play a fictional role. Any essay beginning, "Hello, I'm Douglas Brackman" or "Memo from: Perry Mason" isn't going to get read.

DON'T overuse first-person pronouns. While "I," "me," and "my" are certainly acceptable, the statement, "I think that Mrs. Jones should move to Morganville" is no different from "Mrs. Jones should move to Morganville," and is less concise besides.

DON'T make messy cross-outs. They create a bad first impression. Draw a single, clean line through any text you decide to excise.

DON'T use the "not only/but also" construction more than once in the essay, if you use it at all.

DON'T write over your own head. That is, don't strain to write in "legalese" or sound like William F. Buckley or Susan Sontag or Gore Vidal. Those people have dictionaries and thesauruses at hand, and hours to write and rewrite. You don't. Choose simple, everyday vocabulary and syntax with which you're comfortable.

DON'T become overly ambitious. A modest, well-planned, well-crafted 150 words or so is more impressive than a sprawling, disorganized, stream-of-consciousness "epic." Scale down your task to the thirty minutes you're given.

It's only right that we stop dwelling on the negative for a while, and give you some *positive* suggestions for your Writing Sample:

DO plan your essay carefully. Spend at least six minutes deciding what points you want to make and in which order.

DO use your scratch paper to jot down the points you want to raise, and number them so that you're working with at least a crude outline.

DO assume that your reader is familiar with the overall situation; the topic is there for him or her to consult if necessary.

DO start off with a clear statement of choice—no lengthy, tedious introductions!

DO make sure that each paragraph sticks to one main theme.

DO use keywords in making transitions. Such organizing words and phrases as "because," "therefore," "however," "moreover," "for one thing," and "finally" are no less useful to you than to the author of any Reading Comprehension passage. They are the hallmark of prose that is well thought out.

DO grant that the alternative you've chosen may not be 100 percent perfect, but try to explain away any weaknesses it might have.

DO keep referring to your notes as you write.

DO strive to sound objective and fair minded. Passion and sarcasm are hard to control in thirty minutes and may rub the reader the wrong way. (Besides, how emotionally involved are you in these topics, anyhow?)

DO give your essay at least a cursory, last-minute proof for blatant errors.

Sample Essay

At this point, you'll probably want to try your hand at writing an essay on the above-mentioned topic. Please do so (observing the 30-minute time limit, of course). Then check your essay, making sure it observes the basic principles outlined above.

> You are to write a brief essay on the topic below. You will have thirty minutes in which to plan and write. Read the topic carefully. You will most likely benefit from spending several minutes organizing your response and planning your essay before you begin to write. DO NOT WRITE ON A TOPIC OTHER THAN THE ONE GIVEN. WRITING ON A TOPIC OF YOUR OWN CHOOSING IS NOT ACCEPTABLE.
>
> There is no "correct" and "incorrect" answer to this question. Law schools are primarily interested to see how clearly and carefully you argue your position. No specialized knowledge is required. Schools are interested in the level of vocabulary, organization, and writing mechanics that you employ. They understand the time constraints and pressured condition under which you will write.
>
> Limit your writing to the lined area inside this booklet. You will have sufficient space in which to write if you plan your response carefully. Keep your handwriting and margins to a reasonable size. Do not skip spaces. Be sure to write legibly!

TOPIC

The *Daily Tribune,* a metropolitan newspaper, is considering two candidates for promotion to business editor. Write an argument for one candidate over the other with the following considerations in mind:

- The editor must train new writers and assign stories.
- The editor must be able to edit and rewrite stories under daily deadline pressure.

Laura received a B.A. in English from a large university. She was the managing editor of her college newspaper and served as a summer intern at her hometown daily paper. Laura starting working at the *Tribune* right out of college and spent three years at the city desk covering the city economy. Eight years ago the paper formed its business section and Laura became part of the new department. After several years covering state business, Laura began writing on the national economy. Three years ago, Laura was named senior business and finance editor on the national business staff; she is also responsible for supervising seven writers.

Palmer attended an elite private college where he earned both a B.S. in business administration and an M.A. in journalism. After receiving his journalism degree, Palmer worked for three years on a monthly business magazine. He won a prestigious national award for a series of articles on the impact of monetary policy on multinational corporations. Palmer came to the *Tribune* three years ago to fill the newly created position of international business writer. He was the only member of the international staff for two years and wrote on almost a daily basis. He now supervises a staff of four writers. Last year, Palmer developed a bimonthly business supplement for the *Tribune* that has proved highly popular and has helped increase the paper's circulation.

The following is a sample response to the essay topic above:

Both candidates are obviously qualified, but Laura is the better choice. For one thing, Laura has been working at the Tribune for 11 years, and has therefore had plenty of opportunity to learn the workings of the paper. For another, her experience has been in national rather than international business, and national business will certainly be the focus of the Tribune's financial coverage. In her current capacity, she is responsible for writing and editing articles while simultaneously overseeing the work of a staff of seven. Clearly, then, Laura can work under deadline pressure and manage a staff, a capability she demonstrated at an early age as the managing director of her college newspaper. Although Laura's academic credentials may not measure up to Palmer's, her background in English, her history of steady promotions, and her work as senior national business writer—combined with a solid business knowledge and obvious drive for accomplishment—will certainly spur the department to journalistic excellence.

Palmer's résumé is admirable but is nonetheless inferior to Laura's. True, Palmer has evidently done a fine job managing the international section, but his staff numbers only four, and the scope of the venture is smaller than Laura's. True, Palmer's articles on the impact of monetary policy did win an award in the past, but since he has been working for the Tribune, no such honors have been forthcoming. Not only does Palmer lack the English literature background that Laura has, but he also lacks her long experience at the Tribune. Furthermore, Palmer's editing experience seems slight, considering the length of his current tenure and the size of his staff, and while he demonstrates competence in the area of international business, he has little experience in the national business area.

In light of these circumstances, the newspaper would meet its stated objectives best by promoting Laura to the position of business editor.

This generally well-reasoned and well-written essay would be an asset to any applicant's law school admissions file. The writer states his choice in the first sentence and then substantiates this choice in a paragraph on the winner and a paragraph on the loser. Notice the way this writer acknowledges, yet rebuts, the winner's flaws and the loser's strengths. Whether or not one agrees with the choice of Laura over Palmer, the essay definitely makes a strong, well-reasoned case for the choice—and that, after all, is what the law schools want to see.

CHAPTER 7

Putting It All Together

Wow. We've covered a lot. We first looked at why you need to take the LSAT, its structure, the proper mindset required to master the test, and some strategies for managing each of the sections. Then we discussed in depth the content that makes up each specific section of the LSAT and we focused on the strategies and techniques you'll need for each question, game, and passage. In short, we gave you an overview, then broke down the test into manageable pieces so that you could learn to apply Kaplan's proven strategies.

It's now time to recombine everything you've learned into a powerful set of strategies that you can use to ace the LSAT. Let's begin with the often overlooked—but extremely important—topic of test mentality.

The Four Basics of Good Test Mentality

We've armed you with all of the strategies you'll need to do well on the LSAT. But you must wield those weapons with the right frame of mind and in the right spirit. This involves taking a certain stance toward the entire test. Here's what's involved:

- test awareness
- stamina
- confidence
- the right attitude

The LSAT Mindset Revisited

What makes for good test mentality?

- test awareness
- stamina
- confidence
- the right attitude

Test Awareness

To do your best on the LSAT, you must always keep in mind that the test is like no other test you've taken before, both in terms of content and in terms of scoring. If you took a test in high school or college and got a quarter of the questions wrong, you would probably receive a pretty lousy grade. But on the LSAT, you can get a quarter of the questions wrong (about 25) and still score higher than the

Nobody's Perfect

Remember that the LSAT is unlike any other test you've taken. You can miss a lot of questions and still get a great score. So, on the day of the test, don't get rattled if you blow some questions or even an entire section.

eightieth percentile! The test is geared so that only the very best test takers are able to finish every section. But even these people rarely get every question right. As mentioned earlier, you can get a "perfect" score of 180 and still get a handful of questions wrong.

What does this mean for you? Well, just as you shouldn't let one bad game or passage ruin an entire section, you shouldn't let what you consider to be a below par performance on one section ruin your performance on the entire test. A substandard performance on one single section will not by itself spoil your score. However, if you allow that poor section to rattle you, it can have a cumulative negative effect, setting in motion a downward spiral. It's the kind of thing that could potentially do serious damage to your score. Losing a few extra points won't do you in, but losing your head will.

Remember, if you feel you've done poorly on a section, don't sweat it. Who knows, it could be the experimental. And even if it's not, chances are it's just a difficult section—a factor that will already be figured into the scoring curve anyway. The point is, you must remain calm and collected. Simply do your best on each section, and once a section is over, forget about it and move on.

While we're on the topic of the experimental section, we'd like to reiterate an important point. *Never, never try to figure out which section is unscored.* This practice has caused trouble for countless test takers. They somehow convince themselves that a certain section is the one that doesn't count, and then don't take it seriously. And they're pretty upset when they find out they guessed wrong. You can't know which section is the experimental section, so handle each section as if it counts. That way, you're covered no matter what. If a section you had trouble with turns out to be experimental, it's gravy. If it turns out to be scored—well, think how much worse you'd have done if you blew it off entirely.

Stamina

The LSAT is a fairly grueling experience, and some test takers simply run out of gas before it's over. To avoid this, take full-length practice tests in the week or two before the test. That way, five sections plus a writing sample will seem like a breeze (well, maybe not a breeze, but at least not a hurricane).

Get Tough

You wouldn't run a marathon without working on your stamina would you? And the LSAT lasts longer than it takes to run a marathon! So, build your stamina.

We've given you two full-length, real LSATs (with explanations) in this book. These offer a great opportunity for you to build your endurance for the test. If you want additional practice you should buy PrepTests, which are the actual released exams published by Law Services. These are the same type of exam as those that appear in this book. The available PrepTests are listed in the *LSAT Registration and Information Book,* which is available at most colleges and law schools as well as Kaplan centers, or directly from Law Services at (215) 968-1001. (Try to order them early, since delivery takes two to three weeks.)

Another option, if you have some time, would be to take the full Kaplan course. We'll give you access to every released test plus loads of additional material, so you can really build up your LSAT stamina. As a bonus, you'll also have the benefit of our expert live instruction in every aspect of the LSAT. Call 1-800-KAP-TEST for the Kaplan Center location near you.

Confidence

Confidence feeds on itself, and unfortunately, so does self-doubt. Confidence in your ability leads to quick, sure answers and a sense of well-being that translates into more points. If you lack confidence, you end up reading sentences and answer choices two, three, or four times, to the point where you confuse yourself and get off track. This leads to timing difficulties, which only perpetuate the downward spiral, causing anxiety and a tendency to rush in order to finish sections.

If you subscribe to the LSAT mindset we've described, however, you'll gear all of your practice toward the major goal of taking control of the test. When you've achieved that goal—armed with the principles, techniques, strategies, and methods set forth in this book—you'll be ready to face the LSAT with supreme confidence. And that's the one sure way to score your best on the day of the test.

The Right Attitude

Those who approach the LSAT as an obstacle, and who rail against the necessity of taking it, usually don't fare as well as those who see the LSAT as an opportunity to show off the reading and reasoning skills that the law schools are looking for. Those who look forward to doing battle with the LSAT—or, at least, who enjoy the opportunity to distinguish themselves from the rest of the applicant pack—tend to score better than those who resent or dread it.

Develop an Attitude
Your attitude really does affect your performance. We've given you everything you need. Approach the test with confidence.

It may sound a little dubious, but take our word for it: attitude adjustment is a proven test-taking technique. Here are a few steps you can take to make sure you develop the right LSAT attitude:

- Look at the LSAT as a challenge, but try not to obsess over it; you certainly don't want to psyche yourself out of the game.
- Remember that, yes, the LSAT is important, but this one test will not single-handedly determine the outcome of your life.
- Try to have fun with the test. Learning how to match your wits against the test makers can be a very satisfying experience, and the reading and thinking skills you'll acquire will benefit you in law school as well as in your future legal career.
- Remember that you're more prepared than most people. You've trained with Kaplan. You have the tools you need, plus the know-how to use those tools.

The first year of law school is a frenzied experience for most law students. In order to meet the requirements of a rigorous work schedule, they either learn to prioritize and budget their time or else fall hopelessly behind. It's no surprise, then, that the LSAT, the test specifically designed to predict success in the first year of law school, is a time-intensive test, demanding excellent time-management skills as well as that *sine qua non* of the successful lawyer—grace under pressure.

Strategy Review

Let's recap the most important global principles and strategies for success on the LSAT.

- Attack the questions in any order that strikes you as logical.
- Learn to recognize and seek out questions you're good at.
- Know that the test questions are written to different levels of difficulty
- Control time instead of letting time control you

Answer Grid Expertise

An important part of LSAT test expertise is knowing how to handle the answer grid. After all, you not only have to pick the right answers; you also have to mark those right answers on the answer grid in an efficient and accurate way. It sounds simple but it's extremely important: don't make mistakes filling out your answer grid! When time is short, it's easy to get confused going back and forth between your test book and your grid. If you know the answer, but misgrid, you won't get the points. Here are a few methods of avoiding mistakes on the answer grid.

Always Circle Questions You Skip

Circle in your test book the number of any question you skip (you may even want to circle the whole question itself). When you go back, such questions will then be easy to locate. Also, if you accidentally skip a box on the grid, you can more easily check your grid against your book to see where you went wrong.

Always Circle Answers You Choose

Circle the correct answers in your test booklet, but don't transfer the answers to the grid right away. That wastes too much time, especially if you're doing a lot of skipping around. Circling your answers in the test book will also make it easier to check your grid against your book.

Grid Five or More Answers at Once

Don't transfer your answers to the grid after every question. Transfer your answers after every four to eight questions (about two pages) for Logical Reasoning, at the end of each Reading Comp passage, and after you've finished each Logic Game.

Transferring your answers one at a time is more time consuming than transferring them in blocks. Transferring your answers in a group also reduces the chance that you'll misgrid. Finally, transferring your answers one at a time interrupts your concentration. You'll save time and improve accuracy. Just make sure you're not left at the end of the section with ungridded answers!

Save Time at the End for a Final Grid Check

Leave enough time at the end of every section to make sure you've got an oval filled in for each question in the section. Remember, a blank grid has no chance of earning a point, but a guess does.

What's Next

You are now ready to apply what you've learned to the two real LSATs.

SECTION TWO

Two Real LSATs

How to Take These Tests

The best way for you to use the two real LSATs in this book is to take the tests one at a time. Take the first real LSAT under testlike conditions, then spend several hours carefully reviewing it. After working through Kaplan's exclusive explanations, review the appropriate chapters in this book to relearn or refine your test-taking skills before you tackle the second test. Repeat the process with the second test: take the test under simulated conditions, read through the Kaplan explanations, then review chapters as necessary.

When you're ready to take one of the tests, find a quiet place where you can work uninterrupted for about two and a half hours. Don't have anything on your desk except for a watch, this book, and some pencils. You can't use a ball-point pen or scratch paper on test day, so try to simulate testing conditions by keeping your desk clear.

Both real LSATs include four sections. Keep in mind that on the actual LSAT, there will be an additional multiple-choice section—the experimental section—that will not contribute to your score, plus an unscored writing sample.

Use the grid that precedes each test to record you answers. This will allow you to practice gridding. Once you've started a test, don't stop until you've worked through all four sections. It's OK to take a short break (no more than five minutes) between the third and fourth sections as you will also get a short break on the day of the test. But, make sure you take all four sections in the same sitting. That way, you'll get the most out of the experience. Remember, you can review your work within a section, but you may not change sections.

The answer key and explanations follow each test. Read the explanation for every question, even the ones you get right. For each question, make sure you understand why the right answer is right and why the wrong answers are wrong, but don't stop there. After all, the questions on these tests will not appear on *your* LSAT. However, the concepts tested on these LSATs will be the same concepts tested on your LSAT.

The key to your preparation is to learn those concepts. Don't obsess over your performance on particular questions. Instead, use each practice question to help you prepare for similar questions that you will face on the day of the test. To help you identify the principles that each question has to teach, we've included strategy points after every question explanation. These strategy points tell you, in a nutshell, the "lesson" that we can learn from that question. Use the strategy points to help you learn the concepts and techniques that will lead to a higher score on the day of the test.

After you read the explanations, you should review chapters as necessary to relearn or refine your strategies.

We've given you everything you need to succeed. Good luck.

Real LSAT 1

Answer Sheet

MARK ONE AND ONLY ONE ANSWER TO EACH QUESTION. BE SURE TO FILL IN COMPLETELY THE SPACE FOR YOUR INTENDED ANSWER CHOICE. IF YOU ERASE, DO SO COMPLETELY. MAKE NO STRAY MARKS.

	SECTION 1	SECTION 2	SECTION 3	SECTION 4
1	A B C D E	A B C D E	A B C D E	A B C D E
2	A B C D E	A B C D E	A B C D E	A B C D E
3	A B C D E	A B C D E	A B C D E	A B C D E
4	A B C D E	A B C D E	A B C D E	A B C D E
5	A B C D E	A B C D E	A B C D E	A B C D E
6	A B C D E	A B C D E	A B C D E	A B C D E
7	A B C D E	A B C D E	A B C D E	A B C D E
8	A B C D E	A B C D E	A B C D E	A B C D E
9	A B C D E	A B C D E	A B C D E	A B C D E
10	A B C D E	A B C D E	A B C D E	A B C D E
11	A B C D E	A B C D E	A B C D E	A B C D E
12	A B C D E	A B C D E	A B C D E	A B C D E
13	A B C D E	A B C D E	A B C D E	A B C D E
14	A B C D E	A B C D E	A B C D E	A B C D E
15	A B C D E	A B C D E	A B C D E	A B C D E
16	A B C D E	A B C D E	A B C D E	A B C D E
17	A B C D E	A B C D E	A B C D E	A B C D E
18	A B C D E	A B C D E	A B C D E	A B C D E
19	A B C D E	A B C D E	A B C D E	A B C D E
20	A B C D E	A B C D E	A B C D E	A B C D E
21	A B C D E	A B C D E	A B C D E	A B C D E
22	A B C D E	A B C D E	A B C D E	A B C D E
23	A B C D E	A B C D E	A B C D E	A B C D E
24	A B C D E	A B C D E	A B C D E	A B C D E
25	A B C D E	A B C D E	A B C D E	A B C D E
26	A B C D E	A B C D E	A B C D E	A B C D E
27	A B C D E	A B C D E	A B C D E	A B C D E
28	A B C D E	A B C D E	A B C D E	A B C D E
29	A B C D E	A B C D E	A B C D E	A B C D E
30	A B C D E	A B C D E	A B C D E	A B C D E

General Directions for the LSAT Answer Sheet

The actual testing time for this portion of the test will be two hours and 20 minutes. There are four sections, each with a time limit of 35 minutes. The supervisor will tell you when to begin and end each section. If you finish a section before time is called, you may check your work on that section only; do not turn to any other section of the test book and do not work on any other section either in the test book or on the answer sheet.

There are several different types of questions on the test, and each question type has its own directions. Be sure you understand the directions for each question type before attempting to answer any questions in that section.

Not everyone will finish all the questions in the time allowed. Do not hurry, but work steadily and as quickly as you can without sacrificing accuracy. You are advised to use your time effectively. If a question seems too difficult, go on to the next one and return to the difficult question after completing the section. MARK THE BEST ANSWER YOU CAN FOR EVERY QUESTION. NO DEDUCTIONS WILL BE MADE FOR WRONG ANSWERS. YOUR SCORE WILL BE BASED ONLY ON THE NUMBER OF QUESTIONS YOU ANSWER CORRECTLY.

ALL YOUR ANSWERS MUST BE MARKED ON THE ANSWER SHEET. Answer spaces for each question are lettered to correspond with the letters of the potential answers to each question in the test book. After you have decided which of the answers is correct, blacken the corresponding space on the answer sheet. BE SURE THAT EACH MARK IS BLACK AND COMPLETELY FILLS THE ANSWER SPACE. Give only one answer to each question. If you change an answer, be sure that all previous marks are erased completely. Since the answer sheet is machine scored, incomplete erasures may be interpreted as intended answers. ANSWERS RECORDED IN THE TEST BOOK WILL NOT BE SCORED.

There may be more questions noted on this answer sheet than there are questions in a section. Do not be concerned but be certain that the section and number of the question you are answering matches the answer sheet section and question number. Additional answer spaces in any answer sheet section should be left blank. Begin your next section in the number one answer space for that section.

SECTION I

Time—35 minutes

24 Questions

Directions: The questions in this section are based on the reasoning contained in brief statements or passages. For some questions, more than one of the choices could conceivably answer the question. However, you are to choose the best answer; that is, the response that most accurately and completely answers the question. You should not make assumptions that are by commonsense standards implausible, superfluous, or incompatible with the passage. After you have chosen the best answer, blacken the corresponding space on your answer sheet.

1. Rita: The original purpose of government farm-subsidy programs was to provide income stability for small family farmers, but most farm-subsidy money goes to a few farmers with large holdings. Payments to farmers whose income, before subsidies, is greater than $100,000 a year should be stopped.

   Thomas: It would be impossible to administer such a cutoff point. Subsidies are needed during the planting and growing season, but farmers do not know their income for a given calendar year until tax returns are calculated and submitted the following April.

   Which one of the following, if true, is the strongest counter Rita can make to Thomas' objection?

   (A) It has become difficult for small farmers to obtain bank loans to be repaid later by money from subsidies.
   (B) Having such a cutoff point would cause some farmers whose income would otherwise exceed $100,00 to reduce their plantings.
   (C) The income of a farmer varies because weather and market prices are not stable from year to year.
   (D) If subsidy payments to large farmers were eliminated, the financial condition of the government would improve.
   (E) Subsidy cutoffs can be determined on the basis of income for the preceding year.

2. Modern physicians often employ laboratory tests, in addition to physical examinations, in order to diagnose diseases accurately. Insurance company regulations that deny coverage for certain laboratory tests therefore decrease the quality of medical care provided to patients.

   Which one of the following is an assumption that would serve to justify the conclusion above?

   (A) Physical examinations and the uncovered laboratory tests together provide a more accurate diagnosis of many diseases than do physical examinations alone.
   (B) Many physicians generally oppose insurance company regulations that, in order to reduce costs, limit the use of laboratory tests.
   (C) Many patients who might benefit from the uncovered laboratory tests do not have any form of health insurance.
   (D) There are some illnesses that experienced physicians can diagnose accurately from physical examination alone.
   (E) Laboratory tests are more costly to perform than are physical examinations.

3. Oil analysts predict that if the price of oil falls by half, the consumer's purchase price for gasoline made from this oil will also fall by half.

   Which one of the following, if true, would cast the most serious doubt on the prediction made by the oil analysts?

   (A) Improved automobile technology and new kinds of fuel for cars have enabled some drivers to use less gasoline.
   (B) Gasoline manufacturers will not expand their profit margins.
   (C) There are many different gasoline companies that compete with each other to provide the most attractive price to consumers.
   (D) Studies in several countries show that the amount of gasoline purchased by consumers initially rises after the price of gasoline has fallen.
   (E) Refining costs, distribution costs, and taxes, none of which varies significantly with oil prices, constitute a large portion of the price of gasoline.

GO ON TO THE NEXT PAGE.

1 1 1 1 1 1 1 1 1 1

4. A survey was recently conducted among ferry passengers on the North Sea. Among the results was this: more of those who had taken anti-seasickness medication before their trip reported symptoms of seasickness than those who had not taken such medication. It is clear, then, that despite claims by drug companies that clinical tests show the contrary, people would be better off not taking anti-seasickness medications.

   Which one of the following, if true, would most weaken the conclusion above?

   (A) Given rough enough weather, most ferry passengers will have some symptoms of seasickness.
   (B) The clinical tests reported by the drug companies were conducted by the drug companies' staffs.
   (C) People who do not take anti-seasickness medication are just as likely to respond to a survey on seasickness as people who do.
   (D) The seasickness symptoms of the people who took anti-seasickness medication would have been more severe had they not taken the medication.
   (E) People who have spent money on anti-seasickness medication are less likely to admit symptoms of seasickness than those who have not.

5. Economic considerations color every aspect of international dealings, and nations are just like individuals in that the lender sets the terms of its dealings with the borrower. That is why a nation that owes money to another nation cannot be a world leader.

   The reasoning in the passage assumes which one of the following?

   (A) A nation that does not lend to any other nation cannot be a world leader.
   (B) A nation that can set the terms of its dealings with other nations is certain to be a world leader.
   (C) A nation that has the terms of its dealings with another nation set by that nation cannot be a world leader.
   (D) A nation that is a world leader can borrow from another nation as long as that other nation does not set the terms of the dealings between the two nations.
   (E) A nation that has no dealings with any other nation cannot be a world leader.

Questions 6–7

Rotelle: You are too old to address effectively the difficult issues facing the country, such as nuclear power, poverty, and pollution.

Sims: I don't want to make age an issue in this campaign, so I will not comment on your youth and inexperience.

6. Sims does which one of the following?

   (A) demonstrates that Rotelle's claim is incorrect
   (B) avoids mentioning the issue of age
   (C) proposes a way to decide which issues are important
   (D) shows that Rotelle's statement is self-contradictory
   (E) fails to respond directly to Rotelle's claim

7. Rotelle is committed to which one of the following?

   (A) Many old people cannot effectively address the difficult issues facing the country.
   (B) Those at least as old as Sims are the only people who cannot effectively address the difficult issues facing the country.
   (C) Some young people can effectively address the difficult issues facing the country.
   (D) If anyone can effectively address the difficult issues facing the country, that person must younger than Sims.
   (E) Addressing the difficult issues facing the country requires an understanding of young people's points of view.

GO ON TO THE NEXT PAGE.

8. Political theorist: The chief foundations of all governments are the legal system and the police force; and as there cannot be a good legal system where the police are not well paid, it follows that where the police are well paid there will be a good legal system.

The reasoning in the argument is not sound because it fails to establish that

(A) many governments with bad legal systems have poorly paid police forces
(B) bad governments with good legal systems must have poorly paid police forces
(C) a well-paid police force cannot be effective without a good legal system
(D) a well-paid police force is sufficient to guarantee a good legal system
(E) some bad governments had a good legal systems.

9. Court records from medieval France show that in the years 1300 to 1400 the number of people arrested in the French realm for "violent interpersonal crimes" (not committed in wars) increased by 30 percent over the number of people arrested for such crimes in the years 1200 to 1300. If the increase was not the result of false arrests, therefore, medieval France had a higher level of documented interpersonal violence in the years 1300 to 1400 than in the years 1200 to 1300.

Which one of the following statements, if true, most seriously weakens the argument?

(A) In the years 1300 to 1400 the French government's category of violent crimes included an increasing variety of interpersonal crimes that are actually nonviolent.
(B) Historical accounts by monastic chroniclers in the years 1300 to 1400 are filled with descriptions of violent attacks committed by people living in the French realm.
(C) The number of individual agreements between two people in which they swore oaths not to attack each other increased substantially after 1300.
(D) When English armies tried to conquer parts of France in the mid- to late 1300s, violence in the northern province of Normandy and the southwestern province of Gascony increased.
(E) The population of medieval France increased substantially during the first five decades of the 1300s, until the deadly bubonic plague decimated the population of France after 1348.

10. *Rhizobium* bacteria living in the roots of bean plants or other legumes produce fixed nitrogen, which is one of the essential plant nutrients and which for nonlegume crops, such as wheat, normally must be supplied by applications of nitrogen-based fertilizer. So if biotechnology succeeds in producing wheat strains whose roots will play host to *Rhizobium* bacteria, the need for artificial fertilizers will be reduced.

The argument above makes which one of the following assumptions?

(A) Biotechnology should be directed toward producing plants that do not require artificial fertilizer.
(B) Fixed nitrogen is currently the only soil nutrient that must be supplied by artificial fertilizer for growing wheat crops.
(C) There are no naturally occurring strains of wheat or other grasses that have *Rhizobium* bacteria living in their roots.
(D) Legumes are currently the only crops that produce their own supply of fixed nitrogen.
(E) *Rhizobium* bacteria living in the roots of wheat would produce fixed nitrogen.

11. Current legislation that requires designated sections for smokers and nonsmokers on the premises of privately owned businesses is an intrusion into the private sector that cannot be justified. The fact that studies indicate that nonsmokers might be harmed by inhaling the smoke from others' cigarettes is not the main issue. Rather, the main issue concerns the government's violation of the right of private businesses to determine their own policies and rules.

Which one of the following is a principle that, if accepted, could enable the conclusion to be properly drawn?

(A) Government intrusion into the policies and rules of private businesses is justified only when individuals might be harmed.
(B) The right of individuals to breathe safe air supersedes the right of businesses to be free from government intrusion.
(C) The right of businesses to self-determination overrides whatever right or duty the government may have to protect the individual.
(D) It is the duty of private businesses to protect employees from harm in the workplace.
(E) Where the rights of businesses and the duty of government conflict, the main issue is finding a successful compromise.

GO ON TO THE NEXT PAGE.

12. Leachate is a solution, frequently highly contaminated, that develops when water permeates a landfill site. If and only if the landfill's capacity to hold liquids is exceeded does the leachate escape into the environment, generally in unpredictable quantities. A method must be found for disposing of leachate. Most landfill leachate is sent directly to sewage treatment plants, but not all sewage plants are capable of handling the highly contaminated water.

    Which one of the following can be inferred from the passage?

    (A) The ability to predict the volume of escaping landfill leachate would help solve the disposal problem.
    (B) If any water permeates a landfill, leachate will escape into the environment.
    (C) No sewage treatment plants are capable of handling leachate.
    (D) Some landfill leachate is sent to sewage treatment plants that are incapable of handling it.
    (E) If leachate does not escape from a landfill into the environment, then the landfill's capacity to hold liquids has not been exceeded.

13. The soaring prices of scholarly and scientific journals have forced academic libraries used only by academic researchers to drastically reduce their list of subscriptions. Some have suggested that in each academic discipline subscription decisions should be determined solely by a journal's usefulness in that discipline, measured by the frequency with which it is cited in published writings by researchers in the discipline.

    Which one of the following, if true, most seriously calls into question the suggestion described above?

    (A) The nonacademic readership of a scholarly or scientific journal can be accurately gauged by the number of times articles appearing in it are cited in daily newspapers and popular magazines.
    (B) The average length of a journal article in some sciences, such as physics, is less than half the average length of a journal article in some other academic disciplines, such as history.
    (C) The increasingly expensive scholarly journals are less and less likely to be available to the general public from nonacademic public libraries.
    (D) Researchers often will not cite a journal article that has influenced their work if they think that the journal in which it appears is not highly regarded by the leading researchers in the mainstream of the discipline.
    (E) In some academic disciplines, controversies that begin in the pages of one journal spill over into articles in other journals that are widely read by researchers in the discipline.

14. The average level of fat in the blood of people suffering from acute cases of disease W is lower than the average level for the population as a whole. Nevertheless, most doctors believe that reducing blood-fat levels is an effective way of preventing acute W.

    Which one of the following, if true, does most to justify this apparently paradoxical belief?

    (A) The blood level of fat for patients who have been cured of W is on average the same as that for the population at large.
    (B) Several of the symptoms characteristic of acute W have been produced in laboratory animals fed large doses of a synthetic fat substitute, though acute W itself has not been produced in this way.
    (C) The progression from latent to acute W can occur only when the agent that causes acute W absorbs large quantities of fat from the patient's blood.
    (D) The levels of fat in the blood of patients who have disease W respond abnormally slowly to changes in dietary intake of fat.
    (E) High levels of fat in the blood are indicative of several diseases that are just as serious as W.

15. Baking for winter holidays is a tradition that may have a sound medical basis. In midwinter, when days are short, many people suffer from a specific type of seasonal depression caused by lack of sunlight. Carbohydrates, both sugars and starches, boost the brain's levels of serotonin, a neurotransmitter that improves the mood. In this respect, carbohydrates act on the brain in the same way as some antidepressants. Thus, eating holiday cookies may provide an effective form of self-prescribed medication.

    Which one of the following can be properly inferred from the passage?

    (A) Seasonal depression is one of the most easily treated forms of depression.
    (B) Lack of sunlight lowers the level of serotonin in the brain.
    (C) People are more likely to be depressed in midwinter than at other times of the year.
    (D) Some antidepressants act by changing the brain's level of serotonin.
    (E) Raising the level of neurotransmitters in the brain effectively relieves depression.

GO ON TO THE NEXT PAGE.

16. The current proposal to give college students a broader choice in planning their own courses of study should be abandoned. The students who are supporting the proposal will never be satisfied, no matter what requirements are established. Some of these students have reached their third year without declaring a major. One first-year student has failed to complete four required courses. Several others have indicated a serious indifference to grades and intellectual achievement.

    A flaw in the argument is that it does which one of the following?

    (A) avoids the issue by focusing on supporters of the proposal
    (B) argues circularly by assuming the conclusion is true in stating the premises
    (C) fails to define the critical term "satisfied"
    (D) distorts the proposal advocated by opponents
    (E) uses the term "student" equivocally

GO ON TO THE NEXT PAGE.

Questions 17–18

The question whether intelligent life exists elsewhere in the universe is certainly imprecise, because we are not sure how different from us something might be and still count as "intelligent life." Yet we cannot just decide to define "intelligent life" in some more precise way since it is likely that we will find and recognize intelligent life elsewhere in the universe only if we leave our definitions open to new, unimagined possibilities.

17. The argument can most reasonably be interpreted as an objection to which one of the following claims?

(A) The questions whether intelligent life exists elsewhere in the universe is one that will never be correctly answered.
(B) Whether or not there is intelligent life elsewhere in the universe, our understanding of intelligent life is limited.
(C) The question about the existence of intelligent life elsewhere in the universe must be made more precise if we hope to answer it correctly.
(D) The question whether there is intelligent life elsewhere in the universe is so imprecise as to be meaningless.
(E) The question whether there is intelligent life elsewhere in the universe is one we should not spend our time trying to answer.

18. The passage, if seen as an objection to an antecedent claim, challenges that claim by

(A) showing the claim to be irrelevant to the issue at hand
(B) citing examples that fail to fit a proposed definition of "intelligent life"
(C) claiming that "intelligent life" cannot be adequately defined
(D) arguing that the claim, if acted on, would be counterproductive
(E) maintaining that the claim is not supported by the available evidence

19. The efficiency of microwave ovens in destroying the harmful bacteria frequently found in common foods is diminished by the presence of salt in the food being cooked. When heated in a microwave oven, the interior of unsalted food reaches temperatures high enough to kill bacteria that cause food poisoning, but the interior of salted food does not. Scientists theorize that salt effectively blocks the microwaves from heating the interior.

Which one of the following conclusions is most supported by the information above?

(A) The kinds of bacteria that cause food poisoning are more likely to be found on the exterior of food than in the interior of food.
(B) The incidence of serious food poisoning would be significantly reduced if microwave ovens were not used by consumers to cook or reheat food.
(C) The addition of salt to food that has been cooked or reheated in a microwave oven can increase the danger of food poisoning.
(D) The danger of food poisoning can be lessened if salt is not used to prepare foods that are to be cooked in a microwave oven.
(E) Salt is the primary cause of food poisoning resulting from food that is heated in microwave ovens.

GO ON TO THE NEXT PAGE.

20. Pamela: Business has an interest in enabling employees to care for children, because those children will be the customers, employees, and managers of the future. Therefore, businesses should adopt policies, such as day-care benefits, that facilitate parenting.

Lee: No individual company, though, will be patronized, staffed, and managed only by its own employees' children, so it would not be to a company's advantage to provide such benefits to employees when other companies do not.

In which one of the following pairs consisting of argument and objection does the objection function most similarly to the way Lee's objection functions in relation to Pamela's argument?

(A) New roads will not serve to relieve this area's traffic congestion, because new roads would encourage new construction and generate additional traffic.
Objection: Failure to build new roads would mean that traffic congestion would strangle the area even earlier.

(B) Humanity needs clean air to breathe, so each person should make an effort to avoid polluting the air.
Objection: The air one person breathes is affected mainly by pollution caused by others, so it makes no sense to act alone to curb air pollution.

(C) Advertised discounts on products draw customers' attention to the products, so advertised discounts benefit sales.
Objection: Customers already planning to purchase accelerate buying to take advantage of advertised discounts, and thus subsequent sales suffer.

(D) If people always told lies, then no one would know what the truth was, so people should always tell the truth.
Objection: If people always told lies, then everyone would know that the truth was the opposite of what was said.

(E) Human social institutions have always changed, so, even if we do not know what those changes will be, we do know that the social institutions of the future will differ from those of the past.
Objection: The existence of change in the past does not ensure that there will always be change in the future.

21. Pedro: Unlike cloth diapers, disposable diapers are a threat to the environment. Sixteen billion disposable diapers are discarded annually, filling up landfills at an alarming rate. So people must stop buying disposable diapers and use cloth diapers.

Maria: But you forget cloth diapers must be washed in hot water, which requires energy. Moreover, the resulting wastewater pollutes our rivers. When families use diaper services, diapers must be delivered by fuel-burning trucks that pollute the air and add to traffic congestion.

Maria objects to Pedro's argument by

(A) claiming that Pedro overstates the negative evidence about disposable diapers in the course of his argument in favor of cloth diapers

(B) indicating that Pedro draws a hasty conclusion, based on inadequate evidence about cloth diapers

(C) pointing out that there is an ambiguous use of the word "disposable" in Pedro's argument

(D) demonstrating that cloth diapers are a far more serious threat to the environment than disposable diapers are

(E) suggesting that the economic advantages of cloth diapers outweigh whatever environmental damage they may cause

GO ON TO THE NEXT PAGE.

22. In an experiment, two-year-old boys and their fathers made pie dough together using rolling pins and other utensils. Each father-son pair used a rolling pin that was distinctively different from those used by the other father-son pairs, and each father repeated the phrase "rolling pin" each time his son used it. But when the children were asked to identify all of the rolling pins among a group of kitchen utensils that included several rolling pins, each child picked only the one that he had used.

    Which one of the following inferences is most supported by the information above?

    (A) The children did not grasp the function of a rolling pin.
    (B) No two children understood the name "rolling pin" to apply to the same object.
    (C) The children understood that all rolling pins have the same general shape.
    (D) Each child was able to identify correctly only the utensils that he had used.
    (E) The children were not able to distinguish the rolling pins they used from other rolling pins.

23. When 100 people who have not used cocaine are tested for cocaine use, on average only five will test positive. By contrast, of every 100 people who have used cocaine, 99 will test positive. Thus, when a randomly chosen group of people is tested for cocaine use, the vast majority of those who test positive will be people who have used cocaine.

    A reasoning error in the argument is that the argument

    (A) attempts to infer a value judgment from purely factual premises
    (B) attributes to every member of the population the properties of the average member of the population
    (C) fails to take into account what proportion of the population have used cocaine
    (D) ignores the fact that some cocaine users do not test positive
    (E) advocates testing people for cocaine use when there is no reason to suspect that they have used cocaine.

GO ON TO THE NEXT PAGE.

24. If a society encourages freedom of thought and expression, then, during the time when it does so, creativity will flourish in that society. In the United States creativity flourished during the eighteenth century. It is clear, therefore, that freedom of thought was encouraged in the United States during the eighteenth century.

    An error of reasoning of the same kind as one contained in the passage is present in each of the following arguments EXCEPT:

    (A) According to the airline industry, airfares have to rise if air travel is to be made safer; since airfares were just raised, we can rest assured that air travel will therefore become safer.
    (B) We can conclude that the Hillside police department has improved its efficiency, because crime rates are down in Hillside, and it is an established fact that crime rates go down when police departments increase their efficiency.
    (C) People who are really interested in the preservation of wildlife obviously do not go hunting for big game; since Gerda has never gone hunting for big game and intends never to do so, it is clear that she is really interested in the preservation of wildlife.
    (D) If the contents of a bottle are safe to drink, the bottle will not be marked "poison," so, since the bottle is not marked "poison," its contents will be safe to drink.
    (E) None of the so-called Western democracies is really democratic, because, for a country to be democratic, the opinion of each of its citizens must have a meaningful effect on government, and in none of these countries does each citizen's opinion have such an effect.

S T O P

IF YOU FINISH BEFORE TIME IS CALLED, YOU MAY CHECK YOUR WORK ON THIS SECTION ONLY.
DO NOT WORK ON ANY OTHER SECTION IN THE TEST.

SECTION II

Time—35 minutes
27 Questions

Directions: Each passage in this section is followed by a group of questions to be answered on the basis of what is stated or implied in the passage. For some of the questions, more than one of the choices could conceivably answer the question. However, you are to choose the best answer; that is, the response that most accurately and completely answers the question, and blacken the corresponding space on your answer sheet.

The extent of a nation's power over its coastal ecosystems and the natural resources in its coastal waters has been defined by two international law doctrines: freedom of the seas and adjacent state sovereignty. Until the mid-twentieth century, most nations favored application of broad open-seas freedoms and limited sovereign rights over coastal waters. A nation had the right to include within its territorial dominion only a very narrow band of coastal waters (generally extending three miles from the shoreline), within which it had the authority, but not the responsibility, to regulate all activities. But, because this area of territorial dominion was so limited, most nations did not establish rules for management or protection of their territorial waters.

Regardless of whether or not nations enforced regulations in their territorial waters, large ocean areas remained free of controls or restrictions. The citizens of all nations had the right to use these unrestricted ocean areas for any innocent purpose, including navigation and fishing. Except for controls over its own citizens, no nation had the responsibility, let alone the unilateral authority, to control such activities in international waters. And, since there were few standards of conduct that applied on the "open seas," there were few jurisdictional conflicts between nations.

The lack of standards is traceable to popular perceptions held before the middle of this century. By and large, marine pollution was not perceived as a significant problem, in part because the adverse effect of coastal activities on ocean ecosystems was not widely recognized, and pollution caused by human activities was generally believed to be limited to that caused by navigation. Moreover, the freedom to fish, or overfish, was an essential element of the traditional legal doctrine of freedom of the seas that no maritime country wished to see limited. And finally, the technology that later allowed exploitation of other ocean resources, such as oil, did not yet exist.

To date, controlling pollution and regulating ocean resources have still not been comprehensively addressed by law, but international law—established through the customs and practices of nations—does not preclude such efforts. And two recent developments may actually lead to future international rules providing for ecosystem management. First, the establishment of extensive fishery zones, extending territorial authority as far as 200 miles out from a country's coast, has provided the opportunity for nations individually to manage larger ecosystems. This opportunity, combined with national self-interest in maintaining fish populations, could lead nations to reevaluate policies for management of their fisheries and to address the problem of pollution in territorial waters. Second, the international community is beginning to understand the importance of preserving the resources and ecology of international waters and to show signs of accepting responsibility for doing so. As an international consensus regarding the need for comprehensive management of ocean resources develops, it will become more likely that international standards and policies for broader regulation of human activities that affect ocean ecosystems will be adopted and implemented.

1. According to the passage, until the mid-twentieth century there were few jurisdictional disputes over international waters because

(A) the nearest coastal nation regulated activities
(B) few controls or restrictions applied to ocean areas
(C) the ocean areas were used for only innocent purposes
(D) the "freedom of the seas" doctrine settled all claims concerning navigation and fishing
(E) broad authority over international waters was shared equally among all nations

GO ON TO THE NEXT PAGE.

2. According to the international law doctrines applicable before the mid-twentieth century, if commercial activity within a particular nation's territorial waters threatened all marine life in those waters, the nation would have been

(A) formally censured by an international organization for not properly regulating marine activities
(B) called upon by other nations to establish rules to protect its territorial waters
(C) able but not required to place legal limits on such commercial activities
(D) allowed to resolve the problem at its own discretion providing it could contain the threat to its own territorial waters
(E) permitted to hold the commercial offenders liable only if they were citizens of that particular nation

3. The author suggests that, before the mid-twentieth century, most nations' actions with respect to territorial and international waters indicated that

(A) managing ecosystems in either territorial or international waters was given low priority
(B) unlimited resources in international waters resulted in little interest in territorial waters
(C) nations considered it their responsibility to protect territorial but not international waters
(D) a nation's authority over its citizenry ended at territorial lines
(E) although nations could extend their territorial dominion beyond three miles from their shoreline, most chose not to do so

4. The author cites which one of the following as an effect of the extension of territorial waters beyond the three-mile limit?

(A) increased political pressure on individual nations to establish comprehensive laws regulation ocean resources
(B) a greater number of jurisdictional disputes among nations over the regulation of fishing on the open seas
(C) the opportunity for some nations to manage large ocean ecosystems
(D) a new awareness of the need to minimize pollution caused by navigation
(E) a political incentive for smaller nations to solve the problems of pollution in their coastal waters

5. According to the passage, before the middle of the twentieth century, nations failed to establish rules protecting their territorial waters because

(A) the waters appeared to be unpolluted and to contain unlimited resources
(B) the fishing industry would be adversely affected by such rules
(C) the size of the area that would be subject to such rules was insignificant
(D) the technology needed for pollution control and resource management did not exist
(E) there were few jurisdictional conflicts over nations' territorial waters

6. The passage as a whole can best be described as

(A) a chronology of the events that have led up to a present-day crisis
(B) a legal inquiry into the abuse of existing laws and the likelihood of reform
(C) a political analysis of the problems inherent in directing national attention to an international issue
(D) a historical analysis of a problem that requires international attention
(E) a proposal for adopting and implementing international standards to solve an ecological problem

GO ON TO THE NEXT PAGE.

2 2 2 2 2 2 2 2 2 2

The human species came into being at the time of the greatest biological diversity in the history of the Earth. Today, as human populations expand and alter the natural environment, they are reducing biological diversity to its lowest level since the end of the Mesozoic era, 65 million years ago. The ultimate consequences of this biological collision are beyond calculation, but they are certain to be harmful. That, in essence, is the biodiversity crisis.

The history of global diversity can be summarized as follows: after the initial flowering of multicellular animals, there was a swift rise in the number of species in early Paleozoic times (between 600 and 430 million years ago), then plateaulike stagnation for the remaining 200 million years of the Paleozoic era, and finally a slow but steady climb through the Mesozoic and Cenozoic eras to diversity's all-time high. This history suggests that biological diversity was hard won and a long time in coming. Furthermore, this pattern of increase was set back by five massive extinction episodes. The most recent of these, during the Cretaceous period, is by far the most famous, because it ended the age of the dinosaurs, conferred hegemony on the mammals, the ultimately made possible the ascendancy of the human species. But the Cretaceous crisis was minor compared with the Permian extinctions 240 million years ago, during which between 77 and 96 percent of marine animal species perished. It took five million years, well into Mesozoic times, for species diversity to begin a significant recovery.

Within the past 10,000 years biological diversity has entered a wholly new era. Human activity has had a devastating effect on species diversity, and the rate of human-induced extinctions is accelerating. Half of the bird species of Polynesia have been eliminated through hunting and the destruction of native forests. Hundreds of fish species endemic to Lake Victoria are now threatened with extinction following the careless introduction of one species of fish, the Nile perch. The list of such biogeographic disasters is extensive.

Because every species is unique and irreplaceable, the loss of biodiversity is the most profound process of environmental change. Its consequences are also the least predictable because the value of the Earth's biota (the fauna and flora collectively) remains largely unstudied and unappreciated; unlike material and cultural wealth, which we understand because they are the substance of our everyday lives, biological wealth is usually taken for granted. This is a serious strategic error, one that will be increasingly regretted as time passes. The biota is not only part of a country's heritage, the product of millions of years of evolution centered on that place; it is also a potential source for immense untapped material wealth in the form of food, medicine, and other commercially important substances.

7. Which one of the following best expresses the main idea of the passage?

(A) The reduction in biodiversity is an irreversible process that represents a setback both for science and for society as a whole.
(B) The material and cultural wealth of a nation are insignificant when compared with the country's biological wealth.
(C) The enormous diversity of life on Earth could not have come about without periodic extinctions that have conferred preeminence on one species at the expense of another.
(D) The human species is in the process of initiating a massive extinction episode that may make past episodes look minor by comparison.
(E) The current decline in species diversity is a human-induced tragedy of incalculable proportions that has potentially grave consequences for the human species.

8. Which one of the following situations is most analogous to the history of global diversity summarized in lines 10–18 of the passage?

(A) The number of fish in a lake declines abruptly as a result of water pollution, then makes a slow comeback after cleanup efforts and the passage of ordinances against dumping.
(B) The concentration of chlorine in the water supply of a large city fluctuates widely before stabilizing at a constant and safe level.
(C) An old-fashioned article of clothing goes in and out of style periodically as a result of features in fashion magazines and the popularity of certain period films.
(D) After valuable mineral deposits are discovered, the population of a geographic region booms, then levels off and begins to decrease at a slow and steady rate.
(E) The variety of styles stocked by a shoe store increases rapidly after the store opens, holds constant for many months, and then gradually creeps upward.

GO ON TO THE NEXT PAGE.

9. The author suggests which one of the following about the Cretaceous crisis?

(A) It was the second most devastating extinction episode in history.
(B) It was the most devastating extinction episode up until that time.
(C) It was less devastating to species diversity than is the current biodiversity crisis.
(D) The rate of extinction among marine animal species as a result of the crisis did not approach 77 percent.
(E) The dinosaurs comprised the great majority of species that perished during the crisis.

10. The author mentions the Nile perch in order to provide an example of

(A) a species that has become extinct through human activity
(B) the typical lack of foresight that has led to biogeographic disaster
(C) a marine animal species that survived the Permian extinctions
(D) a species that is a potential source of material wealth
(E) the kind of action that is necessary to reverse the decline in species diversity

11. All of the following are explicitly mentioned in the passage as contributing to the extinction of species EXCEPT

(A) hunting
(B) pollution
(C) deforestation
(D) the growth of human populations
(E) human-engineered changes in the environment

12. The passage suggests which one of the following about material and cultural wealth?

(A) Because we can readily assess the value of material and cultural wealth, we tend not to take them for granted.
(B) Just as the biota is a source of potential material wealth, it is an untapped source of cultural wealth as well.
(C) Some degree of material and cultural wealth may have to be sacrificed if we are to protect our biological heritage.
(D) Material and cultural wealth are of less value than biological wealth because they have evolved over a shorter period of time.
(E) Material wealth and biological wealth are interdependent in a way that material wealth and cultural wealth are not.

13. The author would be most likely to agree with which one of the following statements about the consequences of the biodiversity crisis?

(A) The loss of species diversity will have as immediate an impact on the material wealth of nations as on their biological wealth.
(B) The crisis will likely end the hegemony of the human race and bring about the ascendancy of another species.
(C) The effects of the loss of species diversity will be dire, but we cannot yet tell how dire.
(D) It is more fruitful to discuss the consequences of the crisis in terms of the potential loss to humanity than in strictly biological terms.
(E) The consequences of the crisis can be minimized, but the pace of extinctions cannot be reversed.

GO ON TO THE NEXT PAGE.

Women's participation in the revolutionary events in France between 1789 and 1795 has only recently been given nuanced treatment. Early twentieth-century historians of the French Revolution are typified by Jaurès, who, though sympathetic to the women's movement of his own time, never even mentions its antecedents in revolutionary France. Even today most general histories treat only cursorily a few individual women, like Marie Antoinette. The recent studies by Landes, Badinter, Godineau, and Roudinesco, however, should signal a much-needed reassessment of women's participation.

Godineau and Roudinesco point to three significant phases in that participation. The first, up to mid-1792, involved those women who wrote political tracts. Typical of their orientation to theoretical issues—in Godineau's view, without practical effect—is Marie Gouze's *Declaration of the Rights of Women*. The emergence of vocal middle-class women's political clubs marks the second phase. Formed in 1791 as adjuncts of middle-class male political clubs, and originally philanthropic in function, by late 1792 independent clubs of women began to advocate military participation for women. In the final phase, the famine of 1795 occasioned a mass women's movement: women seized food supplies, held officials hostage, and argued for the implementation of democratic politics. This phase ended in May of 1795 with the military suppression of this multiclass movement. In all three phases women's participation in politics contrasted markedly with their participation before 1789. Before that date some noblewomen participated indirectly in elections, but such participation by more than a narrow range of the population—women or men—came only with the Revolution.

What makes the recent studies particularly compelling, however, is not so much their organization of chronology as their unflinching willingness to confront the reasons for the collapse of the women's movement. For Landes and Badinter, the necessity of women's having to speak in the established vocabularies of certain intellectual and political traditions diminished the ability of the women's movement to resist suppression. Many women, and many men, they argue, located their vision within the confining tradition of Jean-Jacques Rousseau, who linked male and female roles with public and private spheres respectively. But, when women went on to make political alliances with radical Jacobin men, Badinter asserts, they adopted a vocabulary and a violently extremist viewpoint that unfortunately was even more damaging to their political interests.

Each of these scholars has a different political agenda and takes a different approach—Godineau, for example, works with police archives while Roudinesco uses explanatory schema from modern psychology. Yet, admirably, each gives center stage to a group that previously has been marginalized, or at best undifferentiated, by historians. And in the case of Landes and Badinter, the reader is left with a sobering awareness of the cost to the women of the Revolution of speaking in borrowed voices.

14. Which one of the following best states the main point of the passage?

(A) According to recent historical studies, the participation of women in the revolutionary events of 1789–1795 can most profitably be viewed in three successive stages.
(B) The findings of certain recent historical studies have resulted from an earlier general reassessment, by historians, of women's participation in the revolutionary events of 1789–1795.
(C) Adopting the vocabulary and viewpoint of certain intellectual and political traditions resulted in no political advantage for women in France in the years 1789–1795.
(D) Certain recent historical studies have provided a much-needed description and evaluation of the evolving roles of women in the revolutionary events of 1789–1795.
(E) Historical studies that seek to explain the limitations of the women's movement in France during the years 1789–1795 are much more convincing than are those that seek only to describe the general features of that movement.

GO ON TO THE NEXT PAGE.

15. The passage suggests that Godineau would be likely to agree with which one of the following statements about Marie Gouze's *Declaration of the Rights of Women*?

    (A) This work was not understood by many of Gouze's contemporaries.
    (B) This work indirectly inspired the formation of independent women's political clubs.
    (C) This work had little impact on the world of political action.
    (D) This work was the most compelling produced by a French woman between 1789 and 1792.
    (E) This work is typical of the kind of writing French women produced between 1793 and 1795.

16. According to the passage, which one of the following is a true statement about the purpose of the women's political clubs mentioned in line 20?

    (A) These clubs fostered a mass women's movement.
    (B) These clubs eventually developed a purpose different from their original purpose.
    (C) These clubs were founded to advocate military participation for women.
    (D) These clubs counteracted the original purpose of male political clubs.
    (E) These clubs lost their direction by the time of the famine of 1795.

17. The primary function of the first paragraph of the passage is to

    (A) outline the author's argument about women's roles in France between 1789 and 1795
    (B) anticipate possible challenges to the findings of the recent studies of women in France between 1789 and 1795
    (C) summarize some long-standing explanations of the role of individual women in France between 1789 and 1795
    (D) present a context for the discussion of recent studies of women in France between 1789 and 1795
    (E) characterize various eighteenth-century studies of women in France

18. The passage suggests that Landes and Badinter would be likely to agree with which one of the following statements about the women's movement in France in the 1790s?

    (A) The movement might have been more successful if women had developed their own political vocabularies.
    (B) The downfall of the movement was probably unrelated to its alliance with Jacobin men.
    (C) The movement had a great deal of choice about whether to adopt a Rousseauist political vocabulary.
    (D) The movement would have triumphed if it had not been suppressed by military means.
    (E) The movement viewed a Rousseauist political tradition, rather than a Jacobin political ideology, as detrimental to its interests.

19. In the context of the passage, the word "cost" in line 63 refers to the

    (A) dichotomy of private roles for women and public roles for men
    (B) almost nonexistent political participation of women before 1789
    (C) historians' lack of differentiation among various groups of women
    (D) political alliances women made with radical Jacobin men
    (E) collapse of the women's movement in the 1790s

20. The author of the passage is primarily concerned with

    (A) criticizing certain political and intellectual traditions
    (B) summarizing the main points of several recent historical studies and assessing their value
    (C) establishing a chronological sequence and arguing for its importance
    (D) comparing and contrasting women's political activities before and after the French Revolution
    (E) reexamining a long-held point of view and isolating its strengths and weaknesses

GO ON TO THE NEXT PAGE.

2 2 2 2 2 2 2 2 2 2

Art historians' approach to French Impressionism has changed significantly in recent years. While a decade ago Rewald's *History of Impressionism*, which emphasized Impressionist painters' stylistic innovations, was unchallenged, the literature on Impressionism has now become a kind of ideological battlefield, in which more attention is paid to the subject matter of the paintings, and to the social and moral issues raised by it, than to their style. Recently, politically charged discussions that address the Impressionists' unequal treatment of men and women and the exclusion of modern industry and labor from their pictures have tended to crowd out the stylistic analysis favored by Rewald and his followers. In a new work illustrating this trend, Robert L. Herbert dissociates himself from formalists whose preoccupation with the stylistic features of Impressionist painting has, in Herbert's view, left the history out of art history; his aim is to restore Impressionist paintings "to their sociocultural context." However, his arguments are not, finally, persuasive.

In attempting to place Impressionist painting in its proper historical context, Herbert has redrawn the traditional boundaries of Impressionism. Limiting himself to the two decades between 1860 and 1880, he assembles under the Impressionist banner what can only be described as a somewhat eccentric grouping of painters. Cézanne, Pisarro, and Sisley are almost entirely ignored, largely because their paintings do not suit Herbert's emphasis on themes of urban life and suburban leisure, while Manet, Degas, and Caillebotte—who paint scenes of urban life but whom many would hardly characterize as Impressionists—dominate the first half of the book. Although this new description of Impressionist painting provides a more unified conception of nineteenth-century French painting by grouping quite disparate modernist painters together and emphasizing their common concerns rather than their stylistic differences, it also forces Herbert to overlook some of the most important genres of Impressionist painting—portraiture, pure landscape and still-life painting.

Moreover, the rationale for Herbert's emphasis on the social and political realities that Impressionist paintings can be said to communicate rather than on their style is finally undermined by what even Herbert concedes was the failure of Impressionist painters to serve as particularly conscientious illustrators of the social milieu. They left much ordinary experience—work and poverty, for example—out of their paintings, and what they did put in was transformed by a style that had only an indirect relationship to the social realities of the world they depicted. Not only were their pictures inventions rather than photographs, they were inventions in which style to some degree disrupted description. Their paintings in effect have two levels of "subject": what is represented and how it is represented, and no art historian can afford to emphasize one at the expense of the other.

21. Which one of the following best expresses the main point of the passage?

(A) The style of Impressionist paintings has only an indirect relation to their subject matter.
(B) The approach to Impressionism that is illustrated by Herbert's recent book is inadequate.
(C) The historical context of Impressionist paintings is not relevant to their interpretation.
(D) Impressionism emerged from a historical context of ideological conflict and change.
(E) Any adequate future interpretation of Impressionism will have to come to terms with Herbert's view of this art movement.

22. According to the passage, Rewald's book on Impressionism was characterized by which one of the following?

(A) evenhanded objectivity about the achievements of Impressionism
(B) bias in favor of certain Impressionist painters
(C) an emphasis on the stylistic features of Impressionist painting
(D) an idiosyncratic view of which painters were to be classified as Impressionists
(E) a refusal to enter into the ideological debates that had characterized earlier discussions of Impressionism

23. The author implies that Herbert's redefinition of the boundaries of Impressionism resulted from which one of the following?

(A) an exclusive emphasis on form and style
(B) a bias in favor of the representation of modern industry
(C) an attempt to place Impressionism within a specific sociocultural context
(D) a broadening of the term "Impressionism" to include all of nineteenth-century French painting
(E) an insufficient familiarity with earlier interpretations of Impressionism

24. The author states which one of the following about modern industry and labor as subjects for painting?

(A) The Impressionists neglected these subjects in their paintings.
(B) Herbert's book on Impressionism fails to give adequate treatment of these subjects.
(C) The Impressionists' treatment of these subjects was idealized.
(D) Rewald's treatment of Impressionist painters focused inordinately on their representations of these subjects.
(E) Modernist painters presented a distorted picture of these subjects.

GO ON TO THE NEXT PAGE.

25. Which one of the following most accurately describes the structure of the author's argument in the passage?

(A) The first two paragraphs each present independent arguments for a conclusion that is drawn in the third paragraph.
(B) A thesis is stated in the first paragraph and revised in the second paragraph, and the revised thesis is supported with an argument in the third paragraph.
(C) The first two paragraphs discuss and criticize a thesis, and the third paragraph presents an alternative thesis.
(D) A claim is made in the first paragraph, and the next two paragraphs each present reasons for accepting that claim.
(E) An argument is presented in the first paragraph, a counterargument is presented in the second paragraph, and the third paragraph suggests a way to resolve the dispute.

26. The author's statement that Impressionist paintings "were inventions in which style to some degree disrupted description" (lines 57–59) serves to

(A) strengthen the claim that Impressionists sought to emphasize the differences between painting and photography
(B) weaken the argument that style is the only important feature of Impressionist paintings
(C) indicate that Impressionists recognized that they had been strongly influenced by photography
(D) support the argument that an exclusive emphasis on the Impressionists' subject matter is mistaken
(E) undermine the claim that Impressionists neglected certain kinds of subject matter

27. The author would most likely regard a book on the Impressionists that focused entirely on their style as

(A) a product of the recent confusion caused by Herbert's book on Impressionism
(B) emphasizing what Impressionists themselves took to be their primary artistic concern
(C) an overreaction against the traditional interpretation of Impressionism
(D) neglecting the most innovative aspects of Impressionism
(E) addressing only part of what an adequate treatment should cover

S T O P

IF YOU FINISH BEFORE TIME IS CALLED, YOU MAY CHECK YOUR WORK ON THIS SECTION ONLY. DO NOT WORK ON ANY OTHER SECTION IN THE TEST.

SECTION III

Time—35 minutes

24 Questions

Directions: Each group of questions in this section is based on a set of conditions. In answering some of the questions, it may be useful to draw a rough diagram. Choose the response that most accurately and completely answers each question and blacken the corresponding space on your answer sheet.

Questions 1–6

A law firm has exactly nine partners: Fox, Glassen, Hae, Inman, Jacoby, Kohn, Lopez, Malloy, and Nassar.

Kohn's salary is greater than both Inman's and Lopez's.
Lopez's salary is greater than Nassar's.
Inman's salary is greater than Fox's.
Fox's salary is greater than Malloy's.
Malloy's salary is greater than Glassen's.
Glassen's salary is greater than Jacoby's.
Jacoby's salary is greater than Hae's.

1. Which one of the following partners cannot have the third highest salary?

   (A) Fox
   (B) Inman
   (C) Lopez
   (D) Malloy
   (E) Nassar

2. If Malloy and Nassar earn the same salary, at least how many of the partners must have lower salaries than Lopez?

   (A) 3
   (B) 4
   (C) 5
   (D) 6
   (E) 7

3. The salary rankings of each of the nine partners could be completely determined if which one of the following statements were true?

   (A) Lopez's salary is greater than Fox's.
   (B) Lopez's salary is greater than Inman's.
   (C) Nassar's salary is greater than Fox's.
   (D) Nassar's salary is greater than Inman's.
   (E) Nassar's salary is greater than Malloy's.

4. If Nassar's salary is the same as that of one other partner of the firm, which one of the following must be false?

   (A) Inman's salary is less than Lopez's.
   (B) Jacoby's salary is less than Lopez's.
   (C) Lopez's salary is less than Fox's.
   (D) Lopez's salary is less than Hae's.
   (E) Nassar's salary is less than Glassen's.

5. What is the minimum number of different salaries earned by the nine partners of the firm?

   (A) 5
   (B) 6
   (C) 7
   (D) 8
   (E) 9

6. Assume that the partners of the firm are ranked according to their salaries, from first (highest) to ninth (lowest), and that no two salaries are the same. Which one of the following is a complete and accurate list of Glassen's possible ranks?

   (A) fifth
   (B) fifth, sixth
   (C) fifth, seventh
   (D) fifth, sixth, seventh
   (E) fifth, sixth, seventh, eighth

GO ON TO THE NEXT PAGE.

3 3 3 3 3 3 3 3 3 3

Questions 7–11

Each of five illnesses—J, K, L, M, and N—is characterized by at least one of the following three symptoms: fever, headache, and sneezing. None of the illnesses has any symptom that is not one of these three.

Illness J is characterized by headache and sneezing.
Illnesses J and K have no symptoms in common.
Illnesses J and L have at least one symptom in common.
Illness L has a greater number of symptoms than illness K.
Illnesses L and N have no symptoms in common.
Illness M has more symptoms than illness J.

7. Which one of the following statements must be false?

(A) Illness J has exactly two symptoms.
(B) Illness K has exactly one symptom.
(C) Illness L has exactly two symptoms.
(D) Illness M has exactly three symptoms.
(E) Illness N has exactly two symptoms.

8. In which one of the following pairs could the first member of the pair be characterized by exactly the same number and types of symptoms as the second member of the pair?

(A) J and N
(B) K and L
(C) K and N
(D) L and M
(E) M and N

9. If illness L is characterized by a combination of symptoms different from any of the other illnesses, then which one of the following statements must be true?

(A) Fever is a symptom of illness L.
(B) Sneezing is a symptom of illness L.
(C) Headache is a symptom of illness L.
(D) Illnesses K and N are characterized by exactly the same symptoms.
(E) Illnesses M and N are characterized by exactly the same symptoms.

10. The illnesses in which one of the following pairs must have exactly one symptom in common?

(A) J and L
(B) J and M
(C) J and N
(D) K and L
(E) M and N

11. If Walter has exactly two of the three symptoms, then he cannot have all of the symptoms of

(A) both illness J and illness L
(B) both illness J and illness N
(C) both illness K and illness L
(D) both illness K and illness N
(E) both illness L and illness N

GO ON TO THE NEXT PAGE.

Questions 12–17

A street cleaning crew works only Monday to Friday, and only during the day. It takes the crew an entire morning or an entire afternoon to clean a street. During one week the crew cleaned exactly eight streets—First, Second, Third, Fourth, Fifth, Sixth, Seventh, and Eighth streets. The following is known about the crew's schedule for the week:

The crew cleaned no street on Friday morning.
The crew cleaned no street on Wednesday afternoon.
It cleaned Fourth Street on Tuesday morning.
It cleaned Seventh Street on Thursday morning.
It cleaned Fourth Street before Sixth Street and after Eighth Street.
It cleaned Second, Fifth, and Eighth streets on afternoons.

12. If the crew cleaned Second Street earlier in the week than Seventh Street, then it must have cleaned which one of the following streets on Tuesday afternoon?

(A) First Street
(B) Second Street
(C) Third Street
(D) Fifth Street
(E) Eighth Street

13. If the crew cleaned Sixth Street on a morning and cleaned Second Street before Seventh Street, then what is the maximum number of streets whose cleaning times cannot be determined?

(A) 1
(B) 2
(C) 3
(D) 4
(E) 5

14. What is the maximum possible number of streets any one of which could be the one the crew cleaned on Friday afternoon?

(A) 1
(B) 2
(C) 3
(D) 4
(E) 5

15. If the crew cleaned First Street earlier in the week than Third Street, then which one of the following statements must be false?

(A) The crew cleaned First Street on Tuesday afternoon.
(B) The crew cleaned Second Street on Thursday afternoon.
(C) The crew cleaned Third Street on Wednesday morning.
(D) The crew cleaned Fifth Street on Thursday afternoon.
(E) The crew cleaned Sixth Street on Friday afternoon.

16. If the crew cleaned Fifth, Sixth, and Seventh streets in numerical order, then what is the maximum number of different schedules any one of which the crew could have had for the entire week?

(A) 1
(B) 2
(C) 3
(D) 4
(E) 5

17. Suppose the crew had cleaned Fourth Street on Tuesday afternoon instead of on Tuesday morning, but all other conditions remained the same. Which one of the following statements could be false?

(A) The crew cleaned First Street before Second Street.
(B) The crew cleaned Second Street before Fifth Street.
(C) The crew cleaned Third Street before Second Street.
(D) The crew cleaned Sixth Street before Fifth Street.
(E) The crew cleaned Seventh Street before Second Street.

GO ON TO THE NEXT PAGE.

3 3 3 3 3 3 3 3 3 3

Questions 18–24

J, K, L, M, N, and O are square ski chalets of the same size, which are positioned in two straight rows as shown below:

	J	K	L
row 1:	■	■	■
row 2:	■	■	■
	M	N	O

J is directly opposite M; K is directly opposite N; and L is directly opposite O. After a snowstorm, residents shovel a single continuous path that connects all of the chalets and meets the following conditions:

The path is composed of five straight segments, each of which directly connects exactly two of the chalets.
Each chalet is directly connected by a segment of the path to another chalet.
No chalet is directly connected by segments of the path to more than two other chalets.
No segment of the path crosses any other segment.
One segment of the path directly connects chalets J and N, and another segment directly connects chalets K and L.

18. Which one of the following statements could be true?

(A) One segment of the path directly connects chalets M and K.
(B) One segment of the path directly connects chalets M and L.
(C) One segment of the path directly connects chalets M and O.
(D) One segment of the path directly connects chalets J and K and another segment directly connects chalets K and M.
(E) One segment of the path directly connects chalets O and L and another segment directly connects chalets O and N.

19. If one segment of the path directly connects chalets K and N, then the two chalets in which one of the following pairs must be directly connected to each other by a segment?

(A) J and K
(B) K and O
(C) L and O
(D) M and N
(E) N and O

20. If a segment of the path directly connects chalets J and K, then the two chalets in which one of the following pairs must be directly connected to each other by a segment?

(A) J and M
(B) K and N
(C) K and O
(D) L and O
(E) N and O

21. If one segment of the path directly connects chalets K and O, then which one of the following statements could be true?

(A) Chalet J is directly connected to chalet M.
(B) Chalet K is directly connected to chalet N.
(C) Chalet L is directly connected to chalet O.
(D) Chalet L is directly connected to exactly two chalets.
(E) Chalet J is directly connected to exactly one chalet.

22. Which one of the following statements, if true, guarantees that one segment of the path directly connects chalets M and N?

(A) One segment of the path directly connects chalets K and J.
(B) One segment of the path directly connects chalets N and O.
(C) One segment of the path directly connects chalet K and a chalet in row 2.
(D) One segment of the path directly connects chalet L and a chalet in row 2.
(E) One segment of the path directly connects chalet O and a chalet in row 1.

23. Which one of the following chalets cannot be directly connected by segments of the path to exactly two other chalets?

(A) K
(B) L
(C) M
(D) N
(E) O

24. If no segment of the path directly connects any chalet in row 1 with the chalet in row 2 that is directly opposite it, then each of the following statements must be true EXCEPT:

(A) A segment of the path directly connects chalets M and N.
(B) A segment of the path directly connects chalets N and O.
(C) Chalet L is directly connected to exactly one other chalet.
(D) Chalet N is directly connected to exactly two other chalets.
(E) Chalet O is directly connected to exactly two other chalets.

S T O P

IF YOU FINISH BEFORE TIME IS CALLED, YOU MAY CHECK YOUR WORK ON THIS SECTION ONLY. DO NOT WORK ON ANY OTHER SECTION IN THE TEST.

4 4 4 4 4 4 4 4 4 4

SECTION IV

Time—35 minutes

25 Questions

Directions: The questions in this section are based on the reasoning contained in brief statements or passages. For some questions, more than one of the choices could conceivably answer the question. However, you are to choose the best answer; that is, the response that most accurately and completely answers the question. You should not make assumptions that are by commonsense standards implausible, superfluous, or incompatible with the passage. After you have chosen the best answer, blacken the corresponding space on your answer sheet.

1. With the passage of the new tax reform laws, the annual tax burden on low-income taxpayers will be reduced, on average, by anywhere from $100 to $300. Clearly, tax reform is in the interest of low-income taxpayers.

   Which one of the following, if true, most undermines the conclusion above?

   (A) Tax reform, by simplifying the tax code, will save many people the expense of having an accountant do their taxes.
   (B) Tax reform, by eliminating tax incentives to build rental housing, will push up rents an average of about $40 per month for low-income taxpayers.
   (C) Low-income taxpayers have consistently voted for those political candidates who are strong advocates of tax reform.
   (D) The new tax reform laws will permit low- and middle-income taxpayers to deduct child-care expenses from their taxes.
   (E) Under the new tax reform laws, many low-income taxpayers who now pay taxes will no longer be required to do so.

2. If we are to expand the exploration of our solar system, our next manned flight should be to Phobos, one of Mars's moons, rather than to Mars itself. The flight times to each are the same, but the Phobos expedition would require less than half the fuel load of a Mars expedition and would, therefore, be much less costly. So, it is clear that Phobos should be our next step in space exploration.

   Which one of the following, if true, would most help to explain the difference in fuel requirements?

   (A) More equipment would be required to explore Phobos than to explore Mars.
   (B) Smaller spaceships require less fuel than larger spaceships.
   (C) Information learned during the trip to Phobos can be used during a subsequent trip to Mars.
   (D) The shortest distance between Phobos and Mars is less than half the shortest distance between Earth and Mars.
   (E) Lift-off for the return trip from Phobos requires much less fuel than that from Mars because of Phobos' weaker gravitational pull.

3. Scientific research that involves international collaboration has produced papers of greater influence, as measured by the number of times a paper is cited in subsequent papers, than has research without any collaboration. Papers that result from international collaboration are cited an average of seven times, whereas papers with single authors are cited only three times on average. This difference shows that research projects conducted by international research teams are of greater importance than those conducted by single researchers.

   Which one of the following is an assumption on which the argument depends?

   (A) Prolific writers can inflate the number of citations they receive by citing themselves in subsequent papers.
   (B) It is possible to ascertain whether or not a paper is the product of international collaboration by determining the number of citations it has received.
   (C) The number of citations a paper receives is a measure of the importance of the research it reports.
   (D) The collaborative efforts of scientists who are citizens of the same country do not produce papers that are as important as papers that are produced by international collaboration.
   (E) International research teams tend to be more generously funded than are single researchers.

GO ON TO THE NEXT PAGE.

4 4 4 4 4 4 4 4 4 4

4. It is more desirable to have some form of socialized medicine than a system of medical care relying on the private sector. Socialized medicine is more broadly accessible than is a private-sector system. In addition, since countries with socialized medicine have a lower infant mortality rate than do countries with a system relying entirely on the private sector, socialized medicine seems to be technologically superior.

Which one of the following best indicates a flaw in the argument about the technological superiority of socialized medicine?

(A) The lower infant mortality rate might be due to the system's allowing greater access to medical care.
(B) There is no necessary connection between the economic system of socialism and technological achievement.
(C) Infant mortality is a reliable indicator of the quality of medical care for children.
(D) No list is presented of the countries whose infant mortality statistics are summarized under the two categories, "socialized" and "private-sector."
(E) The argument presupposes the desirability of socialized medicine, which is what the argument seeks to establish.

5. Most parents who are generous are good parents, but some self-centered parents are also good parents. Yet all good parents share one characteristic: they are good listeners.

If all of the statements in the passage are true, which one of the following must also be true?

(A) All parents who are good listeners are good parents.
(B) Some parents who are good listeners are not good parents.
(C) Most parents who are good listeners are generous.
(D) Some parents who are good listeners are self-centered.
(E) Fewer self-centered parents than generous parents are good listeners.

6. Lourdes: Dietary fiber is an important part of a healthful diet. Experts recommend that adults consume 20 to 35 grams of fiber a day.

Kyra: But a daily intake of fiber that is significantly above that recommended level interferes with mineral absorption, especially the absorption of calcium. The public should be told to cut back on fiber intake.

Which one of the following, if true, most undermines Kyra's recommendation?

(A) Among adults, the average consumption of dietary fiber is at present approximately 10 grams a day.
(B) The more a food is processed, the more the fiber is broken down and the lower the fiber content.
(C) Many foodstuffs that are excellent sources of fiber are economical and readily available.
(D) Adequate calcium intake helps prevent the decrease in bone mass known as osteoporosis.
(E) Many foodstuffs that are excellent sources of fiber are popular with consumers.

7. A certain retailer promotes merchandise by using the following policy:

> At all times there is either a "manager's sale" or a "holiday sale" or both going on. All sales are run for exactly one calendar month. In any given month, if a manager wishes to clear out a particular line of merchandise, then a manager's sale is declared. If a holiday falls within the calendar month and there is excess merchandise in the warehouse, then a holiday sale is declared.

However, there is no holiday that falls within the month of August and, in that month, the warehouse never contains excess merchandise.

Which one of the following can be concluded from the passage?

(A) If a holiday falls within a given month and there is no extra merchandise in the warehouse that month, then a holiday sale is declared.
(B) If a holiday sale is not being run, then it is the month of August.
(C) If a manager's sale is being run in some month, then there is no excess merchandise in the warehouse in that month.
(D) If there is not a manager's sale being run in some month, then there is a holiday sale being run in that month.
(E) If there is no excess merchandise in the warehouse, then it is the month of August.

GO ON TO THE NEXT PAGE.

8. Prominent business executives often play active roles in United States presidential campaigns as fund-raisers or backroom strategists, but few actually seek to become president themselves. Throughout history the great majority of those who have sought to become president have been lawyers, military leaders, or full-time politicians. This is understandable, for the personality and skills that make for success in business do not make for success in politics. Business is largely hierarchical, whereas politics is coordinative. As a result, business executives tend to be uncomfortable with compromises and power-sharing, which are inherent in politics.

Which one of the following, if true, most seriously weakens the proposed explanation of why business executives do not run for president?

(A) Many of the most active presidential fundraisers and backroom strategists are themselves politicians.
(B) Military leaders are generally no more comfortable with compromises and power-sharing than are business executives.
(C) Some of the skills needed to become a successful lawyer are different from some of those needed to become a successful military leader.
(D) Some former presidents have engaged in business ventures after leaving office.
(E) Some hierarchically structured companies have been major financial supporters of candidates for president.

9. A scientific theory is a good theory if it satisfies two requirements: It must accurately describe a large class of observations in terms of a model that is simple enough to contain only a few elements, and it must make definite predictions about the results of future observations. For example, Aristotle's cosmological theory, which claimed that everything was made out of four elements—earth, air, fire, and water—satisfied the first requirement, but it did not make any definite predictions. Thus, Aristotle's cosmological theory was not a good theory.

If all the statements in the passage are true, each of the following must also be true EXCEPT:

(A) Prediction about the results of future observations must be made by any good scientific theory.
(B) Observation of physical phenomena was not a major concern in Aristotle's cosmological theory.
(C) Four elements can be the basis of a scientific model that is simple enough to meet the simplicity criterion of a good theory.
(D) A scientific model that contains many elements is not a good theory.
(E) Aristotle's cosmological theory described a large class of observations in terms of only four elements.

10. Millions of irreplaceable exhibits in natural history museums are currently allowed to decay. Yet without analyses of eggs from museums, the studies linking pesticides with the decline of birds of prey would have been impossible. Therefore, funds must be raised to preserve at least those exhibits that will be most valuable to science in the future.

The argument presupposes that

(A) if a museum exhibit is irreplaceable, its preservation is of an importance that overrides economic considerations
(B) the scientific analysis of museum exhibits can be performed in a nondestructive way
(C) eggs of extinct species should be analyzed to increase knowledge of genetic relationships among species
(D) it can be known at this time what data will be of most use to scientific investigators in the future
(E) the decay of organic material in natural history exhibits is natural and cannot be prevented

11. Compared to nonprofit hospitals of the same size, investor-owned hospitals require less public investment in the form of tax breaks, use fewer employees, and have higher occupancy levels. It can therefore be concluded that investor-owned hospitals are a better way of delivering medical care than are nonprofit hospitals.

Which one of the following, if true, most undermines the conclusion drawn above?

(A) Nonprofit hospitals charge more per bed than do investor-owned hospitals.
(B) Patients in nonprofit hospitals recover more quickly than do patients with comparable illnesses in investor-owned hospitals.
(C) Nonprofit hospitals do more fundraising than do investor-owned hospitals.
(D) Doctors at nonprofit hospitals earn higher salaries than do similarly qualified doctors at investor-owned hospitals.
(E) Nonprofit hospitals receive more donations than do investor-owned hospitals.

GO ON TO THE NEXT PAGE.

12. The ancient Egyptian pharaoh Akhenaten, who had a profound effect during his lifetime on Egyptian art and religion, was well loved and highly respected by his subjects. We know this from the fierce loyalty shown to him by his palace guards, as documented in reports written during Akhenaten's reign.

    A questionable technique used in the argument is to

    (A) introduce information that actually contradicts the conclusion
    (B) rely on evidence that in principle would be impossible to challenge
    (C) make a generalization based on a sample that is likely to be unrepresentative
    (D) depend on the ambiguity of the term "ancient"
    (E) apply present-day standards in an inappropriate way to ancient times

13. Physician: The patient is suffering either from disease X or else from disease Y, but there is no available test for distinguishing X from Y. Therefore, since there is an effective treatment for Y but no treatment for X, we must act on the assumption that the patient has a case of Y.

    The physician's reasoning could be based on which one of the following principles?

    (A) In treating a patient who has one or the other of two diseases, it is more important to treat the diseases than to determine which of the two diseases the patient has.
    (B) If circumstances beyond a decision maker's control will affect the outcome of the decision maker's actions, the decision maker must assume that circumstances are unfavorable.
    (C) When the soundness of a strategy depends on the truth of a certain assumption, the first step in putting the strategy into effect must be to test the truth of this assumption.
    (D) When success is possible only if a circumstance beyond one's control is favorable, then one's strategy must be based on the assumption that this circumstance is in fact favorable.
    (E) When only one strategy carries the possibility of success, circumstances must as much as possible be changed to fit this strategy.

14. Consumer advocate: Tropical oils are high in saturated fats, which increase the risk of heart disease. Fortunately, in most prepared food tropical oils can be replaced by healthier alternatives without noticeably affecting taste. Therefore, intensive publicity about the disadvantage of tropical oils will be likely to result in dietary changes that will diminish many people's risk of developing heart disease.

    Nutritionist: The major sources of saturated fat in the average North American diet are meat, poultry, and dairy products, not tropical oils. Thus, focusing attention on the health hazards of tropical oils would be counterproductive, because it would encourage people to believe that more substantial dietary changes are unnecessary.

    Which one of the following is a point at issue between the nutritionist and the consumer advocate?

    (A) whether a diet that regularly includes large quantities of tropical oil can increase the risk of heart disease
    (B) whether intensive publicity campaigns can be effective as a means of changing people's eating habits
    (C) whether more people in North America would benefit from reducing the amount of meat they consume than would benefit from eliminating tropical oils from their diets
    (D) whether some people's diets could be made significantly healthier if they replaced all tropical oils with vegetable oils that are significantly lower in saturated fat
    (E) whether conducting a publicity campaign that, by focusing on the health hazards of tropical oils, persuades people to replace such oils with healthier alternatives is a good public-health strategy

GO ON TO THE NEXT PAGE.

4 4 4 4 4 4 4 4 4 4

15. People who take what others regard as a ridiculous position should not bother to say, "I mean every word!" For either their position truly is ridiculous, in which case insisting that they are serious about it only exposes them to deeper embarrassment, or else their position has merit, in which case they should meet disbelief with rational argument rather than with assurances of their sincerity.

Which one of the following arguments is most similar in its reasoning to the argument above?

(A) A practice that has been denounced as a poor practice should not be defended on the grounds that "this is how we have always done it." If the practice is a poor one, so much the worse that it has been extensively used; if it is not a poor one, there must be a better reason for engaging in it than inertia.

(B) People who are asked why they eat some of the unusual foods they eat should not answer, "because that is what I like." This sort of answer will sound either naive or evasive and thus will satisfy no one.

(C) People whose taste in clothes is being criticized should not reply, "Every penny I spent on these clothes I earned honestly." For the issue raised by the critics is not how the money was come by but rather whether it was spent wisely.

(D) Scholars who champion unpopular new theories should not assume that the widespread rejection of the ideas shows that they "must be on the right track." The truth is that few theories of any consequence are either wholly right or wholly wrong and thus there is no substitute for patient work in ascertaining which parts are right.

(E) People who set themselves goals that others denounce as overly ambitious do little to silence their critics if they say, "I can accomplish this if anyone can." Rather, those people should either admit that their critics are right or not dignify the criticism with any reply.

16. Concetta: Franchot was a great writer because she was ahead of her time in understanding that industrialization was taking an unconscionable toll on the family structure of the working class.

Alicia: Franchot was not a great writer. The mark of a great writer is the ability to move people with the power of the written word, not the ability to be among the first to grasp a social issue. Besides, the social consequences of industrialization were widely understood in Franchot's day.

In her disagreement with Concetta, Alicia does which one of the following?

(A) accepts Concetta's criterion and then adds evidence to Concetta's case

(B) discredits Concetta's evidence and then generalizes from new evidence

(C) rejects Concetta's criterion and then disputes a specific claim

(D) disputes Concetta's conclusion and then presents facts in support of an alternative criterion

(E) attacks one of Concetta's claims and then criticizes the structure of her argument

GO ON TO THE NEXT PAGE.

Questions 17–18

Zelda: Dr. Ladlow, a research psychologist, has convincingly demonstrated that his theory about the determinants of rat behavior generates consistently accurate predictions about how rats will perform in a maze. On the basis of this evidence, Dr. Ladlow has claimed that his theory is irrefutably correct.

Anson: Then Dr. Ladlow is not a responsible psychologist. Dr. Ladlow's evidence does not conclusively prove that his theory is correct. Responsible psychologists always accept the possibility that new evidence will show that their theories are incorrect.

17. Which one of the following can be properly inferred from Anson's argument?

    (A) Dr. Ladlow's evidence that his theory generates consistently accurate predictions about how rats will perform in a maze is inaccurate.
    (B) Psychologists who can derive consistently accurate predictions about how rats will perform in a maze from their theories cannot responsibly conclude that those theories cannot be disproved.
    (C) No matter how responsible psychologists are, they can never develop correct theoretical explanations.
    (D) Responsible psychologists do not make predictions about how rats will perform in a maze.
    (E) Psychologists who accept the possibility that new evidence will show that their theories are incorrect are responsible psychologists.

18. Anson bases his conclusion about Dr. Ladlow on which one of the following?

    (A) an attack on Dr. Ladlow's character
    (B) the application of a general principle
    (C) the use of an ambiguous term
    (D) the discrediting of facts
    (E) the rejection of a theoretical explanation

19. Smith: Meat in the diet *is* healthy, despite what some people say. After all, most doctors do eat meat, and who knows more about health than doctors do?

    Which one of the following is a flaw in Smith's reasoning?

    (A) attacking the opponents' motives instead of their argument
    (B) generalizing on the basis of a sample consisting of atypical cases
    (C) assuming at the outset what the argument claims to establish through reasoning
    (D) appealing to authority, even when different authorities give conflicting advice about an issue
    (E) taking for granted that experts do not act counter to what, according to their expertise, is in their best interest

20. The rise in the prosperity of England subsequent to 1840 can be attributed to the adoption of the policy of free trade, since economic conditions improved only when that policy had been implemented.

    The reasoning in the above argument most closely parallels that in which one of the following?

    (A) An exhaustive search of the marshes last year revealed no sign of marsh hawks, so it can be assumed that a similar search this year would reveal equally little sign of that kind of bird.
    (B) Building a circular bypass road around Plainfield probably helped the flow of local traffic in the town center, since a circular bypass road generally cuts a city's through traffic markedly.
    (C) Before the banks raised their interest rates, people on average incomes could almost afford a mortgage for an amount twice their salary, hence the rate increase has now put mortgages beyond their reach.
    (D) Since the improvement in the company's profitability began to occur after the vice president's new morale-building program was put in place, that program can be credited with the improved result.
    (E) The extinction of the dinosaurs was brought about by an asteroid colliding with Earth, so their extinction could not have come before the collision.

GO ON TO THE NEXT PAGE.

21. During construction of the Quebec Bridge in 1907, the bridge's designer, Theodore Cooper, received word that the suspended span being built out from the bridge's cantilever was deflecting downward by a fraction of an inch. Before he could telegraph to freeze the project, the whole cantilever arm broke off and plunged, along with seven dozen workers, into the St. Lawrence River. It was the worst bridge construction disaster in history. As a direct result of the inquiry that followed, the engineering "rules of thumb" by which thousands of bridges had been built went down with the Quebec Bridge. Twentieth-century bridge engineers would thereafter depend on far more rigorous applications of mathematical analysis.

Which one of the following statements can be properly inferred from the passage?

(A) Bridges built before about 1907 were built without thorough mathematical analysis and, therefore, were unsafe for the public to use.
(B) Cooper's absence from the Quebec Bridge construction site resulted in the breaking off of the cantilever.
(C) Nineteenth-century bridge engineers relied on their rules of thumb because analytical methods were inadequate to solve their design problems.
(D) Only a more rigorous application of mathematical analysis to the design of the Quebec Bridge could have prevented its collapse.
(E) Prior to 1907 the mathematical analysis incorporated in engineering rules of thumb was insufficient to completely assure the safety of bridges under construction.

22. Most children find it very difficult to explain exactly what the words they use mean when those words do not refer to things that can be seen or touched. Yet, since children are able to use these words to convey the feelings and emotions they are obviously experiencing, understanding what a word means clearly does not depend on being able to explain it.

Which one of the following principles, if accepted, would provide the most justification for the conclusion?

(A) The fact that a task is very difficult for most people does not mean that no one can do it.
(B) Anyone who can provide an exact explanation of a word has a clear understanding of what that word means.
(C) Words that refer to emotions invariably have less narrowly circumscribed conventional meanings than do words that refer to physical objects.
(D) When someone appropriately uses a word to convey something that he or she is experiencing, that person understands what that word means.
(E) Words can be explained satisfactorily only when they refer to things that can be seen or touched.

Questions 23–24

The brains of identical twins are genetically identical. When only one of a pair of identical twins is a schizophrenic, certain areas of the affected twin's brain are smaller than corresponding areas in the brain of the unaffected twin. No such differences are found when neither twin is schizophrenic. Therefore, this discovery provides definitive evidence that schizophrenia is caused by damage to the physical structure of the brain.

23. Which one of the following is an assumption required by the argument?

(A) The brain of a person suffering from schizophrenia is smaller than the brain of anyone not suffering from schizophrenia.
(B) The relative smallness of certain parts of the brains of schizophrenics is not the result of schizophrenia or of medications used in its treatments.
(C) The brain of a person with an identical twin is no smaller, on average, than the brain of a person who is not a twin.
(D) When a pair of identical twins both suffer from schizophrenia, their brains are the same size.
(E) People who have an identical twin are no more likely to suffer from schizophrenia than those who do not.

24. If the statements on which the conclusion above is based are all true, each of the following could be true EXCEPT:

(A) People who lack a genetic susceptibility for the disease will not develop schizophrenia.
(B) Medications can control most of the symptoms of schizophrenia in most patients but will never be able to cure it.
(C) The brains of schizophrenics share many of the characteristics found in those of people without the disorder.
(D) It will eventually be possible to determine whether or not someone will develop schizophrenia on the basis of genetic information alone.
(E) Brain abnormalities associated with schizophrenia are the result of childhood viral infections that inhibit the development of brain cells.

GO ON TO THE NEXT PAGE.

25. Sixty adults were asked to keep a diary of their meals, including what they consumed, when, and in the company of how many people. It was found that at meals with which they drank alcoholic beverages, they consumed about 175 calories more from nonalcoholic sources than they did at meals with which they did not drink alcoholic beverages.

    Each of the following, if true, contributes to an explanation of the difference in caloric intake EXCEPT:

    (A) Diners spent a much longer time at meals served with alcohol than they did at those served without alcohol.
    (B) The meals eaten later in the day tended to be larger than those eaten earlier in the day, and later meals were more likely to include alcohol.
    (C) People eat more when there are more people present at the meal, and more people tended to be present at meals served with alcohol than at meals served without alcohol.
    (D) The meals that were most carefully prepared and most attractively served tended to be those at which alcoholic beverages were consumed.
    (E) At meals that included alcohol, relatively more of the total calories consumed came from carbohydrates and relatively fewer of them came from fats and proteins.

S T O P

IF YOU FINISH BEFORE TIME IS CALLED, YOU MAY CHECK YOUR WORK ON THIS SECTION ONLY.
DO NOT WORK ON ANY OTHER SECTION IN THE TEST.

LSAT WRITING SAMPLE TOPIC

Ralston, the capital city, is planning its 200th anniversary celebration, which will end with speeches in front of City Hall. The town is considering including a theatrical performance. Write an argument favoring one of the following two productions over the other, with two considerations guiding your decision:

- The town wants to promote significant out-of-town interest in the event.
- The town wants to encourage as much community participation as possible.

First Lady, a serious drama, was written by a local author who is also a community leader in Ralston. It is the story of Ada Jeffers, the controversial, outspoken wife of the first governor. Jeffers' unceasing, uncompromising stance against various forms of oppression was the subject of a nationally broadcast television special last year. Teri Alan, a native of Ralston and famous film actor, will play the lead. She has promised to recruit a small professional cast to perform the parts of the main characters in the play, and all other roles will be filled by area residents. The town's newspaper, the *Ralston Times Daily,* in conjunction with the town historical society, will publish a special anniversary edition featuring Jeffers' many activities.

Ralston Redux is a musical revue based on a fictionalized account of the colorful life and exploits of Herbert Ralston, the town founder and confidence man. Two of the region's leading satirists adapted the script from a popular play. The show includes a children's chorus and a number of crowd scenes, all to be played by community members. Leading roles will be filled through auditions. The director of a successful summer stock company has offered her assistance and the services of her professional technical crew. The Ralston High School Band, which has won the regional competition for the past three years, will provide the music. Local merchants have contributed money for a fireworks extravaganza that will be part of the play's finale.

Compute Your Score

Directions:

1. Use the Answer Key on the next page to check your answers.
2. Use the Scoring Worksheet below to compute your raw score.
3. Use the Score Conversion Chart to convert your raw score into the 120–180 scale.

Scoring Worksheet

1. Enter the number of questions you answered correctly in each section.

Number Correct

SECTION I . . . . . . ._____
SECTION II . . . . . ._____
SECTION III . . . . ._____
SECTION IV . . . . ._____

2. Enter the sum here: . ._____

This is your Raw Score.

Conversion Chart Form 2LSS15

For Converting Raw Score to the 120–180 LSAT Scaled Score

Reported Score	Raw Score Lowest	Raw Score Highest
180	99	100
179	98	98
178	97	97
177	—*	—*
176	96	96
175	95	95
174	94	94
173	93	93
172	92	92
171	91	91
170	90	90
169	88	89
168	87	87
167	86	86
166	84	85
165	83	83
164	81	82
163	79	80
162	78	78
161	76	77
160	74	75
159	72	73
158	70	71
157	68	69
156	66	67
155	64	65
154	63	63
153	61	62
152	59	60
151	57	58
150	55	56
149	53	54
148	51	52
147	49	50
146	47	48
145	45	46
144	44	44
143	42	43
142	40	41
141	38	39
140	37	37
139	35	36
138	34	34
137	32	33
136	31	31
135	29	30
134	28	28
133	27	27
132	25	26
131	24	24
130	23	23
129	22	22
128	21	21
127	20	20
126	19	19
125	—*	—*
124	18	18
123	—*	—*
122	17	17
121	16	16
120	0	15

*There is no raw score that will produce this scaled score for this form.

Answer Key

SECTION I

1. E
2. A
3. E
4. D
5. C
6. E
7. D
8. D
9. A
10. E
11. C
12. E
13. D
14. C
15. D
16. A
17. C
18. D
19. D
20. B
21. B
22. B
23. C
24. E

SECTION II

1. B
2. C
3. A
4. C
5. C
6. D
7. E
8. E
9. D
10. B
11. B
12. A
13. C
14. D
15. C
16. B
17. D
18. A
19. E
20. B
21. B
22. C
23. C
24. A
25. D
26. D
27. E

SECTION III

1. D
2. C
3. D
4. D
5. C
6. D
7. E
8. C
9. A
10. E
11. E
12. B
13. C
14. E
15. A
16. D
17. B
18. E
19. C
20. D
21. A
22. A
23. C
24. B

SECTION IV

1. B
2. E
3. C
4. A
5. D
6. A
7. D
8. B
9. B
10. D
11. B
12. C
13. D
14. E
15. A
16. C
17. B
18. B
19. E
20. D
21. E
22. D
23. B
24. D
25. E

Real LSAT 1: Explanations

Section I: Logical Reasoning

1 (E) is correct. Rita believes that farmers who earn more than $100,000 a year shouldn't receive subsidies, since the original purpose of the subsidies was to give *small* family farmers a stable income. Thomas objects that the income cutoff Rita proposes can't be administered, because farmers don't *know* their income until they file their taxes, long after the season when the subsidies are needed. We're asked to counter Thomas' argument, so we want a choice that weakens the idea that the cutoff is impossible to administer, a choice that shows how a farmer's need for subsidies can be determined before tax time. Choice (E) provides this: the farmers' income from the *previous* year can be used as a gauge for the current year's income, and can be used to determine who qualifies for subsidies.

(A): This is consistent with Rita's argument in that it brings up another problem for small farmers. But it doesn't address Thomas' objection that an income cutoff can't be administered.

(B): The results of (B) may run counter to the intention of Rita's proposal, but (B) doesn't in any way address Thomas' objection to her argument, which is that a $100,000 cutoff would be impossible to administer.

(C): This tends to *strengthen* Thomas' argument. If farmers' income varies from year to year, that fact would substantiate his claim that farmers don't know their yearly income until tax time.

(D): This cites a positive result from the elimination of subsidies to large farmers, which supports Rita, but fails to address Thomas' objection, which again focuses on the supposed impossibility of administering a cutoff point.

In supporting one argument over an objection to it, you might not have to address every issue in each. You should, however, focus on the part of the argument that is *contested.* For this reason, an optional strategy for dialogue questions such as this one is to read the objection first, since the objection determines the scope of our task.

2 (A) is correct. The assumption in this question is the choice that makes the necessary connection between the uncovered lab tests and the decreased quality of medical care discussed in the stimulus. Choice (A) hits the nail on the head: the combination of physical exams and lab tests makes for a *better* diagnosis than do physical exams alone. Therefore, anything that interferes with patients getting lab tests (like insurance companies' refusal to cover them) will decrease the accuracy of the diagnosis, and hence the quality of the care available to those people.

To look at this question another way, suppose that the laboratory tests added *nothing* to the accuracy of a diagnosis (the denial of (A)). In that case, it would be extremely difficult to argue that denying coverage for those tests decreased the quality of medical care. If we deny or negate (A), the argument becomes suspect, thereby confirming (A) as the assumption we seek.

(B): This is outside the scope. The argument never deals with physicians' opinions, so it needn't assume anything about those opinions.

(C): This is totally irrelevant; we're not interested in patients who don't have *any* medical coverage. The argument concerns the value of lab tests, and whether those whose insurance does not cover lab tests are worse off than those whose insurance does cover such tests.

(D): This works against the author's argument by minimizing the importance of lab tests for medical diagnosis, at least in certain cases.

(E): This is an irrelevant comparison. The issue here is the usefulness of laboratory tests, not their cost.

The argument deals with insurance regulations and their supposed effect on medical care. As soon as you see a choice that discusses someone's *opinion* of the regulations, such as (B), you can throw it out. That's a fairly common wrong choice on LSAT Assumption questions: a choice that brings in something about people's motives or opinions although the argument doesn't touch on those issues.

The argument isn't perfect even after you assume (A); you might still have to assume that the lack of insurance coverage means some people won't get lab tests. Still, (A) is necessary to make the argument work (as usual, you can check it with Kaplan's Denial Test), so it is an assumption.

3 (E) is correct. According to the analysts, if oil prices drop by half, then the purchase price of gasoline made from the oil should drop by half, too. We're asked to weaken this simplistic argument, and choice (E) does the job by providing an alternative account of the factors involved in gasoline prices. Choice (E) illuminates many other factors that, taken together, have a significant influence on the price of gasoline. Because these factors are not tied to oil prices, these costs won't decrease simply because oil prices do. Therefore, because gasoline prices are largely based on the independent costs mentioned in answer choice (E), we shouldn't expect gasoline prices to drop by half just because oil prices drop by half.

(A): This has no bearing on the question, which concerns the actual cost of gasoline, not the amount of gasoline consumers purchase. Also, (A) is limited to only *some* drivers, which severely limits its impact on the argument.

(B): If anything, answer choice (B) strengthens the analysts' argument by showing that gas manufacturers won't try to increase profits by deliberately keeping the cost of gas artificially high.

(C): This is awfully vague. We're not told anything about the effect of competition on oil prices, or about how analysts worked this factor into their analysis. If anything, fierce competition suggests that prices will be kept as low as possible, which wouldn't hurt the argument at all. Of course, since none of this is contained in the argument, this is all conjecture on our part, which means we must reject (C) immediately as irrelevant.

(D): The event (D) describes—increased consumption—happens *after* the price has already dropped. The relevant issue, however, is how much prices will drop; what happens afterwards is beside the point.

This is a prime candidate for prephrasing. After reading the argument you might have thought, "That's silly, gas prices must be based on a lot of things other than oil prices." Prephrasing is useful even if you can't come up with something specific enough to be an answer choice; just getting the general idea can be a big help.

Don't question the evidence; accept it for the purposes of the question. However, you must always maintain a healthy skepticism about the *connection* between the evidence and the conclusion, especially in Weaken the Argument and Flaw questions. Recognizing alternative explanations of the evidence is a valuable skill, as authors often miss things that you are expected to notice.

4 (D) is correct. A survey of ferry passengers came up with startling results: symptoms of seasickness were more common among those who *took* anti-seasickness medication than among those who didn't. Based on this, the author concludes that people would be better off *not* taking anti-seasickness drugs. Choice (D), holding that the people who took the drugs would have experienced even harsher symptoms without them, weakens this conclusion by showing that anti-seasickness drugs actually do some good.

(A): First, there's no indication that the weather was rough on this passage. Second, (A) does nothing to explain the curious fact that those who took the medication were disproportionately afflicted with seasickness.

(B): This is simply irrelevant. It doesn't matter who conducted the tests; what's important are the results. (You could argue that who conducted the tests is relevant in some way to the results, but you would have to take this reasoning a number of steps further to actually show how this weakens the stated conclusion.)

(C): This works as a mild strengthener. It suggests that the survey's sample was representative, and therefore supports the accuracy of the results gathered by the survey.

(E): If people who spend money on anti-seasickness drugs are less likely to report symptoms of seasickness, then it's probable that even more people who took the drugs suffered from seasickness than we had previously thought. This can only strengthen the argument.

If you can't prephrase an answer, at least make sure you have a grip on the scope of the argument before you attack the choices. In this case, the argument has many holes, which makes it difficult to prephrase an answer. Still, knowing the scope of the argument allows you to find the right answer quickly.

If you find yourself going out on a limb to justify a particular answer choice, chances are that answer is wrong. There is nothing subtle about the answers to Logical Reasoning questions, so don't waste time trying to create intricate chains of logic in order to rationalize a vague or irrelevant choice.

5 (C) is correct. "World leader" is a term that appears only in the conclusion; we need an assumption that connects that term with the terms or ideas in the evidence of the first sentence. Choice (C) makes that connection: if a nation can't be a world leader when it has the terms of its dealings with another nation set by that other nation, then it's true that a borrower nation (because it has terms set by the lender nation) can't be a world leader. Add (C) and the argument flows smoothly—that is, the conclusion follows perfectly from the evidence if (C) is added to the mix. Deny (C) and the argument falls apart.

(A): According to the stimulus *borrowers* can't be leaders, but for that to be true, we don't have to assume that leaders have to be lenders. A leader might follow Polonius' advice and neither a borrower nor a lender be.

(B): This confuses what is necessary with what is sufficient. Just because it is necessary that world leaders do not have the terms of their dealings set by other nations, the argument needn't assume that setting the terms of dealings with other nations is *sufficient* for a nation to be a world leader.

(D): This actually contradicts the stimulus, which says that lender nations set the terms of dealings with borrower nations. Stated that way it means this is *always* the case—no exceptions. No choice that contradicts the stimulus can be an assumption.

(E): This certainly sounds reasonable, but that doesn't mean it's assumed by the argument. If you deny (E), and say that such an isolationist nation *can* be a world leader, you don't hurt the conclusion that a borrower nation *can't* be a world leader.

Use the Kaplan Denial Test to find necessary assumptions and eliminate wrong choices. In Assumption questions, the negation of the correct answer will defeat the argument. On the other hand, if the negation of an answer choice fails to defeat the argument, then that choice cannot be necessary to the argument.

On Assumption questions, focus on terms. When there's a new term or idea in the conclusion, it needs to be connected to the terms or ideas present in the evidence. That's where the assumption—the necessary *connection*—comes in.

6 (E) is correct. Rotelle claims that Sims is too old to address the important concerns that currently face the country. Sims' reply is that she doesn't want to make age an issue, so she won't comment on Rotelle's youth and lack of experience. How does she counter Rotelle's claim that she is too old? She sidesteps it; she never squarely tackles the issue of her own age, but instead brings up the issue of Sims' age (while pretending not to). So (E) is correct—she fails to respond directly to the claim that she's too old to govern.

(A): On the contrary: Sims doesn't directly address Rotelle's claim, so she can't be said to demonstrate that Rotelle's claim is incorrect.

(B): This answer falls for Sims' little rhetorical trick. She *claims* that she won't make an issue of age, then goes ahead and contradicts herself by referring to Rotelle's inexperience and *youth.* So she definitely mentions age.

(C): Sims only says (hypocritically) that age shouldn't be an issue; she never advances any general method for deciding which issues *are* important.

(D): Sims doesn't even reply to Rotelle's claim, much less show it to be contradictory. In fact, it's Sims' own claim that is contradictory.

Choice (E) is not a complete description of Sims' argument. It never mentions the contradictory nature of her statement. The question stem asks only for *something* Sims does in her argument, not for everything she does, so the correct answer doesn't have to give a complete account. That means that the wrong choices won't merely be incomplete or inadequate descriptions of the argument; they'll be flat out wrong.

7 (D) is correct. Rotelle says that *because* Sims is too old, she can't be effective. In other words, it's Sims' age that precludes her from being effective. Since Rotelle believes that Sims can't face the problems because of her advanced age, he holds that anyone Sims' age or older would be ineffective. Therefore, anyone who *could* be effective at addressing the problems would have to be younger than Sims. That points right to (D): if anyone can effectively address the issues in question, that person must be younger than Sims.

(A): Rotelle assumes that some people (anyone as old as Sims) are too old to address the issues, but that doesn't mean that *many* people are too old. Maybe very few people are so old as to be incapable, and Sims (who might be 105 years old, for all we know) happens to be one of these.

(B): Rotelle says that Sims' age disqualifies her, but that doesn't mean he is committed to believing that advanced age is the *only* thing that can make a person incapable.

(C): All we know is that Rotelle believes that some people are too old to address the issues. We don't know, however, who he believes *can* address the issues. He may believe that *no* young people are fit, but only some middle-aged people, or some old people who aren't quite as old as Sims. Rotelle's argument is too narrow for us to conclude that he's committed to the statement in choice (C).

(E): This is way outside the scope—Rotelle never talks about young people's "point of view." Rotelle says that Sims can't address the issues because she's too old; he never says what it is about advanced age that makes old people ineffective, so he needn't believe answer choice (E).

The contrapositive is the key to many Logical Reasoning questions, even questions that don't appear to be in if/then form. If a statement can be translated into an if/then statement, then the contrapositive applies. In this case, Rotelle basically claims that *if* someone is as old as Sims, *then* that person cannot effectively address the difficult issues facing the country. The right answer, (D) is merely the contrapositive of this statement.

8 (D) is correct. Here, we're looking for something that the argument should have established but didn't. The meat of the argument occurs in the second clause, which concerns the relationship between the police force and the legal system. The evidence: there can't be a good legal system if the police aren't well paid. The conclusion: if the police *are* well paid, there *will* be a good legal system. This is a classic mistake. From the fact that a well-paid police force is *necessary* for a good legal system, the author concludes that a well-paid police force is *sufficient* to guarantee a good legal system. But we don't know that—maybe some other things are needed (like honest judges, fair laws, etcetera) above and beyond a well-paid police force to ensure a good legal system. Choice (D) addresses this defect: the argument never establishes the claim that a well-paid police force by itself is enough, or *sufficient*, to guarantee a good legal system.

(A): No. Even if the argument *did* establish the fact that many governments with bad legal systems happen to have poorly paid police forces, this wouldn't have any bearing whatsoever on the argument in question, namely that a good legal system must automatically follow from a well-paid police force.

(B): This overtly contradicts the argument. The author establishes that a good legal system requires well-paid police, while in answer choice (B) we get a good legal system with poorly paid police. The argument is not sound for a lack of the premise in choice (B); establishing (B) would only confuse matters further.

(C): The author's premise is that good legal systems rely on well-paid police forces. Choice (C) reverses this relationship, and says that a well-paid police force depends for its *effectiveness* (an idea not discussed in the stimulus) on a good legal system. Choice (C) brings in an irrelevant issue, and is therefore far from a notion that the author should have established.

(E): This leaves out the pay status of the police force entirely, which is a good enough reason to reject this choice out of hand. Moreover, a relationship between bad *governments* and good legal systems is outside the scope.

Many LSAT questions test the distinction between what is necessary for a result and what is sufficient. Just because a condition is required for a result doesn't mean that satisfying that condition guarantees that result.

Become adept at recognizing the various ways the test makers can phrase the same question. Notice here that Question 8 could have been worded as an Assumption question. Any argument that fails to establish a key link between evidence and conclusion is logically unsound and incomplete, and the necessary link is the author's assumption.

9 (A) is correct. You may have been struck by the unusual phrase "violent interpersonal crimes"; this indeed turns out to be the argument's weak point. Choice (A) says that the French government's definition of what constituted a "violent interpersonal crime" expanded throughout the 1300s to include crimes that were actually nonviolent. If that's the case, then the evidence that more people were arrested for so-called "violent interpersonal crimes" no longer warrants the conclusion that there was actually a higher level of real violence documented. Choice (A) is therefore our weakener.

(B): This is irrelevant. The fact that there are descriptions of violent attacks in the 1300s has no bearing on an argument discussing the *number* of such attacks as compared with the previous century.

(C): This doesn't hurt the conclusion at all. We don't know how many people actually took the oaths (it might be a very small number like 30, up from a previous count of 20), how many *kept* them, or whether the nonoath takers were bashing each other with more and more gusto.

(D): First of all, the acts of violence that answer choice (D) refers to may very well have been committed in war, which doesn't count. More importantly, though, choice (D) refers to violence increasing, whereas a weakener must suggest that documented interpersonal violence *didn't* increase.

(E): As an account of France's population in the 1300s, (E) is ambiguous (first it increased then it decreased), so we don't know how France's population in that century compared to France's population in the 1200s. Even so, it's also unclear how the supposed population changes are connected to interpersonal violence. In essence, (E) tells us nothing.

Take all the clues you're offered. The scope of the argument is phrased very carefully. The conclusion is only about documented, non-war-related, violent crimes, and specifically excludes false arrests from consideration. Almost the only place that allows any opening for a weakener is that term "violent interpersonal crimes." A strong grip on the scope of the argument also helps you eliminate answer choices that distort the scope, like (C) and (D), and those that steer entirely clear of the scope, like (E).

Notice when conclusions deal with numbers: "higher level" in this case means "more." A choice such as (B) totally evades the issue of "more"—it simply reinforces the notion that "some" existed in the 1300s by virtue of the historical descriptions. This is all well and good, but it in no way infers anything about the numerical comparison between the two centuries. For all we know, there were also plenty of historical descriptions of the violence in question from the 1200s, too.

10 (E) is correct. Fixed nitrogen is an essential nutrient that normally has to be supplied to nonlegumes such as wheat by means of fertilizers. However, *Rhizobium* bacteria living on legume roots produces fixed nitrogen. The author concludes that if we can develop wheat strains that also allow *Rhizobium* bacteria to live on their roots, the need for artificial fertilizers will decline. Why? The author

must also believe (E), that *Rhizobium* growing on wheat will also produce fixed nitrogen (just as it does when it grows on legumes), and the wheat's need for artificially supplied fixed nitrogen will be reduced. But this is an assumption, since the evidence says only that *Rhizobium* growing on legumes produces nitrogen. If we negate or deny (E), and assert that *Rhizobium* would not produce fixed-nitrogen on wheat, we'd then have absolutely no reason to believe, as the conclusion proposes, that the need for fertilizers would be reduced.

(A): This introduces the concept of what biotechnology *ought* to do, which is irrelevant; the conclusion speaks only of what will happen *if Rhizobium*-friendly wheat is produced.

(B): The conclusion merely says that the need for artificial fertilizers will be reduced, not eliminated entirely. It's entirely possible that fertilizers will still be needed to provide other nutrients.

(C): This needn't be assumed. Even if some strain of grass already has *Rhizobium* bacteria living in its roots, and even if that *Rhizobium* produces fixed nitrogen (which (C) neglects to say), the conclusion that the *overall* need for chemical fertilizers would be reduced by the production of further *new* strains of *Rhizobium*-friendly wheat wouldn't thereby be invalidated.

(D): Nothing in the argument requires that no crops other than legumes produce their own fixed nitrogen. If there were rutabagas or tomatoes, for example, that also produced fixed nitrogen, it wouldn't damage the conclusion that *Rhizobium* could reduce wheat's need for artificial fertilizer.

In arguments that don't include proposals, and especially in arguments that merely portray an if/then relationship, steer clear of choices that introduce the concept of "should" or "ought"—these are often wrong. Even if it sounds like the author is discussing a positive step, don't assume the author believes it's a step that ought to be taken unless that's explicitly stated.

11 (C) is correct. The author concludes that current legislation regulating smoking on the premises of privately owned businesses is an unjustifiable intrusion into the private sector. She doesn't deny that inhaling second-hand smoke is dangerous, but claims that this isn't the most important consideration. The most important consideration, she says, is that the laws violate the right of private businesses to determine their own policies free of government intervention. The principle in (C) lends credence to the author's contention that the right of business to be free from regulation should outweigh the government's right to protect nonsmokers. Choice (C) allows one to draw the conclusion that the smoking regulations aren't justified.

(A): This answer misunderstands the author's objection. She never denied that second-hand smoke is dangerous. Choice (A) would imply that regulations to limit second-hand smoke may well be justified.

(B): This is an *au contraire* choice; it favors government regulations on smoking.

(D): This could only weaken the argument. Choice (D) claims that businesses have an obligation to protect employees from harm, which would undermine the conclusion. However, (D) applies only to employees in the workplace, which shifts the scope of the argument. No matter how we slice it, (D) cannot help justify the conclusion.

(E): This answer's reasoning certainly follows a different path from that of the author: it wants to find a compromise, but the author comes down squarely on the side of business against government.

Take an active approach—ask yourself which principle would make you agree with the argument. Try them out.

Always keep the author's stance in mind. If the author favors X over Y, then anything that favors Y over X, or a compromise between the two, certainly can't be of much help to the author or the author's conclusion.

12 (E) is correct. We're introduced to a foul-sounding substance called "leachate," which develops when water permeates a landfill site. The most explicit thing we're told about leachate is that it escapes into the environment *whenever* the landfill's capacity to hold water is exceeded, and it *only* escapes into the environment when the landfill's capacity to hold water is exceeded (that's the meaning of the "if and only if" statement in the second sentence). We're also told that a method to dispose of leachate must be found. Currently, most leachate is sent to sewage treatment plants, but some sewage treatment plants can't handle leachate.

We need a good inference based on this mess, and it comes out of the "if and only if" statement. We know that if the landfill's capacity to hold liquid is exceeded, leachate is certain to escape into the environment, which means that answer choice (E) is inferable: if leachate *doesn't* escape into the environment, the landfill's capacity hasn't been exceeded.

(A): The stimulus does say that leachate generally escapes into the environment in unpredictable quantities, and that not all sewage plants can deal with leachate, but nowhere implies that the two facts are related. There's no reason to think the ability to predict the escape of leachate would help with the disposal problem.

(B): This contradicts the passage, which says leachate only escapes into the environment when a landfill's ability to hold liquids is exceeded.

(C): This is unsupported; the stimulus says "not all" treatment plants can handle leachate, not that none of them can.

(D): The stimulus doesn't say that any leachate is actually sent to any of the plants that can't handle it, only that such non-leachate-friendly plants do exist.

A valid inference need not be an earth-shattering deduction, and so the right answer to an Inference question might be a relatively trivial fact that *must* be true based on the information in the stimulus.

If you find that you can't prephrase a potential answer to a question on your LR section, focus on the scope of the argument and use it to go through all five answer choices quickly.

Pay special attention to conditional statements. In an "if and only if" statement, the presence of one condition ensures the presence of the other, and the absence of one condition ensures the absence of the other.

13 (D) is correct. The author says that academic libraries (used only by academic researchers) will have to cut down their subscription lists; journals are just too expensive. He suggests that subscription decisions in each discipline should be based only on the usefulness of the journal in that discipline, and goes on to say that a journal's "usefulness" can be measured by how frequently it's cited by researchers in published writings. Choice (D) weakens this suggestion by attacking the author's concept of "usefulness." If, as (D) says, researchers will not always cite a journal article that's important in their work, then it's possible that by using the suggested criterion for usefulness, some journals that are useful may *not* appear useful based only on frequency of citation. Thus the proposed response to the problem

would actually be counterproductive—many useful journals could end up being removed from the academic libraries.

(A) and (C): These are irrelevant. The problem under discussion is experienced by libraries that cater only to *academic* researchers, and so the *nonacademic* readership of scholarly journals, (A), and the conditions of *nonacademic* libraries, (C), are out of the scope.

(B): This offers an irrelevant comparison/distinction; there's no necessary connection between the length of a journal article and the number of other articles it cites, or is cited by. Furthermore, in the stimulus, the comparison between journals is only made *within* each discipline—there is no comparison *between* disciplines as stated here.

(E): This doesn't affect the solution. It doesn't matter that controversies spill over from one academic journal to another. So long as all the articles concerned with the controversy cite their sources, the solution in the argument isn't weakened.

The consideration of "scope" finds its way into almost every question type and stimulus type on the LSAT. When you're evaluating a solution, consider the scope of the problem being addressed. If you're attacking the solution, you must find some reason that it's not a good approach to *that particular problem.* Here the problem is experienced by "academic libraries used only by academic researchers;" any choice that doesn't affect those institutions is out.

14 (C) is correct. Despite the fact that people suffering from acute W already have lower-than-average blood-fat levels than the population at large, most doctors believe that *reducing* blood-fat levels is a good way to prevent acute W. This is an apparent paradox. The key lies in the relationship between low blood-fat levels and the disease. Choice (C) says that a person can contract acute W *only* when the agent that causes acute W absorbs large quantities of fat from a person's blood. This tells us two things. First, people must *have* large quantities of fat in their bloodstream to contract acute W—this explains why reducing blood-fat is a good way to avoid contracting acute W. Second, people can contract acute W only *after* the agent has already absorbed a lot of blood fat—this explains why people who actually have acute W have low blood-fat levels. So (C) explains how both statements in the stimulus can be true, and thus resolves the paradox.

(A): This is out of the scope, dealing as it does with people who have already been cured of acute W; (A) says nothing about why their blood-fat was low when they had acute W, or why people should reduce blood fat to keep from contracting the disease.

(B): This contains a double scope shift. It points to a "synthetic fat substitute" (not fat), and says that animals who have been fed that substitute show "several symptoms" of acute W (not the disease itself). So the disease isn't there, the fat isn't there, and (B) isn't anywhere.

(D): It's hard to know what to make of (D); it doesn't explain the correlation between low blood-fat and acute W, and certainly doesn't explain how reducing blood-fat could prevent acute W—these people already have acute W.

(E): This is also out of the scope. The stimulus is interested only in prevention of acute W, not in other diseases. (E) doesn't address the paradox at all.

Any time you have to work hard to see the relevance of an answer choice, eliminate it.

As often happens, the correct answer choice resolves the paradox by arranging the chain of events in its proper sequence. First the high blood-fat level, then the development of acute W by the absorption of fat, and finally a low blood-fat level in those with acute W.

15 (D) is correct. The key to this question is the phrase "in this respect." We're told that carbohydrates increase the brain's level of serotonin, and that "in this respect" carbohydrates act on the brain in the same way as antidepressants. Critical reading tells us that the "respect" in question must be the increase in serotonin; the way the sentence is structured, the author simply can't be referring to anything else. And that leads right to the correct inference in (D): some antidepressants must also boost the brain's level of serotonin.

(A): This introduces a false contrast. The stimulus never compares seasonal depression to any other types of depression.

(B): We know that lack of sunlight can cause seasonal depression. We also know that an increase in serotonin can cheer people up. But we cannot combine these facts to conclude that there's any connection between lack of sunlight and serotonin. The stimulus doesn't specify *why* a lack of sunlight is depressing; it may have nothing to do with serotonin.

(C): This answer, like (A), offers another comparison that the stimulus simply doesn't address: the stimulus never compares midwinter to any other season. There may be other times of the year when other causes, more serious than a lack of sunlight, make more people depressed.

(E): This attempts to slip a scope shift by us. Serotonin is the only neurotransmitter mentioned in the passage that has the stated effect on depression; (E) tries to extend the argument to include *all* neurotransmitters. There's no basis for that—for all we know, some neurotransmitters may even have a depressing effect.

As is often the case, the inference is not based on the whole stimulus, but on one section (notice that the correct inference has absolutely nothing to do with the cookie conclusion in the last sentence). This is what makes Inference questions difficult to prephrase—they can be based on any part of the passage.

Pay attention to sentence structure as well as keywords and keyword phrases such as "in this respect." In some cases, picking up on these clues is all that's needed to pick up a Logical Reasoning point.

16 (A) is correct. Students shouldn't be given more freedom in planning their courses of study; that's the conclusion. The evidence used to support this conclusion is basically an extended attack on the students who support the proposal: they'll never be satisfied, these guys don't know their own majors, that one hasn't completed his courses, they don't care about intellectual achievement, etcetera. The proposal itself is never evaluated on its merits. As (A) says, the author avoids the real issue—the proposal—and instead attacks the proposal's supporters.

(B): The argument may be bad, but it's not circular. The evidence—that the people who support the proposal are bums—is different from the conclusion, which is that the proposal should be abandoned.

(C): Language isn't the problem. It's perfectly obvious what the author means by saying the students will never be "satisfied": she means they'll keep making new demands.

(D): The author doesn't distort the proposal; the proposal isn't discussed at all, except to be dismissed in the conclusion. It's this *lack* of focus on the proposal that's the real problem.

(E): Different students are mentioned, yes, but the argument does not employ the word "student" in different senses.

Any valid argument must be backed by substantive claims. Any time you see the author attacking his or her opponents instead of their argument, you know you have identified a major logical flaw.

Circular reasoning is that in which the author's evidence and conclusion are the same, as in the following example: Cathy is so popular because almost everyone likes her. This tells us nothing about why Cathy is so popular; the evidence is merely a restatement of the conclusion. Circular reasoning appears occasionally on the Logical Reasoning section, but usually in the form of a wrong answer choice, like (B) here.

17 (C) is correct. We're asked to find the claim to which the author is objecting. The stimulus starts by saying that the question of whether there is intelligent life in the universe is "certainly" imprecise. This sounds like a concession to an opposing viewpoint, which suggests that the original claim included this idea that the question about intelligent life on other planets was imprecise. The keyword "yet" then jumps off the page, which signifies disagreement with the original claim: "yet," the author says, we *can't* just decide to define "intelligent life" more precisely, and then a reason for that is given. From this we see that the original claim must have suggested making that definition more precise. So an educated guess would be that the original claim says (1) that the question is imprecise and (2) we should make the question more precise (which is what the author disagrees with). Choice (C) fits this profile of a statement to which the author objects.

(A): This isn't a claim the stimulus rebuts. The stimulus is concerned with weighing considerations of precision and imprecision, not with flatly attacking the idea that the question of intelligent life is unanswerable.

(B): The author would *agree* that our understanding of intelligent life is limited (that's why he counsels us to keep our definition open to new possibilities), so he certainly can't be *objecting* to (B).

(D): If he were trying to counter (D), the author would have to argue that the question of intelligent life in the universe is *not* meaningless, which he simply does not do.

(E): The stimulus doesn't spend any time giving reasons why we *should* bother with the question of intelligent life, so it isn't countering (E).

Reading the question stem first tells us we're not simply being asked for a statement the author is likely to disagree with (like (A) and (D) perhaps) but for a statement the author's argument is actually designed to refute.

The keywords ("certainly" and "yet") are lifesavers here. They tell you how each section of the argument relates to the original claim.

18 (D) is correct. Now we're asked for the *method* by which the stimulus argument objected to the "antecedent claim" (choice (C) of Question 17). The author did two things in his objection: he agreed that the question about the existence of intelligent life in the universe is imprecise as it stands, but he argued that simply to define intelligent life more precisely would limit the possibility of finding and recognizing intelligent life. Thus, he argued that making the definition of intelligent life more precise, in order to aid in the discovery of such life, would actually make it harder to achieve the goal of finding and recognizing that life. As (D) says, narrowing the definition of intelligent life would be counterproductive.

(A): The author doesn't challenge the claim's relevance; he attacks it as counterproductive. He says that making the definition of intelligent life more precise would actually have *negative* results. That's not the same as saying that the claim is irrelevant.

(B): The author doesn't offer any examples; after all, his argument concerns types of intelligent life that we can't imagine, so he can't give examples.

(C): The author doesn't argue that *any* adequate definition of intelligent life is *impossible.* He merely argues that to make the definition "more precise" would make it more difficult to recognize new types of intelligent life. Choice (C) is a distortion of that argument.

(E): The author doesn't attack the antecedent claim's evidence, and he doesn't focus on the claim's support. Instead, he talks about its consequences.

Paraphrase the argument to make it yours. In this case, something like "we can't define intelligent life more precisely because that would make it harder to find," would have pointed you straight to answer choice (D), with it's description of the claim as "counterproductive."

19 (D) is correct. The interiors of unsalted foods that are microwaved get hot enough to kill the bacteria that causes food poisoning, whereas the interiors of salted foods don't get so hot and are therefore more vulnerable to harmful bacteria that could lead to food poisoning. This isn't a difficult situation to imagine encountering in real life. Armed with this knowledge, any reasonable person would feel safer from food poisoning by not adding salt to food before microwaving. This notion is echoed in correct choice (D).

(A): This answer offers a comparison that's impossible to verify from the stimulus. The stimulus never even mentions exterior bacteria, whereas it does state for a fact that there is harmful bacteria on the interior of food. There's simply no basis in the passage for comparing how much bacteria is on the exterior of food to how much is on the interior.

(B): This needn't be true, because the author isn't condemning microwave ovens themselves, just pointing out a risk in the use of microwave ovens with salted foods. For all we know, conventional ovens may do an even worse job of killing bacteria.

(C): Scope shift: the stimulus deals with the effects of adding salt to food before microwaving; this choice is about adding salt *after* microwaving. Be careful!

(E): This is unwarranted. We can't conclude that salt is the primary cause of these problems because other elements may do an even better job of protecting bacteria from microwaves.

Don't be surprised if the credited response to an Inference question does not combine all, or even most, of the statements in the stimulus.

There's often more that we *don't* know and can't figure out from a stimulus than things we *do* know and can deduce. This works well for the test makers, who must generate four wrong choices for every one correct choice. In this case, *we don't know* how salt compares to other elements or spices. *We don't know* how microwaves compare to other forms of cooking. *We don't know* where on various foods bacteria like to hang out. Part of sticking to the scope of the argument is recognizing what you *don't know* about a given situation. If you develop this skill, it will help you eliminate many wrong choices.

20 (B) is correct. Previewing the stem, we see that we're looking for the argument-objection that functions most similarly to Lee's objection to Pamela's argument. Pamela thinks businesses should help employees take care of their children—the future customers and employees—as this will benefit businesses in the long run. Lee's objection is that no given company will have as its patrons and employees only the children of its own employees. Thus, it wouldn't be to a company's benefit to provide parenting services if other companies don't.

Abstracting this into general form, Lee basically says that an individual will not receive any benefit from his or her action unless others also perform the action. The objection in (B) fits this mold: air breathed by each individual has been polluted by others, so it doesn't make sense to act individually against pollution. As in the stimulus, unless everyone pitches in, the individual won't benefit from his or her action.

(A): The first speaker says that some action (building new roads) *won't* be of any use, which is already a departure from the stimulus model. The reply is that the failure to take action would be even worse. This is clearly not parallel.

(C): This is way off; it completely lacks the contrast between individuals performing an action and people in general performing the action, which was the crux of Lee's reply to Pamela.

(D): This does contain a disagreement over the results of a particular course of action (lying), but in both the original statement and the objection, *everyone* is performing the action.

(E): This contains a general statement about human social institutions, and an attack on the logic behind that statement (an attack on the idea that the past is a good predictor of the future). Again, no contrast between everyone doing something and a few people doing something

This might have seemed like an odd chore, but it's just a twist on a Parallel Reasoning question. As always in parallel reasoning, you want to concentrate on the form of the argument rather than its content.

Every LSAT question is designed to be answerable in about a minute and a half. So, when a question seems impossibly long, it probably has a shortcut. In this question, once you know to look for the objection that says, "It doesn't make sense to act alone," the question can be handled quickly and accurately.

21 (B) is correct. Pedro draws a contrast between cloth diapers and disposable diapers: disposable diapers are a threat to the environment while cloth diapers aren't. For evidence, he describes the bad environmental effects of disposable diapers, *without* examining the effects of using cloth diapers. He draws his conclusion (that people should use cloth diapers) by looking at only one side of the story. Maria attacks this shortcoming by pointing out some environmental drawbacks to the use of cloth diapers. As (B) says, she indicates that Pedro's conclusion may be premature, given that he hasn't considered all the evidence about cloth diapers.

(A): Never does Maria argue with the evidence Pedro cites against using disposable diapers. She simply points out that there's *also* evidence against using cloth diapers.

(C): This couldn't be farther from Maria's method of argument. She never even mentions the word "disposable" in her rebuttal to Pedro.

(D): This is trickier, but upon close scrutiny you'll notice that it centers on a comparison that is never made. Maria *does* point out that there are drawbacks to the use of cloth diapers, drawbacks Pedro hasn't considered, but she never argues that cloth diapers are *worse* than disposables. She points out only that the issue isn't as black and white as Pedro thinks.

(E): This is beyond the scope of the argument. Neither Maria nor Pedro discusses the economic advantages of either type of diaper; their concern is the environment alone.

Don't be tricked into going farther than the stimulus goes; Maria never says which type of diaper she believes to be more environmentally sound (as Pedro does). The LSAT will often try to get you to read a comparison into the stimulus where none is explicitly stated.

22 (B) is correct. The upshot of this interesting experiment is that each child associated the term "rolling pin" with only the exact object he had previously encountered, not with a category of objects that all serve the same purpose. So what can we infer from this? Since each boy identified only the rolling pin he and his father had used, and since all the rolling pins are different, we can infer (B): that no two boys associated the term "rolling pin" with the same object.

(A): There's a subtle scope shift happening here; the children are asked to identify the pins, not explain how they're used. The mere fact that they couldn't extend the definition of "rolling pin" to other pins doesn't mean they didn't understand the function of the pin they *did* identify.

(C): This answer, if anything, runs counter to the stimulus, since the children did not seem to understand that the term "rolling pin" can refer to a category of objects. If (C) were true, chances are the boys *would* have been able to identify the other rolling pins in the room.

(D): Mind the scope! The conclusion deals only with rolling pins, so we have no right to extend this conclusion to include *all* the utensils used in the experiment.

(E): This contradicts the stimulus. The children certainly could distinguish their own rolling pins from the others; otherwise, how could each child pick out from the rest of the rolling pins only the one he and his father had used?

Choice (D) is the odd man out here. All the other choices stick to rolling pins, while (D) gets wild and speaks of utensils in general. That earns a quick rejection.

In Inference questions, keep an eye out for *au contraire* choices such as (C) and (E)—choices that, far from inferable, actually run counter to the information in the stimulus.

23 (C) is correct. What's wrong with this picture? The argument doesn't take into account the composition of the random group tested. For example, let's assume a random sample of 100 people, none of them cocaine users. Can we do this? Sure: no restrictions are placed on the "random sample," so why not use a convenient one to test the argument's claim? According to the author, roughly five percent of this group of 100 people—that is, five people—will test positive, *even though none of them uses cocaine.* Does the conclusion make sense in the context of this random sample? Clearly, it doesn't. The point is that the argument's conclusion is valid only if the random sample contains a high proportion of cocaine users; otherwise, it falls apart. Answer choice (C) correctly addresses this reasoning error: the author fails to consider what proportion of the population has used cocaine.

(A): Everything in this argument, from the evidence to the conclusion, is numerical in nature. One would be hard pressed to discern a value judgment from the text. It's simply not there.

(B): It's hard to figure out what (B) is getting at. The "properties" of the so-called average member of the population are never mentioned in the stimulus, and therefore couldn't have been attributed to anyone.

(D): Actually, the author's statistics specifically admit that some cocaine users (roughly 1 out of 100, in fact) do not test positive. Whether the author *ignores* this or not, it plays no real part in the argument and is not the source of the logical flaw.

(E): This is way out of the scope—the argument doesn't advocate anything. The author isn't promoting testing or denouncing it, she's simply giving the facts and coming to a conclusion, erroneous as it may be.

▼▼▼

You might have despaired at figuring out the percentages and proportions. Don't worry. The key to any question like this is understanding the scope of the evidence and conclusion. First we have evidence concerning noncocaine users tested, then we have evidence on cocaine users tested, and finally we have a conclusion about a random sampling. Even if you're mathematically challenged (don't be ashamed), you can tell that the author moves to this last group without showing how it relates to the other two groups. This alone points to (C) as the answer.

In some numerically based questions, especially those involving percentages, it may be helpful to work out a test case, as we did above. If you do this, remember to choose the easiest numbers to work with (10 and 100 are usually good bets) while keeping within the restrictions given in the stimulus.

▲▲▲

24 (E) is correct. Stated algebraically, the argument breaks down as follows: "If X, then Y. Y, therefore X." The only choice that does not exhibit this flaw is answer choice (E). If a country is democratic, then the opinions of each of its citizens must have a meaningful effect on its government. So far, so good—"if X, then Y." But look at the rest of the argument: "In none of these countries does each citizen's opinion have an effect (NOT Y); therefore, Western countries aren't really democratic (NOT X)." This is a valid invocation of the contrapositive; in plainer language, it simply makes logical sense. There is no reasoning error in answer choice (E), which means that answer choice (E) cannot be parallel to the original.

Another approach to this question is to simply recognize that the stimulus argument confuses necessity with sufficiency (see the following sidebar). All of the wrong choices exhibit this common logical flaw as well, and you might have been able to eliminate them on that basis alone rather than resorting to the algebraic treatment described below.

(A): The argument here runs as follows: "If air travel is to be made safer (if X), then airfares have to rise (then Y). Since airfares were raised (Y), air travel will be safer (X)." Same error as the stimulus.

(B): When you figure out the wording, (B) says: "If police increase their efficiency, then crime rates go down" (if X, then Y). Crime rates have gone down (Y), therefore, police have improved their efficiency (X). Same error.

(C): Don't be fooled by the fact that one of the original statements is a negative ("not go hunting"). This negative statement functions as the consequent and it is *affirmed* in the conclusion of the argument: if you are interested in wildlife preservation, then you don't hunt (if X, then NOT Y). Gerda doesn't hunt (NOT Y), therefore she is a wildlife preserver (X).

(D): This answer, like (C) has a negative statement in the consequent, but that statement is *affirmed*. If the contents of a bottle are safe to drink, the bottle will not be marked poison: "If X, then NOT Y." The bottle is not marked poison (NOT Y), so its contents are safe to drink (X). Same logical error, and very dangerous too!

Watch for arguments that mistake what is necessary for a result with what's sufficient for a result. According to the stimulus argument, encouraging freedom of thought guarantees creativity, but that doesn't mean that encouraging freedom of thought is *required* for creativty.

Reading the question stem alerts us to a slight twist. "All are parallel EXCEPT" questions don't show up often, and could prove to be a time-consuming ordeal. Luckily, this was the last question on the section, but it could have come earlier. Remember the crucial doctrine of Logical Reasoning section management: no matter how much work goes into a question, it is still worth only one point. Temporarily bypass questions that look like trouble if you can spend your time picking up points elsewhere.

Section II: Reading Comprehension

Passage 1: Territorial Waters (Questions 1–6)

Topic and Scope

The topic is ocean waters—specifically, efforts to regulate "human activities" on the oceans.

Purpose and Main Idea

The author's purpose is to describe the history of efforts to control human activities on the ocean. Since this passage is descriptive in nature, the author really doesn't have a specific main point in mind. In the last paragraph, however, he does suggest that more international regulation is both desirable and likely.

Paragraph Structure

Paragraphs 1 and 2 provide some historical background on the topic: activities in international waters haven't been subject to any regulation, while activities in coastal waters—while subject to national control in theory—have been largely unregulated in practice.

Paragraph 3 goes on to explain why there has been so little regulation up to now, citing three historical reasons. First, before the middle of this century, pollution wasn't considered to be a serious problem. Second, fishing rights were considered to be protected by the doctrine of "freedom of the seas." Third, technology to exploit other ocean resources such as oil didn't yet exist.

Paragraph 4 contrasts today's situation with the past, noting that there are some encouraging signs that nations are starting to do more to regulate activities in both international and coastal waters, even though much remains to be done. The author ends by proclaiming that it's likely that more will be done in the future. And, even though the overall tone of the passage is mostly descriptive, the author does offer a faint hint that such action is desirable: "the international community is beginning to understand the *importance* of preserving the resources and ecology of international waters. . . ."

The Big Picture

This passage isn't an ideal place to begin work on the Reading Comprehension section. The scope and purpose don't become entirely clear until the end of the passage. In general, it's best to start with a passage in which the author's voice is apparent early on.

As is the case with many Reading Comprehension passages, this one contains a great number of details. Never try to memorize details. Instead always read for the gist of paragraphs. Think more about what purpose the details in each paragraph serve—this will help you to grasp each paragraph's gist. And remember: if a

question requires, you can always go back and reread a detail in more depth.

The Questions

1 (B) is correct. Paragraph 2 opens the discussion of international waters, and as we saw above, the predominant theme was "few restrictions, little control, thus few jurisdictional conflicts between nations." Choice (B) nicely paraphrases the information contained in the end of the paragraph, lines 24–27.

(A): Before the mid-twentieth century, nations had the authority to regulate activities in their coastal waters, not international waters.

(C): This distorts a detail in paragraph 2, which says that nations couldn't interfere with someone's right to use international waters so long as that person used them for an "innocent purpose." That's not the same as saying that the oceans *were* used for only innocent purposes, or, even if we make this leap, that such "innocent" use accounted for the lack of jurisdictional disputes.

(D): It seems quite unlikely that a doctrine consisting of "few standards of conduct" would by itself settle all navigation and fishing claims, and in fact, no evidence is given in support of this. Moreover, lines 26–27 mention that "there were few jurisdictional conflicts between nations" under the "freedom of the seas" doctrine (which implies there were some conflicts), so this choice clearly exaggerates.

(E): *Au contraire.* Lines 22–23 say that "no nation had the responsibility, let alone the unilateral authority," to regulate activities in international waters.

If you read for the gist of each paragraph, choice (B) should have jumped out at you. If (B) didn't immediately stand out, you should have consulted paragraph 2 before attempting to answer the question.

2 (C) is correct. (C) serves up a perfect paraphrase of the terminology offered in the passage. Lines 11–12 say that, prior to the mid-twentieth century, a nation had the *authority*, but not the *responsibility*, to regulate activities in its coastal waters. In other words, a nation would have been *able*, if it so chose, to place legal limits on damaging commercial activity in its territorial waters, but would not have been *required* to do so.

(A): This is beyond the scope of the text. The passage never mentions any international organization, either before the mid-twentieth century or today, with the power to censure nations for not taking care of their own territorial waters.

(B), (D), and (E): All of these choices have a similar problem: they presume that nations were not masters in their own territorial waters under certain circumstances. But the passage indicates that they controlled their own territorial waters under all circumstances.

Some questions test your ability to recognize paraphrasing—a word, phrase, or concept restated in an alternative but synonymous way. "*Able* but not *required*" is a paraphrase of "the *authority* but not the *responsibility*." If you saw the connection between these phrases, you were rewarded with a quick and easy point.

In Reading Comprehension, often two or three—and sometimes all—of the wrong choices will be wrong for much the same reason.

3 (A) is correct. The whole theme of the first two paragraphs is that the nations just didn't seem to care much about regulating their territorial waters, and that the international scene pretty much took care of itself. In other words, "low priority," as stated in correct choice (A). If you were clear on the gist of the first two paragraphs, you shouldn't have needed to go back to the passage to pick up this point, but if you were still a little unsure, it's right there in black and white. The last sentence of paragraph 1 says that, before the mid-twentieth century, most nations didn't bother to regulate activities in their territorial waters. Paragraph 2 says that, during the same period, activities in international waters were basically unregulated as well. Evidently, what went on in the oceans was not of much concern to the international community, which once again points to "low priority."

(B): In this wrong choice, the test makers sneak in a common Logical Reasoning tactic, the scope shift. Nothing in the passage suggests that nations were *uninterested* in their territorial waters—lack of interest in *regulating* these waters doesn't equate to an *overall* lack of interest in them. Further, nothing in the passage suggests that nations felt that international waters held unlimited resources.

(C): Although nations had the authority to regulate activities in their coastal waters, few were actually *interested* in doing so. Moreover, nations were precluded by law, not custom, from regulating activities in international waters.

(D): *Au contraire.* Lines 21–24 indicate that a nation had the right to control the behavior of its citizens (but only its citizens) in international waters.

(E): *Au contraire.* Before the mid-twentieth century, nations could *not* extend their territorial control beyond three miles. Only recently have some extended control beyond this point.

With Inference questions, watch out for answer choices that either flat out contradict the passage or else stray too far from its spirit.

Use your skills developed in regard to one LSAT section on other sections when applicable. There's a great deal of synergy between the reading and reasoning skills tested by the different sections of the LSAT. For example, the "scope shift" is a device used commonly by the test makers in Logical Reasoning stimuli that display faulty logic and also in Logical Reasoning answer choices, but it shows up occasionally in Reading Comprehension as well. Once you master this concept as part of your Logical Reasoning preparation, there will be no reason to fall for a choice such (B) here.

4 (C) is correct. Choice (C) nicely paraphrases the information found in lines 48–52. In fact, it's almost word for word.

(A): "Increased political pressure?" No. According to the author, comprehensive laws governing activities on the sea will arise out of an "international consensus."
(B): This plays on (and distorts) a detail from the wrong paragraph—paragraph 2. The only real info we get on jurisdictional disputes is the second paragraph's description of the *lack* of them. "A *greater* number of jurisdictional disputes" should sound wrong right off the bat.

(D): This plays on (and distorts) a detail from the wrong paragraph—paragraph 3.

(E): This is beyond the scope of the passage, which never makes a distinction between larger and smaller nations.

In Explicit Text questions, watch out for choices that play on information from the wrong part of the passage. In this case, since the question deals with recent developments, the answer must come from paragraph 4.

5 (C) is correct. We know countries didn't care much about regulating territorial waters, but now we're asked, "Why?" It's no secret; we're told the reason in lines 12–15, and (C) nicely paraphrases the explanation.

(A), (B), and (D): All of these choices reflect either beliefs about or the situation in *international*, not territorial, waters.

(E): This choice would be a good commonsense guess if the passage were missing, but since we have the passage right in front of us, we know this was not the reason for the lack of regulation in question. "Jurisdictional conflicts" is a concept relating to the open seas, not territorial waters, so this choice can't help explain anything.

This is an excellent example of why it's important to go back and reread the relevant piece(s) of text before answering Explicit Text questions—all of the answers seem plausible. If you don't go back and reread when faced with this sort of question, you can easily fall for one of the wrong choices.

6 (D) is correct. The passage is a historical analysis—it discusses matters before the mid-twentieth century as well as today—and it is about a problem that requires international attention—the regulation of activities on the oceans.

(A): The passage doesn't mention dates or probe specific events, so "chronology" isn't the right term for the text. Besides, the word "crisis" is a bit strong: a problem isn't the same as a crisis.

(B): The passage certainly can't be called a "legal inquiry," even though it does touch on legal issues. Furthermore, there's nothing in the text about "abuse of existing laws."

(C): This passage doesn't qualify as a "political analysis of the problems inherent in directing national attention to an international issue." It's a historical analysis of an international problem.

(E): The author never sets forth any concrete proposal. He simply states that the problem of exploitation of the oceans needs to be addressed by the international community.

The correct answer to a Global question must be broad enough to encompass the entire passage, yet specific enough to refer to its actual content.

Passage 2: Biological Diversity (Questions 7–13)

Topic and Scope

The topic is species diversity—specifically, the history and consequences of species diversity.

Purpose and Main Idea

The author's purpose is to trace the growth and decline of species diversity throughout history, as well as to argue that declining diversity is harmful to humanity. Her specific main idea is that humanity will suffer serious, though unmeasurable, consequences if it doesn't take measures to halt the current decline of species diversity.

Paragraph Structure

Paragraph 1 introduces the author's opinion about the current "biodiversity crisis." Paragraphs 2 and 3 provide historical background on the topic: paragraph 2 recounts the history of species diversity before the rise of humanity, while paragraph 3 discusses humanity's negative effect on species diversity.

In paragraph 4, the author reiterates her earlier point that there's no way to tell precisely what effects loss of species diversity will have, although it's certain to be harmful. She goes on to note, however, that there are certain to be existential costs—the loss of the earth's heritage—and more concrete costs in the area of food, medicine, and commercial products.

The Big Picture

Note the classic structure of this very straightforward science passage. The author's opinion appears in the first paragraph, and all of the subsequent paragraphs simply serve to justify and strengthen that opinion.

Whenever an author has a definite opinion about a topic, be sure that you're clear about exactly what that opinion is—several of the questions are likely to test whether you've picked up on it.
This passage is an example of why it's foolish to panic at the sight of a passage merely because it's scientific in nature and seems to have a lot of "big words." Sure, "biodiversity" and "multicellular animals," not to mention the "Mesozoic," "Paleozoic," and "Cenozoic" eras might make the passage appear to be complex, but in fact, it's really not. As noted above, the structure is clear, and the author's opinion is crystal clear as well. These are the things that determine a passage's difficulty level, and this passage, despite some scientific jargon, simply isn't very difficult to understand.

The Questions

7 (E) is correct. This choice essentially captures the author's opinion, which is stated very clearly right up front in paragraph 1, and reiterated for good measure again in paragraph 4.

(A): The author never states that the loss of species diversity is an "irreversible process." Paragraph 2 shows that the number of species rises and declines in a cyclical fashion over time. The author does say that the extinction of a *particular* species represents an "irreplaceable" loss; but the loss of a single species is distinct from the larger biodiversity process.

(B): This distorts the comparison between biological wealth and material/cultural wealth. The author states that we understand the latter while we take the former for granted. Even without this, the issue isn't important enough to be the main idea of the passage.

(C): The author never claims that the great variety of life on Earth is attributable to past episodes of mass extinction. She simply notes that these episodes are part of the history of the biodiversity process. In any case, just like (B), this choice omits the most important theme of the passage—the author's concern over the biodiversity crisis.

(D): This is too extreme. While the author suggests that today's biodiversity crisis is a potential disaster, she doesn't imply that it could be worse than past episodes of mass extinction.

Read the choices fully before endorsing any one of them. If you don't, then you could pick an answer that is "half right, half wrong." Choice (D), for instance, looks very good if you don't read through the entire choice.

8 (E) is correct. Does this question remind you of anything? It should; it's just like a Parallel Reasoning question found in Logical Reasoning. According to lines 10–18, species diversity increased rapidly at first, then held pretty much constant for a time, and then began a slow and steady climb later. Choice (E) features the same pattern of development.

(A): The mention of an abrupt decline eliminates this choice immediately.

(B): The mention of an initial fluctuation eliminates this choice quickly.

(C): This is eliminated because of its mention of a cyclical pattern.

(D): The mention of a decrease in the last part of this choice contradicts the pattern in lines 10–18.

Again, use your skills wherever they apply, no matter on which section these skills were developed. Since this question is basically the same as a Parallel Reasoning question from a Logical Reasoning section, it should be tackled in the same way.

9 (D) is correct. In lines 27–29, the author mentions that between 77 and 96 percent of all marine animal species became extinct during the Permian extinction episode. In lines 26–27, the author says that the Cretaceous extinction episode was "minor" in comparison to the Permian. Thus, we can conclude that less than 77 percent of marine animal species became extinct during the "Cretaceous crisis."

(A): Nothing in the passage suggests that it was the second worst extinction episode in history.

(B): This can't be. It was "minor" in comparison to the earlier Permian extinction episode.

(C): This is beyond the scope of passage, which never compares the Cretaceous crisis to the current biodiversity crisis.

(E): Don't be fooled because this extinction period was marked by the disappearance of the dinosaurs; this is only what makes it the "most famous" extinction episode. However, this doesn't necessarily mean that the dinosaurs "comprised the great majority of species that perished during the crisis." For all we know, many more nondinosaur species might have perished during this crisis.

Correct answers will generally be worded somewhat differently than the passage itself.

10 (B) is correct. In lines 38–42, the author refers to the careless introduction of the Nile perch into Lake Victoria as an example of a "biogeographic disaster." Moreover, the example of the Nile perch appears in a paragraph that discusses humanity's negative impact on biodiversity. It follows that this case is presented as an example of how human error, or lack of foresight, using (B)'s wording, resulted in biogeographic disaster.

(A): The Nile perch hasn't become extinct. Rather, this species now threatens the existence of *other* marine species in Lake Victoria because of human carelessness.

(C): The passage doesn't say when the Nile perch first emerged as a distinct species. It could have been long after the Permian extinction episode.

(D): No; the "material wealth" issue comes from an entirely different paragraph—paragraph 4.

(E): *Au contraire.* The Nile perch debacle is cited as an example of an action that has helped to *accelerate* the loss of biodiversity.

Logic questions ask about *why* the author has cited a detail. Hence, the key to solving a Logic question lies in understanding the gist of the paragraph in which that detail appears.

11 (B) is correct. Tricky little test makers, aren't they? Pollution is never explicitly mentioned here as contributing to the extinction of species. But pollution sounds familiar, doesn't it? Where did we see something about pollution? From the previous passage, that's where. Pollution was mentioned there in relation to human activities in international waters. Maybe it stuck in your head from that passage. In any case, the best way to get this point is simply to scan the passage for the choices about which you're unsure. Chances are you were able to recall from memory at least three and possibly all four of the wrong choices as things that were definitely mentioned in the passage.

(A) and (C): Hunting (A) and deforestation (C) are both mentioned in paragraph 3.

(D) and (E): The growth of the human population (D) and human-engineered changes to the environment (E) are both mentioned in paragraph 1.

In "all . . . EXCEPT" questions, use a process of elimination to get rid of incorrect choices. Don't just pick a choice on based on a vague recall of the text.

12 (A) is correct. Back to paragraph 4 for this one. In lines 45–51, the author argues that humans take biological wealth for granted because they don't understand its value. In contrast, she suggests, humans do not take for granted material and cultural wealth because they understand the value of these.

(B) and (E): The distinction in paragraph 4 is between material/cultural wealth, on the one hand, and biological wealth, on the other. The connections offered in choices (B) and (E) distort and expand upon this distinction, and are in no way suggested by the author.

(C): The author implies just the opposite—that preserving our biological wealth will *enhance* our material wealth and *preserve* our cultural heritage.

(D): This serves up an unsupported comparison that isn't implied in the passage. The author doesn't rank the *importance* of material and cultural wealth as opposed to biological wealth (she seems to think that all are important to humanity). She merely contrasts our *understanding* and *appreciation* of each.

When a question focuses on one very specific idea (as this one does), reread the idea to make sure that you're absolutely clear about it. This way you won't fall for choices that use the passage's language but distort its content.

13 (C) is correct. This choice captures the author's uncertain but pessimistic appraisal (especially in lines 6–8) of the biodiversity crisis.

(A): Because the planet's biota is "largely unstudied and unappreciated" and therefore "usually taken for granted," the author wouldn't claim that species loss would affect the material wealth of nations as immediately as their biological wealth. Indeed, she might argue that the effects of this loss on material wealth wouldn't be felt for quite some time.

(B): This plays on a detail in paragraph 2 regarding the end of the dinosaurs during the Cretaceous extinction episode and the consequent rise of humanity. Easy as it might be to supply our own logical leap here, in fact, the author never suggests that the same thing will happen to humans as a result of the current biodiversity crisis.

(D): Even though the author is concerned about the consequences of the biodiversity crisis for humanity, she doesn't go so far as to say that it's more fruitful to discuss the consequences of the crisis in human rather than biological terms. After all, much of the passage does dwell on the biological consequences of species loss.

(E): The first part of this choice is in line with the author's belief, but the second part is not. Nowhere does the author say that "the pace of extinctions *cannot* be reversed." The author seems to suggest just the opposite.

Note how the answer to this question echoes the answer to Question 7. Often two (or more) questions in a set will play on the same point, especially a point that's in essence the overall theme of the passage. Just like in Logic Games, you can and should use the answers to easier questions to help you solve the tougher ones.

Passage 3: French Revolution (Questions 14–20)

Topic and Scope

The topic is scholarship about women in the French Revolution—specifically, recent scholarship about women's role in the French Revolution.

Purpose and Main Idea

The author's purpose is to describe and evaluate recent scholarship about women in the French revolution; his specific main idea is that this recent scholarship has finally given adequate attention to the role of women in the French Revolution.

Paragraph Structure

Paragraph 1 reveals the topic, scope, and purpose of the passage. Paragraph 2 discusses some of the historical findings of the recent scholarship, especially the notion that women's participation in the revolution can be divided into three distinct phases. Paragraph 3 discusses scholarly inquiries into the eventual downfall of the women's movement. Finally, paragraph 4 provides the author's assessment of the recent scholarship.

The Big Picture

This passage is an ideal place to begin work on the section since topic, scope, and purpose are all evident very early on. Moreover, the structure of the passage is very predictable. After the introduction in paragraph 1, the next two paragraphs explore the content of the recent scholarship, while the final paragraph provides the author's assessment of that scholarship.

This passage illustrates the importance of previewing the entire section before attacking any of the passages. Sometimes the third or fourth passage will be the easiest, but you would never know that unless you looked at all of the passages before attacking any one of them. Never underestimate the importance of beginning the Reading Comp section on a high note. This will do wonders for your confidence, which will hopefully spill over to the rest of the section. The same can be said for acing the first games in the Logic Games section; it will make you the feel like, "Hey, I can do these, even on the real test." Previewing both the Reading Comprehension and Logic Games sections before jumping in is the best way to increase your chances of a solid start.

The Questions

14 (D) is correct. This choice encompasses the author's topic, scope, and purpose.

(A) and (C): These focus on details. The different phases of women's participation in the revolution (A) is an issue taken up in paragraph 2, while the alliance between the women's movement and other political movements (C) is an issue probed in paragraph 3.

(B): This distorts information in paragraph 1, which notes that recent studies "signal a much-needed reassessment of women's participation" in the French Revolution. The author also points out that earlier studies ignored the role of women in the revolution.

(E): The author never claims that some studies seek to evaluate the women's movement while others seek only to describe it. He implies that all of the recent studies are both descriptive and evaluative in nature.

In Global questions, watch out for choices that accurately reflect information in the passage but focus on details rather than the main idea.

15 (C) is correct. Lines 16–19 indicate that Godineau believes that literary pieces like Gouze's had no "practical effect" on political matters. "Little impact" in choice (C) is a nice paraphrase of this sentiment.

(A) and (D): These are beyond the scope of the passage. Nowhere does the text discuss what Godineau thinks about the capacity of Gouze's contemporaries to understand her tract (A). Likewise, the text never discusses whether Godineau thinks that Gouze's work was the most compelling written by a woman in the years 1789–1792 (D).

(B): Since Godineau believes that Gouze's tract had no "practical effect" on politics, she would not endorse the notion that this piece contributed to the formation of women's political clubs.

(E): This is also beyond the scope of the passage, which discusses *only* political writings up to mid-1792.

When the question stem cites a specific detail, the answer to the question will almost always be found in the lines immediately before or after that detail.

16 (B) is correct. Lines 19–24 state that the clubs began as philanthropic organizations, but later evolved into political advocacy groups with an agenda that included pushing for women's inclusion in the military. Put differently, they "eventually developed a purpose different from their original purpose."

(A): Lines 25–26 say that the mass women's movement grew out of the famine of 1795.

(C): The clubs were founded for philanthropic reasons; only later did they advocate a military role for women.

(D): The passage doesn't say what the original purpose of male political clubs was, so there's no basis for concluding that women's clubs counteracted this purpose.

(E): This is beyond the scope of the passage, which doesn't say anything about women's clubs in 1795. In fact, there's nothing about the history of these clubs after the end of 1792.

When a question stem provides a line reference, the answer to the question will be found in the lines around the reference.

17 (D) is correct. Paragraph 1 makes the point that recent scholarship about women in the French Revolution has broken new ground on the subject. The remaining paragraphs are devoted to describing and evaluating this scholarship. In other words, paragraph 1 places this scholarship in context.

(A): What argument? The author never makes an argument of his own about women's role in the French Revolution; he simply reports on and assesses the work of others.

(B): What challenges? The author distinguishes recent works from earlier works, but he doesn't ever comment on possible future challenges to recent works.

(C): This plays on (and distorts) a tiny detail in the first paragraph.

(E): This is beyond the scope of the passage, which deals only with scholarship about women in the French Revolution. The text doesn't discuss scholarship about French women in the eighteenth century in general.

This question illustrates why it's so important to read for authorial purpose. If you picked up on the author's overall purpose, choice (D) should have been fairly easy to spot.

Always keep in mind the issue of "who says what"—wrong choices often attempt to fool you into attributing the wrong ideas to the wrong characters in the passage. In this case, the author doesn't express any views about women's role in the French Revolution—the scholars do. The author reports on and assesses the scholars' interpretation.

18 (A) is correct. In lines 41–54, we see that Landes and Badinter attribute the decline of the women's movement partly to its inability to utilize its own political discourse. Adopting the traditional language and vocabularies of the time "diminished the ability of the women's movement to resist suppression." This strongly suggests that Landes and Badinter would agree wholeheartedly with (A), that the movement would have been better off if the women developed their own political lingo in support of their cause.

(B) and (C): *Au contraire.* In lines 49–54, Landes and Badinter link the downfall of the movement directly to its political alliance with Jacobin men (B), while in lines 41–49, they assert that women had no choice but to adopt the established political vocabulary of the day (C).

(D): This is beyond the scope of the passage. There's nothing in paragraph 3 to suggest that Landes and Badinter think that the movement would have survived had it not been suppressed militarily.

(E): This is also beyond the scope of the passage. All paragraph 3 says is that *Landes and Badinter* think that the women's movement had no choice but to align with these political traditions. There's nothing about whether the movement *itself* thought that these alliances were beneficial or harmful.

Prephrasing would have worked well here. If you reread Landes and Badinter's view and then put it into your own words before browsing among the choices, (A) would probably have jumped right out at you.

19 (E) is correct. In the last sentence of the passage, the author reiterates the previously mentioned conclusion of Landes and Badinter—that the women's movement was suppressed as a result of its association with other political traditions. Hence, the word "cost" refers to that suppression.

(A): This refers to Rousseauist political philosophy, not to Landes and Badinter's view of the downfall of the women's movement.

(B): This is a point made at the end of paragraph 2—a point that is unconnected to Landes and Badinter's work.

(C): This answer choice doesn't even go so far as to refer to women in the French Revolution.

(D): This confuses cause and effect: The "cost" to women was the collapse of their movement, not the reason for that collapse.

Vocabulary in Context questions don't appear frequently on the LSAT. "Context" is another word for the overall structure and theme of the passage that supplies the foundation for all of the supporting points. If you understand the gist of the paragraphs and of the passage as a whole, you should be able to understand a particular detail in context with little problem.

20 (B) is correct. The author introduces several new studies about women in the French Revolution in paragraph 1; describes the contents of those studies in paragraphs 2 and 3; and then provides a positive assessment of them in paragraph 4.

(A): The "political and intellectual traditions" mentioned in the passage are discussed only in paragraph 3, and the author doesn't criticize them.

(C) and (D): Both of these choices focus on details. The only chronological sequence (C) in the passage appears in paragraph 2, while the only comparison of women's political activities in different time periods (D) occurs at the end of that paragraph.

(E): The author's purpose is to describe and assess *new* research, not to reexamine "a long-held point of view."

It's not unusual for a question set to contain both a Main Idea and a Primary Purpose question. When this is the case, make sure that the answers to these questions are consistent, and, if necessary, use the answer to the easier question to help you answer the tougher one.

Passage 4: Impressionism (Question 21–27)

Well, isn't France just the popular topic on this LSAT administration? First the Revolution, now French art. As always, start with the basics: pinning down the topic and scope.

Topic and Scope

The topic is art historians' views of French Impressionism—specifically, Herbert's interpretation of French Impressionism.

Purpose and Main Idea

The author's purpose is to describe and take issue with Herbert's analysis of French Impressionism. The author's specific main idea is that Herbert's attempt to set French Impressionism in a "sociocultural context" isn't convincing.

Paragraph Structure

Paragraph 1 argues that criticism of French Impressionism has lately centered on the alleged sociocultural implications of Impressionist paintings rather than on their stylistic merits, and cites Herbert's book as a classic example of this new approach to critiquing Impressionism. In the last sentence of this paragraph, the author dismisses Herbert's analysis as not persuasive.

Predictably, paragraphs 2 and 3 explain why, in the author's view, Herbert's analysis is untenable. According to paragraph 2, Herbert's definition of French Impressionism is off. And, according to paragraph 3, he himself undermines his own analysis by acknowledging that Impressionist paintings don't really reflect the realities of France in the Impressionists' day.

The Big Picture

This passage is a classic "book review" passage in which the author critiques the views of somebody else. If you run into a passage like this one on the day of the test—and there's a good chance that you will—many of the questions will test to see whether you've grasped the nuances of the author's perspective.

Always keep an eye out for sentences in which the author's voice comes through—like the sentence in lines 21–22 here. Not only do they enlighten you about the author's purpose, but they also often help you to predict the direction in which the text is going to move.

The Questions

21 (B) is correct. In lines 21–22, the author calls Herbert's approach to the analysis of French Impressionism "not . . . persuasive," which is simply another way of saying "inadequate." The rest of the passage explains why the author thinks this.

(A): This focuses on a detail in paragraph 3.

(C): This distorts the passage. The author claims that Herbert's work hasn't successfully placed Impressionism in an historical context. That's not the same as saying that historical context is *irrelevant* to interpreting Impressionist works.

(D): This, too, distorts the passage. The "ideological conflict and change" alluded to in the passage concerns the interpretation of Impressionist works, not the works themselves.

(E): The author is critical of Herbert, so it's not likely that she would endorse the notion that future analyses of Impressionism will have to take his work into account.

If you prephrased the author's main idea, choice (B) should have looked good immediately. Prephrasing can often save valuable time by allowing you to zero in quickly on the correct choice.

22 (C) is correct. This choice nicely paraphrases lines 3–5.

(A): The author mentions the substance of Rewald's book, but never comments on its "objectivity."

(B) and (D): The author notes Herbert's "somewhat eccentric" selection of painters, not Rewald's.

(E): Paragraph 1 makes it clear that Rewald's book preceded the "ideological debates" about Impressionism.

Book review passages often contain information and comments about different works. Be sure that you're clear about the differences between (or among) them. The questions will test to see if you are.

23 (C) is correct. Lines 23–25 state that Herbert changed the boundaries of Impressionism in order to put it in its "proper historical context."

(A): Rewald, not Herbert, emphasized "form and style."

(B): The fact that Herbert is associated with a school of art criticism that condemns Impressionism's *failure* to represent industrial life doesn't mean that he personally harbored a *bias* in favor of industrial life.

(D): The author accuses Herbert of redrawing the traditional boundaries of Impressionism in a bizarre manner, but doesn't accuse him of incorporating all of nineteenth-century French painting in his definition of Impressionism. In fact, the author criticizes Herbert for restricting his analysis to the 1860s and 1870s.

(E): The author suggests that Herbert's redefinition of Impressionism stemmed from his dissatisfaction with earlier criticism of that school.

Question stems that are very specific require answers that are equally specific.

24 (A) is correct. This choice nicely paraphrases information in lines 12–13.

(B) and (D): *Au contraire.* Herbert's brand of criticism focuses on content issues, such as the Impressionists' failure to depict industrial life, while Rewald focused purely on stylistic issues.

(C): How could the Impressionists idealize topics that weren't represented in their paintings?

(E): This is beyond the scope of the passage, which is about Impressionists in particular, not modernist painters in general.

Use the information in the stem to isolate the relevant part of the text in your search for the correct answer to an Explicit Text question. Since modern industry and labor are mentioned only in paragraph 1, you can safely ignore paragraphs 2 and 3 for the sake of this point.

25 (D) is correct. In the last sentence of paragraph 1, the author claims that Herbert's arguments are unpersuasive. In paragraphs 2 and 3, she explains why.

(A), (B), and (E): Paragraph 2 doesn't present a second argument (A); revise a thesis (B); or present a counterargument (E). Like paragraph 3, it simply fleshes out an argument made in paragraph 1.

(C): Like paragraph 2, paragraph 3 supports the argument made in paragraph 1. Moreover, this paragraph doesn't contain an "alternative thesis." The author simply suggests that art criticism must take into account both stylistic and content issues. But that hardly qualifies as an "alternative thesis."

When describing the structure of a passage, watch out for answer choices containing features that weren't mentioned—in this case, (A), (B), and (E).

26 (D) is correct. Paragraph 3's general thrust is that not too much about society can be inferred from Impressionist paintings because Impressionists consciously distorted reality for stylistic reasons.

(A) and (C): These touch on a distinction made by the author, not by Impressionists themselves.

(B): This quote comes up in the context of an argument that denies the validity of exclusively concentrating on the *substance* of Impressionist paintings.

(E): If anything, this quote supports the claim that Impressionists ignored certain subjects to concentrate on others.

Always get a sense of the context in which a quote appears before attempting to figure out why the author included the quote in the text.

27 (E) is correct. This choice nicely paraphrases the last sentence of the passage, in which the author says that critiques of Impressionist paintings must take into account both their style and content.

(A): Herbert's book, which is based on the content of Impressionist paintings, wouldn't lead to a book on Impressionist style.

(B): The passage reveals what art historians think about Impressionism; it doesn't provide any genuine insight into what Impressionists themselves thought should be their "primary artistic concern."

(C): The traditional interpretation of Impressionism, like that found in Rewald's book, emphasizes stylistic issues.

(D): The author simply says that critiques of Impressionism must address both stylistic and content issues. She doesn't comment on what constitutes the most "innovative" part of Impressionist painting.

This question highlights the importance of reading the entire passage. The answer to a question or two often appears in the last few sentences of the text.

Section III: Logic Games

Game 1: Lawyers' Salaries (Questions 1–6)

The Action

A quick look at the rules tells you immediately that this is a "free-floating" sequencing game. The rules place entities *in relation* to each other instead of assigning them to specific spots. You are asked to order nine partners in a law firm—Fox, Glassen, Hae, Inman, Jacoby, Kohn, Lopez, Malloy, and Nassar—in relation to each other based on their salaries.

Key Issues

1. What partner can, must, or cannot have a higher/lower salary than what other partner?
2. What partner can, must, or cannot have the same salary as what other partner?

The Initial Setup

Often, the best way to visualize this kind of free-floating sequencing game is vertically. On the top of the page, write "more" and at the bottom write "less." This will serve to remind you that those partners above have a larger salary than those below. That and listing the partners (their letters, actually) off to the side are about all you can do before hitting the rules:

F G H I J K L M N more

less

The Rules

To give yourself an idea where to start, scan the rules and try to spot a partner that is not stated as having a lower salary than another partner. Kohn in Rule 1 isn't explicitly lower than anyone, so put a K at the top of your sketch.

1. From the K draw two lines, one down to an I and one down to an L.

2. From that L draw a line down to an N.

3. Now jump over to the other branch. From the I, draw a line down to an F.

4. From the F, you need a line down to an M.

5. From the M, draw a line down to a G.

6. From the G, draw a line down to a J.

7. And finally, from the J, draw a line down to an H.

Key Deductions

The first thing to do is to check your list of entities and make sure that they're all included in the sketch. In this case they are, so you can fully depend on the master sketch (and redrawings of it, as needed) to answer all the questions.

There are a few things that you should notice right from the start. *Kohn has the largest salary, period. Either Hae or Nassar has the smallest salary.* Here's a common mistake to avoid: just because Lopez and Nassar are connected to a shorter "branch," don't assume that they necessarily make a higher salary than any of the entities in the other "branch." They could both make less than even Hae. As soon as you've taken some time to make sure you understand the sketch, you should be all set to rack up some easy points.

The Final Visualization

And here is our neat, accessible sketch:

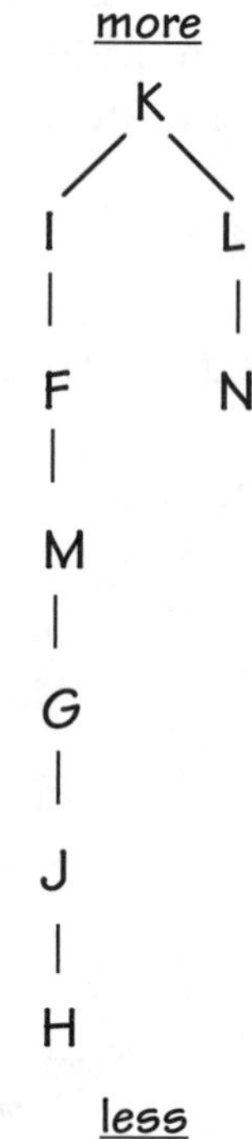

The Big Picture

In a free-floating sequence game, a common mistake is assuming relationships that aren't explicitly stated. If a relationship between two entities is not bound by a rule or deduction, don't assume it.

Time taken up front is especially important in this type of game, but a careless master sketch can turn a straightforward game like this into a nightmare. If your master sketch is accurate, you shouldn't have to use your pencil much in the course of this kind of game, except for an occasional redrawing when necessary.

Picture the lines between the entities as elastic—you can stretch L and N way down below H, or place them practically anywhere between K and H (and L and N don't necessarily have to be near one another, either). This flexibility of the entities' relationships to one another is the key element of the free-floating sequence game.

The Questions

1 (D) is correct. There are two kinds of partners who cannot have the third highest salary: those who must have a higher salary *and* those who must have a lower salary. Who must have a greater salary? Only K, who has the greatest salary, but K isn't one of the choices. So look for those entities that have three or more people *over* them in the sketch (they could be at best fourth highest). The right branch is composed of L and N below K. We noted above that L and N are flexible and can fit anywhere into the left branch, so either of them could have the third highest salary. Eliminate answer choices (C) and (E). On the left branch, count down three people, and anyone after that could be the answer. M, G, J, and H all have three or more people over them, which means that any of them qualifies as a partner who cannot have the third highest salary. The test makers happened to pick M, answer choice (D).

The first question in a question set is often straightforward. This is the test makers' way of rewarding those who took the time up front to carefully work through the setup.

2 (C) is correct. You can probably picture this scenario in your head, but you might have also opted for a quick redrawing of the master sketch including the new information (just draw an "=" sign between M and N):

Now it's simply a matter of counting the people who are definitely below L. The new sketch clearly shows that N, M, G, J, and H are all below L, a total of five people, answer choice (C). I and F could be below L, but they could also be above L. K, as always, is definitely above L.

Never hesitate to redraw a master sketch (especially one as simple as this) when needed. This way the original stays neat, and you can benefit from your previous work in future questions.

3 (D) is correct. To determine all the salaries, you need to connect the L-N branch of the sketch to the longer branch with all of the entities' locations definitely set. Not much to do but check the choices.

(A): L is now above F but could be above or below I, and N could be anywhere below L. Keep on looking.

(B): L is between K and I, but N could be anywhere from third to last.

(C): N is now above F, but L and N are not set in relation to I.

(D): If N is above I, N must be third, following K and L. This leaves I through H fourth through ninth, respectively. All of the partners' rankings are determined, so (D) is the answer.

(E): L and N could assume many positions in the ranking above M and below K, so (E) is no help.

It's good to try to get an idea of what you're looking for in a question (like the need to combine the branches of the sketch), but when you hit a lull, go to the choices. Knowing when to stop looking for deductions and to move on to the choices is a skill that will develop with practice.

4 (D) is correct. If N has the same salary as one other partner, what *can't* be true? At first glance, it appears that there's not much to do here except note the new information and check the choices. However, you might have noticed that L couldn't be the same or less than H because there would be no one left for N to share salaries with. If you recognized this, you could have just scanned the choices and found that choice (D) is impossible for this reason. If you didn't see this, you would need to check each choice, stopping when you found the choice that must be false.

As for the wrong choices, here are orderings that show that each of them is possible:

(A) and (B): K—L—(I=N)—F—M—G—J—H

(C): K—I—F—L—(M=N)—G—J—H

(E): K—I—F—L—M—G—(J=N)—H

Every LSAT question is worth one point, but some take longer than others. Budget your time accordingly. A question that requires you to test each choice may be a good question to put off until later.

5 (C) is correct. What are the minimum number of different salaries? Well, L and N can share salaries with two other partners in the left branch. The entities in the left branch, however, are all separated explicitly by the rules. So all you have to do is count them up (don't forget to count K at the top). There are seven, which is choice (C).

As you work with more questions in a game, you will often find yourself instinctively knowing where to look for the answer. This is the kind of thinking that the test makers reward.

6 (D) is correct. Here we're looking for G's possible rankings, given the fact that no one shares salaries. First count the people who are explicitly placed above G. There are four, which means that G can be fifth but no higher than fifth. Does this eliminate any choices? No, since fifth appears in each answer choice, and no answer choice includes a place higher than fifth. Who else could earn a higher salary than G? The only "wildcards" are L and N who are very flexible. One, both, or neither could be above G. That makes G's possibilities fifth, sixth, and seventh, choice (D).

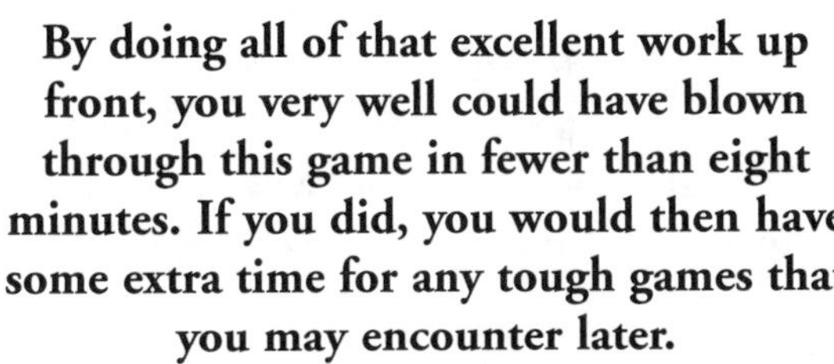

By doing all of that excellent work up front, you very well could have blown through this game in fewer than eight minutes. If you did, you would then have some extra time for any tough games that you may encounter later.

Game 2: Illnesses and Symptoms (Questions 7–11)

The Action

In this one we're asked to match five illnesses—J, K, L, M, and N—with their symptoms: a matching game.

Key Issues

The key issues deal with the typical matching concerns:

1. What symptoms does each illness have?

2. What illnesses can, must, or cannot have the same symptoms as what other illnesses?

The Initial Setup

Either a grid or a list works well with a matching game. You could use a 5 × 3 grid with the illnesses—J, K, L, M, and N—across the top, and the symptoms—f, h, and s—along the side. This way you could put a ✔ when you match a symptom with an illness and an "X" when you know that an illness definitely doesn't have that symptom. However, if you were keeping track of illnesses' symptoms in real life, you would probably just make a list of the illnesses across the page and be ready to fill in the symptoms under each, like so:

f h s

J K L M N

The Rules

1. Very concrete—put an "h" for headache and an "s" for sneezing under the J.

2. Think first, don't just write "J ≠ K." Each illness has at least one symptom, and Rule 1 just said that J has headache and sneezing; therefore K must have only fever. Put an "f" for fever and "no h" and "no s" under K. Also put "no f" under J.

3. L will have at least one (or both) of headache and sneezing. Let's write "at least 1 same" and draw arrows between J and L.

4. Again, think before you draw. You know that K has exactly one symptom, so L must have two or three. Write "2 or 3" over L.

5. L and N don't have any symptoms in common. Write an "≠" with arrows pointing to L and N to serve as a reminder.

6. Don't just write "M > J." Think through the rule first. What did Rule 1 say about J? J has two symptoms, so M must have all three. Write "f, h, s" under M.

Key Deductions

We made a bunch of deductions along the way as we went through the rules above. But there's even another deduction to be made from combining Rules 4 and 5 with what we already deduced about illness L: L has either two or three symptoms (Rule 4), but N has at least one symptom, so L can't have all three symptoms (there would be none left for N—Rule 5). L, therefore, must have exactly two symptoms, and N must have exactly one symptom. Go back and change the "2 or 3" to just "2" over the L and write "1" over N.

Three of the five illnesses (J, K, and M) are entirely filled, and you know the exact number of symptoms for the other two illnesses, L and N. This is a ton of information you've deduced and should lead to some quick and easy points.

The Final Visualization

So, here's what we know heading into the questions (and it's quite a lot):

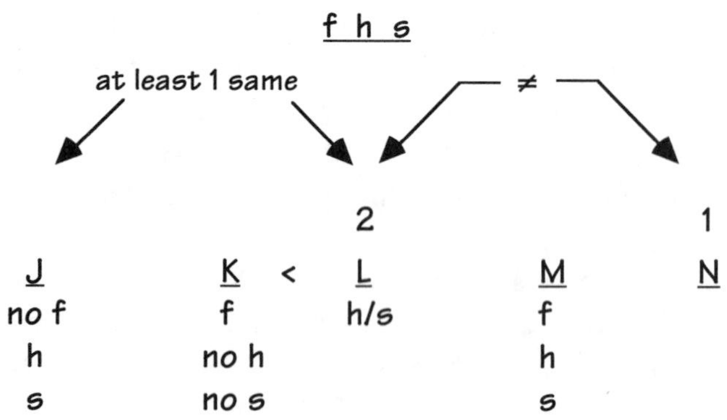

The Big Picture

Again we see how important it is to take the time up front to work out as much as we can about the setup. The more you know about a game before hitting the questions, the better. Anyone armed with the large amount of deductive information described above should be able to blaze through the five questions of this game, saving precious time for the other games in the section.

In Logic Games, numbers are always important. In this game, for example, remembering that each illness has at least one symptom leads to the key deductions. Always paraphrase the rules, asking yourself, "What does this mean?" and not, "What does this say?"

The Questions

7 (E) is correct. After all of our work with the setup, this question should take about ten seconds. Scan the choices against what we've deduced. N has one symptom, not two as choice (E) has it.

An easy first question is the test makers' way of rewarding those who do their work up front. If you did the work, you knew exactly what was right (or wrong) with each answer choice.

If you don't spot the possible deductions up front, often the first question in a question set will subtly inform you that you should have taken the information further than you did. In this case, suppose that initially you didn't work out the numbers the way we did above. Then you come to the first question, which basically tells you that it's possible to deduce a lot about the number of symptoms per illness. Use this as an opportunity to shore up any aspect of the game that you may have overlooked in your initial run-through.

8 (C) is correct. Once you've decoded this question stem, it's just a matter of checking for the pair that could share exactly the same symptoms—that is, the same number *and* type. M is the only illness with all three symptoms so axe any choices that include M—answer choices (D) and (E). We also know the numbers of symptoms for each of the illnesses; the only pairs that can possibly have the same number of symptoms are J and L (they each have two symptoms) or K and N (they each have one). J and L isn't a choice, but K and N is, in answer choice (C).

The "active" way into a question is usually the fastest. But if you can't see it, don't worry. If it doesn't come to you, simply try out the choices. Armed with the information discussed above, it shouldn't have taken long to eliminate everything but (C).

9 (A) is correct. Make abstract information concrete. L's symptoms aren't exactly the same as any other illness. L has two symptoms and so does J, but for this question they can't share both of them. J has headache and sneezing. Rule 3 tells us that L shares at least (and in this question, exactly) one with J. So L's other symptom must be fever, choice (A).

When given new information about an entity, look back to the rules that mention that entity. This will often lead you to the correct answer.

10 (E) is correct. Read carefully here. You may have marked (A) thinking that it was a direct restatement of Rule 3. But the question stem says "exactly" one symptom; Rule 3 states that J and L share *at least* one symptom, which means they can share two. Knowing the number of symptoms in each illness helps enormously here. It may have occurred to you that M, with all three symptoms, and either K or N, with exactly one symptom, would have to share exactly one symptom. Scanning the choices we see that M and N is the pair the test makers chose in (E). If you didn't see this, you could have answered this one fairly quickly by simply checking the choices:

(A): See discussion above.

(B): No, J with two symptoms must share exactly *two* with M.

(C) and (D): Both of these pairs of illnesses could share one symptom, but they can also share none.

Keep thinking actively. Don't automatically try out the choices. Often there is a quicker way.

Critical reading is just as important in Logic Games as in the other sections. Always read critically on the Logic Games section—the difference between "at least one" and "exactly one" is large enough to cost you a point.

11 (E) is correct. What combination of illnesses would force Harold to have all three symptoms? With all the deductions up front, checking each choice is a viable option, but the active way, when available, is always better. If two illnesses have all three symptoms between them, then Walter, who has only two symptoms, cannot have all the symptoms of both. J and K have all the symptoms between them, since J's symptoms are headache and sneezing, and K's symptom is fever.

Unfortunately, J and K isn't a choice. However, L and N also must have all three symptoms between them, since L has two symptoms, N has one, and they have none in common. So Walter, suffering from exactly two symptoms, cannot have all the symptoms of L and N, choice (E). On the day of the test, you wouldn't bother with the other choices. You would just mark (E) and move on. But for the record, here's what's wrong with the other choices:

(A): No, J and L can share headache and sneezing, so forget (A).

(B): N's one symptom could be headache or sneezing; forget (B).

(C): We just saw in Question 9 that L could share one of its two symptoms with K. Walter could have these two, so forget (C).

(D): N's one symptom could be fever, just like K.

Occasionally, when the wording gets a bit obtuse, you'll have to decode or decipher the question stem. Here, the question is not very difficult to answer once you figure out exactly what it's asking. Take the time in an unusual stem to understand exactly what the test makers are looking for before you move on to the solution.

Game 3: Street Cleaning (Questions 12–17)

The Action

This game requires us to order seven streets—1, 2, 3, 4, 5, 6, and 7—based on when they're cleaned—either the morning or afternoon of one Monday through Friday work week. This is a sequencing game with a slight twist. The morning and afternoon aspect means that you've got ten spaces in which to plug the streets.

Key Issues

1. When is each street cleaned?
2. What streets can, must, or cannot be cleaned before or after what other streets?
3. What streets can, must, or cannot be cleaned in the morning?
4. What streets can, must, or cannot be cleaned in the afternoon?

The Initial Setup

If you were keeping track of these days, you would probably make a little calendar. A calendar is just a type of grid, so put the days—M, T, W, Th, and F—across the top of a 5 × 2 grid, and along the side write "AM" and "PM," for morning and afternoon. Since the test makers were kind enough to number the streets, your job simply will be to write the numbers into the squares depending on when each street is cleaned. If you know that no streets can be cleaned on a certain day and time, just put an "X" in that square. Remember to list the streets (in this case, the numbers) off to the side:

1 2 3 4 5 6 7 8

	M	T	W	Th	F
AM					
PM					

The Rules

1. No streets are cleaned on Friday morning, so put a big X in Friday's AM square.
2. Wednesday afternoon is out, so place another X in Wednesday's PM square.
3. Easy enough; write a 4 in Tuesday's AM square, and cross it off the list of streets.
4. And now 7 is definitely set as well. Cross 7 off your list of streets and put it in Thursday's AM square.
5. Make sure you interpret this correctly. For now write, "8 . . . 4 . . . 6," and we'll come back to this rule when discussing key deductions.
6. 2, 5, and 8 are cleaned in the afternoon, so at the far end of the PM row, write "2, 5, and 8."

Key Deductions

Let's now look closer at the fifth rule. Fourth Street is set on Tuesday morning and Sixth Street is cleaned after Fourth. The sixth rule says that Second, Fifth, and Eighth are cleaned in the afternoon. Now, combine the fifth and sixth rules, and the only afternoon slot that is available before Fourth is Monday afternoon. *So Eighth must be cleaned on Monday afternoon;* write an 8 in Monday's PM square. And cross off 8 from the list of afternoon streets.

It's also a good idea to identify the "floaters," those entities that aren't bound by any rules. Here the floaters are First and Third. They can go just about anywhere. However, there is one thing about these two floaters that you might have noticed. Fourth, Seventh, and Eighth are all set. Sixth must be cleaned after Fourth on Tuesday afternoon, Wednesday, Thursday, or Friday. Second and Fifth must be cleaned in the afternoon. So what about Monday morning? *The only streets that can be cleaned on Monday morning are First and Third.* They are the only entities free to be cleaned on Monday (Sixth can't) morning (Second and Fifth can't). Write "1/3" in Monday's AM square. This is a tricky bit of deductive thinking, but if you saw it, you're that much ahead of the game.

The Final Visualization
So this is what the final sketch looks like:

① ~~2~~ ③ ~~4~~ ~~5~~ ~~6~~ ~~7~~ ~~8~~

4 · · · 6

	M	T	W	Th	F	
AM	1/3	4		7	X	
PM	8		X			2, 5

The Big Picture

It's preferable to work a rule directly into the master sketch (such as the fifth rule above). When that's not possible, then it's better to rewrite it than to underline the rule. You will remember it more readily after writing it in your own shorthand.

The scratchwork you choose to use is up to you. You could just as easily have listed M through F across the page with two dashes under each for AM and PM. Whatever kind of sketch you choose, just be sure that it's accurate and neat.

The Questions

12 (B) is correct. Second Street must be in the afternoon (the sixth rule), and the only available afternoon slot before Seventh, which is cleaned on Thursday morning (the fourth rule), is Tuesday afternoon. What street must be cleaned on Tuesday afternoon? Second Street, choice (B).

Early on, you may have to take your time and consult your rules and deductions. As you answer more questions in a game, you will become more accustomed to where you need to look, and what rules are most useful.

13 (C) is correct. The only morning on which Sixth can be cleaned is Wednesday—that's the only morning after Fourth (fifth rule), and Second is under the same conditions as in Question 12: before Seventh, which means Tuesday afternoon. The only streets that we don't know are First, Third (our two floaters), and Fifth. That makes three undetermined streets, answer choice (C).

Get the new information down and work with it. Don't just stare at the page; ask yourself, "What does it mean that Sixth is cleaned in the morning?" Make the abstract information concrete.

Use your past work whenever possible. It's not always this straightforward, having the same condition appear in two questions in a row, but always try to use previous work to your advantage whenever possible.

14 (E) is correct. Fourth, Seventh, and Eighth are all set, so none of them can be cleaned on Friday afternoon. All the other streets (First, Second, Third, Fifth, and Sixth) could be cleaned on Friday afternoon without violating any of the rules. Try it. That's a total of five streets, choice (E).

Don't do more work than necessary. When asked for a maximum, start with the largest number possible and work your way down to the answer. Likewise, when asked for a minimum, start with the smallest number given.

15 (A) is correct. In the discussion of key deductions above, we saw that First or Third must be cleaned on Monday morning (all of the other streets are explicitly prohibited from being cleaned then). This question stem lets you know that Third can't be the street cleaned on Monday morning, so for this question, it has to be First. Let's stop right here and see if that's enough by itself to answer this question. Quickly scan the choices. Answer choice (A) must be false. If First is cleaned before Third, then First must be cleaned on Monday morning, which means First can't be cleaned on Tuesday afternoon. If you hadn't made the "1/3 on Monday AM" deduction before, you could have still checked each of the choices.

(B) and (C): First cleaned on Monday morning, Second cleaned on Thursday afternoon, and Third cleaned on Wednesday morning shows that these two could be true. Eliminate both of them.

(D) and (E): First on Monday morning, Third on Wednesday morning, Fifth on Thursday afternoon, and Sixth on Friday afternoon eliminates (D) and (E).

This question might have taken quite a long time if you had to check each choice. But if you took the time up front and discovered the "1/3 on Monday AM" deduction, this question should have been a snap.

16 (D) is correct. Seventh is set on Thursday morning, so Sixth must be cleaned immediately before that: Wednesday morning (no streets are cleaned on Wednesday afternoon, according to the second rule). Fifth must be cleaned right before Sixth: Tuesday afternoon. That's Fifth, Sixth, and Seventh cleaned in numerical order. We're left with First and Third (one of which is set for Monday morning), and Second (which must be cleaned on one of the remaining afternoons). If First is cleaned Monday morning, then Second and Third are left to float between Thursday and Friday afternoons. That's two possibilities so far. But if Third is cleaned Monday morning, then First and Second are left to float between Thursday and Friday afternoons, giving us another two options. That's four total. Written out, the possibilities look like this:

1: Monday AM—1, Thursday PM—2, Friday PM—3
2: Monday AM—1, Thursday PM—3, Friday PM—2
3: Monday AM—3, Thursday PM—2, Friday PM—1
4: Monday AM—3, Thursday PM—1, Friday PM—2.

There are four possibilities; that's choice (D).

In this question, you were once again aided by the deduction that either First or Third must be cleaned on Monday morning. Even if you didn't see this deduction up front, you might have picked up on it by the time you got to this late question, simply by plotting out the entities over and over again in the previous questions.

Work with concrete information first. You were told that Fifth, Sixth, and Seventh were in numerical order, so it made sense to start with the street that was already set, Seventh, and work your way backwards.

17 (B) is correct. You're given a new rule, so it's not a bad idea to alter your master sketch quickly, moving Fouth Street to Tuesday afternoon. Go back and see how that affects everything else. Eighth is still on Monday afternoon (still the only afternoon before Fourth), and Seventh is still on Thursday morning (the fourth rule hasn't changed). The sixth rule said that Second and Fifth are cleaned in the afternoon. Since Fourth is now in the afternoon that leaves two afternoons for Second and Fifth to split—Thursday afternoon and Friday afternoon. The only place left for Sixth (which must be cleaned after Fourth according to the fifth rule) is Wednesday morning. The only streets left are First and Third, and they'll split Monday morning and Tuesday morning.

Now to the choices. Fifth can be cleaned on Thursday afternoon while Second is cleaned Friday afternoon, showing that choice (B) could indeed be false and is therefore the credited answer.

(A), (C), (D), and (E): All of these must be true, as evidenced by the new master sketch.

Redrawing isn't a waste of time, and it's often the best way to keep a game organized, especially when new rules are added or old ones are changed.

Even if this hadn't been the last question of the game, it would have been a good idea to leave it for last. Whenever you have to change or delete a rule, you're probably best off skipping that question and coming back to it after answering all of the other questions.

Game 4: Ski Chalets (Questions 18–24)

The Action

This is a type of Logic Game that has been absent from the more recent LSATs: a mapping game. Although you might not see one of this type on your test, the methods used to solve this particular type are the same as those needed to solve other types. You are asked to map a single path to each of six chalets—J, K, L, M, N, and O.

Key Issue

1. What chalets can, must, or cannot be directly connected to what other chalets to form a single continuous path?

The Initial Setup

You're given a wonderful sketch in the opening paragraph, so by all means, use it. As you work with the rules, build them right into the given sketch. Here's a reproduction of the diagram that was provided:

row 1: J K L

row 2: M N O

The Rules

There's one very important rule stated in the opening paragraph, and you could have easily missed it. It's stated that "a single continuous path . . . connects all of the chalets." This means that a single line must connect all the chalets with no backtracks (that's one of the implications of the word "continuous.") So a single path will wind around touching all the chalets—very important.

1. The path is composed of exactly five segments, each of which runs between exactly two chalets.

2. This is a basic loophole closer; no chalet is left out of the path.

3. Each chalet is connected to at most two other chalets. This rule hints at the importance of the numbers in the game. When any chalet is connected to two others, then it's maxed out. Write "2 MAX" by the provided sketch to serve as a visual reminder.

4. During the course of winding around to each chalet, the path cannot ever cross itself. Write "none cross."

5. These rules are very concrete, so build them right into the given sketch. Draw a line between J and N, and draw another one between K and L.

Key Deductions

There is something that you should notice just from reviewing the master sketch. Because of the fourth and fifth rules, the only chalets that can be connected with M are J and N (and whichever one is connected to M will be maxed out thanks to the third rule).

The Final Visualization

Here's the master sketch:

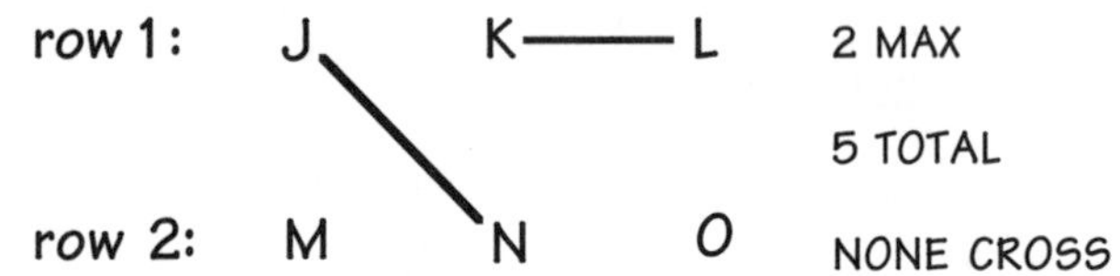

The Big Picture

Rewriting a rule in your own words (when you can't build it directly into your sketch) is the best way to remember it.

Not all rules are in indented form. Some very important rules (like "single continuous path" above) are hidden in the opening paragraph. Be on the lookout for them.

The Questions

18 (E) is correct. There isn't much to do with a "could be true" question offering no new information except check the choices. In (E) we see O connected to L and O connected to N. All we have to do is connect M and J to get an acceptable single continuous path.

(A), (B), (C), and (D): These all try to connect M with a chalet other than J or N, which is not possible.

"Could be trues" like this one often are very time consuming, but those who put in the work up front and took heed of M's situation were probably able to cut through this one much more quickly. If you noticed that four of the choices tried to connect M with a chalet other than J or N, you could have answered this question in 10 seconds.

19 (C) is correct. Since N and K are connected, both are maxed out. M must always be connected to either J or N, so here M must be connected to J and J is maxed out. The only chalet that is left to be connected to O is L. You have a single continuous path and everything is set, so it's a pretty simple task to scan the choices looking for the pair that must be connected. It's L and O, choice (C).

(A), (B), (D), and (E): These are all impossible.

Work with the new information and see where it leads. Don't just stare at a question.

20 (D) is correct. J and K are now maxed out. By now you should be used to looking for a chalet to hook up with M, and here it's N. That's two chalets connected to N, so N is maxed out. Just like in Question 19, L must be connected to O, so choice (D) is correct.

(A), (B), (C), and (E): These are all impossible.

Work with the new information and see where it leads. Sometimes it leads to the same place (L connected to O) twice in a row.

21 (A) is correct. This stem (K to O) maxes out K. As usual, J or N will connect with M. K is maxed and L is off limits to J, M, and N thanks to the fourth rule, so O must be the one that connects the two groups. You don't know whether O is connected to J or N, so move on to the choices. As long as N is the one connected to O, J could be connected to M and (A) could be true.

(B): No, K is maxed out and can't be connected to N.

(C): This would max out O without connecting all of the chalets; a no-no.

(D): The only way for L to be connected to two chalets is if the second one is O (L's path can't cross the K-O path), which would max out O and not connect all the chalets.

(E): No, O is the chalet that has to connect in some way to the J, M, N group, so O must be connected to *two* chalets (K and either J or N), not one.

You may have considered skipping this one if you were running low on time. It's one of the most time consuming of the questions.

22 (A) is correct. We've seen this basic concept before. M can only be connected to either J or N, so in order to force M to connect with N, all we need to do is max out J. This is accomplished by connecting J with either chalet K or chalet O; the test makers chose the former as choice (A).

(B), (C), (D), and (E): These all leave open the possibility that M is connected to J, not K.

By now you should know what to look for in the questions. The "M connected to J or N" deduction has been important in answering every question we've seen so far.

23 (C) is correct. This should have been obvious because of all the previous work with M. The thinking goes like this: M can only be connected to J or N. If M is connected to *both* of them, J and N are both maxed out, leaving no way to connect all the chalets with a single continuous path. M can be connected to only one chalet (J or N), not two, which is choice (C). You could have checked each choice, but that would have taken much longer. If you did have to try out the choices, you could have sped things up by using your previous work, like so:

(A): In Question 21, we saw K connected to two chalets, so forget (A).

(B): In Question 19 (and 20), we saw L connected to two chalets; eliminate (B).

(D): In Question 19, N was connected to two chalets.

(E): In Question 21, we saw that O had to be connected to exactly two chalets.

Try to pursue the answer actively, but if you don't see it, go on to the choices.

Use your previous work whenever possible. If something was true in a previous question, barring a rule change or new hypothetical, it must be true now.

24 (B) is correct. Here we're told that no direct opposites are connected, which means no J to M, no K to N, and no L to O. Where to now? We're used to connecting M to either J or N, so start there. Since M and J can't be connected, it's M and N (N is now maxed out). L and O are not compatible according to this stem, so O can be connected to only J or K. Actually in this case, O must be connected to J *and* K. Otherwise, there would be no way to get our single continuous path. Everything is set. Only (B) contradicts this arrangement.

(A), (C), (D), and (E): All of these follow the new sketch perfectly.

Make the abstract concrete. ". . . no segment of the path directly connects any chalet in row 1 with the chalet in row 2 that is directly opposite it" is not very helpful. However, "No J to M" and so on for the other pairs of opposites lead us right to the answer.

Once again, the numbers of a game prove to be very important. This game was greatly simplified by keeping track of when a chalet was "maxed out" and therefore inaccessible.

Section IV: Logical Reasoning

1 (B) is correct. Sound too good to be true? In real life, our natural skepticism would lead us to ask: "Okay, what's the catch?" And the question stem straight out tells us to be suspicious—we're asked to weaken the conclusion that this tax reform is good for the low-income folks. Well, everyone knows that if you save money in one area but lose more money in another, the overall transaction is a bust.

And that's the result set in motion by choice (B): a low-income taxpayer who saves \$100 to \$300 a year, but has to pay roughly \$40 per month, *or \$480 a year*, in additional rent, certainly isn't benefiting from the tax reform. Based on one positive effect of tax reform, the author concludes that tax reform will have an *overall* positive effect on low-income taxpayers. However, if (B) is true, the tax reform no longer looks like such a good deal.

(A): This could only strengthen the argument, since saving some taxpayers the expense of hiring an accountant would make the new tax reform seem like a positive development. However, (A) fails even as a strengthener, since the argument concerns the interests of low-income taxpayers, whereas (A) would apply to *all* taxpayers.

(C): So what? This choice in no way suggests that tax reform isn't in the interest of low-income taxpayers.

(D) and (E): Both of these strengthen the argument. Allowing low-income taxpayers to take a deduction on child-care expenses (D), or releasing them altogether from the obligation to pay taxes (E) are certainly benefits to those taxpayers.

This stimulus is an excellent example of a type that shows up on the LSAT with some frequency: the author examines only one side of an issue and assumes that there's nothing to be said on the other side. In many cases, results of a policy or an action are assessed as unilaterally good, while any negative impact is minimized or ignored

completely. When you suspect that the argument is lacking because it doesn't include both sides of the story, look for a choice that addresses an issue neglected by the author.

2 (E) is correct. The question stem tells us to concentrate not on the conclusion, but on the seemingly unusual relationship posited in the evidence. That is, although the author concludes that Phobos should be next, the test makers don't really care about that; they're simply looking for a reason why, flight times being equal, the Phobos trip requires so much less fuel than does the Mars trip. If the flight times are equal, odds are there's some *other* difference between the flights that accounts for the difference in fuel requirements. Choice (E) gives us what we want: if lift-off for the return trip from Phobos would use much less fuel than lift-off from Mars would, then the mystery of the difference in fuel requirements is solved.

(A) and (C): These are irrelevant, since neither says anything about the *fuel requirements* of the two trips.

(B): We have no idea what size ship is needed for a Phobos trip or a Mars trip, so (B) doesn't help us understand why the two trips of equal flight times have different fuel requirements.

(D): Huh? This confusing mess is an irrelevant comparison. It doesn't matter in the least how far Phobos is from Mars; the fact that they are relatively close to *each other* doesn't help explain the difference in fuel requirements for a trip from Earth to each of these destinations.

Whenever the question stem gives you information about the stimulus, take it. In this case, reading the question stem first gave valuable information on the scope of the argument. Knowing that the question is concerned with explaining the difference in fuel requirements tells us to focus on that issue as we attack the stimulus.

When you are asked to explain a result or resolve a seeming paradox, don't take issue with the evidence. Accept the evidence as true, but look for an alternative explanation, another way to explain the facts in the passage.

3 (C) is correct. There's a very subtle scope shift in this one. We're told that research involving international collaboration has produced papers of greater *influence* than has noncollaborative research; influence, we learn, is measured by the number of times a paper is cited by subsequent papers. We can accept this definition; it stands to reason that papers used more frequently than others by later researchers can be said to be more "influential."

But then the author expands the scope, hoping we won't notice: she concludes that projects conducted by international research teams are therefore more *important* than projects conducted by single researchers. The evidence is that a paper's influence can be measured by the number of citations, while the conclusion is about a paper's "importance." It might sound like the same thing, but actually it's not. How "important" a paper turns out to be covers a far greater scope than the "influence" it has had on subsequent research as measured by the number of times it's cited. For the conclusion about "importance" to hold, the author must be assuming what's stated in (C): that "importance," like "influence," is indicated by the number of citations a paper receives.

(A): This would weaken the argument by suggesting that the number of subsequent citations might not be a reliable indicator of a paper's importance.

(B): Even if it were impossible to tell whether any given paper is the product of an international collaboration—the denial of (B)—it still might be true that international collaborations are of greater importance, so (B) cannot be an assumption.

(D): This is outside the scope. We don't know anything about collaborative efforts of scientists from the same country; the argument only contrasts international collaborations with single-author papers.

(E): Even if (E) is true, it doesn't indicate that international collaborative efforts are more important than single-author projects; the argument makes no connection between funding and importance.

Pay attention to the scope of the evidence and conclusion. You might not have noticed the subtle shift in focus from a paper's *influence* (explicitly defined in the stimulus) to a work's *importance*. Once you notice the shift, the question practically answers itself.

4 (A) is correct. We're asked to find a flaw in a very specific part of the argument: the claim that socialized medicine is technologically superior to private-sector medicine. Notice that the only evidence the author cites for this claim is the low infant mortality rate in countries that use socialized medicine.

Choice (A) breaks this connection between lower infant mortality and technological superiority by providing an alternative explanation for the lower infant mortality—namely, that the greater access to medical care in countries with socialized medicine, not technological superiority, might be the reason for those countries' lower infant mortality rate. If this is the case, then private-sector care might actually be technologically superior, yet still have a higher infant mortality rate than countries with socialized medicine, due to the limited access to such care.

(B): This is outside the scope. We're not talking about the socialist *economies* and their achievements, but about the alleged technological superiority of socialized *medicine.*

(C): This is a strengthener; it supports the claim that the low infant mortality rate connected to socialized medicine indicates technological superiority.

(D): We don't need a list of countries whose medical systems are socialized or private in order to draw a conclusion about the merits of the different medical systems.

(E): The author doesn't presuppose the desirability of socialized medical systems. She provides evidence (greater accessibility and low infant mortality) that she believes demonstrates that desirability.

Read the question stem first. The earlier you find out your task, the better. Question stems sometimes provide information on an argument's topic and scope, as here.

Don't be fooled into thinking the author uses a circular argument just because the conclusion is stated first. It doesn't matter where the conclusion appears, as long as it is backed up with evidence.

This is another case of weakening the author's explanation by coming up with an alternative explanation. Interestingly, in this case, the alternative explanation for a lower rate of infant mortality (greater access to care) was mentioned by the author herself in a different part of the argument.

5 (D) is correct. The stimulus is a set of formal statements about good parents. The most powerful statement is the one that states that all good parents are good listeners. That means anyone who is a good parent is a good listener. So when the stimulus tells us that most parents who are generous are good parents, and some self-centered parents are good parents, it's also telling us that most parents who are generous are good listeners, and some self-

centered parents are good listeners. The latter statement is what appears in choice (D): if there are some self-centered parents who are good listeners, that's the same as saying that there are some parents who are both self-centered and good listeners.

(A): The stimulus said that all good parents are good listeners, but that doesn't mean, as (A) infers, that every parent who is a good listener must therefore be a good parent. The stimulus allowed the possibility that a lot of parents who are good listeners nevertheless fail to be good parents.

(B): This *could* be true, but it isn't necessarily true. It's *possible* that some parents are good listeners but not good parents; on the other hand, it's also possible that (A) is right and all parents who are good listeners are also good parents. We can't be sure, so (B) cannot be inferred.

(C): We know that most parents who are generous are good parents, so we can conclude that most parents who are generous are good listeners. But we have no reason to believe the opposite—that most parents who are good listeners are generous—so we can't infer (C).

(E): Although we're told that "most" generous parents are good parents, and thus good listeners, and "some" self-centered parents are good parents, and thus good listeners, we can't compare the two groups and conclude (E). Maybe the set of self-centered parents is much larger than the set of generous parents, which could easily make (E) false.

The LSAT often tests whether you understand that "all" statements (like "if/then" statements) can't be reversed; for example, "All dogs are mammals" doesn't translate into, "All mammals are dogs." The same thing goes for "most" statements: "Most dogs are animals that weigh over five pounds," doesn't mean, "Most animals that weigh over five pounds are dogs."

6 (A) is correct. In order for Kyra to conclude that the public should be told to cut down on fiber intake, she must be assuming that public fiber consumption is actually at the high levels that cause problems in absorbing minerals. Choice (A) weakens her argument by attacking this assumption: if the average adult consumption of dietary fiber is only 10 grams a day, then adults aren't even getting enough fiber to meet their daily recommended intake, and, contrary to Kyra's argument, the public shouldn't be warned to cut back on fiber. People seem to be getting too little fiber, not too much.

(B): This is irrelevant. Kyra hasn't said anything about processed foods and their fiber content, so (B) doesn't weaken her claim. Her conclusion concerns total fiber intake in general, not its sources.

(C): This commits the "*can* versus *should*" scope shift. The issue in this argument is the proper level of fiber intake. The availability and/or affordability of that fiber is another question entirely.

(D): This functions more as a strengthener than a weakener. One of Kyra's worries is that calcium won't be absorbed if people eat too much fiber; (D) explains one of the reasons that calcium is important to good health. But you could have dismissed this choice right off the bat because it makes no mention of the argument's most important element, dietary fiber.

(E): This is also irrelevant to the main issue, which is the amount of fiber in the average diet. Fiber's "popularity" has no bearing on Kyra's recommendation that fiber intake should be decreased for health reasons.

This question employs a tried-and-true method of weakening the argument: attack the central assumption. Once you see Kyra is assuming something about how much fiber people eat, the question is a snap.

7 (D) is correct. We're asked for an inference. Fortunately, the credited response is merely a consequence of the first statement in the policy paragraph: every month, there is either a "holiday sale" or a "manager's sale" going on, or both. This means if there is no manager's sale being run in some month, then there must be a holiday sale in that month, which is choice (D).

(A): The stimulus only said that if there's a holiday in a given month *and* there's excess merchandise in the warehouse, a holiday sale is held. We can't assume that only one of these conditions guarantees a holiday sale.

(B): This needn't be true; other months might lack a holiday, or in some month the warehouse might not contain excess merchandise. In that case we could just have a manager's sale.

(C): Nothing in the stimulus says that it's impossible for a manager's sale to run when there's excess merchandise in the warehouse. Even if the excess merchandise gives rise to a holiday sale, we're explicitly told that it's possible for both kinds of sales to run at once.

(E): Although we know there's no excess merchandise in August, we don't know that *only* in August is there no excess merchandise in the warehouse.

It's not uncommon for an inference to be based on only one statement of a tricky stimulus. If you find yourself bogged down in a stimulus, or unable to prephrase any kind of answer, go to the choices for help. You know the answer's there.

Notice that the two if/then statements give some conditions under which the two types of sale take place, but say nothing about the conditions under which either type of sale *doesn't* take place. Once again, the test makers use what we don't know to formulate many of the wrong choices.

8 (B) is correct. The stem tells us what issue is paramount here: why business executives don't run for president. What's the author's explanation? Business executives are used to the hierarchical world of business and are uncomfortable with the compromises and power-sharing that are necessary in politics; the skills and personalities that bring success in business don't necessarily do the same in politics. But we're also told what types of people *do* typically run for president: lawyers, military leaders, and career politicians. We can weaken the author's explanation if we show that any of these ambitious types share the same attitudes towards compromise and power-sharing as business executives.

Choice (B) does just that: military leaders are just as uncomfortable with power sharing and compromise as business executives. Since that discomfort doesn't deter military leaders, the explanation that such discomfort is the main reason business executives don't run for president is seriously weakened.

(A): The author never said that *only* business executives act as fund-raisers or strategists, or even that most people who act in such capacity are business executives. So (A) wouldn't even affect *that* part of the argument, no less weaken the explanation in question.

(C): Could be, but so what? Choice (C) offers an irrelevant comparison while ignoring the crucial character in the explanation in question: business executives.

(D): This is irrelevant. The argument concerns the previous activities of those who seek to become president. The activities of former presidents *after* they leave office is another matter entirely.

(E): The stimulus admits that business executives have acted as fund-raisers and strategists in presidential campaigns, so (E) fits in nicely. Besides, the stimulus drew its conclusion about the character of individual business executives, so the actions of *companies* are irrelevant.

Watch out for irrelevant comparisons. Many wrong answer choices, like (C) in this question, relate two elements in the stimulus (such as lawyers versus military men) in a way that has nothing to do with the true scope of the argument.

Read actively and pay attention to your reactions. You might have thought, "Business is hierarchical? What about military life?" And that's the answer to the question right there.

9 (B) is correct. According to the definition, there are two requirements for a scientific theory to be "good." It must be able to describe a broad set of events using only a few elements, and it must make clear predictions concerning future events. Aristotle's cosmological theory, which claimed that everything was made out of four elements but failed to make any definite predictions, satisfied the first requirement but failed the second. For this reason, the author concludes that Aristotle's cosmological theory was not a good one. All the choices may be inferred from the passage except (B). We don't know anything about the "major concerns" of Aristotle's theory or whether "the observation of physical phenomena" is one of those concerns. Choice (B) shifts the scope of the argument and cannot be inferred.

(A): This simply paraphrases the second condition for a good scientific theory (according to the stimulus): that it must make definite predictions about the results of future observations. So if the stimulus statements are true, (A) necessarily follows.

(C): The author said that Aristotle's theory (which was based on four elements) fulfilled the first requirement of a good scientific theory, the simplicity requirement; therefore, a theory based on four elements must be able to fulfill the simplicity requirement.

(D): The stimulus requires that a good scientific theory must account for many observations with a model that contains *few* elements, so a theory that contains many elements doesn't make the grade.

(E): This is essentially a restatement of the author's evaluation of Aristotle's cosmological theory; the author said it satisfied the first requirement (describing a large class of observations), by accounting for everything in terms of four elements.

When the correct answer is *not* an inference based on the stimulus, it becomes impossible to prephrase the correct answer. You have to go through the choices methodically, using the process of elimination.

All the wrong choices have to be cut-and-dried inferences based on the stimulus. Such inferences are usually purely mechanical, basically restatements of stimulus claims. For that reason, pay special attention to any choice that departs even slightly from the vocabulary of the stimulus, as in choice (B)'s "physical phenomena."

10 (D) is correct. This argument just sounds incomplete, and in fact, the stem tells us as much. We're to find the author's presupposition, that is, the author's assumption. The author is worried because irreplaceable exhibits in natural history museums are being allowed to decay. He gives us an example intended to show the importance of museum exhibits: previously, analysis of eggs from museums aided studies that linked the decline of birds of prey to pesticides. This suggests that other exhibits might lead to other scientific discoveries. Therefore, the author concludes, funds must be raised to protect, if not all exhibits, at least those that will be *most useful to science in the future.*

Choice (D) points out that this conclusion is taking something for granted. It presupposes that *today* we can look at a bunch of exhibits and identify which ones will be useful in *future* scientific experiments. The Denial Test is helpful here: if (D) were false, then it would be impossible to know what data would be of most use in the future, and the author's plan of allocating resources to preserve those most valuable exhibits would be defeated.

(A): This would make *irreplaceability* the criterion for deciding which exhibits must be preserved, but the argument says that future usefulness to science is the criterion that decides what should be preserved. So (A) needn't be assumed.

(B): The purpose of the preservation of museum exhibits is their future usefulness to science, but nothing is assumed about whether or not their use by science might entail their destruction.

(C): This is irrelevant. The author brought in bird eggs only as one example of successful scientific use of museum exhibits; he assumed nothing about how any other eggs (let alone "extinct eggs") can or should be used in the future.

(E): This runs counter to the author's goal of preserving valuable exhibits, since the inevitability of decay tends to weaken the argument that certain exhibits must be preserved.

Use the Denial Test to find necessary assumptions and eliminate wrong answers. Sometimes, it is difficult to see why a choice is necessary to the argument, but easier to see that the argument falls apart if that choice is false.

11 (B) is correct. In this classic scope shift, the author lists some advantages that investor-owned hospitals enjoy over nonprofit hospitals: they don't need as much public investment, use fewer employees, and have higher occupancy levels. Therefore, the author concludes, investor-owned hospitals are better at delivering *medical care* than are nonprofit hospitals. It shouldn't be very hard to weaken this argument, since the evidence concerns administrative advantages in investor-owned hospitals, while the conclusion deals with the sort of medical care one gets at such hospitals.

Choice (B) directly deals with the subject of medical care. If patients at nonprofit hospitals recover faster from *comparable illnesses* than do patients in investor-owned hospitals, then we have a serious reason to doubt the claim that patients in investor-owned hospitals are receiving better medical care.

(A): This actually fits in with the stimulus evidence by suggesting that, in addition to their administrative advantages, investor-owned hospitals are cheaper for the public. This doesn't weaken the conclusion about the quality of medical care.

(C) and (E): Both of these choices fail to deal with medical care, concentrating on advantages that nonprofit hospitals have in raising money. But neither establishes that these money-raising advantages translate into better medical care, so the argument is unaffected.

(D): This falls into the same trap as (C) and (E): it tells us that doctors at nonprofit hospitals are paid better than their counterparts at investor-owned hospitals, but not that they're *better qualified.* Although we may naturally equate "more money" with "better qualified," the information in (D) doesn't allow us to make that jump or infer that care at nonprofit hospitals is better.

The Logical Reasoning sections replay the same topics over and over: comparing types of medical care, describing scientific theories, economic policies, etcetera. That makes it a little easier on the test makers; good topics are hard to find. In the same way, the arguments exhibit the same logical flaws over and over (in this case, different terms in evidence and conclusion). Learn what to expect, and the questions become much easier.

Rely on your common sense in evaluating the arguments. If *you* needed medical care and were choosing between the two alternatives, would the evidence in favor of investor-owned hospitals sway you? Probably not, because that evidence is based purely on administrative issues; you would probably want some medical reassurances as well. Recognizing the lack of such evidence is the key to unraveling this sloppy argument.

12 (C) is correct. We're told that Akhenaten was loved and respected by his subjects. The evidence for this assertion is that reports written during Akhenaten's reign indicate that his palace guards were fiercely loyal to him. Why doesn't this evidence adequately support the conclusion? The evidence speaks only of the attitude of Akhenaten's *palace guards*, who were naturally chosen to be loyal to him (not to mention the fact that their jobs, and possibly their lives, depended on it), yet says nothing about his subjects in general. That's the flaw that (C) points out: the argument makes a general conclusion (about all Akhenaten's subjects) based on a sample (his palace guards) that is likely to be unrepresentative.

(A): The evidence (documents showing the loyalty of the guard) doesn't *contradict* the conclusion that Akhenaten's subjects were loyal; it just fails to establish the conclusion.

(B): This says that the evidence is impossible to challenge *in principle*. But the argument uses historical records, which can always be challenged in principle by other records—documents showing discontent or rebellion in other sections of the pharaoh's kingdom, for instance.

(D): The word "ancient" is used only once in the passage, to describe Akhenaten, and it's used in one sense only: to mean that he lived a very long time ago. There's nothing ambiguous about this term.

(E): This isn't accurate; the argument is interested in what Akhenaten's own people thought of him during his reign, and uses documents written by Akhenaten's own contemporaries as evidence. The author herself doesn't judge the pharaoh; she merely formulates an inappropriate conclusion based on the judgments of the ancient palace guards.

The flaw of the unrepresentative sample can show up in many ways (watch out for it especially on survey questions). Any time the evidence deals with the characteristics of a certain group, and the conclusion concerns a larger group, think about the "representativeness" of the evidence group.

Choices that claim that an argument is flawed because it uses an ambiguous term are almost always wrong.

13 (D) is correct. The physician knows exactly three things: (1) a patient is suffering from disease X or disease Y; (2) there's no test that can distinguish disease X from disease Y; and finally, (3) there is an effective treatment for Y, but not for X. The physician concludes that the patient should be treated as if he has disease Y, and we're asked to identify a principle on which that conclusion could be based. It's easy to follow the physician's thinking: if the patient has disease X, no treatment will help; if he has disease Y, the treatment for disease Y will help; so with nothing to lose and everything to gain, we might as well treat him for disease Y.

Choice (D) describes this principle in general terms. When success is only possible if circumstances beyond one's control are favorable (the patient has the treatable disease Y), one should act as if the circumstances *are* favorable (treat the patient for disease Y).

(A) and (C): These both fail to recognize that it's *impossible* to determine whether a patient has X or Y. Moreover, (A) recommends treating both diseases, while the physician can treat only one, Y.

(B): *Au contraire!* Choice (B) says the physician should act as if circumstances were unfavorable (as if the patient has untreatable disease X), which is the opposite of what the physician recommends.

(E): This correctly identifies one of the problems (only one strategy has a hope of success), but suggests that circumstances should be *altered* to fit that strategy. Here, however, circumstances (the disease) are completely outside the physician's control—he can't ask the patient to switch diseases for his convenience—so (E) suggests the impossible.

With Principle questions, one of the difficulties is seeing how the specific language in the stimulus fits the general language in the answer choices. Don't be satisfied with something that fits in most respects; if the principle in the choice is inapplicable in *any* respect, toss the choice.

14 (E) is correct. The nutritionist isn't exactly crazy about the consumer advocate's suggestion to publicize the disadvantages of tropical oils. She worries that a campaign focusing on tropical oils would do harm, because Americans would make minor changes in their diet (cut down on tropical oils) and ignore more important changes (continue to wolf down meat, poultry, etcetera).

So the focal point of the debate is the publicity campaign: the advocate believes such a campaign would *improve* public health by cutting consumption of tropical oils and hence saturated fat, whereas the nutritionist believes it would lead people to ignore the dangers posed by more harmful sources of saturated fat, in which case public health would actually *suffer.* As (E) says, they disagree over the wisdom of a campaign focusing on tropical oils.

(A): The nutritionist never disputes that large quantities of tropical oil can cause heart disease; she only says North Americans are likely to get more saturated fats from other sources.

(B): The two debaters don't disagree over whether the publicity campaign can change the public's behavior; they just disagree over whether the change caused by an anti–tropical oil campaign will be for the better.

(C): This is wrong because the consumer advocate never compares the effects of reducing tropical oils to the effects of reducing meat; she merely said that it would be possible and beneficial to persuade people to reduce their tropical oil consumption. We have no clue as to the advocate's stance on meat.

(D): This choice is similar to (A), focusing on an issue relating to tropical oils that the nutritionist simply doesn't touch. The nutritionist doesn't deny that replacing tropical oils with healthier alternatives might help some people; she just doubted the wisdom of an ad campaign focusing *only* on tropical oils.

The correct answer to a point-at-issue question must address an issue that's relevant to both arguments. If you are convinced that both speakers address a particular issue contained in a choice, you must then ask yourself if they in fact *disagree* over that issue. If so, you've found a winner. Here, the relevant issue discussed by both speakers is the tropical oils publicity campaign. The advocate is in favor, the nutritionist is opposed —as simple as that.

15 (A) is correct. The first step in this Parallel Reasoning question is to abstract from the specifics of the stimulus. In general terms, the stimulus provides a case in which a statement uttered in response to a particular situation is attacked as an ineffectual response. There are only two possible scenarios, and both expose the futility of the statement: if the original position is wrong, the given response would make matters look worse; if the position is right, the response does nothing to prove it. The parallel choice we're looking for should therefore show that a given

response is poor because the response is ineffective, whether the party under attack is right or wrong.

We don't have to look far. Choice (A) says that when a practice has been denounced, it shouldn't be defended by saying, "this is how we've always done it." The reason for this is exactly parallel to the original's "lose-lose" element: if the practice is a poor one, the response makes matters look even worse; if the practice is wise, the answer doesn't provide good support for it. Choice (A) fits the stimulus form perfectly.

(B): Unlike the stimulus, there's no issue of whether the initial opinion is right or wrong. Instead of being presented with two cases in which a person who eats strange foods is wrong or right to do so, we're given two ways the response will sound unsatisfying.

(C): This also begins with a poor response to a criticism. But instead of showing why the justification in the response is pointless—whether the criticized behavior is good or bad—the argument attacks the response for avoiding the issue.

(D): This also fails to show why the scholars' response is a poor one, whether they are right or wrong, implying instead that they are probably partly right and partly wrong.

(E): This fails because it recommends two *better* ways of responding (admission of error or silence), whereas the stimulus was primarily interested in describing why the response was poor, whether the original statement was right or wrong.

▼▼▼

All Logical Reasoning questions are designed to be answerable in one and a half minutes. This means that questions that seem to require much more time (like this one) must have a shortcut. Read critically, looking for structure. In this case, "whether the party under attack is right or wrong, the response is ineffective," is enough information to recognize the correct choice quickly.

▲▲▲

16 (C) is correct. Alicia's argument is twofold. First she disagrees with Concetta's criterion for a great writer, which is that the person grasps a social issue ahead of her time (in this case industrialization). She offers instead her own criterion, which is that the person has the ability to move people through writing. Then she disagrees with Concetta's claim that Franchot was in fact one of the first to recognize the consequences of industrialization. This is the method that (C) describes: she rejects Concetta's criterion of what makes a great writer, and disputes a specific claim (that Franchot was ahead of her time).

(A): The word "accepts" tells you immediately why (A) is wrong—Alicia doesn't accept *anything* Concetta says, much less her criterion of what makes a great writer.

(B): This is correct in saying that Alicia attacks Concetta's evidence (the claim that Franchot was ahead of her time) but totally misses the major focus of her argument, which is a rejection of Concetta's criterion for a great writer. Moreover, Alicia doesn't generalize from new evidence.

(D): Alicia never offers facts to support the notion that the mark of a great writer is the ability to move people with the written word. She does claim that the consequences of industrialization were well known at Franchot's time, but this merely undermines Concetta's claim, and provides no support for her alternative criterion.

(E): This ignores the fact that Alicia attacks *two* of Concetta's claims (that she was a great writer and ahead of her time) as well as her criterion for great writers. More importantly, Alicia never attacks the *structure* of Concetta's argument (there's little structure to attack).

▼▼▼

In a Method of Argument question, the correct choice must cover the entire method employed by the arguer in question. If a choice is incomplete, it cannot be correct. In this case, all of the wrong

choices not only *miss* an important part of Alicia's argument, but also describe something Alicia doesn't do; that is, the wrong choices here are both incomplete *and* incorrect.

17 (B) is correct. Anson has taken umbrage at Dr. Ladlow's conclusion that his theory is "irrefutably correct." He argues that Dr. Ladlow isn't a responsible psychologist, because a responsible psychologist would *always* realize that no theory can be called irrefutable, since new evidence can always come to light. Answer choice (B) essentially restates Anson's attack on Dr. Ladlow in general terms. Dr. Ladlow didn't fit Anson's criterion of a responsible psychologist because he didn't recognize the possibility that contradictory evidence could refute his theory. Answer choice (B) says that a psychologist who obtains consistent results can't *responsibly* conclude that his theory is irrefutable. This is essentially the principle that Anson's argument rests on, so answer choice (B) can be inferred from Anson's argument.

(A): This is a distortion of the argument. Anson doesn't question the accuracy of Ladlow's evidence, he just points out the possibility (which Ladlow ignored) that new evidence might turn up.

(C): This is relatively tricky. Anson doesn't say that psychologists can never be correct, only that they can never be absolutely *sure* that they're correct. For instance, Ladlow's theory may well be correct, but he can't responsibly claim to *know,* beyond a shadow of doubt, that it's correct.

(D): This has nothing to do with Anson's argument. Anson isn't questioning the content of Ladlow's experiments, only his conclusion that his theory is irrefutable.

(E): This makes a familiar error. Anson says, "If psychologists are responsible, they admit their theories might be disproved." Choice (E) states, "If psychologists admit that their theories might be disproved, they must be responsible." But there might be other requirements for a psychologist to be considered responsible.

Unlike the previous question, which concerns how the second argument related to the first, this question only concerns Anson's argument, which allows you to narrow your focus.

18 (B) is correct. Again we're asked to understand Anson's argument, this time in more general terms. On what does Anson base his conclusion about Dr. Ladlow? He says that responsible psychologists always behave a certain way, and since Ladlow does not behave in that way, he is not a responsible psychologist. As (B) observes, he is taking a *general principle* (about responsible psychology) and applying it to the case of Dr. Ladlow.

(A): Anson doesn't *base* his argument on an attack against Ladlow's character. His *conclusion* could be seen to attack Ladlow's character, but that conclusion is based on an application of the principle that responsible psychologists admit their fallibility.

(C): There's simply no ambiguous term being used in Anson's argument; the term "responsible" is the only candidate, and Anson tells us exactly what he means by it.

(D): Anson never questions the factual validity of Dr. Ladlow's evidence—that is, the facts on which he bases his rat predictions. As we saw in the previous question, Anson doesn't attack Ladlow's actual theory, but Ladlow's belief that his theory is irrefutable.

(E): Again, the theory itself is not the focus of Anson's argument. Anson never discusses Ladlow's theoretical explanation of rat behavior. His point isn't that the theory is wrong, but that it can't be considered irrefutable.

The "ambiguous term" choice shows up often on Method of Argument questions. Don't pick it unless you can point to exactly the term that is being used ambiguously, and you feel sure you can identify the two (or more) different ways the term is used.

19 (E) is correct. Smith tells us that meat must be healthy, because most doctors eat meat, and hey, who knows more about health than doctors do? If doctors knew meat to be unhealthy, he implies, they wouldn't eat it. He's assuming that doctors, because of their great knowledge of nutrition, actually *use* that knowledge to guide their eating habits. As (E) says, he's assuming that the experts (in this case doctors) do not act contrary to what their expertise tells them is in their best interest (that is, do not eat unhealthy foods). That's a questionable assumption, and the basis for the flawed logic here.

(A): On the contrary, the issue of the motives of Smith's opponents (the people who believe meat is unhealthy) never arises.

(B): The doctors are presented as experts, not simply "typical cases," and Smith uses their behavior as a guide precisely *because* they are experts.

(C): This is wrong, because although Smith states his conclusion in the beginning, he isn't *assuming* this conclusion. He provides evidence (the behavior of the doctors). The reasoning is flawed because it's based on a questionable assumption, but not because it's circular.

(D): The only authority mentioned in the stimulus is the doctors and there's no hint that doctors give conflicting advice. Besides, Smith bases his conclusion not on doctors' *advice*, but on their behavior.

Once again, use your common sense and everyday experience to help you whenever possible. If you've ever seen an overweight doctor or a doctor who smokes, you probably were suspicious of this reasoning right off the bat. In fact, you might have encountered any number of situations in your life in which it's evident that a so-called expert apparently does not follow his or her own advice. If personal experience can help you, use it to your advantage, but be sure not to overstep the bounds of the argument when doing so.

20 (D) is correct. The stimulus concludes that the rise in prosperity in England after 1840 was caused by the free-trade policy because the economy improved only after the policy was implemented. The author is assuming a *causal* connection from a *temporal* correlation. The general form of the argument is: Y happened after X; therefore, X must have caused Y. We see that form in (D): an improvement in a company's profitability occurred after a morale-building program was instituted; therefore, that program must have *caused* the improvement. As in the stimulus, the author concludes causation based on a temporal correlation.

(A): This concludes that since no marsh hawks were found in the marsh last year, none will be found this year; that is, (A) reasons that past performance is a good predictor of future performance. There's no assumption of causality, so (A)'s not parallel.

(B): The reason for concluding that a bypass road *probably* helped the flow of traffic is not a temporal coincidence, as in the stimulus. Also, once we see the word "probably," we know that this argument is too qualified to be parallel to the original, which, along with correct choice (D), is not qualified at all. Both arguments conclude that one thing caused another, not that one thing *probably* caused another.

(C): This is simply the observation of an action's effect. The stimulus, on the other hand, *concluded* that a certain action must have been responsible for a certain effect, *because* the effect occurred after that action.

(E): This is the opposite of the stimulus. Choice (E) concludes that because the asteroid collision caused the extinction of dinosaurs, that extinction couldn't have taken place before the collision; that is, since X caused Y, Y couldn't have happened before X. That's just common sense.

The fallacy of inferring a causal connection between two events because one happened after another is quite common on the LSAT. It even has a Latin name, the "*post hoc* fallacy" (from "post hoc ergo propter hoc"—meaning, "after this, therefore because of this").

Qualifications are important on Parallel Reasoning questions. If a choice contains a qualification and the stimulus doesn't, that's enough to show they're not parallel.

21 (E) is correct. We've got a tragic story. Theodore Cooper, designer of the Quebec Bridge, receives word that there's danger on the construction site; he telegraphs immediately, but it's too late, and 84 workers plunge to their death. They didn't die completely in vain, though; as a result of their misfortune, the process of bridge construction was altered. Whereas engineering "rules of thumb" had been used in the past, they were now abandoned in favor of "rigorous applications of mathematical analysis."

Choice (E) is inferable: before the Quebec tragedy in 1907, bridge builders had been accustomed to relying on "engineering rules of thumb" (and thus relying on whatever level of mathematical analysis was incorporated in those rules); as the 1907 disaster showed, these rules didn't ensure complete safety. That's all (E) says.

(A): This is too broad. The Quebec Bridge was unsafe at one period of its construction, but for all we know, plenty of pre-twentieth-century bridges were completely safe for public use, despite their engineers' reliance on nonrigorous "rules of thumb."

(B): We're never told that Cooper's absence from the site led to the disaster; we don't know that he would have made a difference if he had been on site. The stimulus blames the then-customary lack of rigorous mathematical analysis for the disaster.

(C): We're never told *why* nineteenth-century engineers relied on rules of thumb. Maybe their analytical methods were inadequate. On the other hand, maybe it was a matter of time saving or cost cutting.

(D): This is too strong. We don't know that more rigorous application of mathematical analysis was the *only* thing that would have prevented the disaster. Maybe a wholly different bridge design, to take one example, could also have done the job.

You can approach a long, involved stimulus like a reading comprehension passage. Understand the organization, understand how the author links the parts of his or her argument or story, don't get bogged down in details (What's a cantilever?), but remember where they occur so you can go back to them if necessary.

22 (D) is correct. The author concludes that understanding the meaning of a word doesn't depend on being able to *explain* exactly what it means. Her evidence is that children often cannot explain exactly what some words mean (notably, words that don't refer to physical objects), even though they can *use* those words to convey accurately the feelings they are experiencing. Since the children are supposed to be demonstrating that it's possible to understand words without being able to explain them, the author must be assuming that the

children's ability to use words to convey their experiences shows that they *understand* those words. Otherwise, her evidence would have little to do with her conclusion. What principle would justify that assumption, and the conclusion based on it? Clearly it's (D): that appropriate use of a word to convey experience is sufficient evidence that the user has understood the word.

(A): This seems to be talking about some other argument; even if you consider the "difficult task" in (A) to be explaining words that convey feelings, (A) does nothing to justify the conclusion that understanding words doesn't require the ability to explain them (that is, the ability to perform the difficult task).

(B): This certainly doesn't justify the author's argument that understanding of a word does not depend on being able to explain it.

(C): This might help explain why children have difficulty explaining the meaning of words that refer to emotions, but it doesn't justify the belief that they understand these words because they can use them.

(E): This basically says that people cannot explain words that don't refer to physical objects. Again this offers a reason why children can't explain these words, but doesn't justify the author's belief that children understand the words.

▼▼▼

It's always important to isolate the conclusion of every Logical Reasoning question (it's sometimes embedded within a sentence), even if that means drawing a circle around it. When you do that, it becomes easier to see if there are any gaps between evidence and conclusion.

▲▲▲

23 (B) is correct. We're told that identical twins have *genetically* identical brains. Nevertheless, if one of the twins is schizophrenic, the brains show a difference—certain areas of the schizophrenic twin's brains have been found to be smaller than corresponding areas in the healthy twin's brain. The author concludes that some "damage to the physical structure of the brain" *caused* the schizophrenia; that is, that some sort of physical damage caused the small brain areas and resulted in schizophrenia. This is a familiar argument type: the author observes a correlation between small brain areas and schizophrenia, and deduces that the shrunken brain areas *caused* the schizophrenia.

But the causality could just as easily be reversed. As answer choice (B) says, the author assumes that the causal relationship doesn't run the other way around; he's assuming that the schizophrenia, or treatment for schizophrenia, didn't cause the smallness of those areas of the brain. If this is the case, the argument falls apart, which verifies that answer choice (B) is the assumption that this question requires.

(A): The author doesn't assume anything about the overall comparative brain size of schizophrenics and healthy people. His comparison is between *certain areas* in the brains of twins, which would be exactly the same size if it weren't for the disease.

(C): This is out for basically the same reason that (A) is out: the author makes no comparison between the brain size of twins and people in general. The stimulus only compares identical twins (who should have identical-size brains) to each other.

(D): This sounds interesting, but it needn't be true. Schizophrenia could, in accordance with the author's theory, reduce brain size, but it could do so by different amounts in different twins, especially if their brains suffer structural damage of differing severity.

(E): No. Schizophrenia could be more likely to develop in identical twins than in the population at large and this would have no effect on the conclusion.

▼▼▼

Don't confuse correlation with causation. In this case, the evidence is that schizophrenia and the abnormal smallness of certain parts of the brain go together. That's another way of saying that they're correlated. But the author goes on to conclude that one *causes* the other. Remember, it's quite possible that there is no causal connection between correlated events or phenomena. In fact, it's even possible that the causality runs counter to the way the author proposes.

All the wrong choices make a comparison that's beyond the scope of the stimulus: schizophrenic brain to healthy brain; schizophrenic twin to schizophrenic twin, etcetera. This false comparison is a common type of red herring on the LSAT. When authors make specific comparisons in the stimulus, they usually are not assuming further comparisons between other groups.

24 (D) is correct. Now we're looking for a statement that contradicts the stimulus evidence. The stimulus tells us that the brains of identical twins are genetically identical. Thus, their brains contain the *same* genetic information; there are no genetic differences between them. So, in the cases discussed, it would not be possible to determine from genetic information alone that one twin will develop schizophrenia and the other won't. Therefore, genetic information alone isn't enough to indicate whether a person will develop schizophrenia. If the statements in the stimulus are to be believed, (D) is flat-out wrong, and therefore the answer we seek.

(A): This could be true; genetic susceptibility to schizophrenia could be one of its prerequisites. Considering the evidence we're given, it's possible that a pair of identical twins share a genetic *susceptibility* to schizophrenia, but that only one actually develops the disease (for whatever reason).

(B): Nothing in the stimulus refers to the *treatment* of schizophrenia, so there's nothing to contradict (B)'s claim.

(C): The stimulus never says that the brains of schizophrenic twins are completely different from the brains of healthy twins, only that certain areas of the brain are smaller. The brains of schizophrenics might share many characteristics with the brains of people without the disorder.

(E): This provides a cause—viral infections—for the brain abnormalities associated with schizophrenia. This fits the stimulus rather well: maybe viral infections damage the brain and the damage causes schizophrenia. No contradiction.

Question 23 asks for an assumption, which is something that *must* be true for the argument to work. Question 24 asks for something that *couldn't* be true based on the argument. In both cases, any choice that only *could* be true was incorrect.

When LSAT arguments are couched in real-life terms, they generally don't require absurd conclusions. That makes it unlikely that a choice like (C) could be the answer to this question; the argument isn't going to require that the brains of schizophrenics and nonschizophrenics have absolutely nothing in common.

It's important that you see the difference between (D)'s claim that genetics alone are the cause of schizophrenia, and (A)'s claim that genetics has *something* to do with it.

25 (E) is correct. The stimulus study found that when people drank alcoholic beverages with their meals, they consumed about 175 more calories from *nonalcoholic* sources than when they ate meals without consuming alcoholic beverages. In other words, when people are pounding down the booze, they tend to be eating more, or at least consuming more food calories, than they do when they aren't drinking. All of the choices help explain why this is so—all except correct choice (E).

Choice (E) does present a difference between the two types of meals (alcoholic and alcohol free), but it's not a *relevant* difference. The issue isn't what *kind* of calories were consumed, but how *many*. In breaking down the two types of meals into their proportional sources of calories, (E) does nothing to explain why the *total amount* of calories in the two meal situations differ.

(A): If people linger at the table when they consume alcohol, it's not surprising that they spend a lot of that extra time eating, and so tend to consume more calories.

(B): If the alcoholic meals, since they occurred later in the day, were larger meals, then it's no surprise at all that people consumed more calories at those bigger meals.

(C): This says that people eat more when there are a lot of them eating together, and that alcohol tends to be served at meals that include several diners. So here, too, we have an explanation: the large number of diners, which correlates well with the serving of alcohol, results in greater food consumption.

(D): If meals at which alcohol is served tend to be more "enticing" in both preparation and appearance, then it's understandable that diners may be enticed to eat more of those meals.

Sometime it's difficult to convince yourself that a choice really does nothing to contribute to an explanation. Use the process of elimination; it's usually easy to see that two or three choices definitely help the explanation. Then, if you're still stumped, you can guess with favorable odds.

The incorrect choices for this question don't have to offer a full explanation, only *contribute* to one.

All the wrong choices help explain the correlation between alcohol consumption and calorie consumption by linking alcohol consumption to some *other* factor associated with more eating. It helps to see the similarities between wrong choices—that makes the credited response stand out.

Real LSAT 2

Answer Sheet

MARK ONE AND ONLY ONE ANSWER TO EACH QUESTION. BE SURE TO FILL IN COMPLETELY THE SPACE FOR YOUR INTENDED ANSWER CHOICE. IF YOU ERASE, DO SO COMPLETELY. MAKE NO STRAY MARKS.

	SECTION 1	SECTION 2	SECTION 3	SECTION 4
1	A B C D E	A B C D E	A B C D E	A B C D E
2	A B C D E	A B C D E	A B C D E	A B C D E
3	A B C D E	A B C D E	A B C D E	A B C D E
4	A B C D E	A B C D E	A B C D E	A B C D E
5	A B C D E	A B C D E	A B C D E	A B C D E
6	A B C D E	A B C D E	A B C D E	A B C D E
7	A B C D E	A B C D E	A B C D E	A B C D E
8	A B C D E	A B C D E	A B C D E	A B C D E
9	A B C D E	A B C D E	A B C D E	A B C D E
10	A B C D E	A B C D E	A B C D E	A B C D E
11	A B C D E	A B C D E	A B C D E	A B C D E
12	A B C D E	A B C D E	A B C D E	A B C D E
13	A B C D E	A B C D E	A B C D E	A B C D E
14	A B C D E	A B C D E	A B C D E	A B C D E
15	A B C D E	A B C D E	A B C D E	A B C D E
16	A B C D E	A B C D E	A B C D E	A B C D E
17	A B C D E	A B C D E	A B C D E	A B C D E
18	A B C D E	A B C D E	A B C D E	A B C D E
19	A B C D E	A B C D E	A B C D E	A B C D E
20	A B C D E	A B C D E	A B C D E	A B C D E
21	A B C D E	A B C D E	A B C D E	A B C D E
22	A B C D E	A B C D E	A B C D E	A B C D E
23	A B C D E	A B C D E	A B C D E	A B C D E
24	A B C D E	A B C D E	A B C D E	A B C D E
25	A B C D E	A B C D E	A B C D E	A B C D E
26	A B C D E	A B C D E	A B C D E	A B C D E
27	A B C D E	A B C D E	A B C D E	A B C D E
28	A B C D E	A B C D E	A B C D E	A B C D E
29	A B C D E	A B C D E	A B C D E	A B C D E
30	A B C D E	A B C D E	A B C D E	A B C D E

General Directions for the LSAT Answer Sheet

The actual testing time for this portion of the test will be two hours and 20 minutes. There are four sections, each with a time limit of 35 minutes. The supervisor will tell you when to begin and end each section. If you finish a section before time is called, you may check your work on that section only; do not turn to any other section of the test book and do not work on any other section either in the test book or on the answer sheet.

There are several different types of questions on the test, and each question type has its own directions. Be sure you understand the directions for each question type before attempting to answer any questions in that section.

Not everyone will finish all the questions in the time allowed. Do not hurry, but work steadily and as quickly as you can without sacrificing accuracy. You are advised to use your time effectively. If a question seems too difficult, go on to the next one and return to the difficult question after completing the section. MARK THE BEST ANSWER YOU CAN FOR EVERY QUESTION. NO DEDUCTIONS WILL BE MADE FOR WRONG ANSWERS. YOUR SCORE WILL BE BASED ONLY ON THE NUMBER OF QUESTIONS YOU ANSWER CORRECTLY.

ALL YOUR ANSWERS MUST BE MARKED ON THE ANSWER SHEET. Answer spaces for each question are lettered to correspond with the letters of the potential answers to each question in the test book. After you have decided which of the answers is correct, blacken the corresponding space on the answer sheet. BE SURE THAT EACH MARK IS BLACK AND COMPLETELY FILLS THE ANSWER SPACE. Give only one answer to each question. If you change an answer, be sure that all previous marks are erased completely. Since the answer sheet is machine scored, incomplete erasures may be interpreted as intended answers. ANSWERS RECORDED IN THE TEST BOOK WILL NOT BE SCORED.

There may be more questions noted on this answer sheet than there are questions in a section. Do not be concerned but be certain that the section and number of the question you are answering matches the answer sheet section and question number. Additional answer spaces in any answer sheet section should be left blank. Begin your next section in the number one answer space for that section.

SECTION I

Time—35 minutes

25 Questions

Directions: The questions in this section are based on the reasoning contained in brief statements or passages. For some questions, more than one of the choices could conceivably answer the question. However, you are to choose the best answer; that is, the response that most accurately and completely answers the question. You should not make assumptions that are by commonsense standards implausible, superfluous, or incompatible with the passage. After you have chosen the best answer, blacken the corresponding space on your answer sheet.

1. Something must be done to ease traffic congestion. In traditional small towns people used to work and shop in the same town in which they lived; but now that stores and workplaces are located far away from residential areas, people cannot avoid traveling long distances each day. Traffic congestion is so heavy on all roads that, even on major highways where the maximum speed limit is 55 miles per hour, the actual speed averages only 35 miles per hour.

   Which one of the following proposals is most supported by the statements above?

   (A) The maximum speed limit on major highways should be increased.
   (B) People who now travel on major highways should be encouraged to travel on secondary roads instead.
   (C) Residents of the remaining traditional small towns should be encouraged to move to the suburbs.
   (D) Drivers who travel well below the maximum speed limit on major highways should be fined.
   (E) New businesses should be encouraged to locate closer to where their workers would live.

2. College professor: College students do not write nearly as well as they used to. Almost all of the papers that my students have done for me this year have been poorly written and ungrammatical.

   Which one of the following is the most serious weakness in the argument made by the professor?

   (A) It requires confirmation that the change in the professor's students is representative of a change among college students in general.
   (B) It offers no proof to the effect that the professor is an accurate judge of writing ability.
   (C) It does not take into account the possibility that the professor is a poor teacher.
   (D) It fails to present contrary evidence.
   (E) It fails to define its terms sufficiently.

Questions 3–4

Mayor of Plainsville: In order to help the economy of Plainsville, I am using some of our tax revenues to help bring a major highway through the town and thereby attract new business to Plainsville.

Citizens' group: You must have interests other than our economy in mind. If you were really interested in helping our economy, you would instead allocate the revenues to building a new business park, since it would bring in twice the business that your highway would.

3. The argument by the citizens' group relies on which one of the following assumptions?

   (A) Plainsville presently has no major highways running through it.
   (B) The mayor accepts that a new business park would bring in more new business than would the new highway.
   (C) The new highway would have no benefits for Plainsville other than attracting new business.
   (D) The mayor is required to get approval for all tax revenue allocation plans from the city council.
   (E) Plainsville's economy will not be helped unless a new business park of the sort envisioned by the citizens' group is built.

4. Which one of the following principles, if accepted, would most help the citizens' group to justify drawing its conclusion that the mayor has in mind interests other than Plainsville's economy?

   (A) Anyone really pursuing a cause will choose the means that that person believes will advance the cause the farthest.
   (B) Any goal that includes helping the economy of a community will require public revenues in order to be achieved.
   (C) Anyone planning to use resources collected from a group must consult the members of the group before using the resources.
   (D) Any cause worth committing oneself to must include specific goals toward which one can work.
   (E) Any cause not pursued by public officials, if it is to be pursued at all, must be pursued by members of the community.

GO ON TO THE NEXT PAGE

5. Recently, highly skilled workers in Eastern Europe have left jobs in record numbers to emigrate to the West. It is therefore likely that skilled workers who remain in Eastern Europe are in high demand in their home countries.

Which one of the following, if true, most seriously weakens the argument?

(A) Eastern European factories prefer to hire workers from their home countries rather than to import workers from abroad.
(B) Major changes in Eastern European economic structures have led to the elimination of many positions previously held by the highly skilled emigrants.
(C) Many Eastern European emigrants need to acquire new skills after finding work in the West.
(D) Eastern European countries plan to train many new workers to replace the highly skilled workers who have emigrated.
(E) Because of the departure of skilled workers from Eastern European countries, many positions are now unfilled.

6. Historian: Alexander the Great should not be judged by appeal to current notions of justice. Alexander, an ancient figure of heroic stature, should be judged by the standards of his own culture. That is, did he live up to his culture's ideals of leadership? Did Alexander elevate the contemporary standards of justice? Was he, in his day, judged to be a just and wise ruler?

Student: But you cannot tell whether or not Alexander raised the contemporary standards of justice without invoking standards other than those of his own culture.

Which one of the following argumentative strategies does the student use in responding to the historian?

(A) arguing that applying the historian's principle would require a knowledge of the past that is necessarily inaccessible to current scholarship
(B) attempting to undermine the historian's principle by showing that some of its consequences are inconsistent with each other
(C) showing that the principle the historian invokes, when applied to Alexander, does not justify the assertion that he was heroic
(D) questioning the historian's motivation for determining whether a standard of behavior has been raised or lowered
(E) claiming that one of the historian's criteria for judging Alexander is inconsistent with the principle that the historian has advanced

Questions 7–8

Two paleontologists, Dr. Tyson and Dr. Roes, disagree over the interpretation of certain footprints that were left among other footprints in hardened volcanic ash at site G. Dr. Tyson claims they are clearly early hominid footprints since they show human characteristics: a squarish heel and a big toe immediately adjacent to the next toe. However, since the footprints indicate that if hominids made those prints they would have had to walk in an unexpected cross-stepping manner, by placing the left foot to the right of the right foot, Dr. Roes rejects Dr. Tyson's conclusion.

7. The disagreement between the two paleontologists is over which one of the following?

(A) the relative significance of various aspects of the evidence
(B) the assumption that early hominid footprints are distinguishable from other footprints
(C) the possibility of using the evidence of footprints to determine the gait of the creature that made those footprints
(D) the assumption that evidence from one paleontologic site is enough to support a conclusion
(E) the likelihood that early hominids would have walked upright on two feet

8. Which one of the following, if true, most seriously undermines Dr. Tyson's conclusion?

(A) The footprints showing human characteristics were clearly those of at least two distinct individuals.
(B) Certain species of bears had feet very like human feet, except that the outside toe on each foot was the biggest toe and the innermost toe was the smallest toe.
(C) Footprints shaped like a human's that do not show a cross-stepping pattern exist at site M, which is a mile away from site G, and the two sets of footprints are contemporaneous.
(D) When the moist volcanic ash became sealed under additional layers of ash before hardening, some details of some of the footprints were erased.
(E) Most of the other footprints at site G were of animals with hooves.

GO ON TO THE NEXT PAGE

9. It is not known whether bovine spongiform encephalopathy (BSE), a disease of cattle invariably deadly to them, can be transmitted directly from one infected animal to another at all stages of the infection. If it can be, there is now a reservoir of infected cattle incubating the disease. There are no diagnostic tests to identify infected animals before the animals show overt symptoms. Therefore, if such direct transmission occurs, the disease cannot be eradicated by ______.

   Which one of the following best completes the argument?

   (A) removing from the herd and destroying any diseased animal as soon as it shows the typical symptoms of advanced BSE
   (B) developing a drug that kills the agent that causes BSE, and then treating with that drug all cattle that might have the disease
   (C) destroying all cattle in areas where BSE occurs and raising cattle only in areas to which BSE is known not to have spread
   (D) developing a vaccine that confers lifelong immunity against BSE and giving it to all cattle, destroying in due course all those animals for which the vaccine protection came too late
   (E) developing a diagnostic test that does identify any infected animal and destroying all animals found to be infected

10. Auto industry executive: Statistics show that cars that were built smaller after 1977 to make them more fuel-efficient had a higher incidence of accident-related fatalities than did their earlier, larger counterparts. For this reason we oppose recent guidelines that would require us to produce cars with higher fuel efficiency.

    Which one of the following, if true, would constitute the strongest objection to the executive's argument?

    (A) Even after 1977, large automobiles were frequently involved in accidents that caused death or serious injury.
    (B) Although fatalities in accidents involving small cars have increased since 1977, the number of accidents has decreased.
    (C) New computerized fuel systems can enable large cars to meet fuel efficiency standards established by the recent guidelines.
    (D) Modern technology can make small cars more fuel-efficient today than at any other time in their production history.
    (E) Fuel efficiency in models of large cars rose immediately after 1977 but has been declining ever since.

11. No one who lacks knowledge of a subject is competent to pass judgment on that subject. Since political know-how is a matter, not of adhering to technical rules, but of insight and style learned through apprenticeship and experience, only seasoned politicians are competent to judge whether a particular political policy is fair to all.

    A major weakness of the argument is that it

    (A) relies on a generalization about the characteristic that makes someone competent to pass judgment
    (B) fails to give specific examples to illustrate how political know-how can be acquired
    (C) uses the term "apprenticeship" to describe what is seldom a formalized relationship
    (D) equates political know-how with understanding the social implications of political policies
    (E) assumes that when inexperienced politicians set policy they are guided by the advice of more experienced politicians

12. Impact craters caused by meteorites smashing into Earth have been found all around the globe, but they have been found in the greatest density in geologically stable regions. This relatively greater abundance of securely identified craters in geologically stable regions must be explained by the lower rates of destructive geophysical processes in those regions.

    The conclusion is properly drawn if which one of the following is assumed?

    (A) A meteorite that strikes exactly the same spot as an earlier meteorite will obliterate all traces of the earlier impact.
    (B) Rates of destructive geophysical processes within any given region vary markedly throughout geological time.
    (C) The rate at which the Earth is struck by meteorites has greatly increased in geologically recent times.
    (D) Actual meteorite impacts have been scattered fairly evenly over the Earth's surface in the course of Earth's geological history.
    (E) The Earth's geologically stable regions have been studied more intensively by geologists than have its less stable regions.

GO ON TO THE NEXT PAGE

13. That the policy of nuclear deterrence has worked thus far is unquestionable. Since the end of the Second World War, the very fact that there were nuclear armaments in existence has kept major powers from using nuclear weapons, for fear of starting a worldwide nuclear exchange that would make the land of the power initiating it uninhabitable. The proof is that a third world war between superpowers has not happened.

Which one of the following, if true, indicates a flaw in the argument?

(A) Maintaining a high level of nuclear armaments represents a significant drain on a country's economy.
(B) From what has happened in the past, it is impossible to infer with certainty what will happen in the future, so an accident could still trigger a third world war between superpowers.
(C) Continuing to produce nuclear weapons beyond the minimum needed for deterrence increases the likelihood of a nuclear accident.
(D) The major powers have engaged in many smaller-scale military operations since the end of the Second World War, while refraining from a nuclear confrontation.
(E) It cannot be known whether it was nuclear deterrence that worked, or some other factor, such as a recognition of the economic value of remaining at peace.

14. A survey of alumni of the class of 1960 at Aurora University yielded puzzling results. When asked to indicate their academic rank, half of the respondents reported that they were in the top quarter of the graduating class in 1960.

Which one of the following most helps account for the apparent contradiction above?

(A) A disproportionately large number of high-ranking alumni responded to the survey.
(B) Few, if any, respondents were mistaken about their class rank.
(C) Not all the alumni who were actually in the top quarter responded to the survey.
(D) Almost all of the alumni who graduated in 1960 responded to the survey.
(E) Academic rank at Aurora University was based on a number of considerations in addition to average grades.

15. M: It is almost impossible to find a person between the ages of 85 and 90 who primarily uses the left hand.

Q: Seventy to ninety years ago, however, children were punished for using their left hands to eat or to write and were forced to use their right hands.

Q's response serves to counter any use by M of the evidence about 85- to 90-year-olds in support of which one of the following hypotheses?

(A) Being born right-handed confers a survival advantage.
(B) Societal attitudes toward handedness differ at different times.
(C) Forcing a person to switch from a preferred hand is harmless.
(D) Handedness is a product of both genetic predisposition and social pressures.
(E) Physical habits learned in school often persist in old age.

16. The seventeenth-century physicist Sir Isaac Newton is remembered chiefly for his treatises on motion and gravity. But Newton also conducted experiments secretly for many years based on the arcane theories of alchemy, trying unsuccessfully to transmute common metals into gold and produce rejuvenating elixirs. If the alchemists of the seventeenth century had published the results of their experiments, chemistry in the eighteenth century would have been more advanced than it actually was.

Which one of the following assumptions would allow the conclusion concerning eighteenth-century chemistry to be properly drawn?

(A) Scientific progress is retarded by the reluctance of historians to acknowledge the failures of some of the great scientists.
(B) Advances in science are hastened when reports of experiments, whether successful or not, are available for review by other scientists.
(C) Newton's work on motion and gravity would not have gained wide acceptance if the results of his work in alchemy had also been made public.
(D) Increasing specialization within the sciences makes it difficult for scientists in one field to understand the principles of other fields.
(E) The seventeenth-century alchemists could have achieved their goals only if their experiments had been subjected to public scrutiny.

GO ON TO THE NEXT PAGE

17. Sedimentary rock hardens within the earth's crust as layers of matter accumulate and the pressure of the layers above converts the layers below into rock. One particular layer of sedimentary rock that contains an unusual amount of the element iridium has been presented as support for a theory that a meteorite collided with the earth some sixty million years ago. Meteorites are rich in iridium compared to the earth's crust, and geologists theorize that a meteorite's collision with the earth raised a huge cloud of iridium-laden dust. The dust, they say, eventually settled to earth where it combined with other matter, and as new layers accumulated above it, it formed a layer of iridium-rich rock.

    Which one of the following, if true, would counter the claim that the iridium-rich layer described in the passage is evidence for the meteorite collision theory?

    (A) The huge dust cloud described in the passage would have blocked the transmission of sunlight and lowered the earth's temperature.
    (B) A layer of sedimentary rock takes millions of years to harden.
    (C) Layers of sedimentary rock are used to determine the dates of prehistoric events whether or not they contain iridium.
    (D) Sixty million years ago there was a surge in volcanic activity in which the matter spewed from the volcanoes formed huge iridium-rich dust clouds.
    (E) The iridium deposit occurred at about the same time that many animal species became extinct and some scientists have theorized that mass dinosaur extinctions were caused by a meteorite collision.

18. Mary, a veterinary student, has been assigned an experiment in mammalian physiology that would require her to take a healthy, anesthetized dog and subject it to a drastic blood loss in order to observe the physiological consequences of shock. The dog would neither regain consciousness nor survive the experiment. Mary decides not to do this assignment.

    Mary's decision most closely accords with which one of the following principles?

    (A) All other things being equal, gratuitously causing any animal to suffer pain is unjustified.
    (B) Taking the life of an animal is not justifiable unless doing so would immediately assist in saving several animal lives or in protecting the health of a person.
    (C) The only sufficient justification for experimenting on animals is that future animal suffering is thereby prevented.
    (D) Practicing veterinarians have a professional obligation to strive to prevent the unnecessary death of an animal except in cases of severely ill or injured animals whose prospects for recovery are dim.
    (E) No one is ever justified in acting with the sole intention of causing the death of a living thing, be it animal or human.

19. A tree's age can be determined by counting the annual growth rings in its trunk. Each ring represents one year, and the ring's thickness reveals the relative amount of rainfall that year. Archaeologists successfully used annual rings to determine the relative ages of ancient tombs at Pazyryk. Each tomb was constructed from freshly cut logs, and the tombs' builders were constrained by tradition to use only logs from trees growing in the sacred Pazyryk Valley.

    Which one of the following, if true, contributes most to an explanation of the archaeologists' success in using annual rings to establish the relative ages of the tombs at the Pazyryk site?

    (A) The Pazyryk tombs were all robbed during ancient times, but breakage of the tombs' seals allowed the seepage of water, which soon froze permanently, thereby preserving the tombs' remaining artifacts.
    (B) The Pazyryk Valley, surrounded by extremely high mountains, has a distinctive yearly pattern of rainfall, and so trees growing in the Pazyryk Valley have annual rings that are quite distinct from trees growing in nearby valleys.
    (C) Each log in the Pazyryk tombs has among its rings a distinctive sequence of twelve annual rings representing six drought years followed by three rainy years and three more drought years.
    (D) The archaeologists determined that the youngest tree used in any of the tombs was 90 years old and that the oldest tree was 450 years old.
    (E) All of the Pazyryk tombs contained cultural artifacts that can be dated to roughly 2300 years ago.

GO ON TO THE NEXT PAGE

20. Experienced gardeners advise against planting snap peas after late April because peas do not develop properly in warm weather. This year, however, the weather was unusually cool into late June, and therefore the fact that these snap peas were planted in mid-May is unlikely to result in crop failure despite the experts' warnings.

The pattern of reasoning displayed above is most closely paralleled in which one of the following?

(A) According to many gardening authorities, tomatoes should not be planted near dill because doing so is likely to affect their taste adversely; however, since these tomatoes were grown near dill and taste fine, there is clearly no reason to pay much attention to the so-called experts' advice.
(B) Since African violets do not thrive in direct sunlight, it is said that in this region these plants should be placed in windows facing north rather than south; however, since these south-facing windows are well shaded by evergreen trees, the African violets placed in them are likely to grow satisfactorily.
(C) Where flowers are to be planted under shade trees, gardening experts often advise using impatiens since impatiens does well in conditions of shade; however, it is unlikely to do well under maple trees since maple tree roots are so near the surface that they absorb all available moisture.
(D) Most seeds tend to germinate at much higher rates when planted in warm soil than when planted in cold soil; spinach seeds, however, are unlikely to germinate properly if the soil is too warm, and therefore experts advise that spinach should be planted earlier than most vegetables.
(E) House plants generally grow best in pots slightly larger than their existing root systems, so the usual advice is to repot when roots first reach the sides of the pot; this rule should not be followed with amaryllis plants, however, because they are likely to do best with tightly compressed roots.

21. Whenever a major political scandal erupts before an election and voters blame the scandal on all parties about equally, virtually all incumbents, from whatever party, seeking reelection are returned to office. However, when voters blame such a scandal on only one party, incumbents from that party are likely to be defeated by challengers from other parties. The proportion of incumbents who seek reelection is high and remarkably constant from election to election.

If the voters' reactions are guided by a principle, which one of the following principles would best account for the contrast in reactions described above?

(A) Whenever one incumbent is responsible for one major political scandal and another incumbent is responsible for another, the consequences for the two incumbents should be the same.
(B) When a major political scandal is blamed on incumbents from all parties, that judgment is more accurate than any judgment that incumbents from only one party are to blame.
(C) Incumbents who are rightly blamed for a major political scandal should not seek reelection, but if they do, they should not be returned to office.
(D) Major political scandals can practically always be blamed on incumbents, but whether those incumbents should be voted out of office depends on who their challengers are.
(E) When major political scandals are less the responsibility of individual incumbents than of the parties to which they belong, whatever party was responsible must be penalized when possible.

GO ON TO THE NEXT PAGE

22. Once people habitually engaged in conversation; now the television competes for their attention. When the television is on, communication between family members stops. Where there is no communication, family ties become frayed and eventually snap. Therefore, the only solution is to get rid of the television.

Which one of the following is most closely parallel in its reasoning to the flawed reasoning in the argument above?

(A) Once friendships thrived on shared leisure time. But contemporary economic pressures minimize the amount of free time people have and thus jeopardize many friendships.
(B) Once people listened to the radio while pursuing other activities. Now they passively watch television. Therefore, radio was less distracting for most people than television is.
(C) Once sports enthusiasts regularly engaged in sports, but now they watch spectator sports when they could be getting physical exercise. Without physical exercise, health deteriorates. Therefore, the only remedy is to eliminate spectator sports.
(D) Once people were willing to tailor their day to the constraints of a bus or train schedule; now they are spoiled by the private car. The only solution is for government to offer financial incentives to encourage the use of public transportation.
(E) Once people did their shopping in urban retail districts, where they combined their shopping with other errands. Now many people shop in suburban malls, where they concentrate on shopping exclusively. Therefore, shopping has become a leisure time activity.

23. In essence, all rent-control policies involve specifying a maximum rent that a landlord may charge for a dwelling. The rationale for controlling rents is to protect tenants in situations where limited supply will cause rents to rise sharply in the face of increased demand. However, although rent control may help some tenants in the short run, it affects the rental-housing market adversely in the long run because landlords become reluctant to maintain the quality of their existing properties and even more reluctant to have additional rental-housing units built.

Which one of the following, if true, best explains the landlords' reluctance described above?

(A) Tenants prefer low-quality accommodations with rent control to high-quality accommodations without it.
(B) Rent control makes it very difficult for landlords to achieve reasonable returns on any investments in maintenance or in new construction.
(C) Rent control is a common practice even though it does nothing to alleviate shortages in rental housing.
(D) Rent control is generally introduced for political reasons and it takes political action to have it lifted again.
(E) Tenants prefer rent control to the alternative of receiving direct government subsidies toward rents they cannot afford.

GO ON TO THE NEXT PAGE

24. Certain minor peculiarities of language are used unconsciously by poets. If such peculiarities appear in the works of more than one poet, they are likely to reflect the language in common use during the poets' time. However, if they appear in the work of only one poet, they are likely to be personal idiosyncrasies. As such, they can provide a kind of "fingerprint" that allows scholars, by comparing a poem of previously unknown authorship to the work of a particular known poet, to identify the poem as the work of that poet.

For which one of the following reasons can the test described above never provide conclusive proof of the authorship of any poem?

(A) The labor of analyzing peculiarities of language both in the work of a known poet and in a poem of unknown authorship would not be undertaken unless other evidence already suggested that the poem of unknown authorship was written by the known poet.
(B) A peculiarity of language that might be used as an identifying mark is likely to be widely scattered in the work of a poet, so that a single poem not known to have been written by that poet might not include that peculiarity.
(C) A peculiarity of language in a poem of unknown authorship could be evidence either that the poem was written by the one author known to use that peculiarity or that the peculiarity was not unique to that author.
(D) Minor peculiarities of language contribute far less to the literary effect of any poem than such factors as poetic form, subject matter, and deliberately chosen wording.
(E) A poet's use of some peculiarities of language might have been unconscious in some poems and conscious in other poems, and the two uses would be indistinguishable to scholars at a later date.

25. Because of the recent transformation of the market, Quore, Inc., must increase productivity 10 percent over the course of the next two years, or it will certainly go bankrupt. In fact, however, Quore's production structure is such that if a 10 percent productivity increase is possible, then a 20 percent increase is attainable.

If the statements above are true, which one of the following must on the basis of them also be true?

(A) It is only Quore's production structure that makes it possible for Quore to survive the transformation of the market.
(B) Quore will not go bankrupt if it achieves a productivity increase of 20 percent over the next two years.
(C) If the market had not been transformed, Quore would have required no productivity increase in order to avoid bankruptcy.
(D) Because of the transformation of the market, Quore will achieve a productivity increase of 10 percent over the next two years.
(E) If a 20 percent productivity increase is unattainable for Quore, then it must go bankrupt.

STOP

IF YOU FINISH BEFORE TIME IS CALLED, YOU MAY CHECK YOUR WORK ON THIS SECTION ONLY.
DO NOT WORK ON ANY OTHER SECTION IN THE TEST.

SECTION II

Time—35 minutes

24 Questions

Directions: Each group of questions in this section is based on a set of conditions. In answering some of the questions, it may be useful to draw a rough diagram. Choose the response that most accurately and completely answers each question and blacken the corresponding space on your answer sheet.

Questions 1–6

John receives one grade for each of the following six courses: economics, geology, history, Italian, physics, and Russian. From highest to lowest, the possible grades are A, B, C, D, and E. E is the only failing grade. Two letter grades are consecutive if and only if they are adjacent in the alphabet.

John's grades in geology and physics are consecutive.
His grades in Italian and Russian are consecutive.
He receives a higher grade in economics than in history.
He receives a higher grade in geology than in physics.

1. If John receives the same grade in economics and Italian, and if he fails Russian, which one of the following must be true?

(A) John's geology grade is a B.
(B) John's history grade is a D.
(C) John's history grade is an E.
(D) John's physics grade is a B.
(E) John's physics grade is a C.

2. If John passes all his courses and receives a higher grade in geology than in either language, which one of the following must be true?

(A) He receives exactly one A.
(B) He receives exactly one B.
(C) He receives exactly two Bs.
(D) He receives at least one B and at least one C.
(E) He receives at least one C and at least one D.

3. If John receives a higher grade in physics than in economics and receives a higher grade in economics than in either language, which one of the following allows all six of his grades to be determined?

(A) His grade in history is a D.
(B) His grade in Italian is a D.
(C) His grades in history and Italian are identical.
(D) His grades in history and Russian are identical.
(E) His grade in history is higher than his grade in Russian.

4. If John receives a higher grade in physics than in economics and receives a higher grade in history than in Italian, exactly how many of his grades can be determined?

(A) 2
(B) 3
(C) 4
(D) 5
(E) 6

5. Assume that John's grade in physics is higher than his grade in Italian and consecutive with it and that his grades in Russian and physics differ. Which one of the following must be true?

(A) John receives both an A and a B.
(B) John receives both an A and a C.
(C) John receives both a B and a D.
(D) John receives both a B and an E.
(E) John receives both a D and an E.

6. Assume that John receives a lower grade in economics than in physics. He must have failed at least one course if which one of the following is also true?

(A) He receives a lower grade in Italian than in economics.
(B) He receives a lower grade in Italian than in physics.
(C) He receives a lower grade in physics than in Italian.
(D) He receives a lower grade in Russian than in economics.
(E) He receives a lower grade in Russian than in history.

GO ON TO THE NEXT PAGE

2 2 2 2 2 2 2 2 2 2

Questions 7–11

A store sells shirts only in small, medium, and large sizes, and only in red, yellow, and blue colors. Casey buys exactly three shirts from the store.

A shirt type consists of both a size and a color.
Casey does not buy two shirts of the same type.
Casey does not buy both a small shirt and a large shirt.
No small red shirts are available.
No large blue shirts are available.

7. Which one of the following must be false?

(A) Two of the shirts that Casey buys are small and two are red.
(B) Two of the shirts that Casey buys are medium and two are red.
(C) Two of the shirts that Casey buys are large and two are red.
(D) Two of the shirts that Casey buys are small, one is yellow, and one is blue.
(E) Two of the shirts that Casey buys are medium, one is yellow, and one is blue.

8. If Casey buys a small blue shirt, which one of the following must be false?

(A) Casey buys two blue shirts.
(B) Casey buys two red shirts.
(C) Casey buys two yellow shirts.
(D) Casey buys two small shirts.
(E) Casey buys two medium shirts.

9. If Casey does not buy a medium yellow shirt, which one of the following must be true?

(A) Casey buys either a medium red shirt or a small blue shirt.
(B) Casey buys either a medium red shirt or a medium blue shirt.
(C) Casey buys either a large red shirt or a small blue shirt.
(D) Casey buys either a large red shirt or a medium red shirt.
(E) Casey buys either a large yellow shirt or a small yellow shirt.

10. If Casey buys exactly one medium shirt and does not buy two shirts of the same color, then she cannot buy which one of the following?

(A) a medium red shirt
(B) a medium yellow shirt
(C) a medium blue shirt
(D) a large red shirt
(E) a large yellow shirt

11. If neither large red shirts nor small blue shirts are available, which one of the following must Casey buy?

(A) a red shirt
(B) a medium yellow shirt
(C) either a large shirt or a small shirt
(D) either a medium red shirt or a medium blue shirt
(E) either a large yellow shirt or a medium blue shirt

GO ON TO THE NEXT PAGE

2 2 2 2 2 2 2 2 2 2

Questions 12–17

A hobbyist is stocking her aquarium with exactly three fish of different types and with exactly two species of plants. The only fish under consideration are a G, an H, a J, a K, and an L, and the only kinds of plants under consideration are of the species W, X, Y, and Z. She will observe the following conditions:

If she selects the G. she can select neither the H nor a Y.
She cannot select the H unless she selects the K.
She cannot select the J unless she selects a W.
If she selects the K, she must select an X.

12. Which one of the following is an acceptable selection of fish and plants for the aquarium?

	Fish	Plants
(A)	G, H, K	W, Y
(B)	G, J, K	W, X
(C)	G, J, L	X, Z
(D)	H, J, L	W, Z
(E)	H, K, L	Y, Z

13. If the hobbyist selects the H, which one of the following must also be true?

(A) She selects at least one W.
(B) She selects at least one X.
(C) She selects the J but no Y's.
(D) She selects the K, but no X's.
(E) She selects at least one X, but no Y's.

14. If the hobbyist selects both X's and Z's, which one of the following could be the group of fish she selects?

(A) G, H, K
(B) G, J, K
(C) G, K, L
(D) H, J, L
(E) J, K, L

15. The hobbyist could select any of the following groups of fish for the aquarium EXCEPT

(A) G, K, L
(B) H, J, K
(C) H, J, L
(D) H, K, L
(E) J, K, L

16. If the hobbyist selects a Y, which one of the following must be the group of fish she selects?

(A) G, H, K
(B) H, J, K
(C) H, J, L
(D) H, K, L
(E) J, K, L

17. The hobbyist could select any of the following plant combinations EXCEPT

(A) W and X
(B) W and Y
(C) W and Z
(D) X and Y
(E) X and Z

GO ON TO THE NEXT PAGE

Questions 18–24

A committee ranks five towns—Palmdale, Quietville, Riverdale, Seaside, Tidetown—from first (best) to fifth (worst) on each of three criteria: climate, location, friendliness.

For each of the three criteria, none of the five towns receives the same ranking as any other town does.
In climate, Tidetown is ranked third, and Seaside fourth.
In location, Quietville is ranked second, Riverdale third, Palmdale fourth.
In friendliness, Tidetown's ranking is better than Palmdale's, Quietville is ranked fourth, and Seaside fifth.
Riverdale receives a better ranking in climate than in friendliness.
Quietville's three rankings are all different from each other.

18. Which one of the following is a complete and accurate list of the rankings any one of which could be the ranking on climate given to Riverdale?

    (A) first
    (B) first, second
    (C) first, fifth
    (D) second, fifth
    (E) first, second, fifth

19. Which one of the following is a town that CANNOT be ranked fifth on any one of the three criteria?

    (A) Palmdale
    (B) Quietville
    (C) Riverdale
    (D) Seaside
    (E) Tidetown

20. Which one of the following could be true?

    (A) Palmdale is ranked first in both climate and friendliness.
    (B) Quietville is ranked second in both climate and location.
    (C) Riverdale is ranked first in climate and third in both location and friendliness.
    (D) Seaside is ranked fifth in friendliness and fourth in both climate and location.
    (E) Tidetown is ranked third in both climate and friendliness.

21. If Quietville is ranked first in climate, then it must be true that

    (A) Palmdale is ranked second in climate
    (B) Palmdale is ranked third in friendliness
    (C) Riverdale is ranked second in friendliness
    (D) Riverdale is ranked third in friendliness
    (E) Tidetown is ranked fifth in location

22. If Palmdale is ranked second in climate, then which one of the following can be true?

    (A) Palmdale is ranked second in friendliness.
    (B) Quietville is ranked first in climate.
    (C) Riverdale is ranked first in friendliness.
    (D) Riverdale is ranked fifth in climate.
    (E) Tidetown is ranked third in friendliness.

23. If Tidetown is ranked first in location and Riverdale is ranked second in friendliness, then it is possible to deduce with certainty all three rankings for exactly how many of the towns?

    (A) One
    (B) Two
    (C) Three
    (D) Four
    (E) Five

24. Which one of the following statements CANNOT be true?

    (A) Palmdale is ranked first in climate.
    (B) Quietville is ranked fifth in climate.
    (C) Riverdale is ranked third in friendliness.
    (D) Seaside is ranked first in location.
    (E) Tidetown is ranked second in friendliness.

S T O P

IF YOU FINISH BEFORE TIME IS CALLED, YOU MAY CHECK YOUR WORK ON THIS SECTION ONLY.
DO NOT WORK ON ANY OTHER SECTION IN THE TEST.

SECTION III

Time—35 minutes

25 Questions

Directions: The questions in this section are based on the reasoning contained in brief statements or passages. For some questions, more than one of the choices could conceivably answer the question. However, you are to choose the best answer; that is, the response that most accurately and completely answers the question. You should not make assumptions that are by commonsense standards implausible, superfluous, or incompatible with the passage. After you have chosen the best answer, blacken the corresponding space on your answer sheet.

1. Terry: If you want to get a decent job, you should go to college.

   Mark: That is not true. There are other reasons to go to college than wanting to get a good job.

   Mark's response shows that he interpreted Terry's remarks to mean that

   (A) college is one of many places to get trained for a job
   (B) decent jobs are obtained only by persons who have gone to college
   (C) wanting to get a decent job is the only reason for going to college
   (D) training for decent jobs is available only at colleges
   (E) all people who want decent jobs go to college

2. Several studies have shown that hospitals are not all equally successful: patients are much more likely to die in some of them than in others. Since the hospitals in the studies had approximately equal per-patient funding, differences in the quality of care provided by hospital staff are probably responsible for the differences in mortality rates.

   Which one of the following, if true, casts the most doubt on the conclusion drawn above?

   (A) The staff in some of the hospitals studied had earned more advanced degrees, on average, than the staff in the other hospitals.
   (B) Patient populations vary substantially in average severity of illness from hospital to hospital.
   (C) The average number of years that staff members stay on at a given job varies considerably from one hospital to another.
   (D) Approximately the same surgical procedures were performed in each of the hospitals covered in the studies.
   (E) Mortality rates for hospital patients do not vary considerably from one region of the country to another.

Questions 3–4

The United States government generally tries to protect valuable natural resources. But one resource has been ignored for too long. In the United States, each bushel of corn produced might result in the loss of as much as two bushels of topsoil. Moreover, in the last 100 years, the topsoil in many states, which once was about fourteen inches thick, has been eroded to only six or eight inches. Nonetheless, federal expenditures for nationwide soil conservation programs have remained at ridiculously low levels. Total federal expenditures for nationwide soil conservation programs have been less than the allocations of some individual states.

3. Which one of the following best expresses the main point of the argument?

   (A) Corn is not a cost-effective product and substitutes should be found where possible.
   (B) A layer of topsoil only six to eight inches thick cannot support the continued cultivation of corn.
   (C) Soil conservation is a responsibility of the federal government, not the states.
   (D) The federal government's expenditures for soil conservation in the various states have been inequitable.
   (E) The federal government should spend much more on soil conservation than it has been spending.

4. In stating the argument, the author does which one of the following?

   (A) makes a detailed statistical projection of future topsoil loss
   (B) makes a generalization about total reduction in topsoil depth in all states
   (C) assumes that the United States government does not place a high value on its natural resources
   (D) refrains from using slanted language concerning the level of federal expenditures
   (E) compares state expenditures with federal expenditures

GO ON TO THE NEXT PAGE

5. Animals with a certain behavioral disorder have unusually high levels of aluminum in their brain tissue. Since a silicon-based compound binds to aluminum and prevents it from affecting the brain tissue, animals can be cured of the disorder by being treated with the compound.

The argument is based on which one of the following assumptions?

(A) Animals with the disorder have unusually high but invariable levels of aluminum in their brain tissue.
(B) Aluminum is the cause of the disorder rather than merely an effect of it.
(C) Introducing the compound into the brain tissue has no side effects.
(D) The amount of the compound needed to neutralize the aluminum in an animal's brain tissue varies depending upon the species.
(E) Aluminum is never present in normal brain tissue.

6. As air-breathing mammals, whales must once have lived on land and needed hind limbs capable of supporting the mammals' weight. Whales have the bare remnants of a pelvis. If animals have a pelvis, we expect them to have hind limbs. A newly discovered fossilized whale skeleton has very fragile hind limbs that could not have supported the animal's weight on land. This skeleton had a partial pelvis.

If the statements above are true, which one of the following, if also true, would most strongly support the conclusion that the fragile hind limbs are remnants of limbs that land-dwelling whales once had?

(A) Whale bones older than the fossilized hind limbs confirm that ancient whales had full pelvises.
(B) No skeletons of ancient whales with intact hind limbs capable of supporting the mammals' weight have ever been found.
(C) Scientists are uncertain whether the apparently nonfunctioning limbs of other early mammals derived from once-functioning limbs of their ancestors.
(D) Other large-bodied mammals like seals and sea lions maneuver on beaches and rocky coasts without fully functioning hind limbs.
(E) Some smaller sea-dwelling mammals, such as modern dolphins, have no visible indications of hind limbs.

7. The stated goal of the government's funding program for the arts is to encourage the creation of works of artistic excellence. Senator Beton claims, however, that a government-funded artwork can never reflect the independent artistic conscience of the artist because artists, like anyone else who accepts financial support, will inevitably try to please those who control the distribution of that support. Senator Beton concludes that government funding of the arts not only is a burden on taxpayers but also cannot lead to the creation of works of true artistic excellence.

Which one of the following is an assumption on which Senator Beton's argument is based?

(A) Most taxpayers have little or no interest in the creation of works of true artistic excellence.
(B) Government funding of the arts is more generous than other financial support most artists receive.
(C) Distribution of government funds for the arts is based on a broad agreement as to what constitutes artistic excellence.
(D) Once an artist has produced works of true artistic excellence, he or she will never accept government funding.
(E) A contemporary work of art that does not reflect the independent artistic conscience of the artist cannot be a work of true artistic excellence.

GO ON TO THE NEXT PAGE

8. Older United States automobiles have been identified as contributing disproportionately to global air pollution. The requirement in many jurisdictions that automobiles pass emission-control inspections has had the effect of taking many such automobiles out of service in the United States, as they fail inspection and their owners opt to buy newer automobiles. Thus the burden of pollution such older United States automobiles contribute to the global atmosphere will be gradually reduced over the next decade.

   Which one of the following, if true, most seriously weakens the argument?

   (A) It is impossible to separate the air of one country or jurisdiction from that of others, since air currents circle the globe.
   (B) When automobiles that are now new become older, they will, because of a design change, cause less air pollution than older automobiles do now.
   (C) There is a thriving market for used older United States automobiles that are exported to regions that have no emission-control regulations.
   (D) The number of jurisdictions in the United States requiring automobiles to pass emission-control inspections is no longer increasing.
   (E) Even if all the older automobiles in the United States were retired from service, air pollution from United States automobiles could still increase if the total number of automobiles in use should increase significantly.

9. The journalistic practice of fabricating remarks after an interview and printing them within quotation marks, as if they were the interviewee's own words, has been decried as a form of unfair misrepresentation. However, people's actual spoken remarks rarely convey their ideas as clearly as does a distillation of those ideas crafted, after an interview, by a skilled writer. Therefore, since this practice avoids the more serious misrepresentation that would occur if people's exact words were quoted but their ideas only partially expressed, it is entirely defensible.

   Which one of the following is a questionable technique used in the argument?

   (A) answering an exaggerated charge by undermining the personal authority of those who made that charge
   (B) claiming that the prestige of a profession provides ample grounds for dismissing criticisms of that profession
   (C) offering as an adequate defense of a practice an observation that discredits only one of several possible alternatives to that practice
   (D) concluding that a practice is right on the grounds that it is necessary
   (E) using the opponent's admission that a practice is sometimes appropriate as conclusive proof that that practice is never inappropriate

10. The reforms to improve the quality of public education that have been initiated on the part of suppliers of public education have been insufficient. Therefore, reforms must be demanded by consumers. Parents should be given government vouchers with which to pay for their children's education and should be allowed to choose the schools at which the vouchers will be spent. To attract students, academically underachieving schools will be forced to improve their academic offerings.

    The argument assumes that

    (A) in selecting schools parents would tend to prefer a reasonable level of academic quality to greater sports opportunities or more convenient location
    (B) improvement in the academic offerings of schools will be enforced by the discipline of the job market in which graduating students compete
    (C) there is a single best way to educate students
    (D) children are able to recognize which schools are better and would influence their parents' decisions
    (E) schools would each improve all of their academic offerings and would not tend to specialize in one particular field to the exclusion of others

GO ON TO THE NEXT PAGE

11. Professor Smith published a paper arguing that a chemical found in minute quantities in most drinking water had an adverse effect on the human nervous system. Existing scientific theory held that no such effect was possible because there was no neural mechanism for bringing it about. Several papers by well-known scientists in the field followed, unanimously purporting to prove Professor Smith wrong. This clearly shows that the scientific establishment was threatened by Professor Smith's work and conspired to discredit it.

Which one of the following is the central flaw in the argument given by the author of the passage?

(A) The author passes over the possibility that Professor Smith had much to gain should Professor Smith's discovery have found general acceptance.
(B) The author fails to mention whether or not Professor Smith knew that the existence of the alleged new effect was incompatible with established scientific theory.
(C) The author fails to show why the other scientists could not have been presenting evidence in order to establish the truth of the matter.
(D) The author neglects to clarify what his or her relationship to Professor Smith is.
(E) The author fails to indicate what, if any, effect the publication of Professor Smith's paper had on the public's confidence in the safety of most drinking water.

12. The number of North American children who are obese—that is, who have more body fat than do 85 percent of North American children their age—is steadily increasing, according to four major studies conducted over the past 15 years.

If the finding reported above is correct, it can be properly concluded that

(A) when four major studies all produce similar results, those studies must be accurate
(B) North American children have been progressively less physically active over the past 15 years
(C) the number of North American children who are not obese increased over the past 15 years
(D) over the past 15 years, the number of North American children who are underweight has declined
(E) the incidence of obesity in North American children tends to increase as the children grow older

13. Economist: Money, no matter what its form and in almost every culture in which it has been used, derives its value from its scarcity, whether real or perceived.
Anthropologist: But cowrie shells formed the major currency in the Solomon Island economy of the Kwara'ae, and unlimited numbers of these shells washed up daily on the beaches to which the Kwara'ae had access.

Which one of the following, if true about the Kwara'ae, best serves to resolve the apparently conflicting positions cited above?

(A) During festivals they exchanged strings of cowrie-shell money with each other as part of a traditional ritual that honored their elders.
(B) They considered porpoise teeth valuable, and these were generally threaded on strings to be worn as jewelry.
(C) The shells used as money by men were not always from the same species of cowrie as those used as money by women.
(D) They accepted as money only cowrie shells that were polished and carved by a neighboring people, and such shell preparation required both time and skilled labor.
(E) After Western traders brought money in the form of precious-metal coins to the Solomon Islands, cowrie-shell money continued to be used as one of the major media of exchange for both goods and services.

14. School superintendent: It is a sad fact that, until now, entry into the academically best high school in our district has been restricted to the children of people who were wealthy enough to pay the high tuition. Parents who were previously denied the option of sending their children to this school now have this option, since I am replacing the tuition requirement with a requirement that allows only those who live in the neighborhood of the school to attend.

The superintendent's claim about the effect of replacing the tuition requirement relies on the assumption that

(A) the residents of the school's neighborhood tend to be wealthy
(B) people other than those wealthy enough to have paid the old tuition are able to live in the neighborhood of the school
(C) people less wealthy than those who were able to pay the old tuition are in the majority in the district
(D) there are no high schools in the district other than the one referred to by the superintendent
(E) there are many people not wealthy enough to have paid the old tuition who wish to have their children attend the school

GO ON TO THE NEXT PAGE

15. The Scorpio Miser with its special high-efficiency engine costs more to buy than the standard Scorpio sports car. At current fuel prices, a buyer choosing the Miser would have to drive it 60,000 miles to make up the difference in purchase price through savings on fuel. It follows that, if fuel prices fell, it would take fewer miles to reach the break-even point.

Which one of the following arguments contains an error of reasoning similar to that in the argument above?

(A) The true annual rate of earnings on an interest-bearing account is the annual rate of interest less the annual rate of inflation. Consequently, if the rate of inflation drops, the rate of interest can be reduced by an equal amount without there being a change in the true rate of earnings.
(B) For retail food stores, the Polar freezer, unlike the Arctic freezer, provides a consistent temperature that allows the store to carry premium frozen foods. Though the Polar freezer uses more electricity, there is a bigger profit on premium foods. Thus, if electricity rates fell, a lower volume of premium-food sales could justify choosing the Polar freezer.
(C) With the Roadmaker, a crew can repave a mile of decayed road in less time than with the competing model, which is, however, much less expensive. Reduced staffing levels made possible by the Roadmaker eventually compensate for its higher price. Therefore, the Roadmaker is especially advantageous where average wages are low.
(D) The improved strain of the Northland apple tree bears fruit younger and lives longer than the standard strain. The standard strain does grow larger at maturity, but to allow for this, standard trees must be spaced farther apart. Therefore, new plantings should all be of the improved strain.
(E) Stocks pay dividends, which vary from year to year depending on profits made. Bonds pay interest, which remains constant from year to year. Therefore, since the interest earned on bonds does not decrease when economic conditions decline, investors interested in a reliable income should choose bonds.

16. Approximately 7.6 million women who earn incomes have preschool-age children, and approximately 6.4 million women are the sole income earners for their families. These figures indicate that there are comparatively few income-earning women who have preschool-age children but are not the sole income earners for their families.

A major flaw in the reasoning is that it

(A) relies on figures that are too imprecise to support the conclusion drawn
(B) overlooks the possibility that there is little or no overlap between the two populations of women cited
(C) fails to indicate whether the difference between the two figures cited will tend to remain stable over time
(D) ignores the possibility that families with preschool-age children might also have older children
(E) provides no information on families in which men are the sole income earners

17. Being articulate has been equated with having a large vocabulary. Actually, however, people with large vocabularies have no incentive for, and tend not to engage in, the kind of creative linguistic self-expression that is required when no available words seem adequate. Thus a large vocabulary is a hindrance to using language in a truly articulate way.

Which one of the following is an assumption made in the argument?

(A) When people are truly articulate, they have the capacity to express themselves in situations in which their vocabularies seem inadequate.
(B) People who are able to express themselves creatively in new situations have little incentive to acquire large vocabularies.
(C) The most articulate people are people who have large vocabularies but also are able to express themselves creatively when the situation demands it.
(D) In educating people to be more articulate, it would be futile to try to increase the size of their vocabularies.
(E) In unfamiliar situations, even people with large vocabularies often do not have specifically suitable words available.

GO ON TO THE NEXT PAGE

Questions 18–19

Dr. Schilling: Those who advocate replacing my country's private health insurance system with nationalized health insurance because of the rising costs of medical care fail to consider the high human costs that consumers pay in countries with nationalized insurance: access to high-technology medicine is restricted. Kidney transplants and open-heart surgery—familiar life-saving procedures—are rationed. People are denied their right to treatments they want and need.

Dr. Laforte: Your country's reliance on private health insurance denies access even to basic, conventional medicine to the many people who cannot afford adequate health coverage. With nationalized insurance, rich and poor have equal access to life-saving medical procedures, and people's right to decent medical treatment regardless of income is not violated.

18. Dr. Schilling's and Dr. Laforte's statements provide the most support for holding that they would disagree about the truth of which one of the following?

(A) People's rights are violated less when they are denied an available medical treatment they need because they lack the means to pay for it than when they are denied such treatment on noneconomic grounds.
(B) Where health insurance is provided by private insurance companies, people who are wealthy generally receive better health care than do people who are unable to afford health insurance.
(C) In countries that rely primarily on private health insurance to pay for medical costs, most people who would benefit from a kidney transplant receive one.
(D) In countries with nationalized health insurance, no one who needs a familiar medical treatment in order to stay alive is denied that treatment.
(E) Anyone who wants a particular medical treatment has a right to receive that treatment.

19. In responding to Dr. Schilling, Dr. Laforte employs which one of the following argumentative strategies?

(A) showing that the objections raised by Dr. Schilling have no bearing on the question of which of the two systems under consideration is the superior system
(B) calling into question Dr. Schilling's status as an authority on the issue of whether consumers' access to medical treatments is restricted in countries with nationalized health insurance
(C) producing counterexamples to Dr. Schilling's claims that nationalized health insurance schemes extract high human costs from consumers
(D) demonstrating that Dr. Schilling's reasoning is persuasive only because of his ambiguous use of the key word "consumer"
(E) showing that the force of Dr. Schilling's criticism depends on construing the key notion of access in a particular limited way

GO ON TO THE NEXT PAGE

20. A certain viral infection is widespread among children, and about 30 percent of children infected with the virus develop middle ear infections. Antibiotics, although effective in treating bacterial infections, have no effect on the virus. Yet when middle ear infections in children infected with the virus are treated with antibiotics, the ear infections often clear up.

Which one of the following most helps to explain the success of the treatments with antibiotics?

(A) Although some types of antibiotics fail to clear up certain infections, other types of antibiotics might provide effective treatment for those infections.
(B) Children infected with the virus are particularly susceptible to bacteria that infect the middle ear.
(C) Many children who develop middle ear infections are not infected with the virus.
(D) Most viral infections are more difficult to treat than are most bacterial infections.
(E) Among children not infected with the virus, fewer than 30 percent develop middle ear infections.

21. Naturalist: For decades we have known that the tuatara, a New Zealand reptile, have been approaching extinction on the South Island. But since South Island tuatara were thought to be of the same species as North Island tuatara there was no need to protect them. But new research indicates that the South Island tuatara are a distinct species, found only in that location. Because it is now known that if the South Island tuatara are lost an entire species will thereby be lost, human beings are now obliged to prevent their extinction, even if it means killing many of their unendangered natural predators.

Which one of the following principles most helps to justify the naturalists' argumentation?

(A) In order to maximize the number of living things on Earth, steps should be taken to preserve all local populations of animals.
(B) When an animal is in danger of dying, there is an obligation to help save its life, if doing so would not interfere with the health or well-being of other animals or people.
(C) The threat of local extinction imposes no obligation to try to prevent that extinction, whereas the threat of global extinction does impose such an obligation.
(D) Human activities that either intentionally or unintentionally threaten the survival of an animal species ought to be curtailed.
(E) Species that are found in only one circumscribed geographical region ought to be given more care and attention than are other species because they are more vulnerable to extinction.

22. Nursing schools cannot attract a greater number of able applicants than they currently do unless the problems of low wages and high-stress working conditions in the nursing profession are solved. If the pool of able applicants to nursing school does not increase beyond the current level, either the profession will have to lower its entrance standards, or there will soon be an acute shortage of nurses. It is not certain, however, that lowering entrance standards will avert a shortage. It is clear that with either a shortage of nurses or lowered entrance standards for the profession, the current high quality of health care cannot be maintained.

Which one of the following can be properly inferred from the passage?

(A) If the nursing profession solves the problems of low wages and high-stress working conditions, it will attract able applicants in greater numbers than it currently does.
(B) The nursing profession will have to lower its entrance standards if the pool of able applicants to nursing school does not increase beyond the current level.
(C) If the nursing profession solves the problems of low wages and high-stress working conditions, high quality health care will be maintained.
(D) If the nursing profession fails to solve the problems of low wages and high-stress working conditions, there will soon be an acute shortage of nurses.
(E) The current high quality of health care will not be maintained if the problems of low wages and high-stress working conditions in the nursing profession are not solved.

GO ON TO THE NEXT PAGE

3 3 3 3 3 3 3 3 3 3

Questions 23–24

There are about 75 brands of microwave popcorn on the market; altogether, they account for a little over half of the money from sales of microwave food products. It takes three minutes to pop corn in the microwave, compared to seven minutes to pop corn conventionally. Yet by weight, microwave popcorn typically costs over five times as much as conventional popcorn. Judging by the popularity of microwave popcorn, many people are willing to pay a high price for just a little additional convenience.

23. If the statements in the passage are true, which one of the following must also be true?

(A) No single brand of microwave popcorn accounts for a large share of microwave food product sales.
(B) There are more brands of microwave popcorn on the market than there are of any other microwave food product.
(C) By volume, more microwave popcorn is sold than is conventional popcorn.
(D) More money is spent on microwave food products that take three minutes or less to cook than on microwave food products that take longer to cook.
(E) Of the total number of microwave food products on the market, most are microwave popcorn products.

24. Which one of the following statements, if true, would call into question the conclusion in the passage?

(A) More than 50 percent of popcorn purchasers buy conventional popcorn rather than microwave popcorn.
(B) Most people who prefer microwave popcorn do so because it is less fattening than popcorn that is popped conventionally in oil.
(C) The price of microwave popcorn reflects its packaging more than it reflects the quality of the popcorn contained in the package.
(D) The ratio of unpopped kernels to popped kernels is generally the same whether popcorn is popped in a microwave or conventionally in oil.
(E) Because microwave popcorn contains additives not contained in conventional popcorn, microwave popcorn weighs more than an equal volume of conventional popcorn.

25. Situation: In the island nation of Bezun, the government taxes gasoline heavily in order to induce people not to drive. It uses the revenue from the gasoline tax to subsidize electricity in order to reduce prices charged for electricity.
Analysis: The greater the success achieved in meeting the first of these objectives, the less will be the success achieved in meeting the second.

The analysis provided for the situation above would be most appropriate in which one of the following situations?

(A) A library charges a late fee in order to induce borrowers to return books promptly. The library uses revenue from the late fee to send reminders to tardy borrowers in order to reduce the incidence of overdue books.
(B) A mail-order store imposes a stiff surcharge for overnight delivery in order to limit use of this option. The store uses revenue from the surcharge to pay the extra expenses it incurs for providing the overnight delivery service.
(C) The park management charges an admission fee so that a park's users will contribute to the park's upkeep. In order to keep admission fees low, the management does not finance any new projects from them.
(D) A restaurant adds a service charge in order to spare customers the trouble of individual tips. The service charge is then shared among the restaurant's workers in order to augment their low hourly wages.
(E) The highway administration charges a toll for crossing a bridge in order to get motorists to use other routes. It uses the revenue from that toll to generate a reserve fund in order to be able one day to build a new bridge.

S T O P

IF YOU FINISH BEFORE TIME IS CALLED, YOU MAY CHECK YOUR WORK ON THIS SECTION ONLY.
DO NOT WORK ON ANY OTHER SECTION IN THE TEST.

SECTION IV

Time—35 minutes

27 Questions

Directions: Each passage in this section is followed by a group of questions to be answered on the basis of what is stated or implied in the passage. For some of the questions, more than one of the choices could conceivably answer the question. However, you are to choose the best answer; that is, the response that most accurately and completely answers the question, and blacken the corresponding space on your answer sheet.

Governments of developing countries occasionally enter into economic development agreements with foreign investors who provide capital and technological expertise that may not be readily available in such countries. Besides the normal economic risk that accompanies such enterprises, investors face the additional risk that the host government may attempt unilaterally to change in its favor the terms of the agreement or even to terminate the agreement altogether and appropriate the project for itself. In order to make economic development agreements more attractive to investors, some developing countries have attempted to strengthen the security of such agreements with clauses specifying that the agreements will be governed by "general principles of law recognized by civilized nations"—a set of legal principles or rules shared by the world's major legal systems. However, advocates of governments' freedom to modify or terminate such agreements argue that these agreements fall within a special class of contracts known as administrative contracts, a concept that originated in French law. They assert that under the theory of administrative contracts, a government retains inherent power to modify or terminate its own contract, and that this power indeed constitutes a general principle of law. However, their argument is flawed on at least two counts.

First, in French law not all government contracts are treated as administrative contracts. Some contracts are designated as administrative by specific statute, in which case the contractor is made aware of the applicable legal rules upon entering into agreement with the government. Alternatively, the contracting government agency can itself designate a contract as administrative by including certain terms not found in private civil contracts. Moreover, even in the case of administrative contracts, French law requires that in the event that the government unilaterally modifies the terms of the contract, it must compensate the contractor for any increased burden resulting from the government's action. In effect, the government is thus prevented from modifying those contractual terms that define the financial balance of the contract.

Second, the French law of administrative contracts, although adopted by several countries, is not so universally accepted that it can be embraced as a general principle of law. In both the United States and the United Kingdom, government contracts are governed by the ordinary law of contracts, with the result that the government can reserve the power to modify or terminate a contract unilaterally only by writing such power into the contract as a specific provision. Indeed, the very fact that termination and modification clauses are commonly found in government contracts suggests that a government's capacity to modify or terminate agreements unilaterally derives from specific contract provisions, not from inherent state power.

1. In the passage, the author is primarily concerned with doing which one of the following?

(A) pointing out flaws in an argument provided in support of a position
(B) analyzing the weaknesses inherent in the proposed solution to a problem
(C) marshaling evidence in support of a new explanation of a phenomenon
(D) analyzing the risks inherent in adopting a certain course of action
(E) advocating a new approach to a problem that has not been solved by traditional means

2. It can be inferred from the passage that the author would be most likely to agree with which one of the following assertions regarding the "general principles of law" mentioned in lines 16–17 of the passage?

(A) They fail to take into account the special needs and interests of developing countries that enter into agreements with foreign investors.
(B) They have only recently been invoked as criteria for adjudicating disputes between governments and foreign investors.
(C) They are more compatible with the laws of France and the United States than with those of the United Kingdom.
(D) They do not assert that governments have an inherent right to modify unilaterally the terms of agreements that they have entered into with foreign investors.
(E) They are not useful in adjudicating disputes between developing countries and foreign investors.

GO ON TO THE NEXT PAGE

4 4 4 4 4 4 4 4 4 4

3. The author implies that which one of the following is true of economic development agreements?

(A) They provide greater economic benefits to the governments that are parties to such agreements than to foreign investors.
(B) They are interpreted differently by courts in the United Kingdom than they are by courts in the United States.
(C) They have proliferated in recent years as a result of governments' attempts to make them more legally secure.
(D) They entail greater risk to investors when the governments that enter into such agreements reserve the right to modify unilaterally the terms of the agreements.
(E) They have become less attractive to foreign investors as an increasing number of governments that enter into such agreements consider them governed by the law of ordinary contracts.

4. According to the author, which one of the following is true of a contract that is designated by a French government agency as an administrative contract?

(A) It requires the government agency to pay for unanticipated increases in the cost of delivering the goods and services specified in the contract.
(B) It provides the contractor with certain guarantees that are not normally provided in private civil contracts.
(C) It must be ratified by the passage of a statute.
(D) It discourages foreign companies from bidding on the contract.
(E) It contains terms that distinguish it from a private civil contract.

5. It can be inferred from the passage that under the "ordinary law of contracts" (lines 53–54), a government would have the right to modify unilaterally the terms of a contract that it had entered into with a foreign investor if which one of the following were true?

(A) The government undertook a greater economic risk by entering into the contract than did the foreign investor.
(B) The cost to the foreign investor of abiding by the terms of the contract exceeded the original estimates of such costs.
(C) The modification of the contract did not result in any increased financial burden for the investor.
(D) Both the government and the investor had agreed to abide by the general principles of law recognized by civilized nations.
(E) The contract contains a specific provision allowing the government to modify the contract.

6. In the last paragraph, the author refers to government contracts in the United States and the United Kingdom primarily in order to

(A) cite two governments that often reserve the right to modify unilaterally contracts that they enter into with foreign investors
(B) support the assertion that there is no general principle of law governing contracts between private individuals and governments
(C) cast doubt on the alleged universality of the concept of administrative contracts
(D) provide examples of legal systems that might benefit from the concept of administrative contracts
(E) provide examples of characteristics that typically distinguish government contracts from private civil contracts

7. Which one of the following best states the author's main conclusion in the passage?

(A) Providing that an international agreement be governed by general principles of law is not a viable method of guaranteeing the legal security of such an agreement.
(B) French law regarding contracts is significantly different from that in the United States and the United Kingdom.
(C) Contracts between governments and private investors in most nations are governed by ordinary contract law.
(D) An inherent power of a government to modify or terminate a contract cannot be considered a general principle of law.
(E) Contracts between governments and private investors can be secured only by reliance on general principles of law.

8. The author's argument in lines 57–62 would be most weakened if which one of the following were true?

(A) The specific provisions of government contracts often contain explicit statements of what all parties to the contracts already agree are inherent state powers.
(B) Governments are more frequently put in the position of having to modify or terminate contracts than are private individuals.
(C) Modification clauses in economic development agreements have frequently been challenged in international tribunals by foreign investors who were a party to such agreements.
(D) The general principles of law provide that modification clauses cannot allow the terms of a contract to be modified in such a way that the financial balance of the contract is affected.
(E) Termination and modification agreements are often interpreted differently by national courts than they are by international tribunals.

GO ON TO THE NEXT PAGE

4 4 4 4 4 4 4 4 4 4

Nico Frijda writes that emotions are governed by a psychological principle called the "law of apparent reality": emotions are elicited only by events appraised as real, and the intensity of these emotions corresponds to the degree to which these events are appraised as real. This observation seems psychologically plausible, but emotional responses elicited by works of art raise counterexamples.

Frijda's law accounts for my panic if I am afraid of snakes and see an object I correctly appraise as a rattlesnake, and also for my identical response if I see a coiled garden hose I mistakenly perceive to be a snake. However, suppose I am watching a movie and see a snake gliding toward its victim. Surely I might experience the same emotions of panic and distress, though I know the snake is not real. These responses extend even to phenomena not conventionally accepted as real. A movie about ghosts, for example, may be terrifying to all viewers, even those who firmly reject the possibility of ghosts, but this is not because viewers are confusing cinematic depiction with reality. Moreover, I can feel strong emotions in response to objects of art that are interpretations, rather than representations, of reality: I am moved by Mozart's *Requiem,* but I know that I am not at a real funeral. However, if Frijda's law is to explain all emotional reactions, there should be no emotional response at all to aesthetic objects or events, because we know they are not real in the way a living rattlesnake is real.

Most psychologists, perplexed by the feelings they acknowledge are aroused by aesthetic experience, have claimed that these emotions are genuine, but different in kind from nonaesthetic emotions. This, however, is a descriptive distinction rather than an empirical observation and consequently lacks explanatory value. On the other hand, Gombrich argues that emotional responses to art are ersatz: art triggers remembrances of previously experienced emotions. These debates have prompted the psychologist Radford to argue that people do experience real melancholy or joy in responding to art, but that these are irrational responses precisely because people know they are reacting to illusory stimuli. Frijda's law does not help us to untangle these positions, since it simply implies that events we recognize as being represented rather than real cannot elicit emotion in the first place.

Frijda does suggest that a vivid imagination has "properties of reality"—implying, without explanation, that we make aesthetic objects or events "real" in the act of experiencing them. However, as Scruton argues, a necessary characteristic of the imaginative construction that can occur in an emotional response to art is that the person knows he or she is pretending. This is what distinguishes imagination from psychotic fantasy.

9. Which one of the following best states the central idea of the passage?

(A) The law of apparent reality fails to account satisfactorily for the emotional nature of belief.
(B) Theories of aesthetic response fail to account for how we distinguish unreasonable from reasonable responses to art.
(C) The law of apparent reality fails to account satisfactorily for emotional responses to art.
(D) Psychologists have been unable to determine what accounts for the changeable nature of emotional responses to art.
(E) Psychologists have been unable to determine what differentiates aesthetic from nonaesthetic emotional responses.

10. According to the passage, Frijda's law asserts that emotional responses to events are

(A) unpredictable because emotional responses depend on how aware the person is of the reality of an event
(B) weaker if the person cannot distinguish illusion from reality
(C) more or less intense depending on the degree to which the person perceives the event to be real
(D) more intense if the person perceives an event to be frightening
(E) weaker if the person judges an event to be real but unthreatening

11. The author suggests that Frijda's notion of the role of imagination in aesthetic response is problematic because it

(A) ignores the unself-consciousness that is characteristic of emotional responses to art
(B) ignores the distinction between genuine emotion and ersatz emotion
(C) ignores the fact that a person who is imagining knows that he or she is imagining
(D) makes irrelevant distinctions between vivid and weak imaginative capacities
(E) suggests, in reference to the observation of art, that there is no distinction between real and illusory stimuli

GO ON TO THE NEXT PAGE

12. The passage supports all of the following statements about the differences between Gombrich and Radford EXCEPT:

(A) Radford's argument relies on a notion of irrationality in a way that Gombrich's argument does not.
(B) Gombrich's position is closer to the position of the majority of psychologists than is Radford's.
(C) Gombrich, unlike Radford, argues that we do not have true emotions in response to art.
(D) Gombrich's argument rests on a notion of memory in a way that Radford's argument does not.
(E) Radford's argument, unlike Gombrich's, is not focused on the artificial quality of emotional responses to art.

13. Which one of the following best captures the progression of the author's argument in lines 9–31?

(A) The emotional responses to events ranging from the real to the depicted illustrate the irrationality of emotional response.
(B) A series of events that range from the real to the depicted conveys the contrast between real events and cinematic depiction.
(C) An intensification in emotional response to a series of events that range from the real to the depicted illustrates Frijda's law.
(D) A progression of events that range from the real to the depicted examines the precise nature of panic in relation to a feared object.
(E) The consistency of emotional responses to events that range from the real to the depicted challenges Frijda's law.

14. The author's assertions concerning movies about ghosts imply that all of the following statements are false EXCEPT:

(A) Movies about ghosts are terrifying in proportion to viewers' beliefs in the phenomenon of ghosts.
(B) Movies about imaginary phenomena like ghosts may be just as terrifying as movies about phenomena like snakes.
(C) Movies about ghosts and snakes are not terrifying because people know that what they are viewing is not real.
(D) Movies about ghosts are terrifying to viewers who previously rejected the possibility of ghosts because movies permanently alter the viewers' sense of reality.
(E) Movies about ghosts elicit a very different emotional response from viewers who do not believe in ghosts than movies about snakes elicit from viewers who are frightened by snakes.

15. Which one of the following statements best exemplifies the position of Radford concerning the nature of emotional response to art?

(A) A person watching a movie about guerrilla warfare irrationally believes that he or she is present at the battle.
(B) A person watching a play about a kidnapping feels nothing because he or she rationally realizes it is not a real event.
(C) A person gets particular enjoyment out of writing fictional narratives in which he or she figures as a main character.
(D) A person irrationally bursts into tears while reading a novel about a destructive fire, even while realizing that he or she is reading about a fictional event.
(E) A person who is afraid of snakes trips over a branch and irrationally panics.

GO ON TO THE NEXT PAGE

Although bacteria are unicellular and among the simplest autonomous forms of life, they show a remarkable ability to sense their environment. They are attracted to materials they need and are repelled by harmful substances. Most types of bacteria swim very erratically; short, smooth runs in relatively straight lines are followed by brief tumbles, after which the bacteria shoot off in random directions. This leaves researchers with the question of how such bacteria find their way to an attractant such as food or, in the case of photosynthetic bacteria, light, if their swimming pattern consists only of smooth runs and tumbles, the latter resulting in random changes in direction.

One clue comes from the observation that when a chemical attractant is added to a suspension of such bacteria, the bacteria swim along a gradient of the attractant, from an area where the concentration of the attractant is weaker to an area where it is stronger. As they do so, their swimming is characterized by a decrease in tumbling and an increase in straight runs over relatively longer distances. As the bacteria encounter increasing concentrations of the attractant, their tendency to tumble is suppressed, whereas tumbling increases whenever they move away from the attractant. The net effect is that runs in the direction of higher concentrations of the attractant become longer and straighter as a result of the suppression of tumbling, whereas runs away from it are shortened by an increased tendency of the bacteria to tumble and change direction.

Biologists have proposed two mechanisms that bacteria might use in detecting changes in the concentration of a chemical attractant. First, a bacterium might compare the concentration of a chemical at the front and back of its cell body simultaneously. If the concentration is higher at the front of the cell, then it knows it is moving up the concentration gradient, from an area where the concentration is lower to an area where it is higher. Alternatively, it might measure the concentration at one instant and again after a brief interval, in which case the bacterium must retain a memory of the initial concentration. Researchers reasoned that if bacteria do compare concentrations at different times, then when suddenly exposed to a uniformly high concentration of an attractant, the cells would behave as if they were swimming up a concentration gradient, with long, smooth runs and relatively few tumbles. If, on the other hand, bacteria detect a chemical gradient by measuring it simultaneously at two distinct points, front and back, on the cell body, they would not respond to the jump in concentration because the concentration of the attractant in front and back of the cells, though high, would be uniform. Experimental evidence suggests that bacteria compare concentrations at different times.

16. It can be inferred from the passage that which one of the following experimental results would suggest that bacteria detect changes in the concentration of an attractant by measuring its concentration in front and back of the cell body simultaneously?

(A) When suddenly transferred from a medium in which the concentration of an attractant was uniformly low to one in which the concentration was uniformly high, the tendency of the bacteria to tumble and undergo random changes in direction increased.

(B) When suddenly transferred from a medium in which the concentration of an attractant was uniformly low to one in which the concentration was uniformly high, the bacteria exhibited no change in the pattern of their motion.

(C) When suddenly transferred from a medium in which the concentration of an attractant was uniformly low to one in which the concentration was uniformly high, the bacteria's movement was characterized by a complete absence of tumbling.

(D) When placed in a medium in which the concentration of an attractant was in some areas low and in others high, the bacteria exhibited an increased tendency to tumble in those areas where the concentration of the attractant was high.

(E) When suddenly transferred from a medium in which the concentration of an attractant was uniformly low to one that was completely free of attractants, the bacteria exhibited a tendency to suppress tumbling and move in longer, straighter lines.

GO ON TO THE NEXT PAGE

4 4 4 4 4 4 4 4 4 4

17. It can be inferred from the passage that a bacterium would increase the likelihood of its moving away from an area where the concentration of a harmful substance is high if it did which one of the following?

(A) increased the speed at which it swam immediately after undergoing the random changes in direction that result from tumbling
(B) detected the concentration gradient of an attractant toward which it could begin to swim
(C) relied on the simultaneous measurement of the concentration of the substance in front and back of its body, rather than on the comparison of the concentration at different points in time
(D) exhibited a complete cessation of tumbling when it detected increases in the concentration of the substance
(E) exhibited an increased tendency to tumble as it encountered increasing concentrations of the substance, and suppressed tumbling as it detected decreases in the concentration of the substance

18. It can be inferred from the passage that when describing bacteria as "swimming up a concentration gradient" (lines 49–50), the author means that they were behaving as if they were swimming

(A) against a resistant medium that makes their swimming less efficient
(B) away from a substance to which they are normally attracted
(C) away from a substance that is normally harmful to them
(D) from an area where the concentration of a repellent is weaker to an area where it is completely absent
(E) from an area where the concentration of a substance is weaker to an area where it is stronger

19. The passage indicates that the pattern that characterizes a bacterium's motion changes in response to

(A) the kinds of chemical attractants present in different concentration gradients
(B) the mechanism that the bacterium adopts in determining the presence of an attractant
(C) the bacterium's detection of changes in the concentration of an attractant
(D) the extent to which neighboring bacteria are engaged in tumbling
(E) changes in the intervals of time that occur between the bacterium's measurement of the concentration of an attractant

20. Which one of the following best describes the organization of the third paragraph of the passage?

(A) Two approaches to a problem are discussed, a test that would determine which is more efficient is described, and a conclusion is made, based on experimental evidence.
(B) Two hypotheses are described, a way of determining which of them is more likely to be true is discussed, and one is said to be more accurate on the basis of experimental evidence.
(C) Two hypotheses are described, the flaws inherent in one of them are elaborated, and experimental evidence confirming the other is cited.
(D) An assertion that a species has adopted two different mechanisms to solve a particular problem is made, and evidence is then provided in support of that assertion.
(E) An assertion that one mechanism for solving a particular problem is more efficient than another is made, and evidence is then provided in support of that assertion.

21. The passage provides information in support of which one of the following assertions?

(A) The seemingly erratic motion exhibited by a microorganism can in fact reflect a mechanism by which it is able to control its movement.
(B) Biologists often overstate the complexity of simple organisms such as bacteria.
(C) A bacterium cannot normally retain a memory of a measurement of the concentration of an attractant.
(D) Bacteria now appear to have less control over their movement than biologists had previously hypothesized.
(E) Photosynthetic bacteria appear to have more control over their movement than do bacteria that are not photosynthetic.

GO ON TO THE NEXT PAGE

Anthropologist David Mandelbaum makes a distinction between life-passage studies and life-history studies that emerged primarily out of research concerning Native Americans. Life-passage studies, he says, "emphasize the requirements of society, showing how groups socialize and enculturate their young in order to make them into viable members of society." Life histories, however, "emphasize the experiences and requirements of the individual, how the person copes with society rather than how society copes with the stream of individuals." Life-passage studies bring out the general cultural characteristics and commonalities that broadly define a culture, but are unconcerned with an individual's choices or how the individual perceives and responds to the demands and expectations imposed by the constraints of his or her culture. This distinction can clearly be seen in the autobiographies of Native American women.

For example, some early recorded autobiographies, such as *The Autobiography of a Fox Indian Woman,* a life passage recorded by anthropologist Truman Michelson, emphasizes prescribed roles. The narrator presents her story in a way that conforms with tribal expectations. Michelson's work is valuable as ethnography, as a reflection of the day-to-day responsibilities of Mesquakie women, yet as is often the case with life-passage studies, it presents little of the central character's psychological motivation. The Fox woman's life story focuses on her tribal education and integration into the ways of her people, and relates only what Michelson ultimately decided was worth preserving. The difference between the two types of studies is often the result of the amount of control the narrator maintains over the material; autobiographies in which there are no recorder-editors are far more reflective of the life-history category, for there are no outsiders shaping the story to reflect their preconceived notions of what the general cultural patterns are.

For example, in Maria Campbell's account of growing up as a Canadian Metis who was influenced strongly, and often negatively, by the non–Native American world around her, one learns a great deal about the life of Native American women, but Campbell's individual story, which is told to us directly, is always the center of her narrative. Clearly it is important to her to communicate to the audience what her experiences as a Native American have been. Through Campbell's story of her family the reader learns of the effect of poverty and prejudice on a people. The reader becomes an intimate of Campbell the writer, sharing her pain and celebrating her small victories. Although Campbell's book is written as a life history (the dramatic moments, the frustrations, and the fears are clearly hers), it reveals much about ethnic relations in Canada while reflecting the period in which it was written.

22. Which one of the following is the most accurate expression of the main point of the passage?

(A) The contributions of life-history studies to anthropology have made life-passage studies obsolete.
(B) Despite their dissimilar approaches to the study of culture, life-history and life-passage studies have similar goals.
(C) The autobiographies of Native American women illustrate the differences between life-history and life-passage studies.
(D) The roots of Maria Campbell's autobiography can be traced to earlier narratives such as *The Autobiography of a Fox Indian Woman.*
(E) Despite its shortcomings, the life-passage study is a more effective tool than the life-history study for identifying important cultural patterns.

23. The term "prescribed roles" in line 24 of the passage refers to the

(A) function of life-passage studies in helping ethnologists to understand cultural tradition
(B) function of life-history studies in helping ethnologists to gather information
(C) way in which a subject of a life passage views himself or herself
(D) roles clearly distinguishing the narrator of an autobiography from the recorder of an autobiography
(E) roles generally adopted by individuals in order to comply with cultural demands

24. The reference to the "psychological motivation" (line 30) of the subject of *The Autobiogaphy of a Fox Indian Woman* serves primarily to

(A) dismiss as irrelevant the personal perspective in the life-history study
(B) identify an aspect of experience that is not commonly a major focus of life-passage studies
(C) clarify the narrator's self-acknowledged purpose in relating a life passage
(D) suggest a common conflict between the goals of the narrator and those of the recorder in most life-passage studies
(E) assert that developing an understanding of an individual's psychological motivation usually undermines objective ethnography

GO ON TO THE NEXT PAGE

25. Which one of the following statements about Maria Campbell can be inferred from material in the passage?

(A) She was familiar with the very early history of her tribe but lacked insight into the motivations of non–Native Americans.
(B) She was unfamiliar with Michelson's work but had probably read a number of life-passage studies about Native Americans.
(C) She had training as a historian but was not qualified as an anthropologist.
(D) Her family influenced her beliefs and opinions more than the events of her time did.
(E) Her life history provides more than a record of her personal experience.

26. According to the passage, one way in which life-history studies differ from life-passage studies is that life-history studies are

(A) usually told in the subject's native language
(B) less reliable because they rely solely on the subject's recall
(C) more likely to be told without the influence of an intermediary
(D) more creative in the way they interpret the subject's cultural legacy
(E) more representative of the historian's point of view than of the ethnographer's

27. Which one of the following pairings best illustrates the contrast between life passages and life histories?

(A) a study of the attitudes of a society toward a mainstream religion and an analysis of techniques used to instruct members of that religious group
(B) a study of how a preindustrial society maintains peace with neighboring societies and a study of how a postindustrial society does the same
(C) a study of the way a military organization establishes and maintains discipline and a newly enlisted soldier's narrative describing his initial responses to the military environment
(D) an analysis of a society's means of subsistence and a study of how its members celebrate religious holidays
(E) a political history of a society focussing on leaders and parties and a study of how the electorate shaped the political landscape of the society

STOP

IF YOU FINISH BEFORE TIME IS CALLED, YOU MAY CHECK YOUR WORK ON THIS SECTION ONLY.
DO NOT WORK ON ANY OTHER SECTION IN THE TEST.

LSAT WRITING SAMPLE TOPIC

The port city of Cedarville is considering two offers for the purchase of a large waterfront tract just within the city limits. Write an argument for one offer over the other with the following considerations in mind:

- Cedarville wants to reverse recent declines in both employment and population.
- Cedarville wants to boom its dwindling tourist industry.

Excel Glassware Company proposes to build a three-story factory on the site. It will employ 150 people and include a research laboratory. The company, part of an international conglomerate, is known for its extensive training programs and other employee benefits. Excel manufactures glassware for private and commercial use, including a world-famous line of crystal. The offer includes a promise to bring an award-winning crystal collection to be housed in a specially designed gallery built as part of a park next to the factory. Excel promises an advertising campaign promoting guided tours of the gallery and demonstrations of glassblowers at work.

Nature Life, a national conservation organization, wants to turn the site into a wildflower and animal sanctuary. The organization plans a tourist area, complete with slide shows, nature paths, and guided tours. The facility would employ a small staff of naturalists and would include a restaurant and a lodge with accommodations for 100 guests. The organization also plans to use the site as a training center and summer school for high school and college students considering a career in conservation. Since the river contains an extensive variety of marine life, including some rare and endangered species, the state university has expressed an interest in locating a branch of its research facility nearby if the sanctuary is built.

Compute Your Score

Directions:

1. Use the Answer Key on the next page to check your answers.
2. Use the Scoring Worksheet below to compute your raw score.
3. Use the Score Conversion Chart to convert your raw score into the 120–180 scale.

Scoring Worksheet

1. Enter the number of questions you answered correctly in each section.

Number Correct

SECTION I . . . . ._____
SECTION II . . . . . . ._____
SECTION III . . . . ._____
SECTION IV . . . . ._____

2. Enter the sum here: . ._____

This is your Raw Score.

Conversion Chart Form 3LSS16

For Converting Raw Score to the 120–180 LSAT Scaled Score

Reported Score	Raw Score Lowest	Raw Score Highest
180	98	101
179	97	97
178	96	96
177	94	95
176	93	93
175	92	92
174	91	91
173	90	90
172	88	89
171	87	87
170	86	86
169	84	85
168	83	83
167	81	82
166	80	80
165	78	79
164	77	77
163	75	76
162	73	74
161	72	72
160	70	71
159	68	69
158	67	67
157	65	66
156	63	64
155	61	62
154	60	60
153	58	59
152	56	57
151	55	55
150	53	54
149	51	52
148	50	50
147	48	49
146	46	47
145	45	45
144	43	44
143	42	42
142	40	41
141	38	39
140	37	37
139	35	36
138	34	34
137	33	33
136	31	32
135	30	30
134	29	29
133	27	28
132	26	26
131	25	25
130	24	24
129	23	23
128	22	22
127	21	21
126	20	20
125	19	19
124	18	18
123	—*	—*
122	17	17
121	16	16
120	0	15

*There is no raw score that will produce this scaled score for this form.

Answer Key

SECTION I

1. E
2. A
3. B
4. A
5. B
6. E
7. A
8. B
9. A
10. C
11. D
12. D
13. E
14. A
15. A
16. B
17. D
18. B
19. C
20. B
21. E
22. C
23. B
24. C
25. E

SECTION II

1. C
2. D
3. E
4. E
5. C
6. E
7. A
8. B
9. B
10. B
11. D
12. B
13. B
14. C
15. C
16. D
17. B
18. B
19. C
20. C
21. D
22. A
23. E
24. E

SECTION III

1. C
2. B
3. E
4. E
5. B
6. A
7. E
8. C
9. C
10. A
11. C
12. C
13. D
14. B
15. C
16. B
17. A
18. A
19. E
20. B
21. C
22. E
23. D
24. B
25. E

SECTION IV

1. A
2. D
3. D
4. E
5. E
6. C
7. D
8. A
9. C
10. C
11. C
12. B
13. E
14. B
15. D
16. B
17. E
18. E
19. C
20. B
21. A
22. C
23. E
24. B
25. E
26. C
27. C

Real LSAT 2: Explanations

Section I: Logical Reasoning

1 (E) is correct. The problem is traffic congestion; it's heavy on all roads and slows highway speeds down to 35 miles per hour. The *cause* of the problem, as the author sees it, is that people no longer work and shop in the same town where they live. As a result, they have to travel long distances to shop and to work. The correct answer choice must propose a solution (or partial solution) that directly addresses this cause, and only (E) does so. Moving new businesses closer to workers' homes would mean that workers wouldn't have to travel very far and, in turn, that traffic congestion would be eased.

(A): Since highway drivers can't even drive at the present speed limit owing to the congestion, raising the limit isn't going to get them driving any faster.

(B): Congestion is heavy on *all* roads, so moving cars to different roads would not have any positive effect on congestion.

(C): Places of business are located far away from "residential areas," which include suburbs. (C) would move the problem around, not solve it. Also, (C) offers an irrelevant distinction between small towns and suburbs; the issue is the residence relative to the workplace.

(D): This solution would just punish the victims. Drivers haven't been choosing to dawdle; they're driving slowly because of the congestion.

When a question asks for the best solution or best proposal, make sure you understand the *cause of the problem*. Here the problem is specifically blamed on the distance people have to travel from their homes to their places of business. A quick glance at the choices tells you that only two, (C) and (E), make any attempt to deal with that.

On a basic level, always read for—and be sensitive to—sentences that demand evidence, such as the first sentence here (or the first sentence in Question 2, for that matter). *Always read for structure first.*

2 (A) is correct. The professor's argument makes the "assumption of representativeness" without justifying it. She argues that college students *in general* don't write as well as they used to; her evidence is that almost all of *her* students' papers were poorly written. She assumes without evidence that the writing produced by her students is representative of the writing produced by college students in general. But, it needn't be.

(B) and (C): While it's true that no proof of the professor's competence is offered, this is a much less important omission than that mentioned in (A). If we were given the "proof" that (B) mentions, would the professor's conclusion be stronger? No, because (A)'s crucial assumption would still be unsupported. So (B) is far from the biggest flaw. As for her teaching skills, we don't even know whether she teaches writing, so we can't argue, as (C) does, that she is responsible for her students' poor abilities.

(D): There is no contrary evidence. If contrary evidence were presented, we could expect the author to address it. We can't, however, fault her for not presenting evidence against herself.

(E): While it's true that "well" and "poorly" may be somewhat subjective terms, they definitely aren't ambiguous. Moreover, the term "ungrammatical" certainly isn't ambiguous. However, even if you did consider some of the terms to be in need of further definition, this clearly isn't as serious a weakness as that described in answer choice (A).

It's common in Flaw questions for wrong answer choices to fault the argument for failing to do something that's really not necessary—for example, defining a common term, as seen in choice (E), or establishing a speaker's credentials, as shown in choice (B) and choice (C).

The key to any argument's soundness is how well it links the evidence to the conclusion. One way to see the clear superiority of answer choice (A) over answer choices (B) and (C) is to note that even if the argument did what answer choices (B) and (C) required, it would be no stronger than it is now, because the professor's evidence would still be limited to her own students while her conclusion is about *all* students.

3 (B) is correct. Attacking the mayor's claim that he supports the highway because it will help the economy, citizens argue that a business park would attract twice as much business as the highway would and that, therefore, anyone preferring the latter to the former (as the mayor does) must have some other agenda. But they assume (B), that the mayor *agrees* with them in thinking a business park really would be better for the economy. If the mayor doesn't believe this—if he sincerely believes that the highway is the best way to help business—then the accusation of an alternative agenda is unwarranted. So (B) is necessary for the group's logic.

(A): *Au contraire;* the group's contention that a new highway is economically less desirable than a new business park would be stronger if there were already *many* highways leading to Plainsville.

(C): The group's argument is that insofar as attracting business is important, the highway wouldn't be as successful as would a new business park. That argument holds even if the highway would provide other benefits.

(D): This is outside the scope: The city council is never mentioned, nor are the requirements for the mayor's allocating tax revenues.

(E): This distorts the group's argument. They claim that a new business center will attract more business than will the highway, not that a new business center is the *only* thing that will attract new business.

When you deal with a stimulus that identifies a speaker or speakers, make sure you understand the status of each individual statement: who it's said by, whether it's an opinion or a fact, whether it's the opinion of the author or the opinion of a subordinate speaker, and so on. This is another very important element of *always reading for structure.*

Take note of wrong choice (E) as a classic example of confusing sufficiency with necessity.

4 (A) is correct. According to the citizens' group, if the mayor wants to attract business he should build a new business park, the best way (in their view) to attract business. Since he supports the highway, which won't attract as much money, the group says he mustn't really be interested in attracting new business. Answer choice (A) sums that up in abstract language. The group reasons that if the mayor were really pursuing the cause of strengthening business, he would choose the means that would best strengthen business—that is, the business park.

(B): Both plans admit that public revenues are required, so (B) doesn't advance either argument any further.

(C) Irrelevant: nothing in the group's argument implies that they want the mayor to consult taxpayers, or that they have done so themselves in considering the new business park.

(D) This choice is far too vague; it could just as easily justify the mayor's wanting to bring the highway to town.

(E) This is irrelevant to the group's argument, which concerns the mayor's motivation, not who is responsible for attracting new business. There's no hint of suggestion that the citizens build the business park by themselves.

The right answer choice to Principle questions must fit the argument in all its essential elements. Be suspicious of choices that seem too vague, like answer choice (D). Also beware of choices that refer to ideas that the argument doesn't mention, as do answer choices (C) and (E).

5 (B) is correct. Because many highly skilled Eastern European workers have emigrated, the author concludes that there is now great demand for such workers in Eastern Europe. This conclusion depends on the concept of supply and demand, the assumption being that the emigration has left a *shortage* of highly skilled workers in Eastern Europe, which has resulted in a great demand for skilled workers. Choice (B) attacks this assumption by making it likely that the workers who have gone abroad haven't left jobs behind. The jobs are disappearing along with the workers, so there's no shortage of skilled workers for the jobs available and no necessary increase in demand. By weakening the assumption, (B) weakens the argument.

(A): This eliminates the possibility that Eastern European countries would hire foreign skilled workers, so it *strengthens* the argument that the emigration of skilled workers would create high demand for native skilled workers.

(C): This is irrelevant, because it deals only with the workers who have already left Eastern Europe, while the argument is concerned with the workers still there.

(D) and (E): These strengthen the argument. If, as (D) says, there are plans to train many new workers to replace the highly skilled ones who left, then apparently there *is* high demand for skilled workers. And (E) says that many positions are unfilled, which pretty much proves the author's point.

We can't say it often enough: the best way to weaken/strengthen an argument is to attack/support a key assumption in that argument. If you notice a gap in the argument and you approach the answer choices with that gap in mind, chances are you'll recognize the correct answer quickly.

Watch out for *au contraire* choices, which can be tricky because they usually address the key issues, and use the right terms. The best way to guard against them is to take the time to read choices carefully and remember what you're being asked.

6 (E) is correct. The historian argues that Alexander should be judged by the standards of his own culture, not by modern criteria. But he also says that we should examine whether Alexander elevated (improved) contemporary standards of justice. That's where the student nails him. She points out that if Alexander *changed* his culture's standards of justice, we can't judge whether he improved or worsened those standards without appealing to our *own* standards of better and worse justice—something the historian has just told us is unacceptable. The principle of not using modern values is inconsistent with judging whether Alexander improved the standards of justice of his own day. So the student has caught the historian in a contradiction, and (E) is correct.

(A): The student never argues that we don't know enough of the past to judge Alexander.

(B): This is the most tempting of the wrong choices, but the problem isn't that the *principle* of avoiding modern values leads to inconsistencies in and of itself. Rather, it's that (as (E) says) this principle is contradicted by one of the criteria that the professor gives as a supposed application of the principle. That principle doesn't contradict itself, as (B) says.

(C) The student never disputes Alexander's heroism. She attacks the historian's methodology, not his conclusions about Alexander.

(D) This is way, way off. Nowhere does the student criticize the professor or attack his motivation.

This question is a good advertisement for reading all the choices carefully. If you read (E), the faults of (B) become apparent. If (B) looked pretty good to you and you stopped reading, then you never got to (E), and you got the question wrong.

By and large, Method and Flaw questions don't hinge on personal issues. When choices allege sneaky motivation or call someone names, they're usually wrong.

7 (A) is correct. Because of the human characteristics of a certain set of footprints, Tyson claims that the prints belong to early hominids. Rees objects that if a hominid indeed made those prints, it must have walked in an absurd "cross-stepping manner," so Rees rejects Tyson's hominid hypothesis. Choice (A) describes their disagreement accurately. They arrive at different conclusions because each gives prime importance to different elements of the prints—Rees to the cross-stepping gait, and Tyson to the humanlike traits.

(B): On the contrary, the fact that each paleontologist takes a position on whether the prints are those of a hominid shows that each believes that early hominid footprints *can* be distinguished from other prints.

(C): Tyson interprets the characteristics of the prints. Rees speculates about the gait. If Tyson has an alternative view of the gait, we don't hear about it. Anyhow, the stimulus clearly states that if hominids made the prints they would have had to walk in a particular gait. No disagreement there.

(D): Both must accept (D); both have drawn a conclusion from the evidence at this one site.

(E): Neither scientist disputes that early hominids walked upright on two feet.

Point at Issue questions ask you what two people are disagreeing about, and often the two disputants won't confront each other directly. Instead of *denying* the first speaker's evidence, the second speaker will put forth additional evidence that points in a new direction. Keep your eye on topic and scope above all.

8 (B) is correct. To recap: Tyson's conclusion—the one we want to undermine—is that the footprints at site G were those of an early hominid. (B) implies that the paw prints left by the bear would, if considered to be human, look like a human walking in a cross-stepping manner. The bear's toes are in the *reverse* order of a human's, and such a bear, walking normally, would produce the prints as described. So the thrust of (B) is to show that the prints could be those of the bear and not those of an early hominid, in which case Tyson would be wrong and Rees correct. In short, (B) explains the apparent evidence for a weird, cross-stepping hominid by providing a more reasonable—or, at least, equally reasonable—alternative.

(A): This is hard to figure. If it suggests that two hominids made the tracks while walking side-by-side, then the "unexpected cross-stepping manner" cited by Rees would be illusory, her objection to Tyson would collapse, and (A) would support Tyson. The problem is that the passage clearly states that if hominids made the tracks, then they *had* to walk in a cross-stepping manner. So (A) seems to contradict the information we're given. In any case, (A) *accepts* the idea that the tracks were made by hominids, and that's precisely the conclusion we seek to weaken.

(C): The footprints at site M are outside the argument's scope. We don't know whether these *are* human footprints. Moreover, the creature at site M is irrelevant to the findings at site G—it need have nothing to do with the Tyson/Rees creature.

(D): This is too vague. We can't assume that the erased details would have damaged Tyson's claim; for all we know, they'd have supported his claim. Since we don't know the nature of the erased details, (D) won't weaken either argument.

(E): There's no reason why a hominid couldn't have walked on the same ground as hoofed animals, so the prints in question could still be those of a hominid. Choice (E) is irrelevant.

This is a prime candidate for using process of elimination. Each of the wrong choices can be eliminated on specific grounds. Start by eliminating the clear losers, such as irrelevant choice (E) and ambiguous/uninformative choice (D). That already leaves you with a one-in-three chance of guessing right. Furthermore, (C) is outside the scope on grounds of geography, and (A), if it means anything, is an *au contraire* choice. The correct answer probably seemed more than a little farfetched (paleontologists confusing bear prints with human prints), but remember the bear was described as having very humanlike feet. In any case, (B) is the best choice of the field.

When a stimulus generates two questions, take a few seconds between questions to recap the logic. Review and paraphrase the argument. It will help.

9 (A) is correct. Read the fragment of the final sentence carefully: the correct choice must describe a program that *won't* work. Well, if BSE can be transmitted from cow to cow at any and all stages of the disease, then diseased cows without visible symptoms could be passing BSE around unnoticed. And there would be no way to identify those cows, since no diagnostic test can identify cows that have BSE but aren't showing symptoms. Our search for the nonsolution doesn't last long, because (A) is it. Removing and destroying cows that actually show symptoms wouldn't control the disease if it can be spread at any stage. Sick cows would still be passing on the disease *before* they showed symptoms. So (A)'s plan would not fell the disease.

(B): If this drug were given to a cow, the animal would have no disease-bearing agent to spread to other cows, and the disease couldn't spread. So if all cattle that might have the disease were treated, the disease could be eradicated.

(C): This would work like a charm. All the cows that could possibly be carrying the disease would be eliminated. Sad for the cows, but good for eliminating BSE.

(D): This plan, which would immunize the healthy animals and kill off the diseased ones, would have a solid shot at eradicating BSE.

(E): A diagnostic test that could identify the diseased animals right from the start would solve the problem. All diseased animals could be eliminated before they transmitted the disease.

Whenever you're asked to complete a paragraph, don't focus on *merely* the final fragment. Recognize that the question is testing whether you comprehend the logic overall, so be sure to follow the *entire* argument. And don't forget to plug the choice you pick into the paragraph and reread the argument before going on to the next question.

Try to simplify complicated passages by isolating the key ideas. One way to do so is to pick out a couple of key terms. For instance, the passage for Question 9 has only two key ideas: (1) the disease can be carried *without symptoms*; and (2) there's *no diagnostic test* for the disease. So (A)'s phrase, "as soon as it shows the typical symptoms," is an immediate tip-off that (A) won't work.

10 (C) is correct. The auto industry opposes a requirement to make cars that are more fuel-efficient. Why? Because previous attempts at better fuel efficiency led to smaller—but less safe—cars. The exec's implication is that, once again, the search for better fuel efficiency will lead to small, dangerous cars, but (C) rebuts that by asserting that large cars can be made more fuel efficient. More efficient cars needn't be smaller, so it's not true that they will have to be more dangerous.

(A): The fact that large cars were frequently involved in serious accidents doesn't refute the statistics that smaller cars were even *more* dangerous.

(B): *Au contraire.* This strengthens the automaker's argument by confirming that small cars are very unsafe, since the odds of surviving an accident in one have become worse.

(D): This doesn't even address the automaker's argument that progress in fuel efficiency requires dangerously small cars.

(E): This suggests that the fuel-efficient cars on the market today are still those dangerous small cars. Choice (E) might be stretched to imply that cars *can* be made more fuel efficient and remain large, but it's too vague. We don't know why fuel efficiency rose and later fell, nor do we know if large cars could meet the proposed new standards.

This is basically an argument from past to future. In such cases, look for differences in the past scenario and the present or future scenario.

11 (D) is correct. Only veteran politicians are competent to judge whether a policy is fair, says the author, because competence in passing judgment on a subject requires knowledge of that subject, and only veteran politicians have political know-how. But is political know-how the same "subject" as policy fairness? Is political know-how the field of knowledge that deals with the social implications of legislation? The author seems to think so, but must he be right? That's the criticism that (D) makes. It's not obvious that political know-how is the same thing as understanding the social implications of policy, but the argument treats it as such.

(A): This attacks the first statement, which is a premise, but the generalization that unknowledgeable people aren't competent to pass judgment is a very reasonable claim.

(B): Specific examples of how political know-how is acquired aren't necessary. Few of us would dispute the author's claim that it's acquired by watching and working with those who have it.

(C): This isn't a weakness; the author simply uses "apprenticeship" metaphorically to imply that politicians learn the ropes from experienced politicians who already possess "know-how."

(E): This isn't something that the author must be assuming, since the argument concerns who is *competent* to judge policy, not who actually does so and how.

When you're asked to find a weakness or flaw in the argument, you're being asked to critique the *logic* of the argument—how it moves from evidence to conclusion, how it *connects* one point to another. For this reason, choices that simply attack a single term or a single assertion—as (A), (B), and (C) do—won't be any good.

12 (D) is correct. The author sees cause-and-effect in the fact that more craters appear in areas with few "destructive geophysical processes." She believes that low rates of geophysical destruction account for the many craters. Presumably she believes that craters are wiped out in areas with destructive geophysical processes, whereas they survive in stable ones. That's a reasonable explanation, but we only *need* an explanation if (D) is true, if craters are equally distributed over the Earth's surface.

The Denial Test shows you why. If, contrary to (D), meteorites struck the Earth unevenly, then an uneven distribution of craters should be no surprise, and it would be just as likely that coincidence (as opposed to cause-and-effect) is what connects stable regions with high crater counts. Meteors just *happen* to strike more often in the stable regions, and no further explanation is necessary. For the cause-and-effect to be supported, the author has to assume (D).

(A): This is irrelevant. Again, try the Denial Test. It wouldn't hurt the argument if the first crater did still show after a second impact. Choice (A) would only make a difference if cases of double impact occurred disproportionately in different regions, and there's no evidence of that.

(B) and (E): These would weaken the argument, each in a different way. If different regions are stable at different times (B), then the crucial character of the regions—their stability or instability—is lost and can't be used as an explanation. And if (E) is true, then the greater density of craters in stable areas is probably a function of those areas having been better explored to date, and the whole argument should be tabled until the unstable regions get their due.

(C): This just increases the rate at which meteors strike, which is irrelevant. What's important is the places where they strike.

An author seeking to explain a phenomenon generally makes the assumption that there exists *no other explanation for that phenomenon.* So when you're asked what such an argument assumes, look for a choice that rules out some alternative explanation.

13 (E) is correct. The nuclear deterrence policy has worked, says the author, because what it's designed to prevent—nuclear holocaust—hasn't occurred. (Note that the second sentence is mainly there to define nuclear deterrence and provide background. The essential argument is the first sentence's conclusion and the third sentence's evidence ("The proof is. . . ."). Anyway, the problem is that the only evidence offered is time sequence. There hasn't been a nuclear war *since* the deterrence policy; therefore there hasn't been a nuclear war *because of* the deterrence policy. Who's to say that some other, unnamed factors haven't been just as responsible—or more so—for the absence of nuclear war? We couldn't be sure without further evidence. That's (E), in a nutshell.

(A): The author never claimed that the policy of nuclear deterrence was without economic drawbacks, only that it has worked, and we know what "working" means to the author. Implying a downside to the policy doesn't damage the logic.

(B): This is a classic scope error. The possibly uncertain future of the policy has no effect on the past and present success of the policy.

(C): The author is interested in deterrence, and gives no indication that she wishes to see more nuclear weapons produced beyond the minimum needed for deterrence. Moreover, the author discusses nuclear war, not the likelihood of nuclear *accident*—another scope error.

(D): This statement might be seen to strengthen the argument slightly by pointing out that, although wars have occurred since the Second World War, none of them have been nuclear wars. (D) implies that *something* has deterred nuclear war. But that something could be the deterrence policy, as the author believes, or some other factor. And in any case, we're looking for a weakener.

When you're looking for a flaw, you're looking for a place where the argument fails to do what it set out to do. The wrong choices here attack the argument for not addressing issues that are entirely outside its scope: economic drawbacks (A), future wars (B), nuclear accidents (C), and conventional wars (D).

For the record, this argument is an example of the *post hoc* fallacy, the assertion that just because a phenomenon (such as the deterrence policy) has preceded an effect (such as the absence of nuclear war), it must have *caused* that effect. Not necessarily so! You don't have to remember the fancy Latin name, but you should be on the lookout for the fallacy—it comes up often on the LSAT.

14 (A) is correct. How can half of the respondents be among the top quarter of the class? This only *seems* to be a contradiction. If the number of respondents were smaller than the total number of graduates, and if many of those who responded were students with high academic rank, then it's quite possible that half of the respondents graduated in the top quarter of the class. The only "puzzle" here was if you didn't see that the respondents could be a *subset* of the total set of graduates, or if you assumed that everyone in the class responded. (Then it would be a puzzle, all right—see the explanation for (D), below.) Anyhow, (A) makes it all clear: The group of respondents included more than its share of high-ranking graduates.

(B): This reinforces the accuracy of the numbers, without making it clearer how half of the respondents fit into a quarter of the graduates.

(C): This tells us that some of the quarter who graduated at the top of the class weren't respondents, which makes it harder to see how half of the respondents came from the top quarter of the class.

(D): This is even worse than (C). If the number of respondents roughly equals the number of graduates, then we would have more than one-quarter of the graduates saying that they were in the top quarter of the class. Rather than explaining an apparent discrepancy, (D) creates a real one.

(E): This deals with the criteria for academic rank, which is outside the scope of the argument. We need help with the numbers, and (E) gives us no information that explains how half of the respondents can represent one-quarter of the graduates.

Don't let fractions or percents scare you; you won't be asked to do much math in Logical Reasoning. Grasp the idea that "too many" respondents seem to have finished at the top of their class. Then you can prephrase likely solutions: Are they lying? (That happens rarely in Logical Reasoning questions.) Did only the high-ranking graduates respond? Or is the sample otherwise skewed?

In short, watch for skewed samples in arguments that relate to survey results—

especially when, as in this question, you're asked to evaluate a seeming contradiction or paradox.

▲▲▲

15 (A) is correct. This one requires careful analysis of the question stem. This is what it's getting at: M presents evidence that could be used to support some unspoken hypothesis. We are to take it that, without even hearing the hypothesis, Q rebuts it by presenting counterevidence. We're asked to locate the disputed hypothesis.

In sum, we want an answer choice that would be *supported* by M's statement and *rebutted* by Q's statement. That answer choice is (A). M's statement that virtually no one who has lived past the age of 85 is left-handed *could* be used to argue that right-handed people have a survival advantage over (live longer than) left-handers. M's statement could be used, that is, except for Q's reply that most people born left-handers who are now 85 to 90 years old were forced to use their right hands as children. That would mean that many right-handed 85- to 90-year-olds might have been born left-handed and forced to switch. The fact that you can't find old southpaws doesn't mean that they die earlier, but merely that they don't behave like southpaws. And that's how answer choice (A) is supported by M but rebutted by Q.

(B): This speaks about the societal attitudes towards handedness. This is an issue that Q raised and used to rebut M, but we want an issue that M raises that is contradicted by Q.

(C): This answer choice speaks of forcing people to switch from a preferred hand. Again, this is merely an issue raised by Q in his rebuttal of M's likely hypothesis. This is not complete enough for us to select it as the answer.

(D): Nothing in M's remarks indicates M is interested in the origins of handedness. You can eliminate this choice.

(E): M couldn't use (E) as evidence under any circumstances, since M merely attempts to correlate handedness and longevity, though (E) does go along well enough with Q's position.

▼▼▼

One of the chief difficulties is keeping the statements clearly separated in your mind. M doesn't say anything about social attitudes or pressures—answer choices (B), (C), and (D); M discusses left-handedness and *age.* Q brings up social pressure to *attack* M's point about age.

Don't be alarmed by an unusual question stem such as this, but do take the necessary time to work it out. (Even if it means skipping the question temporarily until the easier ones have been attempted.) Unusual question stems need to be read with extra care; as a matter of fact, figuring out the stem is often the only really difficult part of the entire question.

▲▲▲

16 (B) is correct. The conclusion comes in the last sentence: if seventeenth-century alchemists had published the results of their unsuccessful experiments, then eighteenth-century chemistry would have been more advanced than it was. We're asked for a necessary assumption, and answer choice (B) explicitly links the reporting of experimental results, even unsuccessful results, to scientific advance. Choice (B)'s claim allows the conclusion to stand: publication of the poor results of the alchemy experiments would have furthered science, which could very easily have aided the furthering of chemistry in the following century. This is all confirmed by the Denial Test. If (B) were false—if available scientific reports have *no* effect on scientific advances—then eighteenth-century science would not have been changed in the way that the author argues. Since (B), when denied, challenges the author's logic, then (B) *as is* must support it.

(A): This blames historians for slowing the advance of science, but the author argued that scientific progress is impeded by *scientists'* refusal to publish the results of their experiments.

(C): This is an *au contraire* choice; it works *against* the conclusion that publishing unsuccessful results helps scientific progress. Moreover, the status of Newton's work on motion and gravity is beyond the scope of this argument.

(D): This is way off. The author argues that secrecy retards scientific progress, but (D) points the finger at specialization, and implies that scientists would have a hard time understanding one another's work even if they published their results.

(E): This does link publicity to success, but there's no hint that the author of the passage believes alchemy was or is feasible. The argument is that publication would have aided later chemists, not the alchemists themselves.

▼▼▼

Remember your fundamentals. An assumption is a necessary piece of unstated evidence, something that must be true if the evidence is to lead to the conclusion. Settle for nothing less in the choice you select for an Assumption question.

Don't allow yourself to be caught up in irrelevant details. Paraphrasing an argument can help you avoid choices that include these unneeded details, such as Newton's work with motion and gravity in choice (C) and specialization in choice (D).

▲▲▲

17 (D) is correct. The geologists figure that the extra iridium in that rock layer had to come from somewhere. Meteorites are rich in iridium; the geologists reason that a meteor could have hit the earth and produced a huge cloud of iridium-rich dust. This dust would settle on the ground, and the ground would eventually become a rock layer containing a lot of iridium. But (D) provides an equally good, *alternative explanation* for the layer of iridium-rich rock. The iridium didn't have to come from a meteorite; it could have come from the volcanoes.

(A): This is irrelevant. Nowhere in the passage is it implied that the scientists' hypothesis depends on the earth's temperature not falling.

(B): This, too, leaves the argument unscathed. The scientists' hypothesis is that a meteorite hit the earth 60 million years ago, leaving plenty of time, in (B)'s terms, for the dust to settle and a layer of sedimentary rock to form.

(C): The argument concerns only the origin of this one particular layer, not the dating of sedimentary rock in general.

(E): This offers another reason for believing that a meteorite hit the earth at about that time. But we want to *weaken* the meteorite theory, something (E) certainly doesn't do.

▼▼▼

When an argument proposes a theory to explain some phenomenon, one of the most common Weaken the Argument strategies is to provide a likely *alternative* explanation for that phenomenon. So when they throw a scientific theory at you and ask you to undermine it, look for an answer choice that provides an alternate theory.

Dense and lengthy science-based stimuli—like this one—offer a special challenge: can you, the test taker, get to the heart or gist of the matter and not get bogged down in details? (A lot of Reading Comprehension passages offer the same challenge.) Notice how little of the stimulus you need to understand in order to see how (D) counters the logic.

▲▲▲

18 (B) is correct. The general principle that justifies Mary's refusal to carry out the experiment is (B). It provides only two possible exceptions (immediately saving a person, or saving several animals) to a flat injunction against taking an animal's life, and neither of those exceptions pertains to this particular case. So the principle stands: Mary is right in not participating in taking this dog's life.

(A): This wouldn't support her decision, since the dog is anesthetized; it wouldn't feel any pain. Moreover, if there *were* pain involved, such pain wouldn't necessarily qualify as gratuitous, since there would be at least one positive result, namely Mary's increased knowledge.

(C): The experiment is designed to make Mary a more knowledgeable veterinarian, and that increased knowledge might very well prevent some animal from suffering in the future. Thus, by (C)'s own terms, Mary might be wrong in refusing to participate.

(D): This rules out most *unnecessary* death, but who's to say that this dog's death isn't "necessary" in order for Mary to become a competent vet? Moreover, Mary isn't a practicing vet, she's a student, so this one is clearly outside the scope.

(E): This isn't applicable because the "sole intention" of the experiment isn't to kill the dog. It's also designed to teach Mary about the physiological consequences of shock.

In Principle questions, you have to concentrate almost exclusively on topic and scope—and sometimes the devil is in the details. Keep your eye open for details in the choices that don't fit the passage ("suffer pain" (A) versus "anesthetized"; "practicing veterinarians" (D) versus "veterinary student"). Such details are put in the stimulus for one purpose—to help the test makers construct incorrect answer choices.

19 (C) is correct. Archaeologists use the growth rings to determine the *relative* ages of the tombs, made from freshly cut logs of the same type and place (and, thus, all with the same amount of annual rainfall). The number of rings equals the number of years, and the width of a tree's yearly ring depends on how much rain fell that year.

Now, how does all of this help determine which tombs are older? Well, if there were no similarity between the rings on the logs of one tomb and those on the logs of another, it wouldn't help at all. You can determine the relative age of the logs (and thus the tombs) only if there's some overlap to the rings, so that the ring patterns can be compared. Thus, (C) is correct: if every log has the same pattern of 12 rings, then their comparative ages can be determined by how many more rings each log has after the crucial pattern of 12 rings. (Example: A tree with 50 rings after the pattern was cut down 30 years later than a tree with 20 rings after the pattern.)

(A): This tells us that "artifacts" were preserved—which needn't, of course, be logs. Moreover, we've no idea what effect seepage would have on the logs' rings, so (A) is of no help.

(B): This speaks of trees outside the valley, so it's irrelevant. The archaeologists only compare the rings on trees within the one valley.

(D): This gives the extreme dates for the trees used, but provides no clue as to *how* the archaeologists determined these ages or the relative ages of the other trees.

(E): The age of the artifacts doesn't indicate the age of the tombs; plenty of new buildings contain old items.

This was a tough question that required some creative reasoning. If you found yourself floundering, this was a perfect question to skip and come back to later. Make sure you get to the rest of the questions in the section; remember, later ones might be (and often are) easier.

With complicated stimuli, concentrate on the big idea. The big idea here is: "Compare rings; what helps one to compare rings?" When you simplify like that, answer choice (C) stands out as the most likely aid, whereas choices such as (A), (D), and (E) are pretty clearly useless.

Also, when you have a lot of detail, it often helps to make some simple mental images to keep it all clear. This is an especially useful technique when physical processes are described.

20 (B) is correct. The stimulus conclusion is that a particular event is unlikely to occur; that is, a particular group of snap peas is unlikely to fail. None of the choices states its conclusion *precisely* the same way, but since "unlikely to result in crop failure" is tantamount to "likely to grow," it is fair to assert that choice (B)'s conclusion—that a particular group of African violets is likely to grow well—is parallel. And the rest of choice (B) matches up well, too. In both answer choice (B) and the stimulus, the predicted successful botanical event is an exception to the conventional wisdom (post-April peas fail/South-facing violets fail), an exception made possible by an exceptional contributing factor (the unusual June cool/the shade provided by the trees).

(A): This draws a *general* conclusion about expert advice, while the stimulus merely concluded that in one particular case, the experts' advice wouldn't apply.

(C): This presents a general rule (impatiens do well under shade trees), and then qualifies it with another general rule (however, impatiens don't do well under maples). No particular plant is pointed to, as was the case in the stimulus.

(D): This has the same problem. A rule is given about planting seeds, and spinach seeds are exempted from the rule. All of it is gardeners' advice, with no concrete counterexample offered.

(E): This has the same flaw as (C) and (D): one rule is qualified by another rule that applies to a whole set of plants (amaryllis plants). We don't get what the stimulus and answer choice (B) provide: a specific case in which we would expect the original rule to hold, but a prediction is made that it won't.

In Parallel Reasoning questions, it's important to be aware of whether the conclusion is particular or general in nature. The stimulus tells you that some condition generally has a consequence, and then presents a *particular* case in which the condition is present but the consequence *isn't* present. The right answer must have this same relationship of general to particular.

21 (E) is correct. The roster of facts is tough to get through; handle with care, and keep paraphrasing. When voters blame a scandal equally on all parties, almost all incumbents win reelection. But when a scandal is blamed on a single party, incumbents from that party tend to lose. (E)'s principle would explain such behavior. According to (E), if Party X is responsible for a scandal, voters should try to punish Party X by voting out its incumbents; however, if all the parties are responsible, there's not much voters can do—*whomever* they vote for would be a member of one of the offending parties, so they might as well vote for the incumbents. Thus (E) accounts for the contrast in voter reactions.

(A): This deals with what should happen to individual incumbents who are responsible for scandals, but the stimulus just describes how voters treat *parties* or incumbents as members of their parties.

(B): This makes a judgment about the likely accuracy of the judgments of blame, but nothing of the kind is mentioned in the passage.

(C): This makes the mistake of concentrating on individuals, instead of parties. Moreover, (C) runs contrary to the passage. According to (C), in cases where all parties are blamed for a scandal, all incumbents should be turned out.

(D): The passage doesn't imply that voters evaluate the challengers. On the contrary, voters are depicted as making choices depending on what they believe about the incumbents' parties.

The question stem asks for a principle that would account for voters' actions. The last sentence has nothing to do with voters' actions, so it is essentially filler used to create wrong answer choices.

The more complex a stimulus is, the more important it is to paraphrase carefully. Don't get bogged down in the author's verbiage; instead, replace it with your own everyday language and images.

22 (C) is correct. This is something of a slam dunk if you start off by locating the stimulus conclusion and characterizing it. You might call it "a recommendation of an extreme step to solve a problem." Of the choices, only (C) and (D) have any kind of recommendation as their conclusion, so the others can be tossed out. And as you read on, you can see that both the stimulus and (C) have the same character and the same flaws. That a phenomenon (TV/spectator sports) may lead to a problem (less communication/diminished health) doesn't mean that *eliminating* the phenomenon will *eliminate* the problem. (That's called "the fallacy of denying the antecedent," if you're into such terminology.) Also, in neither argument do we have evidence that "the *only* way" to solve the problem is the given proposal. Finally, notice how extreme, even ridiculous, both proposals are. It all adds up to (C).

(A), (B), and (E): These are easily eliminated, because not one of them follows the stimulus in proposing a solution to a problem. (A) concludes that economic pressures jeopardize many friendships, without a hint of a solution. (B) concludes that radio was less distracting than television. There's no prescription, no hint that this problem (if it is a problem) can be solved. (E) concludes that shopping is a leisure activity; again, we don't know whether this is a problem, and if so, there's no solution proposed.

(D): As noted, (D) does offer an "only solution," but would be more parallel if it ended, "Thus, the only solution is to ban private cars." Even then, however, it wouldn't be as good as (C), because (D) would still fail to present what both the stimulus and (C) offer: a clearly stated problem, removal of the cause of which would allegedly solve the problem.

Often the quickest method of attacking a Parallel Reasoning question is to locate and characterize the stimulus conclusion. Here the conclusion proposes *a necessary solution*; only pay attention to choices that do the same.

When the question stem tells you that the stimulus argument is flawed, another great Parallel Reasoning technique is to find the flaw and look for a match.

23 (B) is correct. Why are landlords reluctant, under rent control, to maintain existing rental properties and build additional units? As described, rent control cuts down on a landlord's profits. If profits decrease, then the incentive to maintain the properties that generate the profits would also decrease. According to (B), rent control reduces a landlord's profits so much that it becomes difficult to achieve a reasonable return on his or her investment. So (B) explains the landlords' reluctance to build and maintain units.

(A) and (E): These go astray in talking about the preferences of tenants, whereas we're interested in the actions of landlords. Nothing in the passage explains how tenants' preference for rent control would translate into landlords' abhorrence to same.

(C): This totally fails to address the issues of *how* the "common practice" of rent control contributes to housing shortages and *why* it discourages the maintenance of existing properties, which is what we're interested in.

(D): Information about the political origins of rent control doesn't explain why rent control leaves landlords reluctant to invest in maintenance or new construction.

The answer to this one practically jumps off the page. The question, "Which one . . . explains the landlords' reluctance . . . ?" is followed by choice (B)'s "Rent control makes it very difficult for landlords. . . ." The simplicity of Question 23 demonstrates why you don't want to get bogged down in a difficult question like Question 19. There can be very easy points towards the end of the section, just waiting for you to get to them.

24 (C) is correct. According to the passage, personal linguistic idiosyncrasies can be used to identify a poet's work. So if a poem of unknown authorship shares personal quirks with other poems whose author is known, then all the poems must have the same author. Thus, we can identify the author of the previously anonymous poem.

Why isn't this test conclusive? Consider (C): it's always possible that the peculiarity *isn't* unique to one author. Perhaps it was an error to identify the peculiarity as a *personal* idiosyncrasy; perhaps the previously unknown author had the same peculiarity. We wouldn't have known this, because the author was unknown. Thus it's possible that any supposedly unique peculiarity is shared by other, unknown authors, and no linguistic peculiarities by themselves can conclusively prove the authorship of a poem.

(A): This says that the approach would be used only in certain circumstances, but doesn't point to any reason the approach, when used, is inconclusive.

(B): This might be true, but the passage never claimed the technique can be used to identify the author of every poem discovered, only that it works in cases in which the peculiarity actually appears in a poem of unknown authorship.

(D): The literary effect that a poem has is beyond the scope; we're interested only in identification.

(E): It doesn't matter whether or not the usages were conscious; the issue is whether the usages are unique to certain authors.

When a concept is *defined* in a Logical Reasoning stimulus, pay attention! The precise definition is sure to be important in answering the question. Above, the kernel of the problem is the open-ended definition of "personal idiosyncrasy" (it shows up only in the work of one author). When you concentrate on that, the problem introduced by a new, anonymous poem becomes more obvious.

25 (E) is correct. Without a 10 percent increase, Quore will go bankrupt. Since a 20 percent increase in productivity is every bit as attainable as a 10 percent increase (according to the last sentence in the passage), we can conclude (E): if Quore can't achieve a 20 percent increase, then it goes under. (E) is basically the contrapositive of the stimulus. If Quore can't get a 20 percent increase, then it must be the case that it also can't get a 10 percent increase. If Quore can't get a 10 percent increase, then it goes bankrupt.

(A): We can't say that it's only the production structure that can prevent bankruptcy; we're told that only an increase in productivity (which needn't be due to the production structure alone) can do so.

(B): This confuses necessary and sufficient conditions. The stimulus says that an increase of at least 10 percent is necessary for avoiding bankruptcy, not that such an increase will *ensure* that Quore doesn't go bankrupt.

(C): Although the transformation of the market is what has threatened Quore with bankruptcy, for all we know many other factors could have likewise led to the identical result.

(D): This concludes that Quore will boost productivity and avoid bankruptcy, but there's no grounds for such optimism; the transformation of the market has necessitated, not brought about, an increase in productivity.

▼▼▼

Wrong answer choices that confuse necessary and sufficient conditions, as (B) does, are common; learn to reject them quickly. When the stimulus says "X only if Y," chances are one of the choices will take that to mean "If Y, then X."

This is basically a disguised Formal Logic question: if NOT X (10 percent increase in productivity), then Z (go bankrupt); if X, then Y (increase productivity 20 percent); therefore, what? Given the formality of the stimulus, you can be sure the inference is not going to involve any leap into the hypothetical, like (C), or into analysis, like (A).

▲▲▲

Section II: Logic Games

Game 1: John's Grades (Questions 1–6)

The Action

We are to rank six courses—economics, geology, history, Italian, physics, and Russian—according to grades: A (highest), B, C, D, and E (the only failing grade). John receives one letter grade for each course, a "loophole-closing" rule. The game spells out that grades are "consecutive" if they're next to each other in the alphabet (which is redundant, since that's what "consecutive" means).

Key Issues

1. What course receives what grade?

2. What courses can, must, or cannot receive the same grade as what other courses?

3. What courses can, must, or cannot receive grades that are consecutive with what other courses?

The number limitations are a challenge here. Five grades for six courses means that there aren't enough grades to go around; hence, at least one grade will have to be awarded to at least two courses. But it's also worth noting that there could be certain grades that John doesn't receive for *any* course. In other words, you need to realize up front that some of the five grades need not be used.

The Initial Setup

A natural way to visualize this game is vertically: A through E, with A on top. It's intuitive to work vertically here, isn't it? Remember to list the courses off to the side:

A
B
C
D
E

e g h i p r

The Rules

1. The key here is to recognize that we don't know which course receives the higher grade. Symbolize this by putting g immediately above p, and p immediately above g next to it, as a reminder that it can go either way.

2. As with Rule 1, we don't know which course receives the higher grade, so put r above i, and i above r next to it.

3. That John's grade in economics is higher than his grade in history doesn't mean that they're necessarily consecutive (though they *could* be). Write this in shorthand by drawing an "e," a couple of dots underneath it, and then an "h."

4. Did you recognize these as the same two entities from Rule 1? Combining Rules 1 and 4, we see that g will always be exactly one grade above p. Go back and scratch out the other possibility (p over g).

Key Deductions

The major deduction is the realization that g and p occupy two consecutive grades in that order. It's also worth noting that we have no "floaters" in this game—every entity is mentioned in at least one rule. And you might also notice that the minimum number of grades that need to be used is two (for instance, John could receive As in physics, econ, and Russian, and Bs in geology, history, and Italian), but that it's eminently possible that all *five* grades are used. Very slippery game, this.

The Final Visualization

Here's what we have as we go on to the questions:

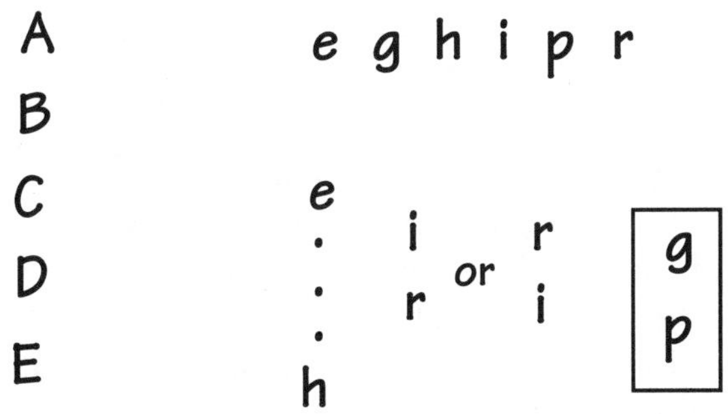

A
B
C
D
E

e g h i p r

e
⋮
h

i
r
or
r
i

g
p

The Big Picture

When the action of a game is to *rank* entities (from best to worst, or from largest to smallest), your best bet is to think and work *vertically*.

Never rush through your work on the opening paragraph and rules. You need a proper foundation in order to make any game work. If, even for a moment, you decide that every grade needs to be used, you're sunk!

Get in the habit of noticing which rules have entities in common (such as Rules 1 and 4 here). That way lies more deductions and more success.

On the actual test, some students had a problem with this game's concept of "consecutivity"—it threw them. Maybe it threw *you* for a minute, too. But if, in a nontest situation, you were asked to name two numbers that are consecutive, would you have any trouble with that concept? Of course not. The moral is that you should

take Logic Games at face value and not get thrown. And if you run across a puzzling term, either use common sense to interpret it, or wait for the test makers to explain it to you (they will). But for Pete's sake, don't panic.

The Questions

1 (C) is correct. The only failing grade is E, so that's what John got in Russian. Rule 2 means that he got a D in Italian. The stem tells us that John receives a D in economics as well, and economics should remind you of Rule 3. Since John's economics grade is higher than his history grade, John has to receive an E in history (there's nothing lower). Choice (C) is what must be true.

(B): This is false.

(A), (D), and (E): These are only possible.

When given two pieces of information, always start with the one that's more concrete ("fails Russian," in this case). Chances are that the more abstract information will make more sense after dealing with the first piece.

2 (D) is correct. John fails nothing, so (E) is out of the picture. Hence (follow this now), the lowest grade that John can receive in geology is (B), since the two languages have to go below it. Geology could receive an A, too. So we have an A or B in geology, and Italian and Russian occupying lower, consecutive grade levels. Now scan your rules and remember Rule 1: physics will receive a B or a C, depending on the geology grade. The upshot is that that block of four courses—geology, physics, and the two languages—has to cover *at least three grades*, whether they be A-B-C or B-C-D, and that makes answer choice (D) true. No matter what, John has to receive a minimum of one B and one C. For this question, you might have found it easier (and quicker) to try out each choice.

(A) and (C): Geology gets a B; physics, Italian, and economics get Cs; and Russian and history get Ds. Possible, and therefore neither of these choices has to be true.

(B): Keep the scenario above, but move economics up to a B. Choice (B) needn't be true, either.

(E): An A in geology, Bs in physics, Italian, and economics, and Cs for Russian and history; this combination eliminates (E).

Don't read rules into a game that aren't there. If you had (for some reason) thought that physics couldn't share a grade with one of the languages, you wouldn't have been able to eliminate choice (E).

This question turns out to be harder than some of those that follow, and in fact, it's common for Logic Games to follow harder questions with easier ones. Don't get bogged down. If an early question is going nowhere, others might be more concrete and hence easier. Move on!

3 (E) is correct. Note how we jotted down Rule 3 (see above). Sketch the same kind of thing as you read this stem, and you get:

p
.
.
.
e
.
.
.
i/r

Then add geology above physics (Rule 1 should be second nature by now) and you will recognize that all five grades will have to be used here: A for geology; B for physics; C for economics; D and E for Italian and Russian in either order. That language ambiguity, and the placement of history, are all that remain for a total ranking, which is what the question is seeking. To solve the problem, you can check out the impact of each choice in turn, or just recognize that since history is always below economics, setting history above one of the languages does the job. Either way, you get to choice (E): it mandates a D in history and an E in Russian (and hence a D in Italian). All six grades are set, and choice (E) is our answer.

(A): We still don't know his definite grades for Italian and Russian.

(B): Russian is set, but his history grade is still undetermined.

(C) and (D): These are wrong for the same reason. If John gets the same grade in history and a language, that grade will be D or E (see above). But what about the *other* language? Too much ambiguity is left.

Deduce as much as you can from the setup, but when you hit a lull, go to the answer choices. Knowing when it's best to stop looking for new deductions and hit the choices is a skill that will develop with practice.

4 (E) is correct. This stem is similar to Question 3's and leads (after using the related rules) to the ranking: geology, physics, economics, history, Italian. Hence all five grades are needed—from geology's A to Italian's E. The only course left is Russian. If John received an E in Italian, he must have received a D in Russian (Rule 2). The grades for all six courses are determined, so choice (E) is correct.

Learn to ask yourself the important questions, such as, "In what rules have I seen this entity?" and "Where does that lead me now (if anywhere)?"

5 (C) is correct. Once this stem is unpacked, it leads to the ranking: geology, physics, Italian, Russian; four classes with different and consecutive grades. This leads to only two possibilities: A-B-C-D and B-C-D-E. We don't have to worry about economics and history, because we are looking for what must be true, and as long as economics is higher than history, those courses can be thrown in nearly anywhere. Which two grades must John receive—in other words, which two grades are in both possibilities? B, C, and D appear in both possibilities above, and B and D are the ones that the test makers put in choice (C).

A quick scan of the answer choices often gives you a hint about where to look for the answer. What do you learn from scanning these five?

Checking each answer choice is always an option, but actively pursuing an answer is almost always the better option, because it's quicker and more direct. It certainly is in this case.

6 (E) is correct. Working with the stem and rules leads to: geology, physics, economics, history. These four courses receive different grades. So far we need not have an E grade awarded, but the question is asking for one. Recognize that anything below history would have to get that desired E. Scan the choices. Choice (E) accomplishes what we want quite nicely: E is the only grade for Russian, if Russian falls below history.

(A) and (B): In either case, an E is not mandated. Note for instance, A for geology, B for physics, Cs for economics and Russian, and Ds for Italian and history.

(C): Moving the Italian-Russian pair *up* certainly can't help: If Italian and geology receive As and Russian and physics receive Bs, John still needn't receive a failing grade.

(D): This is a possibility: A for geology, B for physics, Cs for Italian and economics, and Ds for Russian and history. (D) doesn't do it.

Keep in mind the numbers game. Knowing that you need the courses to span five grades gives you a good idea of what to look for in a choice.

Game 2: Casey's Shirts (Questions 7–11)

The Action

This game asks us to match shirt sizes—small, medium, and large—with shirt colors—red, yellow, and blue. Seems simple enough, but there's a lot of ambiguity, at least at first, in the selection process.

Key Issues

1. What types of shirts does Casey buy?

2. What color of shirt can Casey buy based on what other color and size of shirt is bought?

3. What size of shirt can Casey buy based on what other color and size of shirt is bought?

Note the one bit of precision in this otherwise slippery game: Casey buys exactly three shirts.

The Rules

Let's look over the rules before discussing the initial setup, for convenience's sake.

1. Simply defines the word "type" in the context of the game, so that the term can be used freely in the rules and questions. We are to think of "type" as the size/color combination. Note that there are *nine* possible "types" (three colors multiplied by three sizes): small red, small blue, small yellow, medium red, medium blue, etcetera.

2. Another loophole closer. It means that we must choose three *different* types out of the nine.

3. An injunction against ever picking small and large together. Just underline it for the moment.

4. One "type" is forbidden: small red. Think it through contrapositively: *if a small shirt is chosen, it will have to be blue or yellow. And if a red shirt is chosen, it will have to be medium or large.*

5. Here's another forbidden "type" of shirt: large blue. Therefore, *if a large shirt is chosen, it will have to be red or yellow. And if a blue shirt is chosen, it will have to be small or medium.*

The Initial Setup

As matching games go, this one is pretty loose, and Kaplan has identified three potential ways in which you might have dealt with it on the page. Take note of all three, for future reference. After all, what's important is not this game, but what you can learn *from* this game for later work.

The Grid Approach

This involves setting up a 3 × 3 grid with the characteristics labeled, allowing you the potential to mark with an "X" any combinations rejected and mark with a ✓ the three that are chosen. It would look like so:

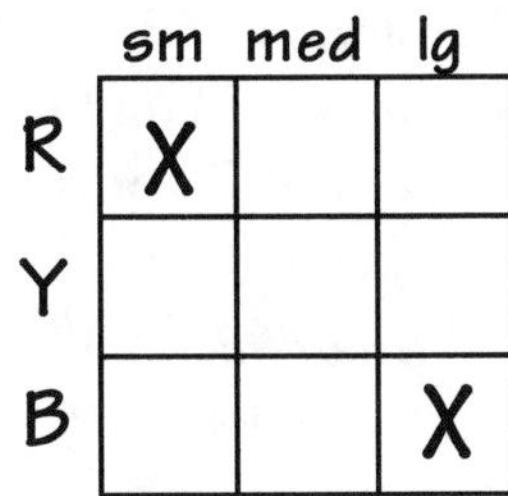

(Notice that we've gone ahead and indicated the upshot of Rules 4 and 5, the rules that toss out two of the nine possible shirt "types.") As needed per question, you would resketch the grid and enter its information, keeping in mind that you need to come up with exactly three ✓s at all times. Some students find such grids counterintuitive and find it difficult to take note, in the grid, of such injunctions as Rules 2 and 3. Those students might prefer the table method.

The Table Method

Using this method, you enter the data through deduction:

size ____ ____ ____

color ____ ____ ____

This might be a more conventional way of working out the information on paper than the grid method. Here, you simply take note of the restrictions on the selection process and refer to them as you go along:

NEVER <u>sm</u> <u>lg</u>

If red → med or lg
If sm → bl or yel
If bl → sm or med
If lg → red or yel

Finally, many students notice that there is only a limited number of possibilities at work in terms of shirt size, and they resolve to use the work-it-all-out method.

The Work-It-All-Out Method

For starters, note that Casey could conceivably buy one of each size, or all three of the same size:

sm med lg   med med med

sm sm sm   lg lg lg

But "sm med lg" violates Rule 3 (she can't buy both small and large together). And "sm sm sm" is out, because it would mean buying one of each color, and she can't buy small red (Rule 4); likewise "lg lg lg" is out, because she'd have to buy a large blue shirt, which is forbidden (Rule 5). So the only possible size combination so far is "med med med"—one of each color.

Now if Casey doesn't buy one of each size *or* three of the same size, what's left? *Two of one size, and one of another.* In other words:

sm sm med   med med sm   lg lg sm

sm sm lg   med med lg   lg lg med

But here again, Rule 3 comes into play rendering "sm sm lg" and "lg lg sm" impossible. In the end, there are only five possibilities for the sizes; here they are, along with what we can deduce about color in each case:

med med med (*obviously, one of each color*)

sm sm med (*one small blue, one small yellow, the medium's color is uncertain*)

med med sm (*the small is blue or yellow, not sure about the two medium*)

med med lg (*the large is red or yellow, not sure about the two medium*)

lg lg med (*one large red, one large yellow, the medium is any color*)

The advantage here is that so much is worked out in advance of the questions that the actual question work becomes a cinch. The disadvantage, of course, is that all of this work is time consuming, providing a lot of opportunities to make mistakes or get discouraged.

Key Deductions

Clearly, the third method above works out the most in advance. Even using the grid or table methods, however, it's possible to realize how limited Casey's choices really are and go into the questions with confidence. Also, we think it's worth noticing how little we are told about the medium-sized shirts: as long as we never choose two of the same "type," the medium-sized shirts offer the most freedom of color choice. But there's one thing we *do* know for sure: no matter what, Casey has to buy at least one medium shirt. Check it out. *That's* a major realization worth making up front.

The Big Picture

If there are only a limited number of possibilities (and you can work them out quickly), it might be worth it to go ahead and work them out up front. This will save you considerable time later. But *do so carefully*—if you rush the job, you're wasting time *and* impeding your performance.

Even in games without many deductions, pay special attention to the numbers aspect. The minimums and maximums required in a game are *always* important.

The Questions

7 (A) is correct. Which one "must be false"—that is, which one is *impossible*? Not much to do but try the answer choices, and the test makers cut us a break, because the very first choice is the one that's a no-go. If Casey buys two small shirts, they must be yellow and blue (Rule 4). The third shirt can be red, either medium or large, but *two* red shirts are impossible. Here are combinations indicating that the other four choices are eminently possible:

(B): medium red, large red, medium yellow
(C): medium red, large red, large yellow
(D): small yellow, small blue, medium red
(E): medium yellow, medium blue, large red

Remember that Logic Game questions are *not* ordered in terms of difficulty. This might be a good candidate for skipping the first time around. If you see complex answer choices, you can usually count on spending some time there.

8 (B) is correct. If, as the stem says, Casey buys a small blue, then Rule 3 means that all large shirts are out. And a glance at the choices tells us that we're looking for what Casey can't buy two of. Since large shirts are out, then only one red shirt—a medium one (according to Rule 4)—can be purchased, and answer choice (B) is our answer. This, the active approach, is the fastest way to get the answer, but you could have tried out each choice until you came upon the right one.

(A): The stem has assigned Casey a small blue shirt, and there's nothing stopping her from buying a second blue one (in medium).

(C): Along with the small blue, she can buy two yellows of any size.

(D) and (E): Given that Casey buys a small shirt, there are two possibilities: either she buys two mediums, in which case (E) is true, or she buys another small and one medium, in which case (D) is true.

The "active" way into a question is usually the fastest. But if you can't see it, don't despair, because you can always try out the choices hands-on. Don't be leery of trial and error. Generally, if you try, you won't err.

9 (B) is correct. All five of the possibilities we worked out (in the work-it-all-out discussion, above) include at least one medium shirt. With medium yellow forbidden, as it is here, then clearly that requisite medium has to be red or blue. And if you scanned the choices, you could have recognized that this is just what (B) is saying. Here are combinations demonstrating that the other choices needn't be true:

(A): large red, large yellow, medium blue
(C): medium red, small yellow, medium blue
(D): small yellow, small blue, medium blue
(E): medium red, large red, medium blue

Get in the habit of scanning the choices before working on the question. Doing so lets you recognize exactly what's being asked and will give you a clue as to how much work will be enough. This saves valuable time. Why do more work, and spend more time, than necessary?

10 (B) is correct. Given that only one medium shirt is purchased, the remaining shirts have to be two small or two large. (We worked all this out above.) If you proceed to match up the sizes with colors, remembering that in this question, each color is used exactly once, you can narrow the selection down to:

- medium blue, large yellow, large red, or
- medium red, small yellow, small blue.

Scanning the choices, notice that (B) is not included in either of our possibilities. And indeed, if Casey buys a medium yellow shirt, either Rule 4 or 5 will be violated. As for the wrong choices, (A) is purchased in the medium red/small yellow/small blue combination above, while (C), (D), and (E) are all purchased in the medium blue/large yellow/large red combination.

When you have narrowed down possibilities to two or three, you can usually quickly eliminate wrong choices, even if the answer doesn't necessarily jump right out at you.

11 (D) is correct. Two more "types" are forbidden: large red and small blue, which narrows things down a lot. Casey can still buy all three medium shirts (which eliminates choice (C), incidentally), and the only other possibilities are one small and two medium or one large and two medium.

Upshot: Casey has to buy either two or three medium shirts, which brings us to answer choice (D). If she buys all three medium shirts, it's obvious that she'll have to buy either a medium red or medium blue (both, actually). But even if she buys only two medium, the only combinations are red and yellow, red and blue, or yellow and blue. In all possible combinations she will buy either a medium red or a medium blue (if not both). So (D)'s our answer.

(A): She needn't buy red. She could buy only blue and yellow in some combination.

(B): She needn't buy a medium yellow. She could buy a medium red, medium blue, and a yellow (small or large).

(C): See above. She could buy three medium.

(E): She can avoid purchasing either a large yellow or a medium blue shirt by going for small yellow, medium red, and medium yellow shirts.

Never turn off your critical reading. The test makers like to stick vital information in the opening paragraph (such as the crucial information that Casey buys exactly three shirts). If you're looking for rules only in indented form, you'll miss the ones in the opening paragraph and be sunk.

Game 3: Fish and Plants (Questions 12–17)

The Action

This game is a straightforward grouping game of selection. There are five kinds of fish to choose from—G, H, J, K, and L—and four kinds of plants—w, x, y, and z. Our job is to select exactly five—three fish and two plants—of the nine entities.

Key Issues

1. What fish and plants are selected?
2. What fish can, must, or cannot be selected with what other fish?
3. What fish can, must, or cannot be selected with what plants?
4. What plants can, must, or cannot be selected with what other plants?
5. What plants can, must, or cannot be selected with what fish?

The Initial Setup

Make a list of the entities, and in each question, circle the ones selected and cross out the ones rejected. This is the classic way to work out selection tasks. As it turns out, this particular game is so basic that most of the questions can be answered simply by looking over the rules with virtually no scratchwork. Perhaps you found that to be the case; if you did, bravo!

Fish	Plants
G H J K L	w x y z
(pick 3)	(pick 2)

The Rules

1. This rule means that selecting G eliminates two other entities. You can write, "If G, then no H and no y," and remember to think through and jot down the contrapositive: "If H or y, then no G."
2. Did you take the necessary time to translate this rule correctly? Read it carefully: choosing K is necessary for choosing H, hence, "If H, then K" and, of course, the contrapositive, "If no K, then no H."
3. This has the same logical structure as Rule 2 and the same need to translate correctly: "If J, then w," and "If no w, then no J."
4. The wording is different from Rules 2 and 3, but the logic is the same: "If K, then x" and "If no x, then no K."

Key Deductions

You could combine Rules 2 and 4 to realize: "If H, then x" and "If no x, then no H." More importantly, give yourself a mental reminder of the numbers in the game before you move ahead: you will always need exactly three of the five fish and two of the four plants.

The Final Visualization

Be sure you've kept all of your notations neat and easily accessible:

Fish	Plants
G H J K L	w x y z
(pick 3)	(pick 2)

If (G) → no H, no y
If (H) or (y) → no G
If (H) → (K)
If no K → no H
If (J) → (w)
If no w → no J
If (K) → (x)
If no x → no K

The Big Picture

The contrapositive is extremely important in all Logic Games, but especially in those with a lot of "if/then" rules.

Endeavor to translate rules into if/then terms whenever possible—*and take the time to translate them correctly!*

Always be sure that your scratchwork is correct and neat. Its purpose, remember, is to remind you of the rules quickly and accurately. Sloppiness, or sloppy thinking, undermines both goals.

The Questions

12 (B) is correct. Check each rule against each choice. Rule 1 axes choice (A). Rule 2 kills choice (D). Choice (C) can be axed because it doesn't obey Rule 3. And (E) violates Rule 4. That leaves (B).

Acceptability questions are your friends. Seek them out. They are straightforward and help to cement the workings of a game.

13 (B) is correct. Jot down your roster, circle H as chosen, and then check your rules. Recognize that H leads to K, and K leads to x (Rules 2 and 4)—meaning answer choice (B). On the day of the test, you wouldn't waste any time on the other choices. For our purposes though, notice that a selection of fish—H, K, L—and plants—x, y—eliminates answer choices (A), (C), (D), and (E). None of them need be true.

To eliminate an answer choice in a "must be true" question, all you have to do is find an exception for it. Here, conveniently, one exception killed all four of the wrong choices.

14 (C) is correct. If x and z are chosen, then the plant quota is filled; w and y (the other plants) can't be selected. According to Rule 3, selecting J requires selecting w, so J can't be one of the chosen fish. That eliminates answer choices (B), (D), and (E) right off the bat, leaving only answer choices (A) and (C). Without J, we're left to choose three fish from the following group of four: G, H, K, and L. G and H can't be selected together (Rule 1), which eliminates answer choice (A). So it must be the case that K and L are selected along with *either* G or H. The only choice that fits this description, and the only choice that remains, is answer choice (C): G, K, L.

Work with what you're given. Don't just stare at a question. Get the information down on the test booklet and see where it leads.

15 (C) is correct. This is an acceptability question, so just check the rules against the choices. The only difference is that ordinarily the four wrong choices violate rules, but here only one—the correct one—is a violator. As it happens, choice (C) violates Rule 2 by selecting an H without a K.

(A): We saw this group in the answer of Question 14, so we know it works.

(B) and (E): Each is acceptable with w and x as the plants.

(D): This combination is acceptable with x and z as the plants.

This acceptability question takes an unusual form, but it's still relatively straightforward. Recognize, once again, that Logic Game questions are in no set order of difficulty—a game can begin with a really tough question and plant an easy one much later.

16 (D) is correct. Selecting y requires crossing G off our fish list (Rule 1). That leaves four fish—H, J, K, and L—from which we need to choose three. J would require the presence of plant w (Rule 3), while K requires the presence of plant x (Rule 4). But the hobbyist can't select *both* plant w and plant x, because she's already taken plant y, and there are only two plants to be selected. Since it's impossible to select both w and x, it's also impossible to select both J and K. The hobbyist can only take one of them, which means that the other two fish, H and L, must both be chosen. And now there's really no ambiguity about the J/K selection—K must get the nod (Rule 2; we need K for H). So the complete group of three fish selected by the hobbyist must be H, K, and L, choice (D).

This question required pretty tricky deductive thinking. If you found it taking a lot of time, you probably should have considered skipping it momentarily and coming back to it later.

17 (B) is correct. Consider the situation. Four of the five choices are pairs of plants that *can* be chosen together. No extra conditions or limitations are specified. That means that any pair we have already seen chosen, in a previous question, can be tossed. In Question 16, we had plants x and y, so cross out (D). The question stem to Question 14 had the hobbyist selecting x and z, so (E) is out; by Question 14's stem alone, we can see that (E)'s pair can be picked! Finally, in Question 12, the correct answer included w and x; that's choice (A).

We're left with only two to check. If you start with (B), you ask yourself, "Can the hobbyist pick both w and y?" Well, having selected y, she can't select G (Rule 1), and having not selected x, she cannot select K (Rule 4). That means she can't select H either, since Rule 2 states that H requires K. G, K, and H are gone; only J and L remain; we've dropped below the three-fish requirement. So it's choice (B) that contains an impossible plant combination.

For the record, plants w and z can be selected along with fish G, J, and L. (C) is acceptable.

When possible, use your work from previous questions to help eliminate choices in later questions. Without doing any new work, we eliminated three answer choices, leaving only two to check. Talk about saving time!

This, of course, is a major argument for not erasing your scratchwork. Leave previous scratchwork there on the page, clean and clear, for later consultation.

Game 4: Five Towns' Rankings (Questions 18–24)

The Action

This is a triple sequencing game—something of a rarity. But that doesn't necessarily make it problematic. Check how much data we're given. We're ranking five towns—Palmdale, Quietville, Riverdale, Seaside, and Tidetown (abbreviated as P, Q, R, S, T)—from first to fifth (best to worst) in three different categories—climate, location, and friendliness. Our job will be to put the towns in order based on the rankings they receive in each of the three categories.

Key Issues

1. How are the towns ranked in each category?
2. How are the towns ranked in each category based on their rankings in the other categories?
3. Which town is ranked higher and lower than which other towns in each category?

The Initial Setup

As with our previous ranking game—Game 1—working vertically seems to make the most sense. It's very intuitive and easy to handle:

	CLI	LOC	FRIEND
1			
2			
3			
4			
5			

P Q R S T

Remember that each town has a rank in each category.

The Rules

1. The first rule is simply a loophole closer. What it's saying is, "There are no ties."
2. In the climate category, enter T third and S fourth. Simple.
3. Here three of the five location rankings are given to us: Q is second, R is third, and P is fourth.
4. As in question stems with more than one piece of information, start with the concrete and then go to the abstract. In the friendliness category, rank Q fourth and S fifth. We're also told that T is better than P in this category. Nearby, jot down a physical reminder that T is ranked higher than P in friendliness (see the figure that follows).
5. R is ranked higher in climate than friendliness. Just make a note of this rule or circle it for now. We'll come back to it under Key Deductions.
6. Q's rankings are already set for location and friendliness, so we can deduce quite a lot from this requirement that Q's rankings all be different. Since Q takes second place in one category and fourth in another, Q's climate ranking—the one remaining—cannot be second or fourth. And the third slot in the climate category is already taken. Therefore, Q must be ranked first or fifth in climate. Make a note of that.

Here's what we've got so far:

Q = 1 or 5

	CLI	LOC	FRIEND
1			
2	no Q	Q	
3	T	R	
4	S	P	Q
5			S

T...P

P Q R S T

Seven out of 15 slots filled. But we can do more.

Key Deductions

Go back to Rule 5, which said that R is ranked higher in climate than in friendliness. Since T and S are third and fourth in climate, respectively, R must be ranked either first or second in climate. (Look at it this way: if R were fifth in climate, there would be no way for its climate ranking to be better than its friendliness ranking.) Make a note of that, too. Meanwhile, note that R will have to be ranked either second or third in friendliness (since the third and fourth slots are taken, and a ranking of first place for R would violate Rule 5).

And we can go even further. In the location category, note that first and fifth place are available to S and T in either order. Jot that down in the sketch.

Finally, we're rewarded if we combine Rules 4 and 5. If T's friendliness ranking is to be higher than P's, and if R can only be ranked second or third in friendliness, then there are no two ways about it: T will have to be ranked first in friendliness. (Nothing else is left!)

The Final Visualization

Here's an extremely helpful sketch of everything that we've determined so far:

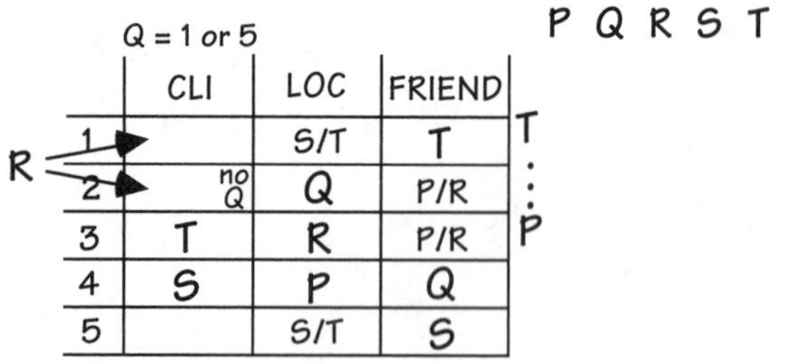

Q = 1 or 5 P Q R S T

	CLI	LOC	FRIEND
1	◄ R	S/T	T
2	◄ R no Q	Q	P/R
3	T	R	P/R
4	S	P	Q
5		S/T	S

T . . . P

Note that the most ambiguity exists in the climate category, where P, Q, and R are yet to be placed—but we know the limitations.

The Big Picture

The prospect of recopying this involved sketch for individual questions might be daunting, but you are likely to find that redrawing isn't necessary, since we already know so much. And as long as you recopy a sketch, doing so shouldn't take much time at all.

Some people think it's a waste of time to commit so much effort up front. They're the ones who end up staring blankly at the questions that they were in such a hurry to get to.

The setup is the time to think, not to draw. The drawing is secondary. Consider the implications of each rule, and if you can build it directly into your master sketch instead of rewriting it (as in Rule 6 and others), then great, do it.

The Questions

18 (B) is correct. We've already done the work on this one. The only climate rankings available for R are first and second, choice (B).

After a time-consuming setup, don't be surprised if the first question is fairly simple. The test makers like to reward you for taking an appropriate amount of time up front to reason out the rules and organize the data.

19 (C) is correct. R must be either first or second in climate, third in location, and either second or third in friendliness. So R can't be ranked fifth in any of the three criteria, answer choice (C). All of the others are open to at least one fifth-place ranking in at least one category.

You should be seeing by now just how valuable that time you spent up front was. If you did the work, you've just blown through the first two questions in about a minute.

20 (C) is correct. Here we simply need to test each choice.

(A): T must be ranked first in friendliness, so P can't be first there.

(B): This violates Rule 6—Q can't have identical rankings in any two categories.

(C): R can be ranked first in climate with P second and Q fifth, and we know for certain that R is ranked third in location (Rule 3). Meanwhile, R can be ranked third in friendliness with T first and P second. (C) is possible and the correct answer. On the day of the test, you would stop and go on to the next question, but for the record:

(D): S can't be ranked fourth in location, because P was assigned that spot by Rule 3.

(E): We deduced above that T must be ranked first in friendliness, not third.

This is a somewhat time-consuming question, but the time required is cut considerably by our fine deductive work up front.

21 (D) is correct. We've seen that R must be ranked either first or second in climate, so if Q is ranked first in climate, as the stem demands, then R is second. But scanning the answers, we see that's not a choice. Since R is second in climate, Rule 5 demands that R be ranked third in friendliness, and that's choice (D). The long road would involve eliminating the wrong choices:

(A) With Q first, R, not P, must be ranked second in climate.

(B): P can't be ranked third in friendliness, since we deduced that R is.

(C): If R is ranked third in friendliness, then it's not ranked second there.

(E): T *could* be ranked fifth in location, but it needn't be. T could be ranked first with S fifth.

However you choose to organize the information in a game, make sure that you keep it neat and readily accessible.

22 (A) is correct. The stem info (that P is second in climate) completes the climate rankings: R must take first and Q is left in fifth, all of which eliminates choices (B) and (D) as statements that can be true. With R first in climate, R can be ranked *either* second or third in friendliness (Rule 5), which means that P can either be ranked second or third in friendliness as well. Choice (A) is possible, and thus the correct answer. T is still ranked first in friendliness, so (C) and (E) are out.

Once again, deductions made from the rules at the beginning of the game (R having to be ranked first or second in climate, and T definitely ranked first in friendliness) allow us to make short work of this question.

23 (E) is correct. Here's a question where—because you're given two concrete pieces of information—you might want to create a unique sketch, with T first in location (leaving S fifth in that category), and R second in friendliness (leaving P third in that category). A new sketch quickly reveals that both of those categories are complete.

What's up with climate? Since R is second in friendliness, R must be ranked first in climate lest we violate Rule 5. Q, we had deduced, is always either first or fifth in climate, so now Q is fifth. That leaves P ranked second. Every town's ranking is determined for each of the three criteria—choice (E).

Get the new information down on paper and work with it. See where it leads.

24 (E) is correct. Several times so far, we've used the deduction we made up front that T must be ranked first in friendliness. It's useful again now: (E), which attempts to place T second, can't be true, and is the answer.

All four of the other choices are things we've seen throughout the game; all of them could be true.

Get used to trusting your deductions. You did the work up front; it makes no sense to waste time second-guessing yourself this late in the game. By the time you got to Question 23 or 24, you may well have forgotten how you figured out that T is first in friendliness, or that R must occupy the first or second slot in the climate category. *But who cares how we learned it?* It's in the sketch; it can be relied upon.

This game, and indeed this very question, dramatically illustrates why it's so important to manage your time well. You don't want to miss an easy question like this at the end of the section simply because you wasted time on an earlier, tougher one.

Section III: Logical Reasoning

1 (C) is correct. This is what we call a crossed-wires question. Mark has misconstrued Terry's claim, and we're asked to find, based on his response, what Mark thinks Terry said. In an attempt to rebut Terry's claim, Mark argues that there are *other* reasons to go to college besides wanting to get a good job. Evidently, he thinks Terry is saying that getting a good job is the *only* reason to go to college, choice (C).

(A): Mark doesn't dispute that college is one of many places where a person can get trained for a good job—he simply disputes that job training is the *only* reason to go to college.

(B), (D), and (E): Mark doesn't deny that getting a good job requires a college background, nor does he deny that everyone who wants a decent job should go to college. He merely denies that getting a good job is the only reason for going to college.

Mark misinterprets Terry's claim. That means that the correct answer can't be simply a rewording of Terry's claim, which eliminates (B), (D), and (E).

On crossed-wires questions, concentrate on the statement of the confused person (in this case, Mark). It's *his* misinterpretation that generates the answer.

2 (B) is correct. The author concludes that the higher patient mortality rates in certain hospitals are probably the result of lower-quality care. The evidence for this includes the fact that the hospitals all had roughly the same per-patient funding; in other words, lack of money didn't account for the high mortality rates. But that eliminates only one other possible explanation for the result. Another, equally plausible explanation why some hospitals are deadlier than others (other than differences in the quality of care provided) would severely weaken the argument. We get this plausible explanation in (B). If those hospitals receive much sicker patients than others, the higher mortality rates at those hospitals might reflect the higher percentage of severely ill patients, rather than low-quality care.

(A): Even if the high death rates in some hospitals are due to the fact that the staff in these hospitals has less training, this would strengthen the argument, by making it plausible that the poorly trained personnel are providing lower quality care.

(C): This is irrelevant, as we have no way of knowing from this statement which hospitals have the most experienced staffs. And even if we did know, we still wouldn't be able to legitimately tie this information to the issue of quality of care. Choice (C) is simply way too vague to damage the argument.

(D): *Au contraire:* (D) slightly strengthens the argument by *eliminating* a possible alternative reason for the difference in death rates—the types of surgery offered.

(E): This essentially does the same thing that (D) does, by eliminating another possible explanation (regional differences not related to quality of care) that otherwise could damage the argument. If mortality rates are the *same* from region to region, then the difference in rates between hospitals can't be due to what region they're in.

Remember: a major way to weaken an argument is to find an alternative explanation for a situation described in a stimulus. In arguments in which an explanation or cause is concluded, the author is assuming that no *other* explanation or cause is at work. An alternative explanation damages the validity of the explanation cited in the conclusion.

Pay attention to how the author makes the argument. Here, the author eliminates one reason for the discrepancy (funding) and concludes that there could be only one other reason (quality of care). That has "alternative explanation" written all over it.

3 (E) is correct. The author has found an exception to the government's policy of conserving valuable natural resources: topsoil, which is eroding at an alarming rate. In many states, 100 years of farming has led to the loss of half the topsoil. The federal government's response has been inadequate. Federal funding is described as "ridiculously low," and we're told that some states actually devote more money to conserving topsoil than the federal government does. The point of all this is expressed in (E): the federal government is spending far too little on soil conservation and it should spend more.

(A): Come on; corn is obviously not the issue. In fact, corn is mentioned only as part of an example of topsoil erosion. This choice fails to even mention the main topic, which is topsoil.

(B) This may or may not be inferable, but it's certainly not the main point. Like (A), this choice focuses on the corn element, and totally ignores the issue in the last two sentences: federal expenditures.

(C) This misses the author's criticism. Instead of merely arguing that the federal government is responsible, she says that the feds aren't doing enough monetarily and should do more. Moreover, she never says conservation isn't the responsibility of the states.

(D) This, too, is a distortion. The author doesn't accuse the feds of making unequal distribution among states; her point is that the federal government is shortchanging all the states.

Paraphrasing the argument is always beneficial, and even more so for Main Point questions. If you tried to summarize the whole argument in a single sentence, would it be (A), "Corn isn't cost effective," or (B), "Six inches of topsoil isn't enough"? No. These choices don't even mention the federal government. A summary of the argument must include the author's criticism of the feds, something like, "The federal government isn't spending enough on soil conservation."

The two main elements of this argument are topsoil and federal expenditures relating to topsoil conservation. Any choice that omits either one of these elements must be wrong.

Don't expect wrong choices on Main Point questions to be flat-out opposed to the main point. Most of them will be incomplete and/or partially erroneous depictions of the argument.

4 (E) is correct. We're looking for an answer that describes something that the author does in her argument. She certainly does what (E) says; she tells us that some individual states spend more money on soil conservation than the entire federal government does.

(A): While the author presents statistics on past topsoil erosion, she doesn't present any detailed statistics relating to future topsoil erosion.

(B): She specifically refers to topsoil loss in *many*, not *all,* states.

(C): Scope shift—the author claims that the natural resource of topsoil is being ignored by the government, not that the government places little value on natural resources *in general.* In fact, this is flatly contradicted by her first sentence.

(D): On the contrary, she does use slanted (or biased) language in reference to the level of federal expenditures. She refers to it as "ridiculously" low.

The word "all" (like the word "none") in an answer choice should act as a red flag. "All" is not an intensifier of "many" or "most." It's an absolute term that isn't used in this stimulus. It might not seem like a big difference at first, but the discrepancy between "many states" in the stimulus and "all states" in choice (B) is enough to nix this choice.

5 (B) is correct. Ah, a classic case of correlation versus causation. The author cites a correlation between a certain animal behavioral disorder and the presence of high levels of aluminum in the animals' brains. He then presents a simplistic conclusion: a compound that prevents aluminum from affecting the brain will cure the afflicted animals. The author assumes that the aluminum *causes* the behavioral disorder, but the evidence shows only a correlation. It's possible that there's no causal connection between the disorder and the aluminum, or even that the connection runs the other way around (the high aluminum level is *a result* of the disease). Therefore, in order to arrive at the conclusion in the last sentence, the author must assume what's stated in (B)—that extra aluminum is the cause, and not a result, of the disorder.

(A): Try the Denial Test: can the unusually high levels of aluminum vary from one afflicted animal to another? Sure, why not? Denying (A) has no effect on the argument, which shows that (A) is irrelevant and therefore not a central assumption.

(C): This is outside the scope. Since the author never makes the claim that the method of cure won't also do some harm, he needn't assume that there will be no side effects. (You could use the denial test here, too, by asking yourself whether the appearance of side effects would doom the logic of the argument.

Since side effects are irrelevant here, the answer is clearly no.)

(D): This may or may not be true (we have no way of knowing), but either way, it isn't an assumption. Even if exactly one dose of the compound cures every organism, the logic of the argument still stands.

(E): The author speaks of "unusually high levels" of aluminum found in animals with the disorder, which implies that *some* level of aluminum is normal.

The fallacy of confusing causation with correlation is common on the LSAT. When the evidence states "whenever A happens, B also happens," all that means is that these two events are *correlated.* That doesn't necessarily mean "A causes B" or "B causes A." Causation must be explicitly stated.

You might have noticed another assumption here: that a compound that prevents aluminum from affecting the brain can cure brains *already* affected. Sometimes a stimulus can afford more than one possible answer; in such cases, of course, only one answer will show up among the choices. If you're prephrasing, don't get so locked into your prephrased answer that you can't recognize a different viable answer should one appear.

6 (A) is correct. The author wants to show that whales must once have lived on land and have had hind legs that could support their weight. She presents evidence: whales have the *remnants* of a pelvis, suggesting that once they had pelvises, and if an animal has a pelvis, we expect it to have hind legs. She also points to a fossilized whale skeleton with hind legs (albeit feeble ones) and a partial pelvis. The skeleton is intended to be an intermediate form: it has more of a pelvis than modern whales, and it has weak hind legs. This makes it likely that even farther back, there were whales with full pelvises and functioning hind legs, and that these lived on dry land. The strengthener for that scenario is in choice (A): bones even older than the fossils mentioned by the author confirm that whales once had full pelvises. As we go back in time then, whales look more and more like animals that walked on land, just as the author argued.

(B): No skeletons confirming the author's theory have been found; this statement is actually a weakener.

(C): The evolution of such limbs in other early mammals is largely irrelevant. But even if we were allowed to turn to this as an analogous case that may have some bearing on the whale/hind limbs issue, it would actually weaken, not strengthen, the conclusion by suggesting that this "uncertainty" regarding the other mammals may extend to the case of whales.

(D): The fact presented here that large mammals don't necessarily need hind limbs to move around on land implies that whales, too, needn't have had hind limbs that could support their weight.

(E): This answer choice is also mostly irrelevant, but if pressed, we would have to say it weakens the argument by weakening the connection between hind limbs and sea-dwelling mammals.

Use the question stem to your advantage! The conclusion in this stem appears to be the conclusion the author is strongly moving towards yet doesn't state explicitly in the argument.

Many choices in Strengthen the Argument questions live in that hazy middle ground between irrelevance and slight weakener. On the day of the test, you need to be able to eliminate these quickly.

7 (E) is correct. Senator Beton claims that government-funded art can't reflect the independent artistic conscience of the artist, because it's designed to please those who pay for it. From this, she concludes in the last sentence that funded art can't be truly excellent. To get from the evidence about independent artistic conscience to the conclusion about truly excellent art, Beton has to be assuming that the *only* truly excellent art is art that's a reflection of the artist's artistic conscience. If a piece of art that's *not* a reflection of the artist's artistic conscience can nonetheless exhibit true artistic excellence, then her argument falls apart. The missing connection, the necessary assumption, is stated in choice (E).

(A): The taxpayers' interests are outside the scope. All Beton says is that funding burdens taxpayers, but that burden isn't necessarily unwillingly accepted.

(B): This offers up an unwarranted and irrelevant comparison between government funding and "other financial support" for artists. Since other types of funding are beyond the scope of the argument, Beton needn't assume anything about how much support these other types of funding provide.

(C) This is a distortion. Beton states that the goal of government support of the arts is to promote the creation of works of artistic excellence. Her point is that this goal won't be attained. She doesn't mention, and therefore needn't assume anything about, what that goal is based on.

(D): Huh? This one is just plain backwards. Beton need not assume what this answer choice states, that artists forego funding *after* they've created excellent art. She simply thinks that government funding makes the production of truly excellent art impossible.

▼▼▼

Many authors and characters portrayed by authors in Logical Reasoning stimuli seem to see the world only in black and white. Recognizing these naive and oversimplistic depictions of situations will help you pinpoint assumptions, logical flaws, strengtheners and weakeners. In this case, the senator assumes that true art can't be produced by an artist who is "just in it for the money." But why can't this happen? Nothing in the stimulus forbids a true work of art that doesn't reflect the artist's independent artistic conscience, but evidently Beton believes this to be an impossibility. Therefore, she must necessarily assume choice (E) in order for her argument to hold water.

▲▲▲

8 (C) is correct. American industry strikes again; this time we're responsible for clogging up the world's air supply thanks to old American cars that contribute disproportionately to global air pollution. The problem is decreasing though, according to the author, because many of these older polluting cars are being taken out of service in the United States for failing emissions tests. The conclusion? Over the next decade, the amount of air pollution contributed by old American cars will decrease.

Did you catch the subtle scope shift? The problem is global, the solution is national. Since the requirement forces these cars out of service *only in the United States,* this leaves the argument vulnerable to a weakener like the one in choice (C). If many old, retired American cars are being shipped to places that lack emissions controls, then the author is overly optimistic. In other words, if (C) is true, then those old junkers aren't as retired as the author thinks, but may still be in service in other countries where they may still contribute significantly to global air pollution.

(A): This answer choice won't weaken the argument because it merely says that the air of different regions can't be separated. That's precisely the author's point; that's why old American cars contribute disproportionately to *global* air pollution even though the cars are located, for the most part, in the United States.

(B): This amounts to the claim that newer automobiles are better for the atmosphere than the old ones, which certainly stands to reason. That's why use of newer American autos will lessen pollution.

(D): So what? Even if the number of such jurisdictions isn't increasing, the jurisdictions that have these standards would still be taking old American cars off the road, and that, according to the author, will decrease the amount of air pollution contributed by old American cars.

(E): The argument predicts a decrease in the air pollution caused only by *older* American cars, not *all* American cars.

Pay attention to regional specifications; some authors shift the scope from one location to another and hope you don't notice. Here we're told that the old gas-guzzlers are taken out of service in the United States, but the problem was one of *global* pollution.

Watch out for choices such as (A) that seem to make a valid point. The test for each choice in a Weaken the Argument question is not, "Is this true?" or "Does this sound reasonable and familiar?" but rather, "Does this *damage* the argument?" The answer must have a definite effect on the argument, so don't get caught on choices that just tell you what you already know.

9 (C) is correct. The author concludes that putting words into people's mouths is permissible because it's better than the alternative, which is to print only the words people actually say. The problem with that alternative is that people usually don't express themselves clearly. Since printing a person's actual remarks wouldn't completely communicate his or her meaning, journalists are entitled to doctor quotes. The problem with this reasoning is that it needn't be an either/or situation. Just because people don't express themselves clearly doesn't mean that the *only* thing to do is manufacture quotes. There are other alternatives; for example, maybe the journalist could write a clear distillation of the interviewee's views, but not put this in quotes. As (C) says, defending the practice against only one alternative isn't enough.

(A): The author never attacks the people who made the charge cited in the first sentence.

(B) This is much too general; the author never argues on the basis of journalism's prestige.

(D) This is what the author *wants* to do—show that inventing quotes is necessary. The problem is that he has only attacked one of many alternatives, and thus he hasn't shown necessity.

(E): No opponent has admitted that the practice is sometimes appropriate.

This is another occurrence of the "false alternatives" theme. A common flaw is that the author ignores the possibility of alternatives beyond those few he or she considers (see the bullet point for Question 7). You have to be more open minded; don't allow yourself to blindly accept the author's view when he or she simplistically asserts "either A or B."

Keywords are helpful, but they can be a little tricky. "However" tells you that the second sentence contains the author's reply to criticism of the journalists. "Therefore" tells you that the last sentence is the conclusion. However, this conclusion is broken up by a piece of evidence signaled by the word "since." Don't let the convoluted sentence structure fool you—you could mentally rearrange the last sentence to read, "therefore, this practice is entirely defensible, since it avoids the more serious. . . ."

10 (A) is correct. Give parents vouchers to pay for their children's education, the author argues, and let them choose the best schools. Then academically underachieving schools will be forced to improve just to stay alive, and the competition will increase the overall level of education. You might have been able to prephrase the assumption, given in choice (A), that parents would use vouchers for the intended purpose: to purchase the best possible education for their kids. Choice (A) presents some reasons why they might not do this. They might prefer a lousy school nearby to a better school farther away, or they might prefer a school that provides high-quality athletics. The argument that letting parents run the show will improve education holds only if parents are primarily interested in procuring a good education for their kids.

(B): The job market is outside the scope. The argument is that parental input, not employer input, is what the schools need.

(C) This needn't be assumed; there could be many effective methods of education, among which parents would choose. All the author assumes is that parents would choose a school because it practices an effective educational method.

(D): The decision making could be left entirely to the parents and the argument would still work fine.

(E): On the contrary, schools might very well want to specialize in certain fields. As long as they do this well and parents are happy with the specialization, these schools could still provide a good education. Since the specific nature of academic improvement is not discussed, nothing as specific as (E) need be assumed for the argument to stand.

Note that the assumption might sound eminently reasonable to you, but if it's unstated, and the logic of the argument depends on it, then it's an assumption nonetheless. An assumption isn't necessarily unreasonable, it's simply a necessary piece of the argument that isn't stated. Choice (C) should have struck you as too "big," or sweeping, a statement to be the correct assumption. The argument is fairly closely argued and unlikely to demand such a big leap. You always want an answer choice that matches the tone of the stimulus.

11 (C) is correct. Nothing unusual for the scientific community here: Smith offers a provocative challenge to an established theory, and other scientists endeavor to prove Smith wrong in defense of the established theory. Our author, however, sees a conspiracy at work. She says the scientific establishment attacked Smith's work merely because they were threatened by Smith's work and wanted to discredit him. Of course, there's no evidence for this; it's just as likely that they honestly believed he was in error. The author assumes without evidence that the scientists' motivation was to discredit Smith rather than to establish the truth of the matter.

(A) and (D): These focus on motivations for claims rather than on the claims themselves. Choice (A) attacks the author for not taking into account the possible gain to Smith should his theory find acceptance, but this is at least one step removed from the argument, and the author has no responsibility to delve this deeply. Choice (D) implies that the author herself is defending Smith for personal reasons, but the author's relationship to Smith plays no part in the logic of the argument.

(B): It's not necessary that the author tell us whether Smith knew that the effect he was reporting was incompatible with established theory. What's necessary is that the author give us some basis for her claim concerning the motivations of the scientists who criticized Smith's claim.

(E): This is outside the scope. The effect, if any, of Smith's paper on the public doesn't help us evaluate the scientific merit of Smith's claim or the logic of the author's defense of that claim.

Logical critique focuses on evidence, conclusion, and reasoning, not on unsupported insinuations about a person's motivations or character.

When looking for a logical flaw, bear in mind that an author is not responsible for covering every little detail of the matter. For example, yes, the author *does* pass over the possibility mentioned in (A), and she *does* neglect to clarify the info in (D). But so what? The author is not *required* to do these things in order for the logic to stand. Don't pick choices like these just because they seem to be "true"; the correct answer must point out the correct logical flaw.

Notice how detecting the author's central assumption gets us the answer to a Flaw question. Remember: the test makers can use an author's central assumption to generate not only Assumption questions, but Flaw, Strengthen the Argument, and Weaken the Argument questions as well.

12 (C) is correct. The stimulus states that the number of obese North American kids has increased over the last 15 years. The crux of the matter is the definition here of "obese"—that is, the fattest 15 *percent* of North American kids. With that standard, you'll always have the same percentage of kids labeled obese, regardless of actual amounts of body fat. Even if every child in North America were emaciated, according to this particular definition, the heaviest 15 percent of them would be labeled "obese." If a number representing 15 percent of all kids has increased, we know that the *total* number of kids must also have increased. So the other, nonobese, 85 percent of the group of kids must also have grown in number. Thus, since there are currently more obese kids, there must also be more nonobese kids. That's choice (C).

(A) This is simply silly; we can't conclude that the agreement of four studies always signals truth.

(B): The issue of physical activity is beyond the scope of the stimulus. Moreover, because the definition of obesity is based on a fixed percentage of kids, we don't even know if kids in general have become fatter than they were. Think about it: even if all the kids *lost* weight, there would still be a group of kids who have more body fat than 85 percent of the children their age. Choice (B) is totally unsupported.

(D): If the term "underweight" refers to a fixed statistical percentage (the way "obese" does), then the number of underweight kids must have *grown* along with the total number of kids. If, unlike being obese, being underweight isn't merely a matter of belonging to a certain percentage of the group of children, then we don't know what to say about (D). Either way, it can't be concluded from the information in the stimulus.

(E): This can't be true, since kids are being compared to other kids their age. By the very definition of obesity, there will always be 15 percent of kids of every age who are obese.

Always pay close attention to definitions on the LSAT. "Obese" here is only a percentage—it isn't an objective measure of fatness. As such it's subject to the usual rules of percentages. If a fixed percentage or fraction of some varying overall quantity increases, then the overall quantity must be increasing.

You may have deduced that the total number of kids increased. That's correct, but the test makers disguise the answer by saying that the number of nonobese kids has increased. You need to be able to recognize

your prephrased answer when it shows up in an unfamiliar form.

In some questions, you either "get it" or you don't. Almost all Kaplan students who took this test remembered this particular question. Some saw what was happening right off the bat; the rest wouldn't have seen it if they stared at the question for the rest of the day. Know when to move on if a question simply baffles you, because, as you know, no question is worth more than any other.

▲▲▲

13 (D) is correct. The economist claims that money derives its value from scarcity, and the anthropologist responds with a supposed exception: the Kwara'ae people used cowrie shells as currency despite the plentiful amount of these shells. We're asked to resolve the apparent discrepancy, so we want to find some way in which the Kwara'ae use of cowrie shells proves to be the use of a scarce thing. Choice (D) does the trick: Kwara'ae did use cowrie shells, but they used only those that were polished and carved by some other people. Such handcrafted shells, because of the time and labor required for their production, couldn't have been very common. So (D) allows us to infer that the shells used as money were indeed likely to be scarce, and thus that the Kwara'ae *aren't* an exception to the economist's claim.

(A): The fact that the Kwara'ae freely exchanged the shells during festivals does nothing to show that the shells were scarce.

(B): This doesn't tell us whether porpoise teeth were rare or whether they were used as currency, nor does it deal with the dispute at hand, which is over the cowrie shells.

(C): This presents a useless distinction. It gives us no reason to think that either type of cowrie shell was scarce, so it has nothing to do with explaining the use of the shells as money despite their apparent abundance.

(E): This is testimony to the enduring use of cowrie shells, even when challenged by Western coins of precious metal. Interesting, but no help in explaining why the common cowrie shell could be used as currency in the first place.

▼▼▼

Paraphrase the argument and try to break it down to its simplest form. Economist: Money becomes valuable by being scarce. Anthropologist: But here's a form of money that isn't scarce. When seen in this form, it's easier to resolve the discrepancy. Simply find the choice that shows that the money cited by the anthropologist actually *is* scarce.

Choice (C) is a fairly common wrong answer choice; it introduces a useless distinction, men versus women. It's the type of choice that can delay you while you try to figure out what bearing it has on the question. It doesn't have any bearing on the question; such choices never do. When you have to puzzle over a distinction made in a choice, chances are you should reject that choice.

▲▲▲

14 (B) is correct. A school superintendent (with either his head or his heart in the wrong place) intends to provide the financially disadvantaged with access to the district's best high school. To that end, he has dropped the tuition requirement; the new requirement for entrance is that you live in the neighborhood near the school. This, the superintendent claims, will give disadvantaged kids' parents the option of sending their kids to this school. But it will help disadvantaged kids only if they can meet the *new* criterion—that is, only if they can afford to live in the school's neighborhood (which might be very exclusive) will they have the option of

attending. The superintendent is assuming what is stated in (B): some people who couldn't have afforded the school's tuition can afford to live nearby.

(A): *Au contraire.* Choice (A) is the opposite of his assumption and tends to *weaken* his claim.

(C): Making the less wealthy the majority in the *district* is of no importance; the issue is whether or not less wealthy people can afford to live in the school's neighborhood. But even if we replace the word "district" in this choice with "neighborhood," there's still no reason that the less wealthy parents need to be in the *majority*, as long as some parents who were previously unable to afford this school now have the option.

(D): This isn't only unnecessary to the argument, it's counterintuitive as well. Where could the other kids, the ones who don't live near the high school, or the ones who previously couldn't afford the high school, go to get their high school education?

(E): This doesn't have to be assumed because the superintendent didn't argue that poor parents *will* send their kids to the high school under discussion. He argues only that they will now have the option.

When evaluating a plan or proposal, make very sure that you always concentrate on that proposal's avowed object. In this case, the superintendent wants to give poor families access that they didn't have before. Clearly, he's *assuming* the residency requirement will provide that access, because he offers no evidence supporting this notion.

15 (C) is correct. The Miser costs more than the Scorpio sports car, but if you drive it 60,000 miles, the author claims, the money you'll save on gas makes up for the extra money you paid when you bought the car. Evidently, the Miser gets more miles per gallon than the Scorpio: after 60,000 miles, you'll have bought fewer gallons of gas, and the savings on these gallons will equal your initial extra investment in the purchase price. Here's the flub: the author argues that if fuel prices fall, you'll recover your initial investment *faster*. Actually, the opposite is true; your savings are nothing other than the money you *don't* spend on gas. So the less gas costs, the less you save per mile and thus the *more* you have to drive before you break even.

So we want a choice that also concludes the exact opposite of the truth. That's (C): the Roadmaker costs more initially (as did the Miser); the other model's drawback is that you need to employ more people (the Scorpio sports car required more gas). Choice (C) concludes that when wages are low (that is, where the competing model's drawback is *less* important), the Roadmaker is more advantageous. Not true. The Roadmaker *saves* on wages, so it's especially advantageous compared to the competing model when wages are high, just as the gas-saving Miser is more advantageous when gas is expensive.

(A): This isn't flawed. Since the true rate of earnings is interest minus inflation, you *can* lower interest when inflation drops and still get the same true rate of earnings, provided both drop by the same amount.

(B): This is also reasonable. The Polar uses more electricity (its drawback) but allows one to stock high-profit items (its plus). If the cost of electricity falls, then you can offset the extra cost of electricity with fewer sales of high-profit items. Unlike the stimulus, (B) diminishes the Polar's drawback, not its advantage.

(D): This compares two strains of apples and then recommends always going with the improved strain. Choice (D) lacks the important idea that after some particular time, one product surpasses another. There's also no mention of the improved strain being more advantageous under certain circumstances. But the most blatant difference, which should have helped you to eliminate this one quickly, is the inclusion of a recommendation, an element absent from the original stimulus.

(E): This does the same thing as (D) does—it includes a recommendation—so it's no good for that reason alone. Moreover, the logic is perfectly reasonable, which also eliminates it.

In Parallel Reasoning questions, you don't have to obsess over each answer choice. Scan the choices in search of parallel features and eliminate those that don't conform. Even if you were lost, you could axe (D) and (E) after seeing that they contained recommendations.

Sometimes it helps to take a situation to the extreme to comprehend fully the effect of a particular factor. Assume that gas prices fell so much that gas was free. Then, having eliminated the Miser's economic benefit, there would be no way to make up the difference in price by fuel savings. Having seen this, it's a short leap to the realization that falling fuel prices are detrimental, not advantageous, to the value of the Miser.

16 (B) is correct. Notice anything odd about the two groups mentioned in the first sentence? They don't necessarily overlap! One group includes women with preschool-age children, the other sole-income earners. Does the latter group include women with preschool-age children? Who knows? Maybe all of them have preschool-age children, maybe none. So how can the author subtract one figure from the other and conclude that there are comparatively very few working women who have preschoolers but aren't their families' sole supporters? If there is substantial overlap between the two groups cited, this would be reasonable. Since we don't know of such an overlap, this is unreasonable, and the flaw is pointed out in (B).

(A): This is unreasonable; a figure taken to a decimal point is precise enough. Also, since the conclusion isn't given in precise language ("comparatively few"), it doesn't require precise figures.

(C): The argument deals with the state of affairs now; there's no need to predict the future.

(D): Older children are irrelevant here—plain and simple.

(E): The scope of the argument is working women; there's no need to discuss working men.

Always be on the lookout for scope shifts! Basically, the test makers are trying to put one over on you. Don't let them.

When you prephrase an answer, don't expect to anticipate the phrasing in the choices. You might not have thought in terms of "overlap"; you probably thought: "What's going on here? You can't just subtract one from the other." Only one choice addresses that.

Even if you didn't see the mistake, you could get this question by process of elimination. Choices (D) and (E) are beyond the scope, which extends only to preschoolers and women. Choice (C) brings in time, which isn't in the stimulus. As for (A), the charge of "imprecise" almost never sticks on the LSAT.

17 (A) is correct. A large vocabulary, the author concludes, is a hindrance to using language articulately because people who have large vocabularies don't have to be creative when they want to get an idea across. So the author's evidence is that a large vocabulary inhibits creative self-expression; she concludes that it hinders articulateness. In order to make the leap from creativity to articulateness she must be

assuming that they're pretty much the same. It's the ability to find a way to get your meaning across, even when you don't know the right words, that the author considers to be the sign of the truly articulate, so (A) is assumed.

(B): This isn't needed for the argument. There's no reason why the truly articulate shouldn't also want large vocabularies—even if they do, the argument still stands.

(C): The argument is that people with large vocabularies are unlikely to exercise creativity. There's no need to assume that the most articulate people are those who possess this unlikely combination of a large vocabulary and creativity.

(D): The claim that a large vocabulary is a hindrance to articulateness doesn't require that every new word added to anyone's vocabulary be futile. Vocabulary enhancement up to a point may aid articulateness; the author just feels that after a certain point, it's a hindrance.

(E): This is too strong. Her argument assumes that those with large vocabularies tend not to express themselves *creatively*; there's no need for her to assume that their vocabularies *often* fail them in "unfamiliar situations."

When you're looking for an assumption, you're looking to link the pieces of the argument. Here, the necessary link comes between "articulateness" and "creative self-expression when no words seem adequate." You may think that the author supplied this link, but upon further inspection, you'll see that this connection is missing, which is why the assumption in (A) is required.

18 (A) is correct. Schilling gripes that national health insurance hurts consumers by rationing high-technology treatments. Laforte responds that medical treatment is also restricted where health insurance is private: people without the money for insurance are denied access even to conventional medicine. Both arguments concern consumer access to medicine. Schilling and Laforte would disagree over choice (A), which says that it's less of a violation of people's rights when they are denied treatment because they can't pay (as happens in private health insurance systems) than it is when people are denied treatment for noneconomic reasons (such as the rationing that occurs with nationalized insurance). Schilling rails against the nationalized system because people are denied treatments due to restricted access—that is, denied on noneconomic grounds. He would therefore agree with (A). Laforte, on the other hand, argues against the private system because some people can't afford it, which means that she would disagree with (A).

(B): This is basically the reason Laforte doesn't like private health insurance. Schilling never disputes this; he just feels that it's less of a drawback than the rationing that results from national health insurance.

(C): Laforte would probably disagree with this; according to her, in the private system, many people can't even afford basic conventional medical procedures. However, we can't determine Schilling's stance on this. While he believes private health insurance provides better access to kidney transplants than does national health insurance, we can't infer that he believes that *most* people who would benefit from a kidney transplant actually get one.

(D): Schilling's last sentence indicates that he would disagree with this statement. However, Laforte's position relative to this statement is ambiguous. She argues that under the national system, rich and poor would have *equal access* to procedures and everyone would be granted the right to *decent* medical treatment. But she doesn't counter Schilling's assertion that access to high-tech medicine is restricted in the nationalized system, so we can't conclude that she would believe that no one in countries with nationalized insurance is *ever* denied a familiar life-saving procedure.

(E): This is too vague. Both talk about life-saving procedures, treatments that people *need.* Perhaps both disputants believe there are limits to a person's right to receive *any* treatment he or she wants. We just don't know.

You're looking for a statement on which both speakers must take a definite stand. If you're not sure about either speaker's reaction to the statement, you can toss it out.

In questions in which we have to consider how a speaker would react to a statement, be especially wary of choices containing words such as "no one" (D) and "anyone" (E). Unless *both* speakers expressed themselves in absolute terms, any statement containing such terms is unlikely to be the correct answer.

19 (E) is correct. "Don't talk to me about access," responds Laforte. "In your private system, many people can't even *afford* basic care." Laforte essentially redefines "access" to mean affordability, as opposed to Schilling's notion that "access" means the availability of certain high-tech procedures. So as (E) says, Laforte's response turns on a rejection of Schilling's definition of "access." Laforte attacks Schilling for considering access only for those who need high-tech care; she expands the notion of access and shows that some in private insurance systems completely lack access. Thus, access to care isn't necessarily an advantage of private insurance—it depends on what *sort* of access you're talking about.

(A): Laforte certainly doesn't accuse Schilling of presenting an irrelevant argument; her argument centers on access and patient rights, just as his does.

(B): This has her questioning Schilling's authority, but she never attacks him personally. Her response centers on drawbacks inherent in private health insurance, specifically lack of access to that care.

(C): No, she never produces counterexamples. Instead, she shows that private insurance *also* extracts high costs, costs that she argues are higher than those demanded by national health insurance.

(D): No, Laforte doesn't attack Schilling's use of the word "consumer" by calling it "ambiguous." She simply points out that the realm of consumers includes those who lack insurance in private systems. But Laforte certainly doesn't accuse Schilling of playing with the word.

You might have found (D) tempting, particularly if you found yourself getting involved in the argument. However, notice that Laforte never even uses the word "consumer," so she can hardly be making a subtle criticism of Schilling's ambiguous use of that word.

In two-question stimuli, use your work from the first question to help you answer the second. Question 18 was tough, but the thinking you put into the stimulus and figuring out the correct answer to that first question should have helped you considerably on Question 19.

Notice that Laforte doesn't *counter* Schilling's claim, but rather Laforte redefines a central issue in order to shift the argument her way. Take a second or two to analyze this type of logical manipulation so that you'll recognize it if it appears on your test.

20 (B) is correct. The key to understanding and explaining the somewhat strange and puzzling result is to realize that the ear infection might not be directly caused by the virus. If, as answer choice (B) has it, children with the virus simply become susceptible to an ear infection caused by bacteria, then we would expect antibiotics (which effectively treat bacterial infections) to be able to clear up the ear infection without having any effect on the virus. That would explain the success of the antibiotics nicely.

(A): *No* antibiotics work against this virus, so this information is completely irrelevant. The mystery of why a side effect of an antibiotic-proof virus is cured by antibiotics still remains.

(C) and (E): Both of these answer choices are outside the scope of the argument. We're concerned only with the surprising effect of antibiotics on children *with* ear infections who *have* the virus. Children without ear infections or without the virus are no concern of ours.

(D): This offers up an irrelevant comparison and is no help in explaining why the middle ear infection is vulnerable to antibiotics when the viral infection isn't.

You're asked to explain the success of the antibiotics. This should send you looking for information about antibiotics. The *only* thing said is that they *can* cure bacterial infections but *can't* cure the virus. So the answer will have to connect the ear infection with bacteria.

This question offers another chance to study the concept of cause-and-effect. The result seems surprising only if we assume that the virus *directly* causes the middle-ear infection. The situation makes more sense once we allow for the possibility of (B)—that the virus *indirectly* causes the ear infection by making the child vulnerable to bacteria.

21 (C) is correct. When it was thought that South Island tuatara were the same species as those found on North Island, the naturalist saw no reason to protect them, even though they were approaching extinction. (After all, there would still be tuataras on North Island.) But now that it has been discovered that the South Island tuatara are a unique species, the naturalist feels we must save them from extinction, even if it means slaughtering their predators. What principle would justify this change of heart? Choice (C), which boils down to this: if a species is being wiped out only in a given area, there's no obligation to save it, but if a species is to be *completely* wiped out, then we must save it.

(A): If she were guided by this principle, the naturalist would have wanted to protect South Island tuatara even before she knew they were a different species.

(B): This speaks of individual animals rather than species. Secondly, it would grant equal rights to tuatara predators, which the naturalist is ready to kill.

(D): There's no hint that human activity is responsible for the declining numbers of South Island tuatara. The naturalist's remedy points to animal predators as a source of danger.

(E): This enjoins us to protect South Island tuatara now that we know they are a separate species, but doesn't justify the idea that when they weren't considered a unique species, it was okay to let them die. Moreover, (E) doesn't mention an "obligation" to save the tuatara, mentioning instead that we should give them "care and attention."

The principle has to justify the *whole* argument, including the naturalist's original idea that it was all right to let the South Island tuatara become extinct. On the LSAT, the correct principle fits *perfectly*.

Be ruthless. Throw out a choice as soon as it fails. (A): "In order to maximize the number of living things on Earth. . . ."

OUT! (B): "When an animal is in danger of dying. . . ." OUT! The perfect principle is there, so don't waste time with these losers.

22 (E) is correct. This Formal Logic stimulus is made up of a string of conditional statements. Nursing schools can't attract more able applicants unless two problems are solved (low wages and bad conditions). It stands to reason, then, that if these two problems are *not* solved, as posited in correct choice (E), then the schools will *not* attract a greater number of able applicants. Add that to what follows. If the applicant pool doesn't increase (and we just saw that in choice (E) it doesn't), then either one of two things will happen: admissions standards will be lowered or there will be a shortage of nurses. Finally, we're told that if either one of *these* things happens (as must be the case according to (E)), then the current high quality of health care cannot be maintained. It takes a few steps, but (E) is inferable from the stimulus.

(A) and (C): These both confuse the necessary condition in the first sentence for a sufficient one. Choice (A) interprets the statement that the number of applicants will not increase unless the problems are solved to mean, "If the problems are solved, the number of able applicants *will* increase." Choice (C) takes it one step further to guarantee the maintenance of high quality health care.

(B) and (D): Both of these fail on the grounds that a nonincrease in applicants can mean *either* a lowering of standards *or* a shortage of nurses. For (B), no increase doesn't necessarily mean lower standards; it could mean a shortage. In (D), failing to solve the problems will prevent an increase, but this need not lead to a shortage—it could lead to lower standards only.

When faced with a string of Formal Logic statements, try to simplify things by paraphrasing. The argument boils down to "either they fix these problems or their applicant level won't increase." The rest tells us the consequences of this state of affairs.

It's difficult to prephrase answers in many Inference questions, so often you'll simply have to test out the choices.

As always, pay attention to the difference between statements that denote *necessity* and those that denote *sufficiency*. The first sentence, correctly interpreted, tells us that it's *necessary* to solve the problems in order to attract a greater number of applicants; this is how we interpret the word "unless." This doesn't mean that simply solving the problems is *sufficient*, or will guarantee a greater number of applicants.

23 (D) is correct. The right answer here is fairly intuitive, even straightforward. The tricky thing, as always, is wading through the wrong choices without getting distracted and seduced by an impostor. Microwave popcorn accounts for over half of the revenues derived from sales of all microwave food products. Microwave popcorn cooks in three minutes or less. Put two and two together, and presto: more money is spent on microwaveable food that prepares in three minutes or less than is spent on microwaveable food that takes more time than that. Stated another way: since microwave popcorn alone accounts for a majority of the money spent on microwaveable food, and since the microwave popcorn prepares in three minutes or less, (D) must be true.

(A): We're given no information about the relative market share of the different brands of popcorn, so we can't infer (A). For all we know, one particular brand of microwave popcorn accounts for the lion's share of microwave popcorn sales, and by extension captures a large share of total microwave food sales.

(B): Nothing allows us to infer this; there could be 1,000 brands of microwave soup.

(C): The stimulus compares the two types of popcorn in terms of cost and preparation time, but never in terms of actual sales by volume.

(E): No. Popcorn accounts for a majority of the *dollars* spent on microwaveable foods, but popcorn needn't represent a majority of all microwave food products.

Don't be surprised if the correct inference is based on a combination of a couple of facts (the first and second sentences here) rather than on the whole stimulus. The cost and the popularity issues in the last two sentences aren't necessary to infer correct choice (D), but they do serve as fodder for the wrong choices.

Many wrong choices ask you to make false comparisons. Choices (B) and (E) make the mistake of comparing actual numbers of products whereas the stimulus compared *money* from sales, and (C) compares volume sales whereas the stimulus compared only preparation time and volume cost. Be wary of such false comparisons; make sure the things compared in answer choices actually are connected in the stimulus.

24 (B) is correct. The author concludes in the last sentence that people are willing to pay more for the convenience of microwave popcorn—presumably, the faster popping time compared to conventional popcorn. But once again, we see an author overlooking the possibility of other factors. If, as (B) has it, most people buy microwave popcorn because it's less fattening, then it's not necessarily true that they're willing to pay more money for the convenience of having their popcorn quickly. They might pay the premium price only to avoid the fat in conventional popcorn.

(A): So what? Even if fewer than 50 percent of consumers buy microwave popcorn, that could still amount to plenty of people, and the conclusion is stated in terms of "*many* people."

(C): The reason microwave popcorn costs so much is irrelevant; the point is that many people pay that extra cost, and the issue to be addressed is why they do so.

(D): We've seen irrelevant distinctions in wrong answer choices; here we have an irrelevant similarity. But what does this do to weaken the claim in the last sentence? Nothing. (If we were told that conventional popcorn results in five times as many unpopped kernels compared to microwave popcorn, then we would have a possible weakener—but even then only as long as we assume that consumers don't like unpopped kernels.)

(E): This tells us that microwave popcorn differs from conventional popcorn in that it contains additives, but instead of going on to tell us that people want the additives, it merely tells us that microwave corn is heavier. Is this heaviness attractive to consumers? Will they pay more for it? We have no idea.

Once again an argument is weakened through the alternative explanation. The author explains consumer willingness to pay for microwave popcorn as a desire for convenience. (B) provides an alternative explanation: the desire to avoid fat.

25 (E) is correct. The situation in the stimulus is one in which a program works against itself. Choice (E) describes the same sort of program. A toll is placed on a bridge to get drivers to use another route. The money from the toll is then

saved to build another bridge. The more they discourage drivers from using the original bridge—the first goal—the less money they raise for the new bridge—the second goal. Just like the situation in the stimulus, the two halves of the project work against each other.

(A): The two halves work towards the same end, reducing overdue books. The more successful the program is in reaching its first goal, the easier it will be to meet the second, because although there will be fewer resources to meet the second goal (reminding tardy borrowers), fewer resources will be required (there will be fewer tardy borrowers).

(B): Again, no conflict between goals: the fewer the number of customers who pay the surcharge, the less money will be required from the surcharge. The surcharge is just a way of passing on costs to the consumer.

(C): The money from the fee isn't earmarked for anything; there's no second, conflicting goal. Moreover, the admission fee isn't intended to dissuade people from using the park.

(D): Same as above: the service charge isn't designed to deter business and, since the money is split among the staff, there's no conflicting program.

Despite the form, this is very much like a Parallel Reasoning question; for the analysis to be appropriate to both situations, the situations must be parallel. In fact, think of this as a Parallel Reasoning question in which the test makers do half of your work for you by analyzing the stimulus.

Always read the question stem first! This stem, which focuses solely on the analysis, hints that you could answer the question without reading the situation at all. Just paraphrase the analysis and then look for a program that works against itself.

Don't panic if and when you come across an unfamiliar or slightly unconventional question type. All LSAT Logical Reasoning questions require basically the same skills. Just take the time to understand the question stem, and then apply Kaplan's tried-and-true methods of evaluating arguments and answer choices.

Section IV: Reading Comprehension

Passage 1: Foreign Investors (Questions 1–8)

Topic and Scope

The topic is the concept of administrative contracts—specifically, flaws in the argument of those who hold that the concept of administrative contracts allows governments to alter contracts unilaterally.

Purpose and Main Idea

The author's purpose is to point out holes in the argument of those who believe that the concept of administrative contracts gives governments the right to alter contracts unilaterally. The author's specific main idea is that, contrary to the opinion of some legal theorists, the concept of administrative contracts does not give governments that right, and this particular concept does not qualify as a "general principle of law."

Paragraph Structure

Paragraph 1 begins with a lot of details about contracts between the governments of developing countries and foreign investors. Not until line 19 does the passage get down to specifics. Lines 19–27 indicate that some legal theorists hold that (1) governments have the right to change the terms of such contracts unilaterally, and (2) this right constitutes a "general principle of law." In lines 28–29, the author's voice finally enters the picture: he argues that this view is flawed on two counts.

Based on lines 28–29, it's predictable that paragraphs 2 and 3 will discuss these flaws in some depth. That's precisely what happens. Paragraph 2 essentially says that the concept of administrative contracts doesn't give governments the right to change contracts to their benefit whenever they feel like it. Paragraph 3, on the other hand, notes that the concept of administrative contracts isn't a "general principle of law." In the United States and Great Britain, for example, if the government wants the right to alter a contract unilaterally, a provision to this effect must be written into the contract itself.

The Big Picture

A passage like this one is not a good place to begin work on the day of the test. The author's purpose isn't evident until lines 28–29—that is, until halfway through the text. On the day of the test, start with a passage in which topic, scope, and *purpose* are clear early on, certainly by the end of the first third of the text.

This passage is a prime example of one in which it's vital to know what the author's *thinking* and *doing* rather than what the text is *saying*. Don't worry about assimilating all of the details—that's not important. What is important is realizing that an argument is outlined (lines 19–27); that the author disagrees with this argument for two reasons (line 28–29); and that these two reasons are then described in paragraphs 2 and 3, respectively.

The Questions

1 (A) is correct. This answer choice very nicely captures the author's purpose as revealed to us in lines 28–29.

(B): This is beyond the scope of the text. What solution? What problem?

(C): The author doesn't offer any "new explanation." He simply marshals evidence to rebut an argument with which he's not in agreement.

(D): This, too, is beyond the scope of the text. What "course of action" does the author supposedly analyze?

(E): Again, what problem? The author's just countering an argument; he's not out to solve any problem.

Don't be thrown by choices phrased in abstract language. In Global questions, always look for the choice that's consistent with the passage's topic, scope, and purpose, however it's phrased.

2 (D) is correct. In paragraphs 2 and 3, the author contends that "general principles of law" don't give governments the right to alter contracts unilaterally.

(A): This is beyond the scope of the text. The author isn't concerned with the "special needs and interests of developing countries" per se. He's interested in the legal relationship between governments and investors in general.

(B): This is also beyond the scope of the text. The passage provides no information about when these principles were first used to settle disputes.

(C): This distorts the text. Paragraph 3 makes it clear that American and British law are more akin to each other than to French law.

(E): The author doesn't take issue with the "general principles of law" themselves. He simply argues that what some consider a general principle of law—the concept of administrative contracts as described in the passage—is not in fact a general principle of law.

In Inference questions, the correct answer will always be close to the spirit of the text. So, make sure you don't stray too far from the text when endorsing any particular answer choice.

3 (D) is correct. In lines 7–11, the author says that an "additional risk" (that is, a risk on top of "normal economic risk") faced by foreign investors that enter into economic development agreements with governments is that some governments may try to alter unilaterally the agreements' original terms to the detriment of foreign investors. That's why some governments, the author notes in lines 11–19, have made these agreements "more attractive" to foreign investors by, in effect, telling investors that they (the governments) won't try to change unilaterally the terms of agreements.

(A): The author never discusses the extent to which either governments or foreign investors benefit from such agreements.

(B): This draws a bogus distinction between the American and British legal systems. Indeed, the text doesn't allude to any differences between these legal systems.

(C): The passage doesn't give any indication that economic development agreements have become more numerous of late, even though it does say that some governments have recently tried to make them more appealing to foreign investors.

(E): Since some governments have tried to make economic development agreements more palatable to foreign investors, chances are that they've become more, not less, attractive to those investors. But there's no hard information in the passage one way or the other.

Any choice that refers to an issue that isn't discussed in the text is wrong. Period.

4 (E) is correct. In lines 36–39, the author notes that contracts designated by French government agencies as administrative contracts include "certain items not found in private civil contracts."

(A): Lines 39–44 reveal that government agencies are only required to pay unanticipated costs if these costs result from a unilateral change in the contract made by the government.

(B): *Au contraire.* If anything, administrative contracts generally provide contractors with fewer guarantees than private civil contracts.

(C): This distorts info in paragraph 2, which says that there are two ways that an administrative contract can be created in France: (1) by statute or (2) through the initiative of a government agency.

(D): The passage says nothing about foreigners being discouraged from bidding on French contracts. What the passage does imply is that some foreigners have been concerned about entering into contracts with governments in developing countries.

Never answer an Explicit Text question on a hunch or a vague recollection of the text. Always go back and reread the relevant piece(s) of text.

5 (E) is correct. Lines 54–56 explicitly state that, under the ordinary law of contracts, governments can unilaterally change the terms of an agreement only if a provision allowing unilateral change is incorporated into the original agreement itself.

(A), (B), and (C): Paragraph 3, the only one that discusses the ordinary law of contracts, doesn't refer to government economic risks (A), costs to foreign investors (B), or increased financial burden to investors (C). Moreover, (A) and (C) distort details from the wrong paragraphs—paragraphs 1 and 2, respectively.

(D): The passage draws no connection between the ordinary law of contracts and "the general principles of law recognized by civilized nations" (mentioned in paragraph 1).

The answer to a question that contains a line reference will be in the lines around the reference. Don't stray too far from the actual line reference when endorsing an answer choice.

6 (C) is correct. In lines 48–51, the author contends that the concept of administrative contracts is not a "general principle of law." He then proceeds to show that contracts in both America and Britain are governed by the ordinary law of contracts in order to support his point with evidence.

(A): *Au contraire.* American and British contract law doesn't allow a government to "reserve the right to modify unilaterally contracts that [it] enter[s] into. . . ." If the government desires this right, it must be explicitly written into the terms of the contract itself.

(B): This is too broad an assertion. While the author does argue that the concept of administrative contracts isn't a "general principle of law," he doesn't conclude that there is *no* general principle of law that governs contracts between governments and private individuals.

(D): If anything, the author is a critic of the concept of administrative contracts. He certainly can't be considered a champion of this notion.

(E): This answer choice is inconsistent with the entire thrust of paragraph 3, which suggests that, under the ordinary law of contracts, government contracts are absolutely no different than private contracts. In fact, answer choice (E) plays on a detail in paragraph 2, which is the wrong paragraph.

It's less important to know the substance of details than to know *why* the author has included them in the text.

7 (D) is correct. This is the only choice that captures the author's topic, scope, and purpose.

(A) and (E): These are beyond the scope of the text. This passage is restricted to a discussion of the concept of administrative contracts as a general principle of law; it's not about the much broader notion of "general principles of law."

(B): This focuses on a detail in paragraphs 2 and 3; it's not the author's main idea.

(C): The only point that the passage makes on this score is that *two* nations—the United States and the United Kingdom—apply ordinary contract law to government contracts.

The correct answer to a Global question must always reflect the author's topic, scope, and purpose.

8 (A) is correct. In lines 57–62, the author argues that "termination or modification clauses" in contracts are proof that government has no *inherent* right to change unilaterally the terms of a contract to which it is a party. If such clauses, however, were a mere acknowledgment of an inherent government right, and had no legal standing of their own, the author's reasoning would be undercut.

(B), (C), (D), and (E): These bring up issues that are not relevant to the author's point about the *lack of an inherent government right* to terminate or modify contracts.

In Strengthen/Weaken the Argument questions, the correct choice must contain a direct reference to the issue brought up in the question stem. Any choice that refers to a different issue is wrong.

Passage 2: Frijda's Law (Questions 9–15)

Topic and Scope

The topic is Frijda's "law of apparent reality"—specifically, the law's inability to account for emotional responses to works of art.

Purpose and Main Idea

The author's purpose is to demonstrate that Frijda's law of apparent reality doesn't account for the full range of human emotional responses; the author's specific main idea is that Frijda's law fails to explain emotional responses to works of art.

Paragraph Structure

Paragraph 1 describes Frijda's law, and provides us with the author's belief that, although it seems plausible, it can't account for emotions brought on by experiences that aren't "appraised as real," such as the emotions brought on by viewing works of art. Paragraph 2 goes into detail about the difference between genuine and contrived experiences, and again points out that Frijda's law can't account for emotional responses caused by the latter type of experience.

Paragraph 3 summarizes the views of other psychologists on the issue of human emotional responses to contrived, or "aesthetic," experiences, and notes that Frijda's law doesn't help to clarify these views. Paragraph 4 describes Frijda's unsatisfactory attempt to cover up that problem by claiming that human imagination turns contrived experiences into genuine ones.

The Big Picture

All of the psychological jargon might have made this passage look difficult, but it really isn't. In fact, it would have been a reasonable place to begin work on the day of the test. Why? Because the author's purpose—to take issue with Frijda's law—is readily apparent early on, from line 6.

Don't let complex language throw you. A simple idea always lies underneath all of the jargon. That's the case here—the important point for you to pick up on is that Frijda's law can't account for all human emotion.

The Questions

9 (C) is correct. This choice nicely encompasses the author's topic, scope, and purpose.

(A): What's the "emotional nature of belief?" This concept isn't discussed in the text.

(B): "Theories of aesthetic response" are discussed in paragraph 3; they aren't the main focus of the author.

(D): The supposedly "changeable nature of emotional responses to art" is never discussed.

(E): This incorrectly expands a detail in paragraph 3 into the main idea. What's important to the author is not what distinguishes "aesthetic from nonaesthetic emotional responses." It's that Frijda's law can't account for emotional responses to aesthetic experiences.

Don't be taken in by choices that use jargon like that used in the passage. Read each choice carefully before choosing one.

10 (C) is correct. Lines 4–6 explicitly state that, according to Frijda's law, "the intensity of . . . emotions corresponds to the degree to which . . . events are appraised as real."

(A): Frijda never says that emotional responses are "unpredictable." He argues that the *intensity* of these responses is affected by the perception of how real events are.

(B): *Au contraire.* Based on the snake/garden hose example, the emotional response should be more intense if a person is unable to distinguish between illusion and reality.

(D) and (E): These are opposite sides of the same counterfeit coin. Both imply that Frijda's law is only about the emotion of fear. But it isn't restricted to fear; it says that the more a person perceives an event to be real, the more intense will be the emotion triggered by that event.

If you didn't reread the exact definition of Frijda's law, all of these choices might have looked tempting. Rereading is often a helpful way to eliminate choices that are wrong for subtle reasons.

11 (C) is correct. This choice nicely paraphrases lines 55–58. The keyword "however" (line 55) signals that the author's about to disagree with Frijda's conclusion.

(A): This misrepresents Scruton's argument. Scruton (with whom the author agrees) says that people are aware that they're using their imaginations when experiencing art. In other words, Frijda ignores the *self-conscious* aspect of the emotional response to art.

(B) and (E): These play on details in paragraph 3, which is the wrong paragraph. Choice (B)'s mention of genuine versus ersatz emotion echoes a distinction made by Gombrich, while (E)'s mention of real versus illusory stimuli plays on Radford's idea.

(D): Frijda never makes any distinction between vivid and weak imaginations.

In passages that contain the views of many individuals, make sure that you know who stands for what.

12 (B) is correct. Lines 32–36 claim that most psychologists believe that aesthetic experiences do generate genuine emotions. dissents from this position (lines 38–41), but Radford endorses it (lines 41–44). Hence, (B) is a false statement.

(A): Gombrich stresses the artificial, not irrational, nature of emotional responses to aesthetic experiences; Radford stresses the genuine but irrational nature of those emotional responses.

(C) and (E): Gombrich does indeed argue that emotional responses to aesthetic experiences are ersatz (or artificial), while Radford argues that these emotional responses are genuine.

(D): According to Gombrich, aesthetic experiences "trigger remembrances of previously experienced emotions," while Radford has nothing to say about memory.

In "All . . . EXCEPT" questions, you're generally asked to look for the answer choice that *isn't* true.

13 (E) is correct. Lines 9–13 demonstrate how Frijda's law accounts for emotional responses to events that are either real or perceived as such. Lines 13–26, in contrast, show that Frijda's law can't account for emotional responses to events that are contrived. Lines 27–31 summarize the inability of Frijda's law to account for all emotional responses.

(A): Not a chance. The issue of "irrationality of emotional response" doesn't even come up until paragraph 3.

(B): This misses the point of paragraph 2, which is to show that Frijda's law fails to account for some emotional responses—those caused by depicted events.

(C): This contradicts the author's opinion that emotional responses to depicted events may be just as strong as emotional responses to real events. Besides, the author's *challenging*, not illustrating, Frijda's law.

(D): This plays on a detail in the second paragraph. The author isn't conducting an inquiry into the nature of panic, but rather portraying the inability of Frijda's law to account for all emotional responses.

It's always a good idea to prephrase an answer to a question that asks about the author's purpose. Think about what the author's trying to do in the passage and then search for the answer that addresses the author's intent.

14 (B) is correct. In lines 13–21, the author argues that emotional responses to movies about imaginary things might be just as intense as emotional responses to movies about real things.

(A): In lines 18–21, the author says that a movie about ghosts might be terrifying even to those who don't believe in ghosts.

(C): In lines 13–21, the author insists that people might be terrified by things that they know aren't real, such as the appearance of ghosts or snakes in movies.

(D): Far from saying that movies permanently alter perceptions of reality, the author implies the opposite, indicating that viewers who enter the theater rejecting the possibility of ghosts don't emerge believing in them.

(E): According to the author, a movie's ability to generate an emotional response in viewers has nothing to do with whether the object shown in the movie actually exists. It's the movie itself that creates the emotional response.

This "All . . . EXCEPT" question is unusual in that you're asked to find the *true* statement. Always read the question stem very carefully to make sure that you're absolutely clear about what it's asking for.

15 (D) is correct. In lines 41–46, Radford argues that emotional responses to art are irrational. Choice (D) outlines a scenario that conforms to his view—a person has an "irrational" emotional response to a work of art, a novel.

(A): This depicts the wrong kind of irrationality—one that results from an inability to differentiate between reality and make-believe. In Radford's world, irrationality occurs when people have an emotional response to something that they know is unreal.

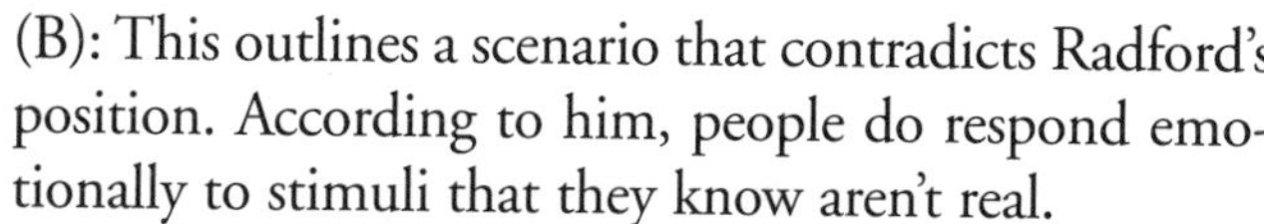

(B): This outlines a scenario that contradicts Radford's position. According to him, people do respond emotionally to stimuli that they know aren't real.

(C): Radford's position, so far as the text is concerned, applies only to people who respond to art, not to people who actually create it.

(E): This scenario doesn't even contain a work of art. Moreover, it incorporates an element of confusion, which isn't part of Radford's position.

In questions like this one, your task is to find the concrete scenario that's analogous to an abstract concept discussed in the text.

Passage 3: Behavior of Bacteria (Questions 16–21)

Topic and Scope

The topic is the movement of bacteria—specifically, the movement of bacteria toward attractants.

Purpose and Main Idea

The author's purpose is to discuss what scientists know about the process by which bacteria move toward attractants. Since this passage is a descriptive one, the author doesn't have a particular main idea in mind.

Paragraph Structure

Paragraph 1 outlines the topic and scope of the passage: how are bacteria able to overcome their seemingly haphazard swimming pattern—a mix of straight runs and uncontrolled tumbles—to move toward attractants? Paragraph 2 begins to answer this question by noting that bacteria have been observed to move along a concentration gradient toward attractants—in other words, to move in a nonrandom fashion. While this paragraph describes the swimming pattern by which bacteria move toward concentrations of attractants, it doesn't explain how bacteria detect concentrations of attractants in order to be able to move toward them.

Paragraph 3 takes up the latter issue. There are two possible methods of detection, both of which are discussed in some detail. The last sentence of the passage concludes that scientists believe that bacteria detect changes in the concentration gradient of attractants by measuring concentrations at different points in time, rather than by measuring concentrations along different parts of their bodies at the same point in time.

The Big Picture

In passages that are built around a relationship, be sure that you're absolutely clear about the nature of the relationship. The questions will certainly focus on it.

Although this science passage isn't especially difficult—all you really have to grasp is the basic relationship between the movement of bacteria and the concentration of attractants—you should probably have left it for later in the section. The author's descriptive purpose isn't entirely clear until you've read the whole thing.

The Questions

16 (B) is correct. Lines 51–57 state that if bacteria detect concentration gradients by measuring concentration simultaneously at different points along their bodies, they wouldn't respond to a sudden jump in concentration because the concentration along different parts of their bodies would be uniform. Choice (B) reflects this scenario.

(A) and (C): Under the conditions stipulated in the question stem, the bacteria shouldn't respond *at all.*

(D): Bacteria tumble less, not more, when they detect higher concentrations of an attractant.

(E): Bacteria tumble more, not less, when they detect lower concentrations of an attractant.

Choice (B) should have been relatively easy to choose if you picked up on the distinction drawn in paragraph 3.

17 (E) is correct. In order to move away from a harmful substance, a bacterium would react in a way that's the opposite of the way that it would react toward an attractant. It would tumble more and make fewer straight runs as the concentration of the harmful substance increased, and it would tumble less and make more straight runs as the concentration of a harmful substance decreased.

(A): This has the bacterium moving fast, but in an uncalculated manner. This pattern of movement wouldn't necessarily increase its likelihood of getting away from a harmful substance.

(B): What if a high concentration of an attractant were to be located in the same area as a high concentration of a harmful substance? There's no guarantee that moving towards an attractant will get a bacterium out of harm's way.

(C): How a bacterium measures concentration changes in substances is not relevant to the problem of moving away from a harmful substance.

(D): If a bacterium ceased tumbling when it detected increased concentrations of a harmful substance, then it would make long, straight runs toward that substance. And that, of course, would not get the bacterium out of harm's way.

It's a very good idea to prephrase answers to questions that test your knowledge of a relationship. If your prephrased answer appears among the choices, you've probably got the relationship straight. If it doesn't, you can go back and rethink the relationship.

18 (E) is correct. A definition of the phrase "swimming up a concentration gradient" appears in lines 39–41. This phrase means that bacteria move from an area where the concentration of a substance is lower to an area where it is higher.

(A): This is beyond the scope of the text. The passage never refers to a "resistant medium."

(B): *Au contraire.* Swimming up a concentration gradient means swimming toward a substance to which bacteria are attracted.

(C) and (D): Swimming up a gradient means swimming toward a substance, not away from it. Nothing in the passage indicates that moving toward an attractant is equivalent to moving away from a harmful substance.

In questions that ask you to figure out the meaning of a word or a phrase in the context of the passage, watch out for choices that are opposite of the correct one.

19 (C) is correct. Bacterial motion is discussed in paragraph 2, where it's stated that the proportion of tumbling to straight runs is determined by relative concentrations of an attractant.

(A), (B), (D), and (E): These are all beyond the scope of the text. The passage says nothing about *different kinds* of chemical attractants (A); about how a bacterium determines the presence (as opposed to the concentration) of an attractant (B); about whether neighboring bacteria affect a bacterium's movement (D); or about "changes" in time intervals between measurements of an attractant's concentration (E).

Use your mental road map of the passage to relocate the information that is relevant to the issue about which the question stem asks.

20 (B) is correct. Lines 33–45 describe two possible methods that bacteria use to detect concentrations of attractants. Lines 45–57 describe an experiment to determine which of the two is more likely. Lines 57–59 point out that one of the two is indeed more likely on the basis of experimental evidence. Choice (B) captures this paragraph structure.

(A): Paragraph 3 doesn't concern itself with the relative efficiency of two methods, but rather with determining which of the two is more likely in use.

(C): Paragraph 3 doesn't point out any inherent flaws. Moreover, the experimental evidence merely "suggests" that one hypothesis is more accurate; confirmation is too strong a sentiment.

(D): Paragraph 3 never asserts that bacteria use two methods to detect concentrations of attractants. It simply notes that scientists have come up with two *hypotheses* about how they detect those concentrations.

(E): This gets the paragraph's structure wrong; the conclusion comes after the evidence, not before it. Besides, like (A), this choice wrongly harps on the theme of relative efficiency.

When you're asked about the organization of a paragraph, it's important to be aware not only of its structure, but also of its content and tone.

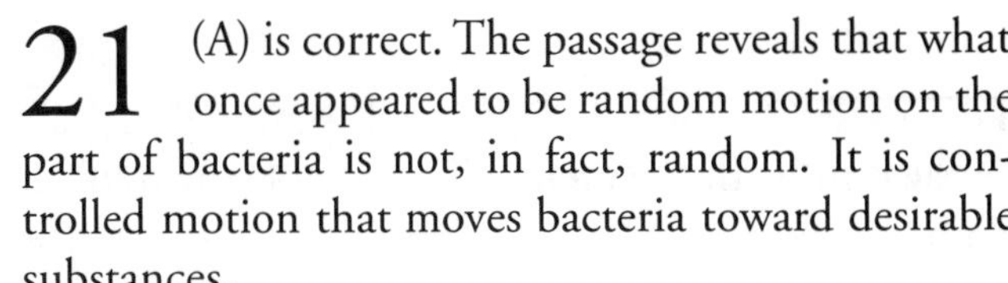

21 (A) is correct. The passage reveals that what once appeared to be random motion on the part of bacteria is not, in fact, random. It is controlled motion that moves bacteria toward desirable substances.

(B): This is beyond the scope of the text. The passage is confined to a discussion of bacteria only, not simple organisms in general. Furthermore, the passage focuses on bacterial motion, not bacterial "complexity."

(C): This is an *au contraire* choice. Lines 57–59 say that "evidence suggests that bacteria compare concentrations [of attractants] at different times." This statement implies that bacteria do retain memories.

(D): This is also *au contraire.* The thrust of the passage is that bacteria now appear to have *more* control than was previously thought.

(E): The passage never compares photosynthetic and nonphotosynthetic bacteria in terms of control over movement.

Even if you're convinced that (A) is correct, check the other choices just to be sure that you're not missing an even better choice.

Passage 4: Life Passage Versus Life History (Questions 22–27)

Topic and Scope

The topic is life-passage and life-history studies—specifically, a comparison of the two types of study.

Purpose and Main Idea

The author's purpose is to compare life-passage and life-history studies; the author's specific main idea is that the differences between them are evident when analyzing the life-passage and life-history studies of Native American women.

Paragraph Structure

The passage's topic, scope, and purpose are all revealed in its first sentence. The rest of paragraph 1 simply goes on to highlight the basic difference between life-passage and life-history studies: the former focuses on the group, while the latter focuses on the individual.

Paragraph 2 describes a typical life-passage study—that by anthropologist Truman Michelson. At the end of this paragraph, the author makes the point that life-passage studies usually emerge when outside recorder-editors such as Michelson prepare the actual studies. In contrast, as paragraph 3 shows, Maria Campbell's study is a life-history study precisely because it's an autobiographical work that relates the experiences of the writer.

The Big Picture

This passage illustrates the importance of previewing the entire section before plunging into it. This passage is the easiest of the lot, and therefore the best place to begin work on the section. But you wouldn't have known that without previewing.

Passages that are based on a comparison—between two theories, two scenarios, two types of study, whatever—are common on the LSAT. Most tests, in fact, have at least one passage of this type. If you run into a comparison passage on the day of the test, make sure that you're clear on the difference between the entities being compared. The questions will surely test to see whether you've grasped the difference.

The Questions

22 (C) is correct. This choice is the only one that encompasses the passage's topic, scope, and purpose.

(A): While the passage distinguishes between life-passage and life-history studies, it never suggests that the latter have rendered the former obsolete.

(B): This is a "half-right, half-wrong" choice. True, life-passage and life-history studies take different approaches to the study of culture, but they don't have similar goals. The former focuses on the group, while the latter focuses on the individual.

(D): The passage never implies that Campbell's study has been influenced by Michelson's. Besides, the text's main idea has nothing to do with the notion of literary influences.

(E): The main idea of the passage isn't to argue that one type of study is superior to the other in providing a certain kind of information, but rather to illustrate what sort of information each type of study provides.

In Global questions, wrong answers are often wrong for subtle reasons. Read each choice *fully* and *carefully* before endorsing any of them.

23 (E) is correct. The first few sentences of paragraph 2 describe the contents of a life-passage study, which, you'll recall, focuses on the group. In this context, then, the term "prescribed roles" refers to the roles that individuals adopt in order to conform to group norms.

(A): "Prescribed roles" refers to the roles played by the subjects of life-passage studies, not to an academic function of the studies themselves.

(B): "Prescribed roles" comes up in the context of a discussion of life-passage studies, not life-history studies.

(C): Life-passage studies focus on how the individual fits into the group, not on the individual him- or herself.

(D): This tempts you by picking up on information from the wrong part of the passage—the end of paragraph 2. "Prescribed roles" refers to the mandated roles played by the subjects of life-passage studies, not to the roles played by narrator and recorder.

When a question asks about the meaning of a word or a phrase, the immediate context in which that word or phrase appears will generally clue you in to the correct answer.

24 (B) is correct. In stating that Michelson's life-passage study "presents little of the central character's psychological motivation" (lines 29–30), the author is making the point that life-passage studies aren't concerned with individuals per se. In other words, the author identifies something that isn't "a major focus of life-passage studies."

(A): The phrase in question refers to a life-passage study, not a life-history study. Furthermore, the author maintains that life-history studies are built around a "personal perspective."

(C): As with choice (A), this choice confuses life-passage and life-history studies. Life-passage studies aren't autobiographical in nature; they are the products of second parties who are interested in relating how societies socialize particular individuals.

(D): This misrepresents the author's purpose in using the phrase in question. "Psychological motivation" refers to the impersonal nature of life-passage studies, not to an alleged conflict between "narrator" and "recorder."

(E): This goes too far. While the author acknowledges that life-passage studies ignore the individual's feelings and perceptions, he doesn't argue that personal views must be discounted if scholarship is to be "objective."

In questions that ask about the *why* of a detail—that is, why the author has included it in the text—read the lines around the detail to get a sense of the context in which it appears.

25 (E) is correct. Paragraph 3 says that, although Campbell's account is a life-history study that concentrates on her own life, the work also reveals much about Native American women, the Metis people, and ethnic relations in Canada. So, "her life history provides more than a record of her personal experience."

(A): Nothing in paragraph 3 suggests either that Campbell was familiar with the *early history* of her people or that she lacked insight into the motives of non–Native Americans.

(B): The passage doesn't say or suggest whether she was familiar with Michelson's work. Nor does it say or suggest whether she had read other Native American life-passage studies.

(C): Paragraph 3 doesn't indicate that Campbell had been trained as a historian. If anything, it creates the impression that she had no formal academic qualifications.

(D): Although the passage says that Campbell wrote about her family, the text doesn't indicate whether (or to what extent) she was influenced by her family. On the other hand, the passage does indicate that Campbell was heavily influenced by the time in which she lived.

Don't be taken in by choices that use the passage's language but distort its ideas. Be on the lookout for these. This wrong answer type is commonly found in Inference questions.

26 (C) is correct. One of the essential differences between life-history and life-passage studies is that the former are made up of autobiographical accounts while the latter are products of "recorder-editors."

(A): This is beyond the scope of the text, which says nothing about the languages in which either life-study or life-history passages are generally written.

(B) and (D): The purpose of the text is to highlight differences between the two types of study, not to rank them in terms of reliability (B) or creativity (D).

(E): The passage never distinguishes between the historian's and the ethnographer's point of view. Besides, life-history studies are personal accounts, and so would not generally be the work of professional historians.

Knowing the gist of each paragraph would have helped with this question. Choice (C) is confirmed at the end of paragraph 2.

27 (C) is correct. One of the basic differences between life-passage and life-history studies is that the former focus on the collective while the latter concentrate on the individual. A study of the way a military organization maintains discipline is analogous to a life-passage study in the sense that it focuses on the collective, while a newly enlisted soldier's narrative about his military experience is analogous to a life-history study in the sense that it concentrates on the individual.

(A), (B), and (E): All of these choices miss the collective-individual distinction. Each pair in these choices focuses on collectives: society and a religious group (A); pre- and postindustrial society (B); and leaders and parties and the electorate (E).

(D): An analysis of society's *means* of subsistence focuses on neither the group nor the individual.

If you don't see a parallel between the text and one of the hypothetical scenarios in the answer choices, eliminate the choices that are similar to *each other* and then guess.

Ten Things You Can Do *Right Now* to Boost Your Chances of Admission to Law School

1. **Do some law-related volunteer work.**

   There's no better way to show the admissions officers that you're serious about the law, and that public service is a priority with you.

2. **Come up with a "theme" for your application.**

   Your application is, in one sense, a marketing tool for yourself. How do you want to be marketed? Who are you? What are you all about? A theme will give your application coherence—and make it stand out.

3. **Familiarize yourself with the LSAT.**

   The LSAT isn't a normal test. If you're unfamiliar with it, you won't do as well as you should. Prep seriously for the test. And begin now.

4. **Send for catalogs and applications.**

   To plan an effective admissions campaign, you've got to know as early as possible what the schools—and their applications—are like. New catalogs appear every September.

5. **Cultivate your recommendation writers.**

   Let them know well in advance that you'll be asking them for a letter. Make sure they know who you are and what you're all about so that their letters will be specific and appropriate.

6. **Visit a variety of schools.**

   Get a sense of what kinds of schools you like—urban or rural, big or small, competitive or easygoing. Talk to students for their perspective.

7. **Register for an early LSAT administration.**

   The June test is probably best. Taking the test that early will allow you to take it again in October—still in advance of application deadlines—if you're not satisfied with your score.

8. **Read Kaplan's book *Law School Admissions Adviser.***

   This book is loaded with helpful tips and information about law schools, essay writing, applications, and financial aid.

9. **Draft several personal statement ideas.**

   Rarely is your first impulse your best impulse. That's why it pays to come up with a few different concepts for your personal statement. Try a funny one, a serious one, one that has nothing to do with the law or your desire to study it. Then put them all aside for later reevaluation.

10. **Read this book!**

    It should be the cornerstone of any comprehensive campaign to get into the law school of your choice. Learn the strategies that will get you a higher score, and practice by taking a couple of real LSATs.

About

Kaplan, Inc. is one of the nation's leading providers of education and career services. Kaplan is a wholly owned subsidiary of The Washington Post Company.

KAPLAN TEST PREPARATION & ADMISSIONS

Kaplan's nationally recognized test prep courses cover more than 20 standardized tests, including secondary school, college and graduate school entrance exams, as well as foreign language and professional licensing exams. In addition, Kaplan offers a college admissions course, private tutoring, and a variety of free information and services for students applying to college and graduate programs. Kaplan also provides information and guidance on the financial aid process. Students can enroll in online test prep courses and admissions consulting services at www.kaptest.com.

Kaplan K12 Learning Services partners with schools, universities, and teachers to help students succeed, providing customized assessment, education, and professional development programs.

SCORE! EDUCATIONAL CENTERS

SCORE! after-school learning centers help K–10 students build confidence along with academic skills in a motivating, sports-oriented environment.

SCORE! Prep provides in-home, one-on-one tutoring for high school academic subjects and standardized tests.

eSCORE.com is the first educational services Web site to offer parents and kids newborn to age 18 personalized child development and educational resources online.

KAPLANCOLLEGE.COM

KaplanCollege.com, Kaplan's distance learning platform, offers an array of online educational programs for working professionals who want to advance their careers. Learners will find nearly 500 professional development, continuing education, certification, and degree courses and programs in Nursing, Education, Criminal Justice, Real Estate, Legal Professions, Law, Management, General Business, and Computing/Information Technology.

KAPLAN PUBLISHING

Kaplan Publishing produces retail books and software. Kaplan Books, published by Simon & Schuster, include titles in test preparation, admissions, education, career development, and life skills; Kaplan and *Newsweek* jointly publish guides on getting into college, finding the right career, and helping children succeed in school.

KAPLAN PROFESSIONAL

Kaplan Professional provides assessment, training, and certification services for corporate clients and individuals seeking to advance their careers. Member units include:

- Dearborn, a leading supplier of licensing training and continuing education for securities, real estate, and insurance professionals
- Perfect Access/CRN, which delivers software education and consultation for law firms and businesses
- Kaplan Professional Call Center Services, a total provider of services for the call center industry
- Self Test Software, a world leader in exam simulation software and preparation for technical certifications
- Schweser's Study Program/AIAF, which provides preparation services for the CFA examination

KAPLAN INTERNATIONAL PROGRAMS

Kaplan assists international students and professionals in the United States through a series of intensive English language and test preparation programs. These programs are offered at campus-based centers across the United States. Specialized services include housing, placement at top American universities, fellowship management, academic monitoring and reporting, and financial administration.

COMMUNITY OUTREACH

Kaplan provides educational career resources to thousands of financially disadvantaged students annually, working closely with educational institutions, not-for-profit groups, government agencies and grass roots organizations on a variety of national and local support programs. These programs help students and professionals from a variety of backgrounds achieve their educational and career goals.

BRASSRING

BrassRing Inc., the premier business-to-business hiring management and recruitment services company, offers employers a vertically integrated suite of online and offline solutions. BrassRing, created in September 1999, combined Kaplan Career Services, Terra-Starr, Crimson & Brown Associates, thepavement.com, and HireSystems. In March 2000, BrassRing acquired Career Service Inc./Westech. Kaplan is a shareholder in BrassRing, along with Tribune Company, Central Newspapers, and Accel Partners.